U•X•L
Protests, Riots, and Rebellions
Civil Unrest in the Modern World

U·X·L
Protests, Riots, and Rebellions
Civil Unrest in the Modern World

VOLUME 1

Tracey Vasil Biscontini, Editor
Kathleen J. Edgar, Project Editor

U·X·L
A part of Gale, a Cengage Company

Farmington Hills, Mich • San Francisco • New York • Waterville, Maine
Meriden, Conn • Mason, Ohio • Chicago

Protests, Riots, and Rebellions: Civil Unrest in the Modern World

Tracey Vasil Biscontini, Editor

Project Editor: Kathleen J. Edgar
Acquisition Editor: Christine Slovey
Editorial: Elizabeth Manar, Mark Mikula
Rights Acquisition and Management: Carissa Poweleit, Ashley M. Maynard
Imaging: John L. Watkins
Product Design: Kristine A. Julien
Composition: Evi Abou-El-Seoud
Manufacturing: Wendy Blurton

© 2018 Gale, a Cengage Company

ALL RIGHTS RESERVED. No part of this work covered by the copyright herein may be reproduced, transmitted, stored, or used in any form or by any means graphic, electronic, or mechanical, including but not limited to photocopying, recording, scanning, digitizing, taping, Web distribution, information networks, or information storage and retrieval systems, except as permitted under Section 107 or 108 of the 1976 United States Copyright Act, without the prior written permission of the publisher.

For product information and technology assistance, contact us at
Gale Customer Support, 1-800-877-4253.
For permission to use material from this text or product, submit all requests online at **www.cengage.com/permissions.**
Further permissions questions can be emailed to
permissionrequest@cengage.com

Cover art, front: Image of Umbrella Revolution, © Chris McGrath/Getty Images; Wounded Knee standoff, © Bettmann/Getty Images; Justice for All march against police violence, © Bill Clark/Getty Images; and child labor protest, courtesy of the Bain Collection/Library of Congress. Cover art, back: Image of sign held at immigration rally, © Jorge Salcedo/Shutterstock.com.

Inside art: Image of cheering crowd, © AlbertBuchatskyy/Shutterstock.com; document icon, © Colorlife/Shutterstock.com; and megaphone, © Gulnar Sarkhanl/Shutterstock.com.

While every effort has been made to ensure the reliability of the information presented in this publication, Gale, a Cengage Company, does not guarantee the accuracy of the data contained herein. Gale accepts no payment for listing; and inclusion in the publication of any organization, agency, institution, publication, service, or individual does not imply endorsement of the editors or publisher. Errors brought to the attention of the publisher and verified to the satisfaction of the publisher will be corrected in future editions.

Library of Congress Cataloging-in-Publication Data

Names: Biscontini, Tracey Vasil, editor. | Edgar, Kathleen J., editor.
Title: UXL protests, riots, and rebellions : civil unrest in the modern world / Tracey Vasil Biscontini, editor ; Kathleen J. Edgar, project editor.
Description: Farmington Hills, Mich. : UXL, a part of Gale, a Cengage Company, [2018] | Includes bibliographical references and index.
Identifiers: LCCN 2017045153 | ISBN 9781410339089 (set : alk. paper) | ISBN 9781410339102 (vol. 1 : alk. paper) | ISBN 9781410339119 (vol. 2 : alk. paper) | ISBN 9781410355874 (vol. 3 : alk. paper) | ISBN 9781410339096 (ebook : alk. paper)
Subjects: LCSH: Protest movements–History–Juvenile literature. | Civil rights movements–History–Juvenile literature. | Political participation–History–Juvenile literature.
Classification: LCC HM883 .U95 2018 | DDC 303.48/4–dc23
LC record available at https://lccn.loc.gov/2017045153

Gale
27500 Drake Rd.
Farmington Hills, MI 48331-3535

978-1-4103-3908-9 (set)   978-1-4103-3911-9 (vol. 2)
978-1-4103-3910-2 (vol. 1)   978-1-4103-5587-4 (vol. 3)

This title is also available as an e-book.
978-1-4103-3909-6
Contact your Gale sales representative for ordering information.

Printed in the United States of America
1 2 3 4 5 6 7 22 21 20 19 18

Table of Contents

Events by Topic of Protest (A Thematic Table of Contents) **ix**
Reader's Guide **xiii**
Chronology **xv**
Words to Know **xxxiii**

VOLUME 1

Chapter 1: Animal Rights **1**
 UCR Lab Raid to Protest Animal Testing **7**
 Bilbao Anti-bullfighting Protest **12**
 Global March for Elephants and Rhinos **18**
 Blackfish Documentary and SeaWorld Protests **25**

Chapter 2: Civil Rights, African American **35**
 Montgomery Bus Boycott **42**
 Little Rock Nine Crisis **47**
 Freedom Rides **54**
 Lunch Counter Protest, McCrory's **59**
 March on Washington for Jobs and Freedom **63**

Chapter 3: Civil Rights, Hispanic and Latino **71**
 East LA Blowouts **77**
 A Day without Immigrants **83**
 Mexican Indignados Movement **90**

Chapter 4: Economic Discontent **99**
 Secret Document of the Farmers of
  Xiaogang **105**

TABLE OF CONTENTS

    Porkulus Protests, Tea Party **111**
    15-M Movement **116**
    Brexit **122**

Chapter 5: Environment **133**
    Forward on Climate Rally **139**
    Copenhagen Protests **144**
    Global Frackdown **151**
    Pacific Climate Warriors Blockade **157**
    March for Science **163**

Chapter 6: Free Speech **171**
    Harry Potter Book Burning **177**
    Muslim Protests of Danish Cartoons **183**
    "Je Suis Charlie" Protests **189**
    Yale Student Protests on Free Speech **194**

Chapter 7: Globalization **203**
    Battle in Seattle: World Trade Organization Protests **209**
    Occupy Wall Street **216**
    March against Monsanto **223**

VOLUME 2

Chapter 8: Gun Control/Gun Rights **233**
    Black Panthers Carry Guns into California Legislative Building in Protest of Mulford Act **239**
    March on Washington for Gun Control **246**
    "I Will Not Comply" Rally **252**
    Democratic Congressional Representatives Sit-in for Gun Control Legislation **256**

Chapter 9: Human Rights **263**
    Attica Prison Riot **270**
    Capitol Crawl **276**
    March to Abolish the Death Penalty **284**
    Dalit Protests in India **290**
    Armenian Genocide Protests **297**

Chapter 10: Immigrant Rights **305**
    1844 Nativist Riots **311**

TABLE OF CONTENTS

    Pro-Migrant Rallies in Europe and Australia **318**

    Protests against President Trump's Travel Ban **325**

Chapter 11: Independence Movements **335**

    Grito de Lares **342**

    Gandhi Leads Salt March **346**

    The Velvet Revolution **352**

Chapter 12: Indigenous Peoples' Rights **361**

    AIM Occupation of Wounded Knee **367**

    Aboriginal Land Rights Protest **375**

    Preservation of Amazon Rain Forest Awareness Campaign **379**

    Dakota Access Pipeline Protest **384**

Chapter 13: Labor Rights **393**

    Mother Jones's "Children's Crusade" **399**

    Flint Sit-Down Strike against General Motors **407**

    Delano Grape Strike and Boycott **414**

    Fast-Food Workers' Strike **422**

Chapter 14: LGBTQ Rights **429**

    Stonewall Riots **435**

    White Night Riots **441**

    Westboro Baptist Church Protests of Matthew Shepard **445**

    Shanghai Pride Festival **452**

    Protests of North Carolina House Bill 2 **458**

VOLUME 3

Chapter 15: Political/Government Uprisings **467**

    Tiananmen Square Protests **473**

    Fall of the Berlin Wall **478**

    Arab Spring and the Syrian Civil Uprising **486**

    Tahrir Square Protests (Egyptian Revolution) **493**

    Umbrella Revolution **498**

Chapter 16: Racial Conflict **509**

    Zoot Suit Riots **518**

    Detroit Riots **524**

    Soweto Uprising **530**

    Justice for All March **539**

TABLE OF CONTENTS

Chapter 17: Reproductive Rights **549**
    March for Women's Lives **556**
    Operation Rescue **562**
    One-Child Policy Riots **568**
    Planned Parenthood Protests **574**

Chapter 18: Resistance to Nazis **585**
    White Rose Movement **592**
    Holocaust Resistance in Denmark **597**
    Warsaw Ghetto Uprising **602**
    Treblinka Death Camp Revolt **607**

Chapter 19: Slavery **617**
    Louisiana Rebellion (German Coast) **623**
    Nat Turner's Rebellion/Anti-slavery Petitions **628**
    Christmas Rebellion/Baptist War **634**
    Harpers Ferry Raid **638**
    Fight to Stop Human Trafficking **643**

Chapter 20: War **651**
    International Congress of Women **657**
    Student Armband Protest of Vietnam War **663**
    Student Protest at Kent State **669**
    Candlelight Vigils against Invasion of Iraq **676**
    Chelsea Manning and WikiLeaks **684**

Chapter 21: Women's Rights **693**
    Hunger Strikes by Suffragettes in Prison **701**
    Women's Suffrage Protest at the White House **707**
    Baladi Campaign **714**
    Malala Yousafzai All-Girls School **718**
    Women's March on Washington **724**

Research and Activities Ideas **xlv**

Where to Learn More **li**

General Index **lxix**

Events by Topic of Protest
(A Thematic Table of Contents)

The main entry events in *Protests, Riots, and Rebellions* are organized by theme and type in the list that follows. Entries may appear under more than one heading when numerous factors were involved. Boldface indicates volume numbers.

Animal Rights
Bilbao Anti-bullfighting Protest	**1:** 12
Blackfish Documentary and SeaWorld Protests	**1:** 25
Global March for Elephants and Rhinos	**1:** 18
UCR Lab Raid to Protest Animal Testing	**1:** 7

Children/Young Adult Issues
East LA Blowouts	**1:** 77
Harry Potter Book Burning	**1:** 177
Little Rock Nine Crisis	**1:** 47
Mother Jones's "Children's Crusade"	**2:** 399
Soweto Uprising	**3:** 530
Yale Student Protests on Free Speech	**1:** 194

Civil Rights
Baladi Campaign	**3:** 714
Day without Immigrants	**1:** 83
East LA Blowouts	**1:** 77
Freedom Rides	**1:** 54
Hunger Strikes by Suffragettes in Prison	**3:** 701
Little Rock Nine Crisis	**1:** 47
Lunch Counter Protest, McCrory's	**1:** 59
March on Washington for Jobs and Freedom	**1:** 63
Mexican Indignados Movement	**1:** 90
Montgomery Bus Boycott	**1:** 42
Women's Suffrage Protest at the White House	**3:** 707

Climate Change
Copenhagen Protests	**1:** 144
Forward on Climate Rally	**1:** 139
March for Science	**1:** 163
Pacific Climate Warriors Blockade	**1:** 157

Economic Issues
Battle in Seattle: World Trade Organization Protests	**1:** 209
Brexit	**1:** 122
Day without Immigrants	**1:** 83
Fast-Food Workers' Strike	**2:** 422
15-M Movement	**1:** 116
March on Washington for Jobs and Freedom	**1:** 63
Occupy Wall Street	**1:** 216
Porkulus Protests, Tea Party	**1:** 111
Secret Document of the Farmers of Xiaogang	**1:** 105

Education
East LA Blowouts	**1:** 77
Little Rock Nine Crisis	**1:** 47

ix

EVENTS BY TOPIC OF PROTEST (A THEMATIC TABLE OF CONTENTS)

Malala Yousafzai All-Girls School   **3:** 718
Soweto Uprising   **3:** 530
Yale Student Protests on Free Speech   **1:** 194

Energy, Power

Dakota Access Pipeline Protest   **2:** 384
Global Frackdown   **1:** 151
Pacific Climate Warriors Blockade   **1:** 157
Preservation of Amazon Rain Forest Awareness Campaign   **2:** 379

Environment

Battle in Seattle: World Trade Organization Protests   **1:** 209
Copenhagen Protests   **1:** 144
Dakota Access Pipeline Protest   **2:** 384
Forward on Climate Rally   **1:** 139
Global Frackdown   **1:** 151
March for Science   **1:** 163
Pacific Climate Warriors Blockade   **1:** 157
Preservation of Amazon Rain Forest Awareness Campaign   **2:** 379

Free Speech

Harry Potter Book Burning   **1:** 177
"Je Suis Charlie" Protests   **1:** 189
Muslim Protests of Danish Cartoons   **1:** 183
Yale Student Protests on Free Speech   **1:** 194

Globalization, Corporations

Battle in Seattle: World Trade Organization Protests   **1:** 209
March against Monsanto   **1:** 223
Occupy Wall Street   **1:** 216

Guns

Black Panthers Carry Guns into California Legislative Building in Protest of Mulford Act   **2:** 239
Democratic Congressional Representatives Sit-In for Gun Control Legislation   **2:** 256
"I Will Not Comply" Rally   **2:** 252
March on Washington for Gun Control   **2:** 246

Health Issues

Capitol Crawl   **2:** 276
March against Monsanto   **1:** 223
March for Women's Lives   **3:** 556
Planned Parenthood Protests   **3:** 574

Human Rights

Armenian Genocide Protests   **2:** 297
Attica Prison Riot   **2:** 270
Capitol Crawl   **2:** 276
Dalit Protests in India   **2:** 290
Gandhi Leads Salt March   **2:** 346
March to Abolish the Death Penalty   **2:** 284
Mexican Indignados Movement   **1:** 90

Immigration

Brexit   **1:** 122
Day without Immigrants   **1:** 83
1844 Nativist Riots   **2:** 311
Pro-Migrant Rallies in Europe and Australia   **2:** 318
Protests against President Trump's Travel Ban   **2:** 325

Income Inequality

Battle in Seattle: World Trade Organization Protests   **1:** 209
Delano Grape Strike and Boycott   **2:** 414
Fast-Food Workers' Strike   **2:** 422
Flint Sit-Down Strike against General Motors   **2:** 407
March on Washington for Jobs and Freedom   **1:** 63
Occupy Wall Street   **1:** 216

Independence Movements

Gandhi Leads Salt March   **2:** 346
Grito de Lares   **2:** 342
Velvet Revolution   **2:** 352

Indigenous Peoples' Rights

Aboriginal Land Rights Protest   **2:** 375
AIM Occupation of Wounded Knee   **2:** 367
Dakota Access Pipeline Protest   **2:** 384

Labor

Preservation of Amazon Rain Forest Awareness Campaign	**2:** 379
Battle in Seattle: World Trade Organization Protests	**1:** 209
Day without Immigrants	**1:** 83
Delano Grape Strike and Boycott	**2:** 414
Fast-Food Workers' Strike	**2:** 422
15-M Movement	**1:** 116
Flint Sit-Down Strike against General Motors	**2:** 407
March on Washington for Jobs and Freedom	**1:** 63
Mother Jones's "Children's Crusade"	**2:** 399
Secret Document of the Farmers of Xiaogang	**1:** 105

Land Rights

Aboriginal Land Rights Protest	**2:** 375
AIM Occupation of Wounded Knee	**2:** 367
Preservation of Amazon Rain Forest Awareness Campaign	**2:** 379

LGBTQ Issues

Protests of North Carolina House Bill 2	**2:** 458
Shanghai Pride Festival	**2:** 452
Stonewall Riots	**2:** 435
Westboro Baptist Church Protests of Matthew Shepard	**2:** 445
White Night Riots	**2:** 441

Police Brutality

Detroit Riots	**3:** 524
Justice for All March	**3:** 539
March on Washington for Jobs and Freedom	**1:** 63
Stonewall Riots	**2:** 435

Political Uprisings

Arab Spring and the Syrian Civil Uprising	**3:** 486
Fall of the Berlin Wall	**3:** 478
Tahrir Square Protests (Egyptian Revolution)	**3:** 493
Tiananmen Square Protests	**3:** 473
Umbrella Revolution	**3:** 498

Race Issues

Black Panthers Carry Guns into California Legislative Building in Protest of Mulford Act	**2:** 239
Detroit Riots	**3:** 524
East LA Blowouts	**1:** 77
Freedom Rides	**1:** 54
Justice for All March	**3:** 539
Little Rock Nine Crisis	**1:** 47
Lunch Counter Protest, McCrory's	**1:** 59
March on Washington for Jobs and Freedom	**1:** 63
Montgomery Bus Boycott	**1:** 42
Soweto Uprising	**3:** 530
Zoot Suit Riots	**3:** 518

Religion

"Je Suis Charlie" Protests	**1:** 189
Muslim Protests of Danish Cartoons	**1:** 183
Protests against President Trump's Travel Ban	**2:** 325

Reproductive Issues

March for Women's Lives	**3:** 556
One-Child Policy Riots	**3:** 568
Operation Rescue	**3:** 562
Planned Parenthood Protests	**3:** 574

Resistance to Nazis

Holocaust Resistance in Denmark	**3:** 597
Treblinka Death Camp Revolt	**3:** 607
Warsaw Ghetto Uprising (Poland)	**3:** 602
White Rose Movement	**3:** 592

Revolutions

Grito de Lares	**2:** 342
Tahrir Square Protests (Egyptian Revolution)	**3:** 493
Umbrella Revolution	**3:** 498
Velvet Revolution	**2:** 352

EVENTS BY TOPIC OF PROTEST (A THEMATIC TABLE OF CONTENTS)

Segregation/Desegregation

Freedom Rides	**1:** 54
Little Rock Nine Crisis	**1:** 47
Lunch Counter Protest, McCrory's	**1:** 59
March on Washington for Jobs and Freedom	**1:** 63
Montgomery Bus Boycott	**1:** 42

Slavery

Christmas Rebellion/Baptist War	**3:** 634
Fight to Stop Human Trafficking	**3:** 643
Harpers Ferry Raid	**3:** 638
Louisiana Rebellion (German Coast)	**3:** 623
Nat Turner's Rebellion/Anti-slavery Petitions	**3:** 628

Student Movements and Protests

East LA Blowouts	**1:** 77
15-M Movement	**1:** 116
Little Rock Nine Crisis	**1:** 47
Soweto Uprising	**3:** 530
Student Armband Protest of Vietnam War	**3:** 663
Student Protest at Kent State	**3:** 669
Tiananmen Square Protests	**3:** 473
Yale Student Protests on Free Speech	**1:** 194

Suffrage (Voting Rights)

Baladi Campaign	**3:** 714
Hunger Strikes by Suffragettes in Prison	**3:** 701
March on Washington for Jobs and Freedom	**1:** 63
Women's Suffrage Protest at the White House	**3:** 707

Violence

Bilbao Anti-bullfighting Protest	**1:** 12
Democratic Congressional Representatives Sit-In for Gun Control Legislation	**2:** 256
Global March for Elephants and Rhinos	**1:** 18
"Je Suis Charlie" Protests	**1:** 189
Justice for All March	**3:** 539
March on Washington for Gun Control	**2:** 246
March to Abolish the Death Penalty	**2:** 284
Mexican Indignados Movement	**1:** 90
White Night Riots	**2:** 441

War, Genocide, Ethnic Cleansing

Arab Spring and the Syrian Civil Uprising	**3:** 486
Armenian Genocide Protests	**2:** 297
Candlelight Vigils against Invasion of Iraq	**3:** 676
Chelsea Manning and WikiLeaks	**3:** 684
Holocaust Resistance in Denmark	**3:** 597
International Congress of Women	**3:** 657
Student Armband Protest of Vietnam War	**3:** 663
Student Protest at Kent State	**3:** 669
Treblinka Death Camp Revolt	**3:** 607
Warsaw Ghetto Uprising (Poland)	**3:** 602
White Rose Movement	**3:** 592

Women's Issues

Baladi Campaign	**3:** 714
Hunger Strikes by Suffragettes in Prison	**3:** 701
International Congress of Women	**3:** 657
Malala Yousafzai All-Girls School	**3:** 718
March for Women's Lives	**3:** 556
One-Child Policy Riots	**3:** 568
Operation Rescue	**3:** 562
Planned Parenthood Protests	**3:** 574
Women's March on Washington	**3:** 724
Women's Suffrage Protest at the White House	**3:** 707

Reader's Guide

The ancient Greek philosopher Heraclitus (535 BCE–475 BCE) once wrote that the only constant thing in life is change. Change is a natural part of human existence. It has driven everything from biological evolution to cultural advancement for thousands of years. Yet, despite the desire for change, accomplishing it can be difficult. Old ideas and prejudices are hard to overcome, and people often resist efforts to alter the current state of affairs.

For some, change involves the fight for human rights. Others seek to end war, to express ideas freely, or to live a lifestyle of their own choosing. Those who seek change use various forms of protest or civil unrest to make their voices heard. Although many protests are peaceful, some escalate into full-scale riots or rebellions. Nevertheless, the people involved in these movements strongly believe that their cause is worth fighting for.

U•X•L Protests, Riots, and Rebellions: Civil Unrest in the Modern World presents a detailed look at many of these efforts to enact change in the world. This 21-chapter work examines a wide range of diverse issues from the environment to free speech and racial conflict. Each chapter begins with a comprehensive overview designed to introduce readers to the topic. The text details 88 events as well as numerous sidebars that focus on various protests, conflicts, or social movements.

The entries are written in a style that makes complicated subjects easy for younger readers to understand. Each event is framed in the context of the historical period in which it occurred, examining not only the social forces that shaped the event but also the motivations of those who participated in it. Rather than solely focusing on what happened, each entry delves deeper into why it happened.

The chapters feature more than 200 photos and illustrations that help bring each event into sharper focus. In addition, each chapter includes a helpful

"Words to Know" box that defines key terms, and another box featuring questions designed to spark critical thinking. The set also includes 42 primary sources that provide additional information helpful in understanding the topic.

Additional Features

Protests, Riots, and Rebellions also contains a substantial and detailed chronology of events to help place each topic in its historical context. A "Where to Learn More" section lists books, periodicals, and websites to find additional information. The section "Research and Activity Ideas" provides students with ways to discuss and explore the topics further. Also included is a general glossary and a subject index.

Acknowledgments

The editors would like to acknowledge the following writers and editors at Northeast Editing, Inc. for their work on this volume: Tyler Biscontini, Eric Bullard, Cait Caffrey, Josephine Campbell, Mark Dziak, Angela Harmon, Jack Lasky, Elizabeth Mohn, Joanne Quaglia, Lindsay Rohland, Michael Ruth, Richard Sheposh, and Rebecca Zukauskas.

Special thanks to Susan Edgar, senior vocabulary editor at Cengage Learning, for sharing her expertise on historical events as we created the topic list. Additional thanks go to Justine Carson for her work on the index.

Suggestions Are Welcome

We welcome your comments on *U•X•L Protests, Riots, and Rebellions: Civil Unrest in the Modern World* and suggestions for other history topics to consider. Please write: Editors, *U•X•L Protests, Riots, and Rebellions* Gale, 27500 Drake Rd., Farmington Hills, MI 48331-3535; call toll free: 1-800-877-4253; fax to 248-699-8097; or send e-mail via http://www.gale.cengage.com.

Chronology

The chronology that follows contains a sampling of important events, protests, riots, and rebellions that occurred in the modern world.

c. 1760 to 1840	Period of transition beginning in Great Britain (and later spreading to Western Europe and North America) when manufacturing changed from hand to machine production. Some workers protested the loss of their jobs to machines during the Industrial Revolution.
1811	On January 8, several hundred slaves on Louisiana's German Coast near New Orleans stage an uprising that lasts for three days before military forces finally put it down.
1811	An anti-industrialization movement led by a group of angry textile workers and weavers called the Luddites begins in Great Britain.
1831–1832	A series of petitions sent to the Virginia General Assembly leads to a debate about the future of slavery in the state.
1835	On January 24, an uprising of Muslim slaves called the Malê revolt begins in Brazil.
1838	Author and poet Ralph Waldo Emerson (1803–1882) writes a letter to President Martin van Buren (1782–1862) in protest of the forced removal of the Cherokee in Georgia. The removal takes place and becomes known as the Trail of Tears.

McConnel & Company mills in England during the Industrial Revolution, c. 1820. PUBLIC DOMAIN

xv

CHRONOLOGY

Ruins of the mission church destroyed during the Taos Revolt, 1847. © MATT RAGEN/SHUTTERSTOCK.COM

1844 In May and July, anti-immigrant mobs attack Irish immigrants in a series of riots that rock the city of Philadelphia, Pennsylvania.

1847 In January, a band of New Mexicans and Pueblo Indians revolt against the United States' occupation of northern New Mexico during the Mexican-American War (1846–1848). It becomes known as the Taos Revolt.

1848 The first women's rights convention in US history takes place in Seneca Falls, New York.

1859 Antislavery activist John Brown (1800–1859) leads an armed slave revolt at the US arsenal in Harpers Ferry, Virginia (now West Virginia).

1861 The US Civil War begins.

1863 In July, riots break out in New York City after Congress passes laws that allow the government to draft young men to serve in the US Civil War.

1865 The US Civil War ends.

1868 On September 23, Puerto Rican revolutionaries stage a brief uprising called the Grito de Lares in hopes of gaining their independence from Spain.

1880 Growing resentment of incoming Chinese immigrants leads to rioting in Denver, Colorado.

1886 On May 4, a labor rally near Haymarket Square in Chicago, Illinois, turns violent after someone throws a bomb at police.

1887 Pioneering female journalist Nellie Bly (Elizabeth Cochran Seaman, 1864–1922) goes undercover as an inmate in a New York mental hospital to expose the many abuses occurring there. Her report is published in the *New York World* newspaper and later in the book *Ten Days in a Mad-House*. Bly's type of investigation is the first of its kind.

1890 On December 29, tensions between the US Army and the Sioux on the Pine Ridge Reservation become intense. After a shot is fired, the army goes on to kill at least 150 Sioux men, women, and children in what becomes known as the Wounded Knee Massacre.

1898 The Spanish-American War begins in April after the USS *Maine* explodes in Havana Harbor, Cuba, in February. The war ends in August with the United States taking control of Guam, Puerto Rico, and the Philippines.

1903 In July, reformer Mary Harris "Mother" Jones (1837–1930) leads the Children's Crusade, also known as the March of the Mill Children, from Philadelphia, Pennsylvania, to Oyster Bay, New York, to bring attention to the problem of child labor.

1909 Women's rights activists imprisoned in Great Britain begin using hunger strikes to bring awareness to their cause.

1911 From September 14 to 22, El Primer Congreso Mexicanista, the first civil rights meeting for Mexican Americans, is held in Laredo, Texas.

1914 World War I begins in Europe.

1915 The International Congress of Women meets at The Hague in the Netherlands and creates several resolutions for peace.

1918 A group of National Women's Party members protest in front of the White House in Washington, DC, and call on the president to help women gain the right to vote.

1918 Between July and September, the anti-government Rice Riots break out in Japan in response to economic problems caused by low wages and high prices on goods such as rice.

1918 World War I ends.

1921 In August, thousands of frustrated West Virginian coal miners march on Blair Mountain and clash with coal company supporters and police for nearly a week in one of the largest labor uprisings in US history.

CHRONOLOGY

1929	In November, women in Nigeria revolt against British colonial administrators in the Aba Women's War.
1930	Indian independence movement leader Mohandas Gandhi (1869–1948) leads his famous Salt March in protest of the British Raj government's abuses of the Indian people.
1933	On May 10, the Nazi Party holds a massive book burning in Germany, during which any books that do not support Nazi thinking or politics are destroyed.
1936	General Motors employees in Flint, Michigan, go on a 44-day sit-down strike for better pay and improved working conditions.
1939	World War II begins in Europe.
1942	In February, President Franklin Roosevelt signs an executive order calling for people of Japanese ancestry on the West Coast to be relocated to internment camps. In March 1945 detainees at an internment camp near Santa Fe, New Mexico, rebel against guards in what becomes known as the Santa Fe Riot.
1942	German medical student Hans Scholl (1918–1943) founds the White Rose movement, a resistance effort aimed at creating opposition to the Nazi Party.
1943	People in Nazi-occupied Denmark begin resisting German rule and protecting Danish Jews from being sent to concentration camps.
1943	On April 19, Jewish prisoners held in Poland's Warsaw Ghetto revolt against Nazi forces it what becomes known as the Warsaw Ghetto Uprising.
1943	On June 3, chaos breaks out in Los Angeles, California, as angry American servicemen attack Mexican American and other minority youths in the Zoot Suit Riots.
1943	In August, Jewish prisoners held by the Nazis at the Treblinka death camp in Poland revolt.
1945	World War II ends.

People of Japanese descent are sent to internment camps, 1942. COURTESY OF LIBRARY OF CONGRESS.

CHRONOLOGY

1950 The Korean War begins.

1953 The Korean War ends.

1954 The Vietnam War begins.

1955 African Americans in Montgomery, Alabama, begin boycotting the public bus system after Rosa Parks (1913–2005) is arrested for refusing to give up her seat to a white passenger.

1957 In September, riots and other protests erupt in Little Rock, Arkansas, when nine African American students are admitted to the desegregated Little Rock Central High School.

1960 In April, a student uprising in South Korea known as the April Revolution leads to the overthrow of the First Republic of South Korea and the resignation of President Syngman Rhee (1875–1965).

1960 Chaos erupts in November when six-year-old Ruby Bridges (1954–) of Tylertown, Mississippi, becomes the first African American child to attend an all-white elementary school in the South.

Scene from the April Revolution in South Korea, 1960. © AP IMAGES.

1961 In January, nine African Americans stage a sit-in at a McCrory's lunch counter in Rock Hill, South Carolina, to protest the store's refusal to serve African American customers.

1961 Beginning In May, bus trips through the American South called the Freedom Rides are held in protest of Jim Crow laws and segregation at interstate bus stations.

1963 On August 28, about 250,000 people participate in the March on Washington for Jobs and Freedom in protest of racial segregation and other forms of discrimination. Civil rights icon the Rev. Dr. Martin Luther King Jr. (1929–1968) delivers his famous "I Have a Dream" speech.

1964 Between June and August, civil rights groups organize a voter registration drive called the Mississippi Summer Project in an effort to increase voter registration in that state.

CHRONOLOGY

Fannie Lou Hamer at Democratic National Convention. COURTESY OF LIBRARY OF CONGRESS.

1964 In August, voting rights and civil rights activist Fannie Lou Hamer shocks the nation during a speech at the Democratic National Convention in Atlantic City, New Jersey. She details the abuse she suffered at the hands of white citizens and police while trying to help register African American voters.

1964 The Free Speech Movement takes off at the University of California, Berkeley.

1965 On September 8, grape pickers in Delano, California, begin a labor strike with the help of the Agricultural Workers Organizing Committee and the United Farm Workers. The movement, which is led by César Chávez (1927–1993), continues until 1970.

1965 In December, students at several schools in Des Moines, Iowa, begin wearing black armbands to protest the Vietnam War.

1967 On May 2, members of the Black Panther Party stage a protest at the California State Capitol over a proposed gun control law that would prohibit them from conducting armed patrols of African American neighborhoods.

1967 On July 23, a race riot begins in Detroit, Michigan, after a police raid on an after-hours bar. The riot quickly becomes one of the worst of its kind in US history, resulting in 43 deaths, 7,200 arrests, and 2,000 damaged buildings.

1968 On March 1, Chicano students in Los Angeles, California, stage the first of a series of walkouts known as the East LA Blowouts in protest of unequal conditions at local high schools.

1968 On April 4, Martin Luther King Jr. is assassinated in Memphis, Tennessee.

1968 In May, civil unrest sweeps across France as student protests and widespread labor strikes temporarily disrupt the nation's government and economy.

May 1968 French student protest poster that reads "Be young and shut up." © ROGER VIOLLET/GETTY IMAGES.

CHRONOLOGY

1968 — On September 7, several hundred feminists stage a protest against the Miss America Pageant on the Atlantic City boardwalk in New Jersey.

1968 — In October, during the Olympic Games in Mexico City, Mexico, African American sprinters Tommie Smith (1944–) and John Carlos (1945–) raise their fists as they receive their medals in a gesture meant to promote human rights.

Protest of the Miss America Beauty Pageant, 1968. © BETTMANN/GETTY IMAGES.

1969 — On June 28, a police raid on a New York City gay nightclub called the Stonewall Inn leads to a series of violent protests and riots.

1969 — On November 20, a group of 89 Native Americans go to Alcatraz Island in San Francisco Bay and claim it as their own "by right of discovery." Their occupation of the island continues until June of 1971.

1970 — On May 4, a protest against the Vietnam War at Kent State University turns deadly when members of the Ohio National Guard open fire on demonstrators and kill four students.

Bob Dylan and Joan Baez protested the Vietnam War through song. © TRINITY MIRROR/MIRRORPIX/ALAMY.

1971 — Whistle-blower Daniel Ellsberg (1931–) reveals details from a secret US government report about US involvement in the Vietnam War to the *New York Times*. The report comes to be known as the Pentagon Papers.

1971 — On September 9, prisoners demanding better living conditions and political rights at Attica Correctional Facility in upstate New York begin a violent four-day revolt. A total of 43 people are killed in the uprising.

1972 — On January 30, British soldiers shoot and kill 28 unarmed people participating in a peaceful protest over the arrest of more than 300 people accused of working with the Irish Republican Army (IRA). This event soon becomes known as Bloody Sunday.

The Pentagon Papers were released in 1971. © MPI/GETTY IMAGES.

1973 — On February 27, about 200 Native Americans led by members of the American Indian Movement (AIM) take control of Pine Ridge Reservation in South Dakota. Their occupation of the reservation continues until May 8.

CHRONOLOGY

1975 The Vietnam War ends.

1976 On June 16, hundreds are killed in Soweto, South Africa, when a student protest turns violent. The violence brings attention to the problem of racism in South Africa and plays an important role in eventually ending the apartheid system.

1977 Chicago-based neo-Nazis attempt to hold a march in Skokie, Illinois, but are blocked by local officials. The case eventually reaches the US Supreme Court, where it is decided that the neo-Nazis' right to march is protected by the 1st Amendment. The march in Skokie is never held.

1979 On May 21, the White Night Riots erupt in San Francisco, California, after convicted killer Dan White (1946–1985) is given a light sentence for the murders of Mayor George Moscone (1929–1978) and gay rights activist and politician Harvey Milk (1930–1978).

1979 On October 14, as many as 125,000 people participate in the National March on Washington for Lesbian and Gay Rights.

1980 On August 14, shipyard workers in Gdańsk, Poland, stage a successful strike that leads to a strong anti-communism movement in the country.

1985 On April 20, animal rights activists break into a laboratory at the University of California, Riverside, to free animals used in experiments.

1986 In March, a pair of reproductive rights rallies called the March for Women's Lives are held in Washington, DC, and Los Angeles, California.

1988 On January 26, thousands of Australian Aboriginals hold a peaceful equal rights rally in Sydney during the 200th anniversary of Australia Day.

1989 Kayapo chief Raoni Metuktire (c. 1930–) leads a campaign against the building of a dam in the Amazon rain forest with the help of rock star Sting (1951–).

CHRONOLOGY

1989 On November 9, the Berlin Wall falls.

1989 On November 17, a political movement called the Velvet Revolution begins in Czechoslovakia and ends just over a month later with the end of communism in that country.

1990 On March 12, disabled activists protest delays in passing the Americans with Disabilities Act (ADA) by crawling up the steps of the US Capitol in an event called the Capitol Crawl.

1990 In October, a Jewish group wants to lay a cornerstone for a temple at the site of the Al-Aqsa Mosque, a Muslim holy place in Jerusalem on a hill known as the Temple Mount. A group of Palestinians respond by throwing rocks and bottles at border police as well as at Jews, who are praying at the Western Wall just below the mosque on the hill. Israeli troops respond and kill 23 Palestinians; several hundred others are injured in the riots.

Temple Mount Riots, 1990.
© MENAHEM KAHANA/AFP/GETTY IMAGES.

1991 In December, the collapse of the Soviet Union is complete.

1992 The pro-life organization Operation Rescue holds an anti-abortion protest called the Spring of Life.

1992 On April 29, riots break out in Los Angeles, California, after several city police officers are found not guilty in a criminal case concerning the beating of an African American man named Rodney King (1965–2012) during an arrest.

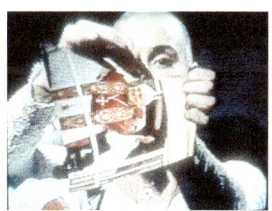

Sinead O'Connor causes a stir when she rips the pope's picture in 1992 on SNL. © YVONNE HEMSEY/HULTON ARCHIVE/GETTY IMAGES.

1992 In October, Irish singer Sinead O'Connor (1966–) appears on NBC's *Saturday Night Live* and sings Jamaican artist Bob Marley's (1945–1981) song "War." As she concludes her performance, she rips up a picture of Pope John Paul II (1920–2005), saying "fight the real enemy." She was protesting sexual abuse in the Catholic Church.

1994 Members of Greenpeace send two ships in an attempt to stop Norwegian ships from hunting whales.

1995 On October 16, Nation of Islam leader Louis Farrakhan (1933–) leads the Million Man March in Washington, DC, to raise awareness of the importance of American family values, unity, and civil rights.

Million Man March in Washington, DC, in 1995.
© JAMES LEYNSE/GETTY IMAGES.

U•X•L Protests, Riots, and Rebellions: Civil Unrest in the Modern World   xxiii

CHRONOLOGY

1998 On October 16, members of the Westboro Baptist Church protest at the funeral of Matthew Shepard (1976–1998), a young man who was murdered for being gay.

1999 On November 30, a series of protests known as the Battle for Seattle break out in Seattle, Washington, during the World Trade Organization (WTO) Ministerial Conference.

2000 On October 15, the first March to Abolish the Death Penalty is held in Austin, Texas. The inaugural event is called the March on the Mansion.

2001 On September 11, terrorists hijack airplanes that crash into the World Trade Center in New York City; the Pentagon in Washington, DC; and a field in western Pennsylvania. Almost 3,000 people are killed.

2001 In response to the September 11 attacks, the United States forms a coalition of nations and begins a war in Afghanistan on October 7.

2001 On December 30, Pastor Jack Brock of the Christ Community Church in Alamogordo, New Mexico, organizes a book burning at which copies of the Harry Potter series are destroyed.

2002 On November 30, various people in the United Kingdom protest the materialism rampant before the holidays by having a "Buy Nothing Day."

Organizer of Buy Nothing Day, Michael Smith, in 2002.
© ROGER BAMBER/ALAMY.

2002 Surfers against Sewage, a group in the United Kingdom, stages a protest to raise awareness about ocean pollutants, including plastics, and the need to keep the coasts clean.

2003 On March 16, thousands of candlelight vigils are held across the world in protest of the impending invasion of Iraq. The war begins on March 19.

Participant in the Surfers against Sewage protest, 2002.
© SION TOUHIG/GETTY IMAGES.

2004 On August 29, a group called One Thousand Coffins participates in a march held in New York City to protest the Iraq War.

CHRONOLOGY

2005 On September 30, the Danish newspaper *Jyllands-Posten* publishes several cartoons depicting the Muslim prophet Muhammad. Many Muslims voice concern over the portrayals and some protests turn violent.

2005 On December 3, the first Global Day of Action is held worldwide to protest climate change.

2006 On May 1, protests called a Day without Immigrants are held in cities across the United States. The event is also called the Great American Boycott.

2006 In late November and early December, damage to a statue of a Dalit hero triggers violent protests near Mumbai, India.

2007 In May, thousands of people riot in China against the government's controversial one-child policy.

2008 The women's rights group Soroptimist International of Great Britain and Ireland begins its Purple Teardrop campaign to combat human trafficking.

2008 In February, several Danish newspapers reprint the 2005 cartoon depicting the prophet Muhammad. At least 200 people are killed as protests flare in Denmark and several other nations.

2009 The conservative anti-tax Tea Party movement begins with protest rallies in cities across the United States.

2009 In June, the first Shanghai Pride Festival is held. The event is the first LGBTQ festival to take place on the Chinese mainland.

2009–2010 About 110 people are killed in ongoing protests in Iran over the election of President Mahmoud Ahmadinejad (1956–), which the protesters claim was fraudulent. The protests are known as the Iranian Green Movement.

2009 On October 11, thousands of members of the LGBTQ community and their supporters stage the National Equality March in Washington, DC.

2009 On December 16, about 1,700 people are arrested as thousands of protesters try to disrupt the United Nations Climate Change Conference in Copenhagen, Denmark.

Participants during the Global Day of Action, 2005, to fight climate change.
© PHOTOFUSION/GETTY IMAGES.

CHRONOLOGY

2010   Classified information stolen by US Army soldier Chelsea Manning (then Bradley Manning, 1987–) is first released on the website WikiLeaks.

2010   On August 21, protesters stage an anti-bullfighting rally in front of the Guggenheim Museum in Bilbao, Spain.

2010   In November in Nigeria, people march in conjunction with the Movement for the Survival of the Ogoni people. They are marking the 15th anniversary of the deaths of the Ogoni martyrs, who were executed by the government amid controversy.

March by the Movement for the Survival of the Ogoni People, 2010. © PIUS UTOMI EKPEI/GETTY IMAGES.

2010   On December 17, a Tunisian street vendor named Mohamed Bouazizi (1984–2011) sets himself on fire in a protest against the government.

2011   In January, ongoing protests inspired by Mohamed Bouazizi's actions force Tunisia's president to resign. The protests spread to other nations in northern Africa and the Middle East, beginning a movement known as the Arab Spring.

2011   In January and February, massive anti-government demonstrations take place in Egypt's Tahrir Square.

2011   On March 11, a powerful earthquake strikes Japan, unleashing a massive tsunami. The earthquake and tsunami kill about 19,000 people and severely damage the Fukushima Daiichi Nuclear Power Station.

2011   In March, an uprising begins in Syria. It eventually turns into a brutal civil war that was still ongoing as of early 2018.

2011   The first "Slutwalk" is held after a police officer in Toronto, Canada, suggests women should stop dressing like "sluts" to avoid sexual assault. The protest took on rape culture, which includes blaming or shaming the victims of sexual assault.

Slutwalk, first held in 2011, is an annual event, shown here in 2014. © TYLER MCKAY/SHUTTERSTOCK.COM.

2011   The March 28 killing of his son prompts Mexican poet Javier Sicilia (1956–) to organize several protest marches against drug violence in Mexico.

2011   On April 25, demonstrators hold several marches in France and Germany to protest the use of nuclear power.

CHRONOLOGY

2011	On May 15, more than 80,000 people take part in a series of economic protests known as the 15-M movement in Spain.
2011	On September 17, a global protest against economic inequality called Occupy Wall Street starts in New York City and spreads throughout the country and other parts of the world.
2011	The Iraq War ends.
2011	In December, residents of Wukan, China, protest illegal land grabs in their fishing village. Claiming that local officials sold communal land and provided no compensation to residents. the protesters become outraged when a local village leader is killed while in police custody.
2012	Starting in March, protesters in Fukushima, Japan, begin to meet in front of the prime minister's house to protest the use of nuclear power.
2012	On November 29, fast-food workers at McDonald's and other restaurants begin going on strike to protest low wages.
2012	Students in Montreal, Canada, take to the streets to protest a tuition hike and other rising fees at the country's universities.
2013	On January 26, about 1,000 protesters take part in the March on Washington for Gun Control in honor of the 20 children and 6 staff members who were murdered in the Sandy Hook Elementary School shooting several weeks earlier.
2013	On February 17, more than 40,000 environmentalists rally in front of the White House as part of the Forward on Climate rally in Washington, DC.
2013	On May 25, people in 436 cities around the world protest against Monsanto, a multinational corporation that produces and promotes genetically modified foods.
2013	In July, the Black Lives Matter movement forms.
2013	On November 21, protests called the Euromaidan demonstrations begin to sweep across Ukraine and eventually lead to the 2014 Ukrainian revolution.

Wukan, China, residents protest illegal communal land sales, 2011. © STR/GETTY IMAGES.

Students protest tuition hikes in Montreal, 2012. © ROGERIO BARBOSA/AFP/GETTYIMAGES.

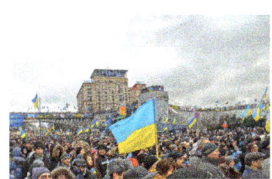

People participating in the Euromaiden protests in the Ukraine, 2013. © PROCESS/SHUTTERSTOCK.COM

CHRONOLOGY

2014	*Blackfish*, a documentary alleging the abuse of orca killer whales at SeaWorld, causes a significant number of animal rights activists to campaign against the parks.
2014	In February, activists around the world protest against the Russian government's harsh policies on homosexuality days before the start of the Sochi Olympic Games.
2014	On April 15, Islamist militants violently kidnap several hundred teenage girls from a boarding school in Nigeria. People around the world respond with the Bring Back Our Girls campaign.
2014	In September, thousands of protesters in Hong Kong clash with police when China announces it will still not allow Hong Kongers to freely select their own leaders. This event is known as the Umbrella Revolution.
2014	On October 3 and 4, animal rights activists around the world continue their annual protests against the poaching of elephants and rhinos in Africa.
2014	On October 11, thousands of environmental activists march in protest of expanded fracking practices.
2014	On October 17, Pacific Climate Warriors attempt to blockade Newcastle Harbor in Australia with kayaks, dinghies, and canoes to prevent coal ships from leaving the harbor.
2015	Saudi Arabia allows women to vote and run in municipal elections for the first time in the country's history.
2015	In January, tens of thousands of people attend rallies throughout France in response to a terrorist attack at the offices of the French magazine *Charlie Hebdo*.
2015	On April 4, people protest the passage of the Religious Freedom Restoration Act in Indiana. They are concerned that the act will allow people to legally discriminate against people based on their sexual orientation or their gender identity.

Participants at the Religious Freedom Restoration Act protest in Indiana, 2015.
© AP IMAGES/DOUG MCSCHOOLER.

CHRONOLOGY

2015   On April 24, protesters around the world march to mark the 100th anniversary of the Armenian genocide. The protesters demand that Turkey acknowledge its role in the Armenian genocide.

2015   Malala Yousafzai (1997–), who was shot by the Taliban for speaking out for girls' education, opens an all-girls school for Syrian refugees. A year earlier, she became one of the youngest people ever to win the Nobel Peace Prize.

2015   On October 13, demonstrators in Turkey protest a double suicide bombing that occurred during a peace rally in Ankara several days earlier. The protesters hold signs of people killed by the blasts.

Anti-terrorism protest in Turkey, 2015. © ADEM ALTAN/GETTY IMAGES.

2015   On November 21, following terror attacks in Paris, France, earlier that month, Muslims in Italy stage a rally to protest terrorism and violence. Many carry signs reading "Not in My Name."

2015   In November, students at Yale University protest in response to racial issues at their school. The protests occur after the university issues advice on what types of Halloween costumes might be considered offensive to others.

Italian Muslims rally against terrorism, 2015. © EUGENIO MARONGIU/SHUTTERSTOCK.COM.

2016   In January, armed anti-government militia members take over the Malheur National Wildlife Refuge near Burns, Oregon. They demand the federal government return the land to the people and release two local ranchers who were put in prison for committing arson on public land. Most of the protesters are not from Oregon but have traveled to the state from Arizona, Montana, and Idaho, among others.

Armed participants at the Malheur National Wildlife Refuge in Oregon, 2016. © ANADOLU AGENCY/GETTY IMAGES.

2016   On January 24, activists in Greece hold a pro-migrant rally.

U•X•L Protests, Riots, and Rebellions: Civil Unrest in the Modern World

CHRONOLOGY

Participants protest lead in the water in Flint, Michigan, 2016. © BILL PUGLIANO/GETTY IMAGES.

Candelight vigil to protest deaths of Tibetans, 2016. © MANJUNATH KIRAN/AFP/GETTY IMAGES.

Counterprotesters urge people to reject hate at Stone Mountain protest, 2016. © AP IMAGES/BEN GRAY.

2016 On February 19, the Rev. Jesse Jackson (1941–) leads a national mile-long march in Flint, Michigan, to raise awareness and demand help to combat the water crisis in the city. A change in the city's water source had led to the corrosion of water pipes that began leaching harmful levels of lead into residents's tap water.

2016 In March, after the self-immolation of two Tibetans in Bangalore, India, a candlelight vigil is held. A schoolboy and a monk had set themselves on fire and died in protest of Chinese rule in the region of Tibet.

2016 Beginning in April, Native Americans and other protesters rally against the Dakota Access Pipeline in North Dakota.

2016 In April, dozens of pro-LGBTQ rights and anti-LGBTQ rights protesters demonstrate in Raleigh, North Carolina, after the passing of the state's Public Facilities Privacy and Security Act. The act pertains to which bathrooms transgender people can use.

2016 In April, white supremacists hold a protest at Stone Mountain, a monument to Confederate leaders, in Georgia. Their white power rally is interrupted by counterprotesters who urge people to reject hate and racism.

2016 On June 22, congressional Democrats stage a sit-in to protest the House of Representatives' refusal to vote on gun control.

2016 On June 23, the United Kingdom votes to leave the European Union. Thousands of people in London take to the streets to protest the decision.

2016 In the fall, San Francisco 49ers quarterback Colin Kaepernick (1987–) begins a protest against racial injustice and police brutality in the United States. He first sits and then later kneels when the national anthem is played at the team's games. Eventually, other athletes join his protest.

2016 In November, following the surprise victory of Republican candidate Donald Trump (1946–) in the US presidential election, protesters take to the streets in various cities to demonstrate against him. Many voice concerns about the negative remarks and promised policies that Trump made during the campaign that would impact women, Hispanics and Latinos, African Americans, Muslims, immigrants, gays, and others.

2017 On January 21, more than two million women march for women's rights and other issues in Washington, DC, on the first day of Donald Trump's (1946–) presidency.

2017 On January 28, protesters across the United States march against President Trump's immigration policy known as the travel ban.

2017 Protests erupt periodically at the University of California, Berkeley, in an attempt to stop controversial speakers from appearing at events on campus. Protests also erupt between pro-Trump supporters and counterprotesters.

2017 On February 11, antiabortion activists throughout the United States protest against Planned Parenthood. Counterprotests in support of Planned Parenthood funding are also held.

2017 On April 22, activists around the world gather in support of government funding for science. The event is known as the March for Science.

2017 On June 25, protesters march in Washington, DC, in support of traditional marriage.

2017 In August, white supremacist protesters and counterprotesters violently clash in Charlottesville, Virginia. The incident results in the death of counterprotester Heather Heyer (c. 1985–2017).

2017 In October, people use the hashtag #MeToo to raise awareness of sexual assault and harassment. Many people, especially women, document the various ways in which they have been victimized by sexual predators. The discussion prompts some of the accused people to resign from their jobs; others are fired.

2017   In December, protests erupt in the Middle East when President Donald Trump announces that the United States will recognize Jerusalem as the capital of Israel. The move stokes the Israeli-Palestinian conflict.

Words to Know

Ableism: Discrimination against disabled people.

Abolition: The act of ending or stopping something.

Abolitionist movement: A campaign held during the 19th century to end slavery in the United States.

Aboriginal: A member of the native people of region, such as Australia or Canada.

Accessibility: How easy or difficult it is for physically disabled individuals to navigate a building.

Activist: One who takes action to support or oppose an issue.

Advocate: One who defends a certain cause.

Allied powers: The group of nations that fought Nazi Germany and other Axis powers during World War II.

Amendment: A change in the wording of a law or bill.

Anarchist: A person who rebels against authority and believes governments should be overthrown.

Animal welfare: To assure the care and comfort of animals.

Apartheid: A series of laws in South Africa that legalized discrimination and ordered the separation of people by race.

Armory: A place where military weapons are made and stored.

Aryan: Adolf Hitler's idea of a master race of people who were tall and had blond hair and blue eyes.

Ashram: A religious retreat.

Assassination: The killing of someone for political reasons.

Asylum: Protection given to refugees that grants them the right to stay in a new country.

Austerity: Conditions of extreme spending cuts at a national level.

Autonomy: Self-government.

Background check: The process that allows authorities to examine the history of a person before he or she can purchase a gun.

Bill: A draft of a law that is presented to lawmakers for a vote.

Bloc: A group of nations that work together toward a common interest.

Boycott: A refusal to buy or use certain items, products, or services as a form of protest.

Bribery: Offering someone a gift in return for a favor.

Candlelight vigil: An assembly of people who hold candles to show support or opposition for a cause or event.

Capital punishment: A death sentence issued by a court to an individual found guilty of committing a serious crime; also known as the death penalty.

Capitalism: An economic system in which land and wealth are mostly owned by private individuals.

Captivity: The state of being held under the control of someone and not allowed to leave.

Cartridge: A tube that contains a bullet that the user puts into a gun.

Caste system: A system that groups people into different social classes based on wealth, occupation, or other factors.

Censorship: The act of removing any content considered harmful or offensive from books, newspapers, or other media.

Census: Provides a count of a population for specific information about the people living in a country.

Chemical weapons: Weapons that use chemicals to kill or seriously injure people.

Chicano: A term used to describe a Mexican American individual.

Christianity: A religion based on the teachings of Jesus Christ.

Civil disobedience: A public refusal to follow certain laws as a peaceful form of protest.

Civil rights: Guarantees of equal political, social, and economic freedoms to all citizens of a country.

Civilian: A person who is not active in the military or a member of law enforcement.

Climate change: Long-term, significant, measured change in the climate as seen in temperature, wind patterns, precipitation, and other factors. The term is often used today to describe any changes to global weather patterns that result from human practices.

Climate refugee: Any person who has been forced to leave his or her home as a direct result of changes to the environment.

Colonialism: An economic system in which Western European nations controlled various underdeveloped countries located around the world.

Colony: A country or other area that is controlled by a more powerful country.

Communism: A political system in which private ownership of property is eliminated and government directs all economic production. The goods produced and accumulated wealth are, in theory, shared relatively equally by all.

Conception: The moment when a male's sperm fertilizes a female's ovum.

Conservative: A view that favors traditional beliefs concerning social issues and wants limited government spending.

Constitution: A country's document of laws.

Consumerism: An economic concept based on buying and using goods.

Contraceptive: A method or device used to prevent pregnancy.

Corporatism: Occurs when big businesses become powerful enough to take control of the state.

Crusade: An important mission, usually involving moral beliefs and often requiring a long journey.

WORDS TO KNOW

D

Dalit: A member of the lowest social class in India's caste system. They were previous known as Untouchables, a term that is considered derogatory.

Death camp: Prison camps where Nazis killed hundreds of thousands of Jews and other prisoners from across Europe during World War II.

Deforestation: The clear-cutting of forests for such human purposes as homes, businesses, and farms.

Delegate: A person at a meeting who represents others.

Democracy: A form of government in which people choose leaders by voting.

Deport: To remove immigrants from a nation and send them back to their home country.

Depression: A period in which economic activity is limited and joblessness is widespread.

Desegregate: To end the practice of keeping different groups of people separated by joining them together as one.

Desertification: A process in which land becomes increasingly dry and unusable due to climate change.

Developing countries: Poor nations that are looking to advance economically and socially.

Dictator: Ruler who has total power over a country.

Disability: A physical, developmental, or mental condition that limits a person's activities in certain areas of life.

Discrimination: Unfair treatment based on one's race, ethnicity, or other distinction.

Draft: A process by which young men are required to serve in the armed forces. Some countries also draft women.

Drug cartel: A group that produces and sells illegal drugs.

E

Economic inequality: A large difference in income between the poor and the wealthy.

Economy: The combined wealth and other resources of a country.

Electoral votes: Votes cast by a select group of people from each state to elect the president of the United States.

Embassy: The office in one country where a representative of another country lives and works.

Endangered: A plant or animal that is in danger of becoming extinct.

Environmentalism: The idea that people must actively take part in political and social movements to bring about positive changes that improve the health of the planet.

Ethnicity: A division of human beings by culture, language, or home country.

Etiquette: A social custom or skill that guides the way people behave in the presence of others.

Execution: The killing of a person who has been sentenced to die.

Extinct: A term to describe a species that has completely died out.

F

Factory farm: A farm where many animals are raised, often indoors, for food.

Fetus: An unborn, developing human.

Final Solution: A plan for killing all Jews in Nazi-controlled areas.

Fiscal responsibility: When the government taxes just enough to pay for necessary expenses.

Force-feed: To make a person eat by forcefully putting food down his or her throat.

Fossil fuels: Energy sources such as gas, oil, and coal that result from ancient natural processes, such as the decay of ancient plants and animals.

Fracking: A method of getting natural gas and oil from rock by injecting water at high pressure into the ground.

Free trade: The buying and selling of goods and services between nations without any special taxes or rules to limit trade.

G

Gender expression: Individuals' external presentation of gender, including how they dress, style their hair, and refer to themselves.

Gender identity: Individuals' personal inner experience of their gender, which may not match the sex they were assigned at birth.

Genocide: The killing of many members of the same race, religion, ethnicity, or culture.

Ghetto: Poor area of a city where certain groups of people live.

Global warming: Rising temperature of Earth's atmosphere caused by an increase of greenhouse gases.

Globalization: Occurs when countries do business on an international level.

Greenhouse gases: Gases that collect in the upper atmosphere of Earth and are believed to be responsible for changes to the planet's climate and weather patterns.

Gun control: Any attempt to create policies that offer more protections from gun violence.

Gun rights: A term used to describe attempts to protect the ability of Americans to own and use guns.

H

Handgun: A firearm that can be held and fired with one hand.

Hate crime: A crime committed against a person because of his or her race, religion, national origin, gender, sexual orientation, or disability.

Hate group: A group that supports hatred, anger, or violence toward members of a certain race, religion, national origin, gender, or sexual orientation.

Hispanic: A person who is from or who has ancestors from a Spanish-speaking country.

Hitler Youth: Nazi Germany's children's organization that taught Nazi ideas to youths so they would grow up supporting the Nazi Party.

Holocaust: Nazi Germany's mass killing of European Jews and others during World War II.

Hostage: A person who is captured and held against his or her will until certain demands are met.

Housing bubble: An increase in housing prices caused by high demand that eventually decreases, causing values of properties to decline sharply.

Human trafficking: The practice of forcing people to perform labor or participate in sex work.

Humane: Acting in a caring or considerate manner.

Hunger strike: The act of refusing to eat to bring about a desired change.

Hydroelectric energy: Energy that is generated from the force of moving water.

I

Idol worship: The worship of a false god.

Immigrant: A person who enters a new country after leaving his or her home country.

Impoverished: Extremely poor.

Indentured servant: A person who works for another person in exchange for travel, food, and housing for a specified amount of time.

Indigenous: Originating in or living naturally in a certain region.

Industry: The production of goods from raw materials in factories.

Integration: The practice of combining different groups in society to make them equal.

Islamization: A shift in a society's culture toward the religion of Islam.

Ivory: The hard, white substance that makes up the tusks and some teeth of certain animals.

J

Jim Crow laws: Laws created mostly in the American South in the late 19th and early 20th centuries that kept black citizens from enjoying the same rights as white Americans.

L

Labor union: An organization of workers that is formed to protect their rights and interests.

Latin America: A region south of the United States that includes Mexico, Central America, South America, and islands in the Caribbean.

WORDS TO KNOW

Latino: A person who is from or who has ancestors from a Latin American country.

Legislature: A group of people responsible for making laws.

Liberal: A view that favors new ideas.

M

Market economy: An economic system of free competition in which prices are determined by supply and demand.

Maroons: Freed Spanish slaves who lived in the mountains of Jamaica.

Migrant: A person who moves from one place to another in search of work.

Militant: Using violent or aggressive means in support of a cause.

Militia: A group of citizens with military training who are called to service only in the event of emergencies.

Minimum wage: The lowest hourly rate that an employer can pay a worker.

Monopoly: When a single company or person is the sole provider of a product or service.

Mortgage: Payments made on a loan from a bank to help pay for the purchase of a home.

Multinational company: A company that does business in many countries around the world.

Muslim: A follower of Islam, a religion founded by the prophet Muhammad.

N

National Guard: A branch of the armed forces that usually deals with problems within the United States.

Nativism: A policy that protects the rights of a country's native people over immigrants' rights.

Natural resources: Water, soil, minerals, and other materials that are found in nature and are important to humans.

Nazi Party: A political party that controlled Germany from 1933 to 1945 under the leadership of Adolf Hitler.

Negotiate: To discuss something in hopes of making a deal.

North Atlantic Treaty Organization (NATO): A military partnership of the United States, Canada, and various European countries.

O

Occult: Matters that deal with the supernatural or magic.

Ovum: A female reproductive cell, sometimes called an egg.

P

Pacifist: Someone who is strongly opposed to war and fighting.

Parliament: A lawmaking body.

Partisans: Members of armed organizations that fight against forces that are controlling their country.

Pepper spray: A spray made from cayenne pepper that can cause a burning feeling in a person's eyes and throat when applied.

Petition: A written request made to an official person or organized body.

Picket: A protest that involves a group of people marching at a site with signs on posts or pointed sticks.

Pipeline: A system of connected pipes that are used to transport liquids and gases over a long distance.

Plantation: A large area of land that is usually worked by manual labor.

Poaching: The illegal hunting or killing of an animal.

Police brutality: The use of more force than necessary by police.

Political correctness: The act of avoiding certain language or activities that could offend a particular person or group.

Pork barrel spending: Funds attached to legislation for projects that benefit a lawmaker's home district.

Pro-choice: A term used to describe people who support a woman's right to choose whether or not to have an abortion.

Pro-life: A term used to describe people who are against abortion.

Prophet: A messenger of God.

R

Racial diversity: To include people from various racial backgrounds.

Racial insensitivity: A lack of understanding of the experiences of people of other races.

Racism: The belief that one human being is better than another because of his or her race.

Radical: Someone who favors extreme measures to make a point or bring about change.

Recession: A period when trade and economic production slow.

Reformer: A person who tries to bring changes to society.

Refugee: A person who leaves his or her home country because of war or mistreatment based on race, religion, or political opinion.

Renewable energy: Sources of energy that can be naturally replaced by the environment and include solar, wind, and water sources.

Repeal: To cancel or withdraw something, especially a law.

Reservation: An area of land set aside for use by certain people.

Reservoir: A human-made lake created to store water for use by a community.

Resistance: The effort to fight against a powerful force.

Revolution: The overthrow of one type of government in favor of another.

S

Sanction: An official punishment usually imposed on a country by another nation or group of nations.

Sanctuary: A refuge for animals where they are protected from harm and able to roam freely.

Segregation: The separation of groups of people.

Semiautomatic weapon: A type of gun that allows the user to fire bullets quickly due to an automatic reloading process.

Sexual orientation: A person's sexual identity, which relates to whom a person is attracted. Sexual orientation includes gay, lesbian, bisexual, straight, and asexual.

Sexual reproduction: Occurs when two individuals have sex and produce an offspring.

Sharia: Islamic law based on the teachings of the Koran.

Sit-down strike: A protest in which a group of workers sit down on the job and refuse to complete any work.

Sit-in: A peaceful protest in which people occupy a place for long periods, often in a seated position, to call attention to a certain social issue.

Slave driver: A slave who is responsible for organizing and punishing other slaves.

Socialism: A political system in which the central government provides goods and services to all members of a society equally.

Sperm: A male reproductive cell.

Stimulus: An action that causes another action to take place.

Strike: An organized work stoppage to force employers to meet certain demands.

Suffocate: To die from not being able to breathe.

Suffrage: The right to vote.

Suffragist: A person who works to gain voting rights for people who are not allowed to vote.

Sustainable: A method of using natural resources without depleting them or damaging them permanently.

Sweatshop: A small factory where people work long hours for low pay.

T

Tactic: Something used to effect change.

Tariff: A tax or fee added to foreign products to make them more expensive.

Terrorism: The use of fear and violence to achieve political goals or social change and to create fear.

Terrorist: Someone who uses fear and violence to influence others.

Trafficking: The act of buying or selling an illegal product or service.

Traitor: Someone who has betrayed his or her country.

Transgender: A term used to describe a person whose gender identity differs from the sex he or she was assigned at birth.

Tribunal: A decision-making body that has authority in a specific area.

Trimester: A period of pregnancy lasting about three months, during which the fetus develops.

U

Unconstitutional: Going against the US Constitution.

Undocumented or unauthorized immigrants: Immigrants who enter a country without permission or who stay longer than they are allowed.

Union: An organized group that protects workers' rights.

Universal Declaration of Human Rights: A document that defines the rights that the United Nations believes should belong to every person in the world.

US Supreme Court: The highest court of the federal government.

V

Visa: A government document that allows a person from another country to stay in the United States.

Voluntary manslaughter: A sentence for a crime in which a person has no previous intent or plans to kill another person, which usually happens in the moment.

W

Weapons of mass destruction (WMD): Powerful weapons that can destroy entire cities or regions.

Whistle-blower: A person who publicly reports the illegal or unethical activities of an organization or a government.

White supremacist: A person who believes the white race is superior to other races.

Z

Zoot suit: A flashy oversized suit that was popular in the 1940s.

1

Animal Rights

UCR Lab Raid to Protest Animal Testing 7

Bilbao Anti-bullfighting Protest 12

Global March for Elephants and Rhinos 18

Blackfish Documentary and SeaWorld Protests 25

The animal rights movement focuses on protecting the rights of non-human animals. Animal rights have been a topic of debate for thousands of years, but people have different views on this issue. Many animal rights activists, or people involved in the movement, believe animals should have the same rights as humans. Some people feel that all animals should have some rights, but others view animals as property.

Humans use animals in many ways. Some animals are used for entertainment, such as in circus acts. Some are used for food. Animals are also used in medical and scientific studies. For example, some companies test products, such as shampoos, on animals to determine if the items are safe for people to use. Many drugs are also tested on animals to see how certain medicines might affect humans.

Opinions on how animals should be treated vary. Some people believe that animals are meant to help people. Others think that humans should protect and care for animals. Animal rights activists believe animals should never be used in experiments. Some activists have even broken laws and damaged property to free animals from laboratories and research buildings.

In most countries, the law treats animals as property. Something that is considered property does not have the same legal rights that people do. However, some laws protect animals from cruelty, even though they are still legally property. Many of these laws date from the 19th century.

History of the animal rights movement

Some of the earliest legal battles concerning animal rights were about bullbaiting. Bullbaiting was a sport in which dogs were trained to attack a bull. The animals kept attacking until either the dogs or the bull were killed. Before the match, people bet money on which animal would win. Efforts to outlaw bullbaiting began around 1800.

Animal Rights

> ### WORDS TO KNOW
>
> **Activist:** One who takes action to support or oppose an issue.
>
> **Advocate:** One who defends a certain cause.
>
> **Animal welfare:** The care and comfort of animals.
>
> **Captivity:** The state of being held under the control of someone and not allowed to leave.
>
> **Endangered:** A plant or animal that is in danger of becoming extinct.
>
> **Extinct:** A term to describe a species that has completely died out.
>
> **Factory farm:** A farm where many animals are raised, often indoors, for food.
>
> **Humane:** Acting in a caring or considerate manner.
>
> **Ivory:** The hard, white substance that makes up the tusks and some teeth of certain animals.
>
> **Poaching:** The illegal hunting or killing of an animal.
>
> **Sanctuary:** A refuge for animals where they are protected from harm and able to roam freely.
>
> **Terrorist:** Someone who uses terror to influence others.

Irish politician Richard Martin (1754–1834) fought against bullbaiting and other violent animal sports. He also tried to protect farm animals. Martin helped pass the Act to Prevent the Cruel and Improper Treatment of Cattle in the United Kingdom in 1822. The law, which is also called Martin's Act, made it illegal to treat cattle, horses, and sheep cruelly.

After Martin died, his struggle to protect animals used in sports became successful. Bearbaiting, a sport similar to bullbaiting, was outlawed in 1835 when Martin's Act was expanded to include protections for sport animals. The broader law, which became known as Pease's Act, also protected pets. In addition, it included rules for how to care for animals used for food.

Cockfighting is another violent animal sport. Two roosters are trained to fight each other until one kills the other. The owners often put sharp metal spikes on the roosters' legs. When they fight, the roosters attack each other with their beaks and claws or the metal spikes. The 1835 bearbaiting law also made cockfighting and dogfighting illegal in the United Kingdom. Although cockfighting is illegal in many countries, including the United States, it is still popular in some parts of the world in the 21st century.

The rise of animal rights organizations Over the years, many people have worked to pass laws to protect animals. Some individuals formed groups to fight for animal rights. For instance, Richard Martin was also a founder of the Royal Society for the Prevention of Cruelty to Animals

(RSPCA), which formed in the United Kingdom in 1824. At first, members of this group tried to help working animals, such as pit ponies. These ponies pulled heavy carts in coal mines and were not treated well. The RSPCA later went on to take up other animal welfare causes.

The American Society for the Prevention of Cruelty to Animals (ASPCA) was founded in 1866 by US activist Henry Bergh (1811–1888). Bergh had seen animal cruelty while traveling in Europe as a diplomat, or a representative of America. In Spain he witnessed a bullfight, an event in which a bullfighter stabs a bull with knives until the animal dies. On an 1863 trip to Russia, Bergh stopped a carriage driver from beating his horse after it fell and could not get up.

Bergh later met the president of the RSPCA in England. When he returned home to New York City, Bergh began working to protect animals. He wrote a Declaration of the Rights of Animals and asked his friends to sign it. Bergh then founded the ASPCA. The 1866 New York Act, which passed a week later, increased protections for animals. The 1867 New York Act made animal fighting illegal and defined humane, or considerate, animal care. Following this, other states also passed laws expanding animal rights.

Both the RSPCA and the ASPCA fought to protect farm animals, working animals, and pets. Both groups also worked to help animals raised for their fur and animals used in experiments. The ASPCA supported the Animal Welfare Act of 1966, a US federal law stating that animals used in research and exhibition must be treated humanely.

In addition, the RSPCA and the ASPCA have helped animals used for entertainment, such as in circus acts, and creatures exhibited at zoos and aquariums. The groups offered guidelines for how to care for these animals. Members of the RSPCA and the ASPCA believe zoos and aquariums should educate people about animals, not just entertain them. The animals should live in areas, which include enclosures, that help them stay physically and mentally healthy. The organizations also noted that animals that live in groups, such as elephants, should not be kept alone because this causes the creatures to have anxiety.

The modern animal rights movement Australian philosopher Peter Singer (1946–) helped start the modern animal rights movement. He was living in England when he became a vegetarian, or a person who does not eat meat. In 1975 he wrote a book called *Animal Liberation: A New Ethics for Our Treatment of Animals*. Singer wrote about how animals were treated on factory farms, which are farms where large numbers of animals are raised for food. He also described research laboratory conditions. Singer's book helped people learn about how animals are mistreated in many parts of the world. Five years after the book was published, People for the Ethical Treatment of Animals (PETA), an animal rights activist group, formed in the United States.

In 1983 American philosopher Tom Regan (1938–2017) wrote *The Case for Animal Rights*. In his book, Regan examined the ethics, or moral ideas about behavior, of how animals are treated. He said that humans should never use animals. This includes using them for food, entertainment, research, or labor. Many people agreed with Regan's ideas.

As awareness of animal rights increased, people organized protests to bring more attention to the issue. Others went even further and broke the law. Some animal rights groups have been called terrorists, or people who use violence for political purposes. These groups often target research laboratories where scientists use animals in experiments. Some activists in the United States and Europe have broken into labs and released research animals. Others have set fire to businesses or even set off bombs.

> ### Why Are Some Children Cruel to Animals?
>
> Researchers give the following reasons why some children abuse animals:
>
> - **Curiosity:** Some children mistreat animals out of curiosity or exploration, not realizing their actions can hurt the animal. Most children stop the mistreatment once they understand the animal can feel pain.
> - **Repeating Violence:** Some children who are subjected to violence or witness violence treat others (including animals) with violence.
> - **Revenge:** Some children abuse animals for revenge against someone they dislike or want to hurt emotionally.
> - **Gaining a Sense of Power:** Some children who feel powerless over situations in their lives abuse animals to feel a sense of control.
> - **Gangs and Initiations:** Some gangs or other groups require future members to prove their toughness by torturing an animal.
> - **Sign of Mental Illness:** For some children, animal cruelty indicates a mental disorder that if left untreated could lead to continued abuse of animals and even future violence against humans.
>
> SOURCES: The Humane Society of the United States and the National Link Coalition.
>
> © 2018 CENGAGE®.

Activists have also targeted businesses that use animal fur or leather (made from animal hides) for clothing. Some groups, including PETA, have created ads using famous people who are against wearing fur or leather. In other instances, activists have thrown red paint, which is meant to resemble blood, on people who are wearing fur.

The continued fight for animal rights

Animal rights continue to be an important issue in the 21st century. Over the years, activists have made documentary films about how animals are treated in circuses, testing labs, and aquariums. Some of these efforts have inspired other people to action. One such documentary was *Blackfish*. This 2013 film focuses on an orca, also called a killer whale, named

Animal Rights

CRITICAL THINKING QUESTIONS

1. What sorts of rights should animals have?

2. In what ways can animals be used humanely to benefit people?

3. Is it fair to experiment on animals to develop drugs and medical treatments that will help people? Why or why not?

4. Do you believe that the actions of groups like ALF and ELF are terrorism? Why or why not?

5. Should animals be used in shows for human entertainment? Why or why not?

6. Are peaceful protests good methods of trying to bring about change in society? Are violent protests? Explain.

Tilikum (pronounced TIL-i-kum). When he was only a few years old, Tilikum was captured and taken to an aquarium. The orca spent the rest of his life in captivity, which is like imprisonment, at various sea parks. The people who made *Blackfish* argued that keeping orcas in small concrete tanks was cruel. Many people agreed and pushed marine parks and aquariums to stop capturing and keeping orcas to entertain people.

Animal rights activists have also protested circuses that include animal acts. PETA targeted the Ringling Bros. and Barnum & Bailey Circus because the company used elephants in its shows. The group claimed that these animals were being abused and mistreated. Due to pressure from such groups, the circus announced the elephants would retire in 2016. A year later, the company ended its shows after 146 years.

Protests abroad and at home Protesters around the world have continued the fight for animal rights in the early 21st century. For example, many animal rights activists protest the ivory trade in Africa and other parts of the world. Ivory is the hard material found in the tusks of certain animals, including elephants and walruses. For years, people killed these animals for their tusks. They then used the ivory to make many products, such as jewelry and artwork.

The sale of ivory was limited in 1989 by the Convention on International Trade in Endangered Species of Wild Fauna and Flora (CITES). However, people in many countries still kill elephants and other animals illegally for their tusks. This is known as poaching. A 2016 documentary called *The Ivory Game* drew attention to elephant poaching. People across the globe have protested the ivory trade. These actions have encouraged many governments to pass laws to stop ivory from being imported, or brought, into their countries.

Animal Rights

Animal rights activists sometimes put on dramatic protests to raise awareness of their causes. Here, an activist lies on the ground covered with fake blood during a protest against bullfighting in Madrid in April 2012. © PIERRE-PHILIPPE MARCOU/AFP/GETTY IMAGES.

Animal rights activists also protest against bullfighting in Spain. Bullfighting has divided many people in Spain. Some citizens believe it is part of their country's culture. Others say it is violent and cruel to stab a bull until it dies. PACMA, an animal rights political party in Spain, has organized protests against the sport. Some members of PACMA secretly filmed a young bull being stabbed and killed in front of children. Such activities helped pressure some local governments to make bullfighting illegal. Still, the sport remains legal in certain regions of Spain.

Another area of concern has been the rights of chimpanzees, gorillas, and orangutans. In the United States, the Nonhuman Rights Project (NhRP) has fought a legal battle in New York City to recognize the rights of chimpanzees that were kept in cages on private property. In March 2017 NhRP argued that two captive chimpanzees named Tommy and Kiko should have legal rights that give them protection under the law but not human rights. The group wanted the chimps sent to an animal sanctuary, a place where animals are protected but free to move around. A court ruled in June that the chimps were not legal persons. It denied the request that the animals be moved to a sanctuary.

Attitudes concerning animal rights continue to change. More people have started to view animal rights as a serious issue. In fact, many law schools in the United States have added animal law courses so future lawyers can learn about protecting animals. Despite this progress, many individuals and organizations around the world continue to protest what they believe to be the unfair treatment of animals.

UCR Lab Raid to Protest Animal Testing

LOCATION: University of California, Riverside, California

DATE: April 20, 1985

On April 20, 1985, a group of animal rights activists broke into a laboratory at the University of California, Riverside (UCR). The group's goal was to free hundreds of animals that were being used in experiments involving blindness, cancer, and human behavior. The group was well known for its use of illegal methods to assist animals. Members called themselves the Animal Liberation Front (ALF). Sixteen group members entered the school's scientific lab overnight. ALF took approximately 460 animals from the lab. Among the stolen animals was a baby monkey named Britches, whose eyes had been sewn shut.

ALF's actions were condemned by the school and the scientists running the studies. They argued that ALF caused $700,000 in damage and ruined many helpful experiments. One such experiment was intended to help blind humans. ALF believed that the experiments were cruel and unnecessary. The raid received a great deal of publicity. In the weeks that followed, this event started an animal rights debate. People argued about whether it was fair to hurt animals to create treatments that might help humans.

Background to the raid

Like many universities, UCR had labs dedicated to medical research. This type of research often uses animals in experiments. Scientists rely on animal subjects because they do not want to test unproven treatments on humans. Many animals have body systems that are similar to humans. As a result, animals are used to examine the effects of drugs or foods, to test the safety of products such as makeup, to understand how creatures think or behave, and to study other important scientific ideas.

The forms of medical experiments can vary broadly. Some researchers use methods that can cause pain to animals. Other testing does not cause animals to suffer at all. However, in some experiments, the animals may be killed once the testing portion of the study is complete. After the animal has been euthanized, which is a painless way of killing an animal, scientists will examine the body to see what effects the experiment had. The goal of these scientists is to create medicines or make products safer for humans. The researchers also may want to see how certain activities or products affect humans.

In the mid-1980s, UCR was using animals in several experiments. After the raid, one experiment involving a group of 24 monkeys became particularly well known. The monkeys were part of a three-year study on vision loss and the effectiveness of a travel aid for blind people. Scientists taped the travel aid device to the heads of several monkeys. These monkeys had undergone procedures to mimic the symptoms of blindness.

Britches, the baby monkey freed by ALF, had been taken from his mother when he was a few days old and placed in a cage by himself. His eyes were sewn shut. Britches' eyes were also covered with patches to prevent him from seeing light. Scientists wanted to observe how Britches responded to having the device attached to his head while not being able to see. The weight of the heavy device meant Britches was unable to lift his head. At the end of the experiment, all of the animals would be euthanized, and the scientists would study their brains.

The Animal Liberation Front (ALF)

Britches, the baby monkey freed by ALF, had been taken from his mother when he was a few days old and placed in a cage by himself. His eyes were sewn shut.

ALF was created in 1976 by British animal rights activist Ronnie Lee (1951–). Lee had been a member of other animal rights groups. These groups included the Hunt Saboteurs Association, a British group that tried to end foxhunting by directly interfering with hunts. Lee believed that violence was sometimes necessary to save animals. In 1975 he was jailed for setting fire to a drug lab in England that experimented on animals. After his release from prison, Lee founded ALF. In the United Kingdom, ALF began stealing animals from labs, farms, and circuses that the group claimed were mistreating animals.

ALF became active in the United States in the early 1980s. Its goals were to stop experiments that caused pain to animals and to steal any animals that the group believed were being harmed. In May 1984 the group raided the University of Pennsylvania's Head Injury Lab. Members caused $60,000 in damage and stole videos of lab workers causing brain damage to baboons. A raid at the City of Hope National Medical Center near Los Angeles, California, resulted in $400,000 in damage. Both break-ins affected many experiments at these facilities. These attacks brought attention to the methods ALF used. The group's actions were condemned by the US government and some scientists but praised by other animal rights activists.

The raid on the University of California, Riverside

In early 1985 a student at UCR became aware of the experiments on Britches and other animals. Upset by how these animals were being treated, the student reported what was happening to an animal rights group. ALF heard about these studies and decided to rescue the animals. On the night of April 20, 1985, the group broke into UCR. Members wore white lab coats and black hooded masks. Although a student saw the ALF activists, he was unable to identify them later.

Over several hours, ALF's members destroyed equipment and stole as many animals as they could. Britches the monkey was taken to a retired doctor, who removed the stitches on Britches' eyes. ALF members made a video documenting the monkey's condition. This tape was later released to the public. At five months old, Britches was given to a foster mother at a monkey sanctuary in Mexico. He lived for 20 years before passing away in 2005 at a sanctuary in Texas.

Effects of the raid

ALF's video showing the condition of the baby monkey was called *Britches*. It created a wave of bad press for UCR. The head of the American Council of the Blind released a statement noting the organization's horror at Britches' treatment. Other scientists said that the experiments at UCR were poorly thought out. Reports by scientists at UCR later showed that they knew they were causing pain to the animals in their experiments but denied it at the time.

UCR announced that many of its experiments had been ruined. The news about Britches' treatment brought the school much unwanted attention. UCR was investigated by the National Institutes of Health

Animal Rights

An ALF activist holds a cat, with an electrode implanted in its head, shortly after the group rescued it from the veterinary school at the University of Philadelphia. The cat was being monitored in tests at the school until it was stolen by ALF.
© BETTMANN/GETTY IMAGES.

(NIH) to see if its experiments were unnecessarily cruel and whether the animals had proper care. After an eight-month investigation, the NIH determined that UCR had not broken federal laws. Nonetheless, 8 of the 17 studies that were in progress at UCR ended because of the raid. UCR said these studies were canceled due to the damage caused by ALF. The activists believed the experiments ended because of the bad press UCR received.

Despite ALF's efforts, experiments involving monkeys continued. Changes were made to how the animals were treated, though. Scientists no longer sewed their eyes shut. The monkeys' outdoor cages were heated, and their treatment was regularly reviewed. Experiments on monkeys eventually did lead to the creation of a tool called the Sonicguide. This device used sounds to alert blind people to possible obstacles around them.

After the raid at UCR, ALF continued to interfere with animal experiments at medical labs. The group also protested other organizations that it believed were treating animals cruelly. The group's methods became increasingly violent over time. In 1987 ALF began using arson, which involves setting a property on fire, to spread its message. One such arson attack at the University of California, Davis, in 1987 caused $5.1 million in damage. Later attacks were directed at McDonald's restaurants, US Forest Service buildings, mink farms, and fur stores. More than 50 such raids by ALF and a related organization called the Earth Liberation Front (ELF) occurred in the United States between 1985 and 2016.

Although several members of these groups were arrested, both ALF and ELF continue to raid farms and free animals in the 21st century. They engage in activities that the US government calls ecoterrorism. Ecoterrorism includes any illegal or dangerous activity done in the name of either environmental or animal rights. These groups are successful in part due to their loose membership. The various chapters of ALF do not organize on a national level and do not have a single leader. This way, if members from one group are arrested, they do not have information about other groups or members.

Some individual members of ALF and ELF have threatened scientists and placed people at risk with their tactics. Overall, the various chapters of ALF have been accused of causing more than $100 million in damage between 1985 and 2006. The US government views both ALF and ELF as terrorist organizations.

Debate over ALF's methods

ALF's methods have been the focus of regular debate. Many animal rights activists have credited ALF for freeing animals from painful lives. The organization's videos and activities have brought greater attention to how animals used in scientific studies are treated. PETA, which does not use violence in its campaigns, has supported ALF's efforts. Some animal rights groups have credited ALF with helping to change attitudes and laws. For instance, the cages used to house cats in scientific studies are now required to be larger.

Others have argued that ALF actually endangers animals. For instance, ALF has freed hundreds of minks from fur farms and released them into the wild. Some animal welfare organizations state that because these animals were born in captivity, they are unable to survive in the wild. As a result, the animals may starve and suffer painful deaths after being freed. Other animal welfare groups, such as the Humane Society of the United States and the ASPCA, have condemned the actions of ALF and ELF. They point out that the sometimes violent actions of ALF and ELF generate bad press for all animal rights groups. Many scientists also believe that ALF has done great damage to important experiments that could have helped humans. Some of these experiments were even designed to create drugs to help animals.

Animal Rights

PETA Antifur Campaign

People for the Ethical Treatment of Animals (PETA) is an animal rights organization. The group is against using animal products such as crocodile skin, silk, leather, goose down, or wool for clothing. However, PETA's most high-profile campaigns have involved fur. Various types of animal fur are used in clothing. The animals most commonly used to make fur coats or other items of clothing are coyotes, foxes, minks, muskrats, rabbits, raccoons, and seals. PETA says that the millions of animals used to make clothing each year suffer needlessly. Captive animals used for their fur often live in small cages for their entire lives.

In the 21st century, most fur comes from China. Few laws exist in China to protect the welfare of animals. Even animals that are considered pets elsewhere, such as dogs and cats, are sometimes killed and their fur mislabeled as some other kind of fur. The methods used to kill the animals can be very painful. PETA believes that by showing how animals suffer, the group can help end the practice of killing animals for their fur. The organization supports the use of artificial fabrics in clothing. For instance, it argues that faux (fake) fur, which is made from nonanimal products, is a good alternative. It looks like animal fur, but it does not cause animals harm.

PETA has used many methods over the years to urge people not to wear fur. Perhaps its best-known campaign involved famous actors and singers who appeared without clothes in posters and commercials. These ads suggested that the celebrities would rather wear nothing than wear fur. PETA members have also been known to throw buckets of red paint on people promoting the use of fur or wearing fur. These activists often appear at fashion shows to protest designers who use animal furs in their clothing lines.

During the 21st century, PETA has even gone so far as to purchase shares, or small portions, of various clothing companies. This allows members to attend board meetings where they can express their concerns about the use of animals in company products. PETA says that its campaigns have been effective. Clothing companies such as Calvin Klein and Zara no longer use animal fur, and designers like Stella

Bilbao Anti-bullfighting Protest

LOCATION: Guggenheim Museum, Bilbao, Spain

DATE: August 21, 2010

Bullfighting is one of the world's oldest and most debated forms of entertainment. For many years, people in Spain and other countries have taken part in this unique spectacle that is often seen as more of an art form than a

McCartney (1971–), Vivienne Westwood (1941–), and Hannah Weiland (1990–) advertise their brands as being fur free. PETA suggests that its efforts have even reduced the number of Angora rabbits being used to make clothing in China by 80 percent.

Twin sisters Lisa (left) and Jessica Origliasso (right), who perform with the band the Veronicas, unveil their new PETA ad. The picture on the poster shows the pair holding fake skinned rabbits with the caption, "Here's the Rest of Your Fur Coat." © TORSTEN BLACKWOOD/AFP/GETTY IMAGES.

sport by some people. Although it has become less popular over time, bullfighting is considered an important part of Spanish culture and has many supporters. Because it involves injuring and even killing bulls, many others view bullfighting as a cruel practice that should be banned. Opponents of bullfighting often stage protests designed to highlight the brutal nature of bullfighting and encourage government officials to end the practice.

One of the most notable protests took place in front of the Guggenheim Museum in Bilbao, Spain, on August 21, 2010. On this day, a group of protesters held an anti-bullfighting demonstration to highlight the cruelty of the sport. The protest did not lead directly to any bullfighting bans, but it did raise awareness about the sport's brutal nature.

What is bullfighting?

Bullfighting has a long history that dates back many centuries. It is believed that the practice first appeared around 711. Experts also think that bullfighting may have started out as a type of hunting. The modern version of bullfighting probably did not emerge until sometime in the 12th century. Some alternative forms of bullfighting, in which the bulls are not killed, are practiced in different places around the world. However, the traditions of Spanish bullfighting have remained mostly unchanged.

A customary Spanish bullfight is called a corrida (pronounced koh-REE-thuh). The main participant in a bullfight is the matador (pronounced MA-ta-door). The matador is accompanied by a six-person cuadrilla (pronounced kwa-DREE-yuh), which is a team of assistants that plays different roles in the bullfight. The cuadrilla is made up of two picadors (pronounced PEE-ka-doors) who ride on horseback, three banderilleros (pronounced ban-de-ree-YER-os) who stab the bull with a type of dart called a banderilla (pronounced band-de-REE-ya), and a special assistant in charge of equipment known as the *mozo de espadas* (pronounced MO-zo de ESS-pa-das), or sword page. Throughout each performance, the cuadrilla helps the matador as he or she works toward killing the bull at the end of the fight.

Bullfights typically occur in three stages after a special ceremony in which the participants parade around the bullfighting ring. Once the parade is finished, the first of at least three bullfights begins. In the first stage of the fight, the bull enters the ring and is tested by the matador. The matador tempts the bull with a cape. By making the bull run through the cape several times, the matador can get a feel for the bull's behavior. It also helps the matador determine how violent the bull is likely to be during the fight. After this, the picadors enter the ring on horseback and jab the bull in the neck with long-handled weapons called lances. This is meant to weaken the neck muscles so the bull will hold its head lower than normal. As this happens, the matador continues to judge the bull's behavior to develop a plan for making the rest of the fight as entertaining to the audience as possible.

In the second stage of the fight, the banderilleros enter the ring and plunge their banderillas into the bull's shoulders. Thrusting these weapons into the bull's shoulders weakens the animal in preparation for the final stage. It also serves to stir up the crowd and build excitement for the fight's end. By the time the banderilleros are finished, the bull is typically left with several banderillas hanging from the back of its neck.

The matador returns in the third stage of the fight to finish off the bull. He or she begins by getting the bull to charge through a cape several times. This further tires the bull and makes it safer for the matador to approach it. With each successful charge, the matador moves closer to the bull until he or she is in the ideal position to strike the final blow. The matador eventually attempts to kill the bull by thrusting a sword between its shoulder blades and into its heart. On rare occasions, this may require several attempts. Afterward, the bull's ears and tail may be cut off and given to the matador as a trophy.

Arguments against bullfighting

Although its supporters say that bullfighting is an important part of Spanish culture that should be preserved, opponents argue that it is a cruel practice that amounts to torturing animals for entertainment. The biggest problem that animal rights activists have with bullfighting is that the bull is killed at the end of the event. To activists, killing animals for sport or entertainment is unacceptable in any situation. The violent way that bulls are killed in bullfights is particularly troublesome to people against the practice.

The death of the bulls is not the only part of bullfighting that animal rights advocates protest. Many also point out that the bulls suffer needlessly during the earlier stages of the fight. During these early attacks, bulls are often injured to the point that they lose a large amount of blood. Animal rights supporters argue that such acts are cruel and painful for the bulls.

In calling for a ban on bullfighting, animal rights activists also note that the suffering that bulls endure starts well before the event begins. Because a normal, healthy bull would be too strong and too dangerous to be used in a bullfight, fighting bulls suffer several days of mistreatment designed to weaken them before they step in to the ring. Bulls are often kept in a dark box for days before the event so they will be confused by the time the bullfight starts. People responsible for preparing the bulls before fights often stuff newspaper into the animals' ears and rub ointment into their eyes to weaken their senses. Sometimes these workers stuff the bulls' noses with cotton to make it difficult for the animals to breathe. Some bulls are given drugs meant to calm them down or give them extra energy. These practices cause a great deal of pain and make it almost impossible for a bull to defend itself against its attackers during a fight.

To activists, killing animals for sport or entertainment is unacceptable in any situation. The violent way that bulls are killed in bullfights is particularly troublesome to people against the practice.

Animal Rights

Interview with an Ex-Bullfighter

In this primary source excerpt from Vice, *Álvaro Múnera of Colombia talks about being a bullfighter, getting gored by a bull in 1984, and how the incident left him in a wheelchair.*

Vice: How did you decide to be a bullfighter?

Álvaro Múnera: I was born in Medellín, where my dad had taken me to see bullfights since I was four years old. The atmosphere at home was totally pro-*taurino* [*taurino* is the Spanish adjective for everything relating to bullfighting culture].... I fought 22 times in Spain until on September 22 of 1984, I was caught by a bull. It gored me in the left leg and tossed me in the air. This resulted in a spinal-cord injury and cranial trauma. The diagnosis was conclusive: I would never walk again. Four months later I flew to the US to start physical rehab, and I seized the opportunity to go to college. The US is a totally anti-*taurino* country, and due to my former profession I felt like a criminal. I became an animal rights defender. Since then I've never stopped fighting for every living being's right not to be tortured. I hope I will continue to do so until the very last day of my life....

Many animal rights defenders applauded your decision, but many others say they can't forgive you. They even call you "mass murderer" to this day....

But as for the people who cannot forgive me for what I did to so many bulls? I have to say that I understand them and agree, to some extent. My only hope is to have a long life so that I can amend my many crimes. I wish to have the pardon of God. If He doesn't pardon me, He has good reasons not to do so....

In your articles you've associated tauromachy with a lack of culture and sophistication on the part of its aficionados. Isn't this a bit simplistic? How do you explain that intelligent people like Ernest Hemingway, Orson Welles, John Huston, and Pablo Picasso were into bullfighting?

Look, to be a talented person doesn't make you more human, more sensible, or more sensitive. There are lots of examples of murderers with a high IQ. But only those who have a sense of solidarity with other living beings are on their way to becoming better people. Those who consider the torture and death of an innocent animal a source of fun or inspiration are mean-spirited, despicable people. Never mind if they paint beautiful pictures, write wonderful books, or film great movies. A quill can be used to write with ink or blood, and many terrorists and drug dealers of the 21st century have university diplomas hanging on the wall. The virtues of the spirit, that's what really counts in God's eyes.

SOURCE: Querol, Toni L. "Anti-Bullfighting." *Vice* (October 1, 2008). Available online at https://www.vice.com/en_us/article/wdz8vz/bullfighter-152-v15n10 (accessed October 12, 2017). Courtesy of Vice Media, Inc.

The protest

Animal rights groups have taken a more active interest in speaking out against bullfighting. Many people have held protests to raise awareness about the abuse fighting bulls suffer and to call on governments to ban

Animal Rights

Members of AnimaNaturalis, Equanimal, and CAS International join together to create a giant bull shape with their painted bodies during the Bilbao protest in 2010. They sent a strong message about the cruelty of bullfighting. © RAFA RIVAS/AFP/GETTY IMAGES.

the practice. One such protest that took place on August 21, 2010, was especially distinctive. On that day, members of three animal rights groups gathered at the Guggenheim Museum in Bilbao, Spain, to protest the sport.

The Bilbao protest was the work of animal rights groups Anima-Naturalis, Equanimal, and CAS International. It was designed to highlight the brutal nature of bullfighting ahead of Bilbao's bullfighting festival, which was set to begin. Held every year, the event typically ended with the death of more than 50 bulls. As it happened, the 2010 festival was already set to be one of the last. Earlier that year, the government of Catalonia, the region of Spain where Bilbao is located, passed a bill to outlaw bullfighting starting in 2012. In recognition of this accomplishment, animal rights activists decided to hold the demonstration.

On the day of the protest, activists gathered at the Guggenheim Museum, which houses a famous bullfighting art exhibit. Once there, the protesters removed most of their clothes and smeared themselves with brown and red paint. Then they began lying on the ground and arranging themselves into the shape of a bloodied bull. The protesters sent a powerful message about the abuse that fighting bulls are forced to endure.

Animal Rights

Results

Like other demonstrations of its kind, the Bilbao protest helped bring attention to the violent nature of bullfighting. It also increased anti-bullfighting feelings among the Spanish people. Spanish attitudes about bullfighting had started to change over the years. Bullfighting was once one of Spain's most popular art forms. In the 21st century, however, more people saw the sport as a dated practice that no longer had a place in a modern society. As a result, bullfighting has become less common.

Even though it appears to be in decline, the fight over the future of bullfighting continues. Those who support the practice remain committed to making sure it maintains its place in Spanish culture. Pro-bullfighting advocates won an important victory in 2016 when the Constitutional Court of Spain overturned, or canceled, Catalonia's bullfighting ban. Some government officials vowed to keep bullfighting out of the region. The debate over bullfighting in Catalonia remained unsettled in 2017.

Global March for Elephants and Rhinos

LOCATION: More than 130 cities worldwide

DATE: First weekend of October beginning in 2013

An annual event, the Global March for Elephants and Rhinos (GMFER) was first held in 2013 in cities around the world. These marches draw thousands of people in an effort to stop the poaching of elephants and rhinoceroses for their valuable tusks and horns. In some places in the world, elephant tusks are used as jewelry and rhino horns are used in medicines. Most elephants and rhinos live in Africa, where many countries have laws that protect these animals. Still, laws have not stopped hunters from tracking and killing these creatures. About 27,000 elephants and 1,000 rhinos are killed each year for their tusks and horns. At that rate, wildlife experts believe the animals may be extinct, or no longer in existence, by 2034.

The value of ivory

Over the years, many people have prized ivory. Researchers discovered that ancient people used ivory to make tools and decorations as far back as 25,000 to 35,000 years ago. Ivory is the hard, white material that makes up the tusks of elephants and other animals. Elephants use their tusks to dig, lift objects, strip bark from trees to eat, and protect themselves.

Elephant ivory was very valuable to early human civilizations. In the areas that became modern-day China, India, and northern Africa, ivory was worth more than food or clothing because it was seen as a symbol of wealth and power. For many centuries, kings and nobles prized objects made from ivory. From the 17th century throughout much of the 20th century, ivory was used to make piano keys, game pieces, sculptures, and many other items.

The demand for ivory has continued into the 21st century. It is used to make jewelry and religious sculptures, although the ivory trade is illegal in many countries. Most of the illegal ivory is sent to China. Ivory is still very expensive. In 2015 the material sold for about $1,000 a pound in China. In some African nations, the tusks from a fully grown elephant are worth more money than a person can make by working an average job for a year.

The value of rhino horn

The horns of a rhinoceros, or rhino, are made of a substance called keratin. This is the same substance found in hair and fingernails. The horns are similar to the beaks of turtles and the hooves on horses. Centuries-old Chinese medical writings show that ground rhino horns have been used for thousands of years to treat fevers, upset stomachs, headaches, and other illnesses. Other ancient people believed the horns could make water safe to drink or help determine if a liquid contained poison. The horns have also been used as drinking cups and as handles for small swords.

In the early 21st century, rhino horn is still used in some places to treat illnesses. It is especially common in Asian nations such as China and Vietnam. Scientists and doctors have studied the horns and proven that they do not help in curing sickness. However, some people in Asia still hold on to old beliefs that the horns have healing powers. Rhino horns are so valuable in some parts of Asia that they sell for as much as $1,700 to $2,800 an ounce. This was higher than the price of gold (about $1,261 per ounce) in early August 2017.

Centuries-old Chinese medical writings show that ground rhino horns have been used for thousands of years to treat fevers, upset stomachs, headaches, and other illnesses. Other ancient people believed the horns could make water safe to drink.

Animal Rights

Dian Fossey and the Poaching of Gorillas

Dian Fossey was a zoologist who studied endangered mountain gorillas in Rwanda for nearly 20 years. In this primary source excerpt from National Geographic, *she describes the death of one of her subjects at the hands of poachers. Fossey would later be killed by poachers herself.*

It was Digit, and he was gone. The mutilated body, head and hands hacked off for grisly trophies, lay limp in the brush like a bloody sack.

Ian Redmond and a native tracker took the initial shock. They stumbled on the spear-stabbed and mangled body at the end of a line of snares set by antelope poachers. Stunned with grief and horror, Ian composed himself and set out to find me in another part of the forest. An outstanding student helper, he shared my aim to balance research with the goal of saving the imperiled mountain gorillas that I was studying from my base camp in the Virunga Mountains of Rwanda, in central Africa.

For me, this killing was probably the saddest event in all my years of sharing the daily lives of mountain gorillas, now diminished to only about 220 individuals—a reduction by half in just 20 years. Digit was a favorite among the . . . gorillas I was studying: In fact, I was unashamed to call him "my beloved Digit."

And now, through our sorrow, anger welled up—rage against the poachers who had committed this slaughter. Yet poaching is only one of many pressures—human encroachment, land clearing, illicit collecting, tourist presence—that have brought the mountain gorilla to the edge of extinction.

Digit's sad end in 1977 was sheer tragedy. . . .

In the daytime on New Year's Eve 1977, Digit was indeed needed. As watchdog of his natal group, he held off six poachers and their dogs who unexpectedly ran into the gorillas at the end of their trapline set for antelope in the saddle area west of Mount Visoke. Allowing the other 13 members of his group to escape, Digit took five spear wounds, yet in ferocious self-defense managed to kill one of the poachers' dogs before he died for his group. . . .

Tradition and circumstance complicate the poacher's motivation in gorilla killing. Sometimes he inadvertently catches gorilla young in traps set for antelope or buffalo. Other times, bolstering his courage with hashish for a hunt after buffalo or elephant, he meets a gorilla and kills the formidable "foe" for killing's sake. Not infrequently, a poacher is promised money to capture a young gorilla for exhibit in a foreign zoo or for sale as a pet to local Europeans.

SOURCE: Fossey, Dian. "The Imperiled Mountain Gorilla: A Grim Struggle for Survival." *National Geographic* (April 1981): 501+. Available online at http://www.nationalgeographic.com/magazine/1981/04/mountain-gorillas-virunga-peril-dian-fossey/ (accessed October 12, 2017). Courtesy of National Geographic Society.

The toll on the animals

Wildlife experts believe about 3 million to 5 million elephants existed in Africa in the early 20th century. According to *National Geographic*, by

1969 the number of elephants in Africa had fallen to 1.3 million. Because of the demand for ivory, by 1979 about 600,000, or almost half of Africa's elephant population, had been killed by poachers. Around the mid-1970s, many countries agreed to join the Convention on International Trade in Endangered Species of Wild Fauna and Flora (CITES). This treaty made the killing of elephants and the sale of ivory illegal.

Rhino populations have also been hurt by years of illegal hunting. In the early 20th century, hundreds of thousands of rhinos lived in Africa and Asia. According to the environmental group Save the Rhino, by 1970 the rhino population in Africa was about 70,000. Within 25 years, that number dropped by 96 percent to about 2,400. By 2016 the rhino population in Africa had bounced back a bit. The two main species of African rhinos are the southern white rhino and the black rhino. According to Save the Rhino, the number of southern white rhinos in Africa in 2015 was believed to be between 19,966 and 21,085. The number of black rhinos was between 5,040 and 5,458. According to the World Wildlife Fund, the largest type of Asian rhino, the greater one-horned rhino, was reduced to a population of about 600 in the year 1975. Conservation efforts helped raise the greater one-horned rhino's numbers to about 3,500 by 2015.

The northern white rhino, a relative of the southern white rhino, has been driven close to extinction by poaching. There were about 2,000 northern white rhinos in Africa in 1960. By 2017 only three remained. The lone male rhino is watched 24 hours a day by armed guards to keep poachers away.

By the early 21st century, efforts to stop the illegal killing of elephants and rhinos found some success. Populations of elephants and rhinos in Africa had grown, and several threatened species of Asian rhinos had recovered. The nation of South Africa, which is home to most of Africa's rhinos, reported that about 36 rhinos were killed each year from 1990 to 2007.

However, a growing demand for ivory and rhino horn in Asia led to a large increase in poaching starting in 2008. Suddenly, more elephants were being killed than at any other time since the 1980s. Wildlife experts believe about 100,000 African elephants were killed for their ivory between 2010 to 2012. By 2016 about 27,000 elephants were being killed each year. An official count by the World Conservation Congress found the total population of African elephants fell to about 352,000 in 2016. Rhino poaching also grew in Africa during this time. In 2014 South Africa reported 1,215 rhinos had been killed. The number fell

Animal Rights

Greenpeace Takes on Norwegian Whalers

For many centuries, humans hunted whales for their meat, oil, and blubber. The oil of a whale is considered valuable because people make items like soap, perfume, and candles from it. Blubber is a thick layer of fat on a whale that is used as food by some people. From the 1600s to the 1900s, so many countries hunted whales that the animals were in danger of dying out.

In 1986 the International Whaling Commission (IWC), a group that monitors whaling around the world, ordered a complete stop to commercial whale hunting. Commercial hunting is done to make money. Most nations agreed to stop whaling, but officials in Japan, Norway, and Iceland refused. Japan said it would continue to hunt whales for scientific reasons.

Norway and Iceland disagreed with the commission and continued to hunt whales. Norwegians said whaling was part of their culture, and it was not fair that IWC was telling them to stop. Norwegian officials said the nation would set limits on the number of whales that could be hunted.

Many environmental organizations, including Greenpeace, opposed Norway's decision. Members of Greenpeace travel around the world to try to prevent people from hurting the environment. The organization is active in efforts to stop whaling. In 1994 Greenpeace sent two ships, the *Solo* and the *Sirius*, to the region where Norwegian ships were hunting whales. Ships from other organizations were in the area as well.

The Greenpeace ships and members in rafts tried to block the paths of the Norwegian ships to prevent them from getting to any whales. Greenpeace members tried to climb onboard the whaling ships to steal the harpoon guns used in hunting. A harpoon is a large spear tied to a rope. Other Greenpeace members cut the ropes connecting the harpoon to the gun.

Eventually, the Norwegian government passed a law allowing its coast guard to arrest any Greenpeace member who tried to stop the

slightly to 1,054 in 2016. Poaching has put the elephants and rhinos on the path to extinction.

The march and its goals

In response to the killing of elephants and rhinos, a group of animal rights activists called for a worldwide march to help bring attention to the issue in 2013. The David Sheldrick Wildlife Trust, a group that rescues orphaned elephants and protects them from poachers, organized the march. The group is located in the African nation of Kenya. The first event was called the International March for Elephants and was held on October 4, 2013. The date was chosen because it was also World Animal

whaling. Greenpeace continued to protest in Norway for several years, but its efforts did not stop whale hunting. By the late 1990s, Greenpeace stopped targeting the ships and tried to prevent whaling through other methods.

Members of Greenpeace take direct action against Norwegian whalers in the North Sea in 1994. © PHOTOFUSION/UIG VIA GETTY IMAGES.

Day, a day meant to bring attention to endangered animal species around the world.

The march was held in 15 large US cities, including New York City; Washington, DC; Los Angeles; and San Francisco. International cities involved in the march included London, UK; Rome, Italy; Paris, France; Toronto, Canada; Melbourne, Australia; Cape Town, South Africa; Nairobi, Kenya; and Bangkok, Thailand. Thousands of people took part in the event. The organizers called it the largest human march for another species in the history of the world.

In October 2014 the event was renamed the Global March for Elephants and Rhinos (GMFER). It took place in more than 130 cities

Animal Rights

Hundreds of Kenyans join conservationists and activists in the march in 2014 as they demand action to stop soaring rhino and elephant poaching. The march was part of global protests held in more than 130 cities across the globe, asking people to shun ivory and rhino horn as commodities. The goal was to raise awareness and ask each government around the world to publicly destroy its stockpiles of illegal wildlife products and to show zero tolerance for illegal trading. © SIMON MAINA/AFP/GETTY IMAGES.

around the world. Marches were also held on the first weekend of October in 2015 and 2016. In 2016 the number of cities grew to more than 140, and tens of thousands of people participated.

The organizers of the GMFER had several goals. First, they wanted to bring the issue of elephant and rhino poaching to worldwide attention. Second, they also wanted world leaders and governments to do more to stop the illegal selling of animal parts. One way to do this is to encourage countries to pass laws that prohibit the sale of any part of an endangered animal. These laws would apply both within a country and in trade with other countries.

Another of the group's goals was to call on all countries to shut down businesses or factories that sell or process ivory or rhino horns. The group also wanted countries where poaching is a problem to do a better job at enforcing their laws. In addition, organizers called for tougher punishments for people caught poaching or buying illegal animal parts.

Continued concern

The problem of poaching in Africa remains very serious. Yet, some progress has occurred since the GMFER marches began. The number of elephants and rhinos killed in Africa is still high but has been slowly dropping. In 2016 the United States passed a law that stopped the buying and selling of almost all ivory products. The only items made of ivory that can be bought or sold are antiques.

Also in 2016, Chinese officials said they would close down all businesses that buy or process ivory by the end of 2017. The first factories closed in March 2017. China's decision to close its ivory businesses had an effect on the price of ivory. The same ivory that sold for about $1,000 a pound in 2015 dropped in value to about $331 a pound by February 2017.

Blackfish Documentary and SeaWorld Protests

LOCATION: Orlando, Florida; New York City; Pasadena and San Diego, California

DATE: 2013–2014

The 2013 documentary *Blackfish* inspired people throughout the United States to begin protesting SeaWorld parks. Located in various cities in the United States, SeaWorld is a theme park chain that features trained sea animals performing stunts for family entertainment. *Blackfish* criticized SeaWorld for using captured orcas, also known as killer whales, for entertainment. The film claimed that the captive orcas live in cramped and unhealthy conditions. It further argued that these conditions sometimes drove these creatures to kill humans.

Blackfish earned international attention after its release in 2013. Activists went to SeaWorld parks in the United States to tell the company to stop using animals for entertainment. The activists wanted the animals to live freely in sanctuaries. Police arrested numerous people at anti-SeaWorld protests in 2014. Public concern over SeaWorld's treatment of animals continued into the late 2010s. Critics of SeaWorld believed the theme parks were mistreating the orcas by keeping them in tanks.

SeaWorld employees did not believe keeping the orcas in their parks was harming the animals, however.

Blackfish background

The *Blackfish* documentary focused on two main subjects: a male orca named Tilikum that was kept at SeaWorld in Orlando, Florida, and the ways orcas suffer in captivity. The documentary used the story of Tilikum to highlight this point.

Tilikum was born in the North Atlantic Ocean in 1981. He was captured in his youth and sent to a sea-animal theme park in Canada. It was there that he became involved in the first of three human deaths. In 1991 he and two other orcas drowned a trainer who had fallen into their tank. Tilikum was transferred to SeaWorld in Orlando a year later.

In 1999 SeaWorld staff found the body of a 27-year-old man in Tilikum's tank. The man had stayed at the park after closing and then approached the orca tank. Authorities did not know whether the man had fallen into the water or if Tilikum had pulled him in. The man's cause of death was later ruled to be hypothermia caused by the tank's cold water. Hypothermia is a serious medical condition in which the body's temperature drops to extremely low levels and can lead to death.

The third human death involving Tilikum eventually became the most famous. The orca was performing at SeaWorld in February 2010 with 40-year-old trainer Dawn Brancheau (1969–2010). At one point during the show, Brancheau turned her head away from Tilikum. The orca took her long ponytail in his mouth and dragged her into the pool. Tilikum then started swinging Brancheau around wildly. Brancheau died from drowning and blunt trauma, or physical force against the body. SeaWorld took Tilikum out of its shows for a time following the trainer's death.

Blackfish examines SeaWorld orcas

In 2013 American director Gabriela Cowperthwaite's documentary *Blackfish* was released. Cowperthwaite had originally intended the film to be about SeaWorld. *Blackfish* would attempt to find out why the theme park's sea-animal shows were so popular with the public.

However, the nature of the documentary changed as Cowperthwaite worked on it. Her research showed how SeaWorld kept its orcas. Cowperthwaite came to believe that the orcas suffered mentally from being

SeaWorld trainer Dawn Brancheau and Tilikum, a popular orca "killer whale," are shown during a 2009 performance at the park. Brancheau was killed in 2010. © LOUIS JOHNNY/SIPA/NEWSCOM/SIPA PRESS/ORLANDO FL USA.

kept in small tanks for years. Wild orcas enjoy traveling great distances every day. They are also social animals that benefit from being with other orcas. At SeaWorld the only contact some orcas experienced was being attacked by other orcas in their tanks.

In addition, Cowperthwaite noticed that the dorsal fins of many captured orcas started to droop over time. Dorsal fins are triangular body structures on the backs of fish, whales, porpoises, and dolphins. The dorsal fins of most wild orcas are straight. Scientists have suggested that the dorsal fins of captive orcas sag because the orcas cannot swim freely. This weakens the tissues in the fins and makes them flop to the side.

Cowperthwaite decided to call attention to the suffering of Sea-World's orcas. She used the story of Tilikum to do this. The documentary argued that Tilikum's many years in captivity at SeaWorld had driven the orca to kill people.

The response

Cowperthwaite had made *Blackfish* for about $76,000. The film was released in only a few theaters throughout the United States in July 2013. It eventually made more than $2 million at the box office.

Critics praised the film. Journalist Michael O'Sullivan of the *Washington Post* was one of them. He wrote in his review that *Blackfish* succeeded because it would probably convince people not to attend orca shows at SeaWorld parks anymore.

SeaWorld management responded to *Blackfish*'s claims about the company just days after the film's release. The theme park chain listed 69 reasons why the public should not believe what *Blackfish* said about the parks' orcas. For example, SeaWorld rejected *Blackfish*'s argument that it still captured wild orcas. SeaWorld said it had not done this for more than 30 years. SeaWorld also questioned the authority of the people interviewed in *Blackfish*. It claimed that the former SeaWorld trainers in the film had not worked at the park in 20 years. According to SeaWorld, these trainers did not know how the parks kept their orcas in the 2010s.

SeaWorld's arguments could not reverse the damage that *Blackfish* had done. Performers, such as the American rock band the Beach Boys, canceled shows scheduled at SeaWorld's Florida locations. About a year after the film's release, attendance at the company's parks had fallen. SeaWorld also started losing money and sponsors, or companies or people who fund organizations in return for advertising.

Cultural responses and protests *Blackfish* also affected certain aspects of American culture. About a month after the film was released, the American computer animation company Pixar Animation Studios changed parts of the story for its film *Finding Dory* in response to *Blackfish*. *Finding Dory* is a 2016 animated film about fish and other sea creatures. It is the sequel to the 2003 film *Finding Nemo*. Pixar changed *Finding Dory* so that some of the characters were no longer forced to stay at a sea-animal park at the end of the film.

Blackfish also inspired some Americans throughout the United States to protest SeaWorld and orca captivity in general. One of the first notable protests took place at the Macy's Thanksgiving Day Parade in New York City in November 2013. The Macy's department store chain presents the parade every year to celebrate the holidays of Thanksgiving and Christmas. SeaWorld had a float in the 2013 parade. A 12-year-old girl named Rose McCoy walked into the street with a sign as the SeaWorld float

Circus Animals

SeaWorld was not the only US organization criticized for using animals in live performances. For years, People for the Ethical Treatment of Animals (PETA), the American Society for the Prevention of Cruelty to Animals (ASPCA), and other animal rights groups had called on Ringling Bros. and Barnum & Bailey Circus to stop using animals such as elephants in its shows. Such groups claimed that the animals were kept in poor conditions while traveling with the circus.

Feld Entertainment, the owner of Ringling Bros. and Barnum & Bailey, defended the circus. The company claimed its employees were professionals who cared for the elephants and other animals at all times. Feld stated that it used some of the profits from circus ticket sales to help protect wild animals such as elephants and tigers.

Ringling Bros. and Barnum & Bailey Circus fought the claims of animal rights groups in numerous court cases. The circus even won a multimillion-dollar case against the ASPCA in 2015. However, the activists' claims about the circus animals had already influenced the American public. Attendance gradually dropped at the circus, and Ringling Bros. was not making as much money.

Ringling Bros. finally responded to public pressure by removing elephants from its shows in May 2016. This actually made circus attendance decline even more. This financial loss finally became too high. Ringling Bros. and Barnum & Bailey Circus gave its last performance in May 2017. PETA called this a great victory for animal rights.

Circus elephants were featured on a US postage stamp. © NEFTALI/SHUTTERSTOCK.COM.

passed. The sign called for people to boycott, or refuse to go to, SeaWorld. The animal rights organization People for the Ethical Treatment of Animals (PETA) was planning to protest the float as well. Both McCoy and PETA wanted to speak out against SeaWorld because they believed it treated orcas poorly. Plans for that larger protest fell through, however.

More protests followed in 2014. The first of these was a protest by PETA at the Rose Parade, which is held every year in Pasadena, California, on New Year's Day. PETA tried to stop SeaWorld's float in that parade. The float depicted orcas swimming as families in the ocean. PETA claimed this was a false image because SeaWorld separated orca families and kept orcas in small tanks.

About 100 people, including McCoy, protested the float. Police arrested 19 of the protesters who sat down in the street in front of the float. Many singers had refused to perform at the parade because SeaWorld was allowed to have a float. These artists included American country singer Willie Nelson (1933–) and American rock bands Cheap Trick and Heart. PETA said it had protested the float because it wanted what was best for the orcas. SeaWorld responded by saying it cared about the animals more than PETA did.

Protests against SeaWorld continued. In mid-January 2014, about 50 people protested the company at its park in San Diego, California. They held signs referring to the company's treatment of orcas. Many of the protesters admitted that *Blackfish* had inspired them to protest SeaWorld. McCoy and members of PETA returned to the Macy's Thanksgiving Day Parade in November 2014 to protest SeaWorld again, and police removed the protesters from the street.

PETA tried to stop SeaWorld's float in the parade. The float depicted orcas swimming as families in the ocean. PETA claimed this was a false image because SeaWorld separated orca families and kept orcas in small tanks.

Tilikum and the future of SeaWorld

SeaWorld eventually made some changes in response to pressure from animal rights groups. In 2016 the company said it would stop breeding its orcas, or forcing them to mate. SeaWorld also promised to end orca shows at its various parks within a few years. The shows ended in the San Diego park in 2017. The shows in Orlando and San Antonio, Texas, were scheduled to end in 2019. SeaWorld said it would rework the shows to provide visitors with natural orca experiences. These shows would be designed to educate people rather than entertain them. New rides were also planned.

SeaWorld announced in early January 2017 that Tilikum had died. PETA noted the news, saying the orca had passed after a long life in captivity. At this time, SeaWorld was still making less money at its parks than in the past, and fewer people were visiting. Many news reports claimed the *Blackfish* protests were responsible for this. In July 2017 SeaWorld reported that the last orca born in captivity at one of its parks had also died.

For More Information

BOOKS

Hardouin-Fugier, Elisabeth. *Bullfighting: A Troubled History*. Translated by Sue Rose. London: Reaktion Books, 2010.

Kennedy, A. L. *On Bullfighting*. New York: Anchor Books, 2001.

McCormick, John. *Bullfighting: Art, Technique and Spanish Society*. New Brunswick, NJ: Transaction Publishers, 1998.

Newkirk, Ingrid. *Free the Animals: The Amazing True Story of the Animal Liberation Front in North America*. 20th anniversary ed. New York: Lantern Books, 2012.

Regan, Tom. *The Case for Animal Rights*. 2nd ed. Berkeley: University of California Press, 2004.

Riese, Juliane. *Hairy Hippies and Bloody Butchers: The Greenpeace Anti-Whaling Campaign in Norway*. New York: Berghahn Books, 2017.

Singer, Peter. *Animal Liberation: The Definitive Classic of the Animal Movement*. 40th anniversary ed. New York: Open Road Media, 2015.

Weisberg, Zipporah. "Animal Liberation Front." In *Cultural Encyclopedia of Vegetarianism*, edited by Margaret Puskar-Pasewicz, 27–31. Santa Barbara, CA: Greenwood, 2010.

PERIODICALS

Abend, Lisa. "In Spain, Human Rights for Apes." *Time* (July 18, 2008). Available online at http://content.time.com/time/world/article/0,8599,1824206,00.html (accessed July 10, 2017).

Belcher, Jerry, and Steven R. Churm. "Animals Taken in 'Rescue' at Research Lab." *Los Angeles Times* (April 21, 1985). Available online at http://articles.latimes.com/1985-04-21/news/mn-13126_1_research-animals (accessed July 10, 2017).

Burgen, Stephen. "Spanish Court Overturns Catalonia's Bullfighting Ban." *Guardian* (October 20, 2016). Available online at https://www.theguardian.com/world/2016/oct/20/spanish-court-overturns-catalonia-bullfighting-ban (accessed July 12, 2017).

Franklin, Ben A. "Going to Extremes for 'Animal Rights.'" *New York Times* (August 30, 1987). Available online at http://www.nytimes.com/1987/08/30/weekinreview/going-to-extremes-for-animal-rights.html (accessed July 10, 2017).

Leaper, Caroline. "PETA Opens London Fashion Week with a Protest on Designers' Use of Animal Skins." *Telegraph* (February 17, 2017). Available online at http://www.telegraph.co.uk/fashion/london-fashion-week/peta-opens-london-fashion-week-protest-designers-use-animal/ (accessed July 10, 2017).

Minder, Raphael. "Animal Welfare Activists to Protest Bullfighting in Spain." *New York Times* (August 20, 2010). Available online at http://www.nytimes.com/2010/08/21/world/europe/21iht-spain.html (accessed July 12, 2017).

Schoon, Nicholas. "When Baiting Bears and Bulls Was Legal. . . ." *Independent* (June 16, 1997). Available online at http://www.independent.co.uk/news/when-baiting-bears-and-bulls-was-legal-1256374.html (accessed July 11, 2017).

Steyn, Paul. "African Elephant Numbers Plummet 30 Percent, Landmark Survey Finds." *National Geographic* (August 31, 2016). Available online at http://news.nationalgeographic.com/2016/08/wildlife-african-elephants-population-decrease-great-elephant-census/ (accessed July 11, 2017).

Wheeler, Duncan. "It Was Spain's 'National Fiesta.' Now Bullfighting Divides Its People." *Guardian* (October 24, 2015). Available online at https://www.theguardian.com/world/2015/oct/25/bullfighting-spain-national-fiesta-now-divides-its-people (accessed July 12, 2017).

WEBSITES

Allen, Greg. "Ringling Bros. Curtain Call Is Latest Victory for Animal Welfare Activists." National Public Radio, May 21, 2017. http://www.npr.org/2017/05/21/528982484/ringling-bros-curtain-call-is-latest-victory-for-animal-welfare-activists (accessed July 14, 2017).

Badcock, James. "Will Spain Ever Ban Bullfighting?" BBC News, December 3, 2016. http://www.bbc.com/news/world-europe-38063778 (accessed July 12, 2017).

"Breaking News: The Last Generation of Orcas at SeaWorld." SeaWorld Cares. https://seaworldcares.com/2016/03/Breaking-News-The-Last-Generation-of-Orcas-at-SeaWorld/ (accessed November 10, 2017).

"Bullfighting." People for the Ethical Treatment of Animals (PETA). https://www.peta.org/issues/animals-in-entertainment/cruel-sports/bullfighting (accessed July 12, 2017).

Connor, Richard. "Spanish Protesters Go Naked to Rally against Bullfights." Deutsche Welle, August 22, 2010. http://www.dw.com/en/spanish-protesters-go-naked-to-rally-against-bullfights/a-5932696 (accessed July 12, 2017).

Convention on International Trade in Endangered Species of Wild Fauna and Flora (CITES). https://www.cites.org/ (accessed July 10, 2017).

"Dramatic Changes in China's Ivory Trade." Save the Elephants, March 29, 2017. http://www.savetheelephants.org/about-ste/press-media/?detail=dramatic-changes-in-china-s-ivory-trade (accessed July 11, 2017).

"The Early History of Animal Rights Extremism." Understanding Animal Research, last edited November 18, 2014. http://www.understandinganimal

research.org.uk/policy/animal-rights-extremism/the-early-history-of-animal-rights-extremism/ (accessed July 10, 2017).

"Ethics Guide—Animal Rights." BBC, 2014. http://www.bbc.co.uk/ethics/animals/rights/rights_1.shtml (accessed July 14, 2017).

"The Fur Industry." People for the Ethical Treatment of Animals (PETA). https://www.peta.org/issues/animals-used-for-clothing/fur/ (accessed July 10, 2017).

Global March for Elephants and Rhinos. http://march4elephantsandrhinos.org/ (accessed July 10, 2017).

"Greater One-Horned Rhino: Overview." World Wildlife Fund. https://www.worldwildlife.org/species/greater-one-horned-rhino (accessed August 2, 2017).

Karimi, Faith. "With 1 Male Left Worldwide, Northern White Rhinos under Guard 24 Hours." CNN, March 3, 2017. http://www.cnn.com/2015/04/16/africa/kenya-northern-white-rhino/index.html (accessed July 12, 2017).

MacInnes, Judy, and Jesus Buitrago. "Spain Anti-bullfighting Groups Protest in Bilbao." Reuters, August 21, 2010. http://uk.reuters.com/article/oukoe-uk-spain-bullfighting-idUKTRE67K22O20100821 (accessed July 12, 2017).

"Our History." Royal Society for the Prevention of Cruelty to Animals (RSPCA). https://www.rspca.org.uk/whatwedo/whoweare/history (accessed July 11, 2017).

"Position Statement on Zoos and Aquariums." American Society for the Prevention of Cruelty to Animals (ASPCA). https://www.aspca.org/about-us/aspca-policy-and-position-statements/position-statement-zoos-and-aquariums (accessed July 11, 2017).

Save the Rhino International. https://www.savetherhino.org/ (accessed July 10, 2017).

OTHER

Blackfish. Documentary. Directed by Gabriela Cowperthwaite. New York: Magnolia Pictures, 2013.

Britches. Documentary. Directed by Lori Gruen. Norfolk, VA: PETA, 1986.

The Ivory Game. Documentary. Directed by Richard Ladkani and Kief Davidson. Vienna, Austria: Terra Mater Factual Studios, 2016.

2

Civil Rights, African American

The African American civil rights movement took place in the 1950s and 1960s. Its goal was to persuade the US government to give full civil rights to black citizens. Civil rights are rights that all US citizens should have. These rights are stated in the US Constitution and its amendments. The right to speak freely and the right to vote are examples of civil rights.

African Americans began fighting for civil rights in the late 19th century. This is when slavery ended throughout the country after the American Civil War (1861–1865). The North and South fought the Civil War in large part because of slavery. The North wanted slavery to end, but the South wanted it to continue for economic reasons. The federal government freed all slaves after the war, but some individual states passed other laws to keep African Americans from having the same civil rights as white citizens. This was racial discrimination, which is unfair treatment based on a person's race. African Americans formed groups to fight for their civil rights. These groups included the National Association for the Advancement of Colored People (NAACP) and the National Urban League (NUL). Both groups formed in the early 20th century.

Even though African Americans began fighting for civil rights after the Civil War, the civil rights movement did not actually begin until the early 1950s. At this time, African Americans wanted to change the unfair laws passed by some states. They held many protests, gathering together to try to change the laws. One protest was the Montgomery bus boycott of 1955 and 1956. When people boycott something, they refuse to buy or use it. At this time in Alabama, black citizens could only sit in certain seats on a bus. These seats were usually in the back of the bus. White citizens sat in different seats. To boycott this practice, African Americans stopped riding buses. They believed they should be able to sit in any seat on a bus. The bus companies lost money because of this protest.

Montgomery Bus Boycott **42**

Little Rock Nine Crisis **47**

Freedom Rides **54**

Lunch Counter Protest, McCrory's **59**

March on Washington for Jobs and Freedom **63**

Civil Rights, African American

The Rev. Dr. Martin Luther King Jr. (left), director of the segregated bus boycott, outlines boycott strategies with his advisers and organizers. They include (seated, left to right) the Rev. Ralph Abernathy and Rosa Parks. © DON CRAVENS/THE LIFE IMAGES COLLECTION/GETTY IMAGES.

Civil rights leader the Rev. Dr. Martin Luther King Jr. (1929–1968) encouraged African Americans to protest peacefully. King's speeches and protests helped the civil rights movement reach important goals by the late 1960s. At that time, the US government had created new laws that protected African Americans' civil rights. The civil rights movement ended around 1968 although activists have continued to take on civil rights causes when needed.

Unfair laws against African Americans

African people began arriving in the British colonies in what became the United States as slaves in 1619. Some Europeans who wanted to settle in the British colonies brought African slaves with them. Colonies are regions of the world controlled by other countries. The settlers needed laborers to tend to crops and build settlements. As colonies grew, the

Civil Rights, African American

> ## WORDS TO KNOW
>
> **Activist:** One who takes action to support or oppose an issue.
>
> **Boycott:** A refusal to buy or use certain items, products, or services as a form of protest.
>
> **Civil rights:** Guarantees of equal political, social, and economic freedoms to all citizens of a country.
>
> **Desegregate:** To end the practice of keeping different groups of people separated by joining them together as one.
>
> **Discrimination:** Unfair treatment based on one's race, ethnicity, or other distinction.
>
> **Integration:** The practice of combining different groups in society together.
>
> **Jim Crow laws:** Laws created mostly in the American South in the late 19th and early 20th centuries that kept black citizens from enjoying the same rights as white Americans.
>
> **Segregation:** The separation of groups of people; often used to describe separating people by race.
>
> **Sit-in:** A peaceful protest in which people occupy a place for long periods, usually in a seated position, to call attention to a certain social issue.
>
> **Unconstitutional:** Going against the US Constitution.
>
> **US Supreme Court:** The highest court of the federal government.

number of slaves in America increased. Slavery remained a part of American culture until the end of the Civil War.

Before the Civil War, the country was divided on the issue of slavery. The South wanted to keep its slaves, but many in the North thought slavery was wrong. The North won the war in 1865. Later that year, the 13th Amendment to the US Constitution was ratified. An amendment is a change or an addition to a set of laws. The 13th Amendment ended slavery. Other amendments created over the next few years made African Americans citizens of the United States and gave black men the right to vote. (American women did not gain the right to vote nationally until 1920.)

Many Southern states did not like these amendments, however. In the late 19th and early 20th centuries, these states passed their own laws to work around the amendments. For example, some Southern states did not want African Americans to vote in elections. These states passed laws saying that people could vote only if they were literate, or able to read and write. Many African Americans at that time had received little or no education; in fact, educating slaves had often been illegal. These laws kept African American men from voting, even though the US Constitution gave them that right. Such laws were known as Jim Crow laws. The term *Jim Crow* was a derogatory, or insulting, nickname for African Americans.

CRITICAL THINKING QUESTIONS

1. How did centuries of slavery influence white Americans' opinions of African Americans after slaves were freed?

2. What do you think of the idea of "separate but equal"? Is it possible for two groups of people to be equal while legally separated from each other?

3. Why was it so important to African American civil rights leaders that their protests be peaceful instead of violent?

4. Why do you think African Americans continued protesting for their civil rights when they knew the dangers of being arrested or beaten for their actions?

5. Why do you think the Friendship Nine were forgiven for their 1961 sit-in in 2015? What does this say about attitudes on race in the United States in the early 1960s and in the mid-2010s?

6. Why was it important for the 1963 March on Washington to take place so physically close to the US Capitol Building and other buildings of the US government?

Origins of the civil rights movement

African Americans became increasingly angry about Jim Crow laws in the 20th century. The laws kept them from going to certain schools, getting jobs, and using the same public places as white Americans. This separation of black Americans from white Americans is called segregation. Segregation keeps certain groups of people apart.

African Americans started banding together to resist segregation. They formed groups such as the NAACP and NUL. These groups worked to make life better for African Americans, especially those in the South. However, the Jim Crow laws continued.

African Americans kept demanding civil rights into the 1930s and 1940s, but they made little progress during those decades. A goal of civil rights activists was to make American schools equal for both white and black Americans. Some activists did not necessarily want African American and white students to attend the same schools. Rather, they wanted to establish all-black schools that were of the same quality as all-white schools. Other activists wanted African American children to attend the same schools as white children. Those who opposed African Americans' protests sometimes burned down their homes and churches and even tried to kill protesters.

In the 1940s and 1950s, the NAACP hired lawyers to fight for civil rights in court. The group succeeded in this area. One of the NAACP's most important wins was the 1954 US Supreme Court case *Brown v. Board of*

Civil Rights, African American

Education. In this court case, NAACP lawyers led by Thurgood Marshall (1908–1993) proved that it was unconstitutional, or against the US Constitution, for states to have separate schools for black students and white students. The case was an important victory for African Americans, but the major protests of the larger civil rights movement were just beginning.

Main civil rights movement

African Americans held many protests against segregation throughout the civil rights movement. The Freedom Rides of 1961 was a group of famous protests. Activists known as Freedom Riders rode interstate buses throughout the American South. They wanted to convince bus companies to treat white riders and black riders equally. The Freedom Riders were sometimes attacked by white Americans who opposed integration. The Freedom Rides eventually succeeded. Interstate bus seating became integrated later in 1961.

One of the most famous events of the civil rights movement was the March on Washington for Jobs and Freedom in 1963. Some 250,000 African Americans and white Americans gathered in Washington, DC. They asked the government to grant black citizens full civil rights. Martin Luther King Jr. delivered his famous "I Have a Dream" speech against segregation at the march. Many people consider it to be one of the most important speeches in American history.

People carry signs during the March on Washington demanding voting rights, jobs, and an end to police brutality.
COURTESY OF THE LIBRARY OF CONGRESS.

Civil Rights, African American

Results of the civil rights movement

The protests of the civil rights movement eventually led President Lyndon B. Johnson (1908–1973) to call on Congress to pass civil rights acts. The US Congress is the part of the government that makes national laws. The first of these acts was the Civil Rights Act of 1964. It banned racial segregation in all public places in the United States. These included parks, restaurants, theaters, arenas, hotels, and courthouses. If the act passed and was made into a law, African Americans would be able to go to any restaurant or other business without being refused service because of their race. The act also made it illegal for employers to discriminate against African Americans or members of other races when hiring employees. The Civil Rights Act of 1964 did become a law, but the process was not an easy one.

To become law, a proposed bill must first be approved by both houses of Congress: the House of Representatives and the Senate. The House has 435 voting members, while the Senate has 100. Southern members of the House opposed the Civil Rights Act. They said it took away US states' rights to make their own laws. In the end, however, the House approved the bill.

The bill then needed the Senate's approval. This was another challenge. Southern senators tried to delay voting on the bill by speaking and debating for many hours. President Johnson eventually convinced more senators to support the bill. Seventy-three senators voted for the bill. The bill passed both houses of Congress. President Johnson signed the Civil Rights Act of 1964 into law on July 2.

The civil rights movement had not yet ended, though. Racial discrimination still existed in other parts of US society. Voting was still a problem. Some states had created voting requirements that made it difficult for African Americans to vote. To protest the continued denial of their right to vote, in March 1965 African American and other activists peacefully marched from Selma, Alabama, to the state capital in Montgomery. State police blocked the activists from completing their march and beat some of them with clubs. President Johnson soon heard about these events and started working to pass another civil rights law through Congress.

After much debate, both houses of Congress approved the Voting Rights Act in the summer of 1965. Johnson signed it into law on August 6, 1965. The act banned literacy tests or other state programs designed to prevent African Americans from voting. Three years later, Johnson signed the Fair Housing Act of 1968, also known as the Civil Rights Act of 1968. This law banned racial discrimination in the selling, buying, or renting of housing.

Major Civil Rights Acts in the 1950s and 1960s

Civil Rights Act of 1957
Signed into law by President Dwight Eisenhower in September 1957, this act created a six-member Commission on Civil Rights and established the Civil Rights Division in the US Department of Justice. The commission's job is to investigate reports of voting rights and other civil rights violations.

Civil Rights Act of 1960
Signed into law by President Dwight Eisenhower in May 1960, this act gave expanded enforcement power to the Civil Rights Act of 1957. It introduced criminal penalties for obstructing the implementation of federal court orders. It also gave judges the authority to appoint people who could assist African Americans who wanted to register to vote in federal elections. The 1960 act also prohibited efforts to try to intimidate African American voters through acts of mob violence or bombings.

Civil Rights Act of 1964
Signed into law by President Lyndon Johnson in July 1964, this act ended the Jim Crow segregation laws practiced in the southern United States. The act prohibited discrimination in public accommodations, facilities, and schools. It outlawed discrimination in federally funded projects, and it created the Equal Employment Opportunity Commission to monitor discrimination in employment, public and private. It also strengthened the voting rights of African Americans.

Voting Rights Act of 1965
Signed into law by President Lyndon Johnson in August 1965, this act outlawed the use of literacy tests and poll taxes, among other devices, that were used as voting requirements to keep people, especially African Americans, from voting. It allowed the use of federal examiners to supervise voter registration in states that used tests or in which less than half of the voting-eligible residents registered or voted. The act also provided criminal penalties for individuals who were found to have violated the act.

Civil Rights Act of 1968 (Fair Housing Act)
Signed into law by President Lyndon Johnson in March 1968, this act prohibited discrimination in the sale or rental of approximately 80 percent of the housing in the United States. Often called the Fair Housing Act, it addressed discrimination based on race, national origin, color, and religion.

SOURCE: Adapted from "Constitutional Amendments and Major Civil Rights Acts of Congress Referenced in *Black Americans in Congress*." History, Art & Archives, US House of Representatives. http://history.house.gov/Exhibitions-and-Publications/BAIC/Historical-Data/Constitutional-Amendments-and-Legislation/ (accessed October 18, 2017).

© 2018 CENGAGE®

After the civil rights movement

The civil rights movement ended around 1968. By that year, African Americans had been granted many of the civil rights they had spent decades fighting to achieve. However, the movement suffered a major setback during this year. King, one of the most famous civil rights activists, was assassinated in April. King's murder resulted in a decrease in African American civil rights protests. Yet, at the same time, African Americans were being integrated into schools, workplaces, and other areas.

The civil rights movement of the 1950s and 1960s accomplished many important goals. Still, tensions between white Americans and black Americans continued into later decades. Many African Americans, especially in the South, continued to live in poverty. Many white people still had racist views but were more discreet about it. For example, although public schools could not legally turn away African American students, some did this anyway without calling attention to it. Even so, the protests and other struggles during the civil rights movement gave African Americans protection of their civil rights as equal members of society into the 21st century.

Montgomery Bus Boycott

LOCATION: Montgomery, Alabama

DATE: 1955–1956

The Montgomery bus boycott was a large protest in which African Americans refused to ride public buses in Montgomery, Alabama, during parts of 1955 and 1956. The protest took place because of racial segregation on the buses. Segregation is the separation of groups of people, often based on race. In Montgomery, African Americans had to sit in a section of the bus that was away from white Americans.

Montgomery's buses were segregated in the 1950s as a form of racial discrimination. Discrimination against African Americans had existed in the United States for centuries before the bus boycott. White Americans had kept African Americans as slaves in the United States prior to the US Civil War. The slaves were eventually freed, but many white Americans still did not want black citizens to be able to participate equally in society. They made laws that separated African Americans from white Americans.

One of these laws stated that African Americans could not sit in the white sections of public buses. Black citizens saw this as a denial of their civil rights. For decades, African Americans had been asking the US government to pass laws to treat them equally. The early 1950s saw this kind of political activity increase. African Americans started protesting their unfair treatment more forcefully than in the past. The period of African American civil rights protests that lasted from about 1954 to 1968 became known as the civil rights movement.

The Montgomery bus boycott began after police arrested Rosa Parks (1913–2005), an African American civil rights activist. Parks was sitting in the section of the bus for black citizens. Then a white person got onto the bus and did not have a seat. The bus driver told

Civil Rights, African American

Rosa Parks Describes Arrest

In this primary source, Rosa Parks describes her arrest after she refused to give up her seat to a white passenger on a bus in Montgomery, Alabama, in 1955. This is a transcription of what Parks wrote down on paper. It is part of the Rosa Parks Papers at the Library of Congress.

I had been pushed around all my life and felt at this moment that I couldn't take it anymore. When I asked the policeman why we had to be pushed around? He said he didn't know. "The law is the law. You are under arrest." I didn't resist.

SOURCE: Parks, Rosa. Image 27 of the Rosa Parks Papers. Library of Congress. Available online at https://www.loc.gov/resource/mss85943.001810/?sp=27 (accessed October 18, 2017). Courtesy of the Library of Congress.

Parks to get up and give the white person her seat. Parks refused and was arrested. News of Parks's arrest quickly spread throughout the city. Many African Americans protested the segregation on Montgomery's buses. Their protests led to the Montgomery bus boycott, during which African Americans in the city refused to ride public buses. The boycott lasted more than a year. The city lost money. The boycott stopped in December 1956, when Montgomery ended the segregation of its bus system. African Americans considered the boycott a great success in their fight for civil rights.

Jim Crow laws

African Americans had been slaves in the United States for nearly 250 years before the practice was abolished by the 13th Amendment to the US Constitution in 1865. Further amendments gave African Americans citizenship in the United States and, for men, the right to vote. However, many states in the South ignored the amendments and treated blacks poorly.

Some Southern states created what became known as Jim Crow laws to continue racial segregation in their territories. "Jim Crow" was an insulting term for African Americans in the 19th century. The laws were designed to prevent blacks from enjoying the same rights as whites. Many white people believed their race was superior to that of blacks. They thought whites were smarter and more advanced socially than black people were. As a result, many white Americans did not want the two races mixing together.

Civil Rights, African American

Jim Crow laws legally separated whites and African Americans in almost every aspect of life. Blacks had to use separate public restrooms, eat in separate restaurants, and sit in designated sections on public transportation such as buses. Often the public places reserved for African Americans were in poor condition, while the places reserved for white Americans were well kept. Jim Crow laws angered African Americans, but they could do little to change the laws for the first several decades of the 20th century.

Civil rights movement and Rosa Parks

In the 1940s and early 1950s, African American civil rights groups such as the NAACP started challenging Jim Crow laws in court. Victories in cases such as *Brown v. Board of Education* (1954), which proved that segregated schools were unconstitutional, encouraged blacks to organize more protests against unfair laws.

The following year, an African American civil rights activist named Rosa Parks became famous for disobeying Jim Crow laws. Parks had joined the NAACP in Montgomery in 1943. She eventually became secretary of the organization's Montgomery chapter. Parks strongly supported African American civil rights. She had struggled for years to live with Montgomery's Jim Crow laws. By the early 1950s, Parks was finally ready to resist the laws in the name of the civil rights movement.

Parks's arrest begins boycott

Under Montgomery's Jim Crow laws of the mid-1950s, African Americans had to ride in the back of city buses. White people rode in the front. Blacks were expected to give up their seats in their own section if a bus became too crowded and white passengers had nowhere to sit. The Montgomery NAACP had been planning to boycott the city's buses as a protest against this segregation. Yet by late 1955, the group had not followed through on this plan.

On December 1, 1955, Parks boarded a Montgomery bus after working all day at a local department store. She sat in the first row of seats reserved for African Americans. The bus later became crowded, and a white passenger came on board and had nowhere to sit. The bus driver, James F. Blake (1912–2002), asked Parks and three other African Americans in her row to move farther back in the bus to make room for white passengers. The others quickly moved, but Parks refused. Blake

After her arrest for refusing to give up her seat on a bus to a white passenger, Rosa Parks was fingerprinted. Her decision to remain seated touched off the Montgomery bus boycott in 1955. © UNDERWOOD ARCHIVES/GETTY IMAGES.

told Parks that he would call the police if she did not move. Parks remained seated. Blake then called the police, who arrested Parks for breaking the city's law.

Parks called some fellow civil rights activists to pay her bail, which allowed her to leave jail. These activists knew Parks's arrest would inspire the rest of Montgomery's black community to protest the city bus system's segregated seating. Local civil rights groups called for a bus boycott to begin on December 5, 1955, four days after Parks's arrest. African American ministers told people in their churches about the plan, and a local newspaper printed a front-page story on the event. The idea behind the boycott was simple. African Americans were to stop riding city buses to work, school, or other locations on December 5. On that day, about 40,000 African Americans suddenly stopped riding the Montgomery city buses.

The boycott

Later on December 5, civil rights activists formed the Montgomery Improvement Association (MIA) to manage the boycott. The group chose Baptist minister the Rev. Dr. Martin Luther King Jr. as its leader. Twenty-six-year-old King was pastor of the local Dexter Avenue Baptist

Church. King and other members of the MIA decided the boycott should continue until the Montgomery city government started respecting black passengers on buses. The group wanted the city to hire black bus drivers and not force any passengers to give up their seats for others. The MIA originally did not intend to change the bus segregation laws completely.

African Americans knew they made up between 70 and 75 percent of the city's daily bus riders. The loss of so many customers every day would cost Montgomery a great deal of money over time. African Americans therefore helped one another continue the boycott by arranging other means of transportation throughout the city.

Some arranged carpools, in which groups of African Americans shared rides in single vehicles. Others took taxis. African American taxi drivers helped their black passengers by charging them only 10 cents for a ride. This was the same price as a ride on a city bus. Many other African Americans walked wherever they needed to go. Not being able to ride the buses caused some challenges for African Americans, but they persisted. The bus boycott angered Montgomery's government because it cost the city thousands of dollars in income. Police arrested King and other civil rights leaders, but the activists did not stop boycotting the buses.

By early 1956, the MIA had begun attempting to outlaw Montgomery's bus segregation laws entirely. On February 1, the group claimed in a US district court that the laws were unconstitutional. In early June, the court ruled that the laws were indeed unconstitutional because they violated the US Constitution's 14th Amendment. This 1868 amendment said that all American citizens were to enjoy equal protection under the law. This meant that the laws of the United States applied to all citizens equally, regardless of race. The Montgomery government disagreed with this decision and asked the US Supreme Court to review the case.

In November 1956, the Supreme Court agreed that Montgomery's bus seating laws were unconstitutional. In late December, the court ordered the Montgomery government to desegregate, or end its separate bus seating. The city did this immediately. King praised the decision as a victory for African American civil rights. He quickly announced the end of the boycott. He encouraged all African Americans in Montgomery to resume riding on city buses the following day. The Montgomery bus boycott had ended after more than a year.

The loss of so many customers every day would cost Montgomery a great deal of money over time. African Americans therefore helped one another continue the boycott by arranging other means of transportation throughout the city.

Aftermath

The Montgomery bus boycott accomplished what it had set out to do. Bus seating in the city had become fully integrated. African Americans could sit in any empty seat on a city bus, including in the front. Many white city residents disliked the fact that African Americans had earned this right. The city still tried to keep African Americans separate from white citizens in some ways. For example, African Americans had to wait at their own bus stops even though seating on the buses had been integrated.

Some white citizens responded violently to the bus integration. They fired guns into city buses, hoping to hit African Americans. In January 1957, members of the Ku Klux Klan (KKK) bombed four African American churches and the homes of various civil rights leaders. The KKK is an organization whose members believe that white people are superior to blacks. The KKK had targeted King's home for bombing, but the bomb was defused before it could explode.

The boycott quickly made King a nationally recognized hero of the African American civil rights movement. He went on to lead African Americans' fight to obtain full civil rights into the late 1960s. Parks avoided public attention after the boycott. White citizens started threatening her in Montgomery, so she and her husband moved to Detroit, Michigan. From the mid-1960s to the 1980s, she worked in the office of US Representative John Conyers Jr. (1929–). Parks later wrote a memoir of her life, focusing on her time fighting for African American civil rights. She died in 2005. Americans remember the Montgomery bus boycott as an early victory of the civil rights movement.

Little Rock Nine Crisis

LOCATION: Little Rock, Arkansas

DATE: 1957

The Little Rock Nine crisis refers to riots and other protests that surrounded nine African American students. The students were supposed to enter Little Rock Central High School in Little Rock, Arkansas, in September 1957. However, white mobs in Little Rock angrily protested against the nine teenagers going to the school because they did not want

African Americans in school with white students. The protesters preferred to keep their schools segregated, with white and black students attending separate schools. The nine African American students became known as the Little Rock Nine.

Segregation had existed in Arkansas and other places in the American South for decades before the Little Rock Nine crisis. Segregation kept African Americans from using the same public areas as white residents. Blacks had their own schools, restaurants, and public restrooms. Many white citizens in the South preferred to live this way because they believed they were superior to blacks. The laws that kept the two races segregated were called Jim Crow laws.

Jim Crow laws began to change in the 1950s. The 1954 US Supreme Court decision in *Brown v. Board of Education* ordered the integration of public schools across the United States. The order meant that African American students could attend the same schools as white students.

In early September 1957, nine African American students attempted to enter Little Rock Central High School under the new law. Arkansas Governor Orval Faubus (pronounced FAW-buss; 1910–1994), who supported segregation, ordered the Arkansas National Guard to stop the black students from entering. The National Guard is part of the US military reserves, which states can call upon in emergencies. To uphold the US Supreme Court decision to desegregate schools, President Dwight D. Eisenhower (1890–1969) later sent federal soldiers to Little Rock to guard the students as they entered the school. The Little Rock Nine attended their first full day of classes on September 25, 1957. African Americans praised the integration of public schools as an important victory for civil rights.

The Jim Crow South

The Little Rock Nine crisis was important because it marked a serious change in social life in the American South. In the late 19th and early 20th centuries, many southern states had Jim Crow laws that prevented blacks from associating with whites. For instance, African Americans could not use the same public areas or facilities as white Americans. This included restrooms, transportation, drinking fountains, schools, restaurants, and hotels. Jim Crow laws required this segregation because many white Americans did not want to be near African Americans.

An especially important event in the history of Jim Crow laws was the 1896 US Supreme Court case *Plessy v. Ferguson*. In this case, the court ruled that Jim Crow laws did not violate the US Constitution because the white and black races were "separate but equal." The case arose when an African American man claimed that the 14th Amendment to the US Constitution protected him from being made to sit in an all-black train car. The 14th Amendment guarantees all Americans equal protection under the law. This means that laws apply to all Americans in the same ways.

Plessy v. Ferguson contended that white Americans and African Americans received equal treatment despite their separation. African Americans disagreed because the public areas reserved for them were often in poor condition. The court case allowed Jim Crow laws to expand in the South over the next few decades.

Southern states used *Plessy v. Ferguson* to deny black students the right to attend white public schools into the 1950s. The states argued that the 14th Amendment permitted them to segregate the schools under the "separate but equal" ruling. In the early 1950s, the NAACP challenged this idea in the Supreme Court. The court ruled in the 1954 case *Brown v. Board of Education* that the racial segregation of public schools was unlawful because it violated the 14th Amendment. The court, therefore, decided that public schools across the United States would immediately start to be integrated.

Little Rock Central High School

Brown v. Board of Education caused much disagreement among Americans in 1954. Many citizens still opposed allowing whites and blacks to mix in society. These feelings were so strong that white public schools throughout the South and in other areas of the country simply refused to obey the court's decision. They would not integrate African Americans into their white student populations. The court passed another ruling, known as *Brown II*, in 1955. This ruling ordered public schools to desegregate quickly.

The school board in Little Rock, Arkansas, soon created a plan to desegregate. A school board is a local organization that manages the public schools in its area. The Little Rock board planned to integrate its high schools first, starting in September 1957. Even during this planning stage, however, local groups formed to oppose the integration of the city's schools.

The US Supreme Court ruled in the 1954 case **Brown v. Board of Education** *that the racial segregation of public schools was unlawful because it violated the 14th Amendment. The court, therefore, decided that public schools across the United States would immediately start to be integrated.*

Civil Rights, African American

Little Rock Nine Exactly which black students would be among the first to attend a newly integrated high school in Little Rock received much local attention. NAACP leaders in Little Rock knew the identities of these students would be important. The students would have to be prepared for the protests opposing school integration. Therefore, in the summer of 1957, Daisy Bates (1914–1999), at one time the president of the Arkansas NAACP, worked to find the best African American students to attend integrated Little Rock schools for the first time.

More than 500 African American students lived in Little Rock Central High School's district in mid-1957. Eighty of these students wanted to attend Little Rock Central High School in September. The members of the Little Rock school board spoke with each of the 80 students. From these candidates, the board members selected 17 finalists. In the end, eight of these students chose to attend an all-black high school. The other nine students would be the first African Americans to enter the integrated Little Rock Central High School. The students were Minnijean Brown (1941–), Elizabeth Eckford (1941–), Ernest Green (1941–), Thelma Mothershed (1940–), Melba Pattillo (1941–), Gloria Ray (1942–), Terrence Roberts (1941–), Jefferson Thomas (1942–2010), and Carlotta Walls (1942–).

Bates and her fellow civil rights activists from the NAACP then thoroughly interviewed the nine students. Bates had to prepare them mentally to enter the school that fall. She knew people would be at Little Rock Central High School to protest the students' entrance into the school. Bates needed to make sure the Little Rock Nine could handle the pressure of attending school when so many people did not want them there. The students met Bates's expectations and were set to enter Little Rock Central High School on September 4, 1957.

The plan soon met with challenges. On September 2, Governor Faubus declared that the Arkansas National Guard would be at the school on September 4 to stop the Little Rock Nine from entering. Faubus claimed that he had the students' best interests in mind. He said he did not want angry crowds at the school to injure any of the students. Still, the nine students planned to attend classes on September 4.

On that day, Bates and eight of the nine students arrived at the school together. Eckford arrived alone because she had not been aware that the others had grouped together. A mob of white students and adults at the school verbally attacked Eckford as she approached the

Letter from Daisy Bates about the Little Rock Nine

This primary source excerpt is from a letter written by Daisy Bates, who was a mentor to the Little Rock Nine. She is writing to Roy Wilkins with the National Association for the Advancement of Colored People (NAACP) on December 17, 1957, to tell him about how the students are being treated.

Conditions are yet pretty rough in the school for the children. Last week, Minnie Jean's mother, Mrs. W. B. Brown, asked me to go over to the school with her for a conference with the principal, and the two assistant principals. Subject of conference: "Firmer disciplinary measures, and the withdrawal of Minnie Jean from the glee club's Christmas program." The principal had informed Minnie Jean in withdrawing her from the program that "When is it definitely decided that Negroes will go to school here with the whites, and the troops are removed, then you will be able to participate in all activities." We strongly challenged this statement, which he denied making in that fashion.

We also pointed out that the treatment of the children had been getting steadily worse for the last two weeks in the form of kicking, spitting, and general abuse. As a result of our visit, stronger measures are being taken against the white students who are guilty of committing these offenses. For instance, a boy who had been suspended for two weeks, flunked both six-weeks tests, and on his return to school, the first day he knocked Gloria Ray into her locker. As a result of our visit, he was given an indefinite suspension.

The superintendent of schools also requested a conference the same afternoon. Clarence and I went down and spent about two hours. Here, again we pointed out that a three-day suspension given Hugh Williams for a sneak attack perpetrated on one of the Negro boys which knocked him out, and required a doctor's attention, was not sufficient punishment. We also informed him that our investigation revealed that there were many pupils willing to help if given the opportunity, and that President Eisenhower was very much concerned about the Little Rock crisis. He has stated his willingness to come down and address the student body if invited by student leaders of the school....

SOURCE: "Daisy Bates to Roy Wilkins, December 17, 1957, on the treatment of the Little Rock Nine." African American Odyssey. Library of Congress Manuscript Division. Courtesy of Library of Congress.

---

building. Someone even spat on her. Meanwhile, the Arkansas National Guard surrounded Little Rock Central High School. Guardsmen stopped the nine students from entering. The Little Rock Nine were forced to leave the grounds. The mob continued to threaten the students with violence as they left.

Faubus said that he would allow school integration in Arkansas if the people of the state supported it. However, a federal judge later ruled that Faubus had improperly used the National Guard to stop

Elizabeth Eckford is turned away from Central High School by members of the Arkansas National Guard, called out by Governor Orval Faubus.
© POPPERFOTO/GETTY IMAGES.

integration from taking place. President Eisenhower ordered Faubus to remove the National Guard and allow the students to enter. Faubus eventually did this.

The Little Rock Nine tried to attend classes again on September 23. An angry mob formed outside, however, and police led the nine students out of the school. Eisenhower then sent some 1,000 members of the US Army to the school to restore order and escort the Little Rock Nine to class. The students attended their first true day of classes on September 25.

Soldiers guarded Little Rock Central High School for the rest of the school year. People still physically attacked the Little Rock Nine whenever they could. One of the nine was suspended later that year for fighting with a white student. The other eight continued attending classes. In 1958 Ernest Green became the first African American to graduate from Little Rock Central High School.

Effects

In the fall of 1958, Faubus closed the three high schools in Little Rock to stop integration from proceeding. In 1959 a federal court ordered him to reopen the schools. Student integration continued in the city's high schools from that point. Several members of the Little Rock Nine later enjoyed notable careers, such as serving in the military and working for the US government. In 1999 President Bill Clinton (1946–) presented each of the nine with Congressional Gold Medals. These are awards given by the US Congress to American citizens to show appreciation for major achievements.

The Little Rock Nine crisis was an important event of the civil rights movement. It marked one of the first times that black students joined white students in the classrooms of an American public school. More schools across the southern United States integrated their student populations over time.

Civil Rights, African American

Ruby Bridges Breaks a Barrier at Age Six

Ruby Bridges (1954–) was involved in a victory for African American civil rights in 1960. Six-year-old Bridges became the first African American to attend a previously segregated elementary school in the American South. Until that point, public high schools had been integrated, but elementary schools had not.

Bridges was born in 1954 in Mississippi. She moved to New Orleans, Louisiana, with her family when she was two. She attended a segregated kindergarten in 1959. Schools were still segregated in the late 1950s because many southern states, such as Louisiana, resisted the US government's orders to integrate public schools. In 1960, however, a federal court demanded that Louisiana integrate its schools immediately.

Bridges's parents were unsure whether they wanted their young daughter to go to an integrated school. Bridges's father worried about what white mobs might do to African American students. Ultimately, Bridges's parents decided to let their daughter attend the previously segregated William Frantz Elementary School. The school district was slow to accept her at first. It finally admitted Bridges to the school in mid-November 1960.

Federal officers escorted Bridges inside the school every day for the entire school year. Angry mobs often surrounded her as she entered the school. They shouted angry words at her and tried to scare her away from the school. Bridges continued attending,

Guarded by several deputy US marshals, young Ruby Bridges enters the newly integrated William Frantz Elementary School in December 1960. She attended class by herself because many white parents kept their children home or threatened to send them to another school rather than integrate. © AP IMAGES.

however. She was taught in a class by herself, ate lunch alone, and had her own recess.

Bridges eventually graduated from an integrated high school and became a travel agent. She later married and had four sons. In the 1990s, Bridges became a speaker on civil rights issues. She wrote about her childhood story in several books. Bridges remained a civil rights activist into the 21st century.

Civil Rights, African American

Freedom Rides

LOCATION: United States
DATE: 1961

The Freedom Rides were a series of bus trips made by white and black activists into the American South throughout 1961. The riders protested racial segregation on interstate buses and in bus stations. Interstate buses are those that travel among multiple US states. At that time in the South, blacks were forced to use their own public spaces, including blacks-only restrooms and waiting rooms. Jim Crow laws banned blacks from sitting in the front section of buses and using other public services that had been reserved specifically for whites. Some of these laws were in conflict with rulings by the US Supreme Court.

The Freedom Rides were organized protests against Jim Crow laws. African Americans rode the buses from Washington, DC, or other northern cities to various places throughout the South. Once the Freedom Riders arrived at their destination, they began violating Jim Crow laws that kept blacks separate from whites. Freedom Riders used restrooms and restaurants reserved for white customers in bus stations. These actions angered many white citizens, and some acted violently toward the riders along the bus routes.

The Freedom Rides continued into the late summer of 1961. White violence against blacks during the rides eventually made international news. With the chaos growing, President John F. Kennedy (1917–1963) ordered the Interstate Commerce Commission (ICC) to declare that racial segregation on interstate buses was unconstitutional. The ICC was a federal agency that oversaw transportation and trade among US states. The ICC delayed following Kennedy's orders for several months. Finally, in November 1961, the agency banned racial segregation on interstate buses and in bus stations. African American civil rights leaders praised the Freedom Rides as a victory in the fight against racial segregation in the United States.

Origins of the Freedom Rides

The Freedom Rides were a product of an African American civil rights group called the Congress of Racial Equality (CORE). The organization formed at the University of Chicago in 1942. CORE's goal was to end racial segregation through nonviolent means.

The segregation of black citizens had been part of American life since the late 19th century. During this period, states in the South introduced Jim Crow laws. These laws made life unfair for blacks by preventing them from using the same public areas and facilities as whites. African Americans were restricted in what restrooms, restaurants, and seats on public transportation they could use. Jim Crow laws existed because many white Americans did not see African Americans as equal members of society. They believed they were superior to blacks.

At first, CORE struggled to do much in the fight against segregation. One reason was because the group was based in the North, while Jim Crow laws existed mostly in the South. Additionally, most members of CORE were white. CORE leaders knew the group could succeed if it moved into the South and found black members willing to protest segregation.

An early CORE protest was the 1947 Journey of Reconciliation. In this event, members of CORE rode on commercial interstate buses to see whether authorities would enforce the decision made in the 1946 US Supreme Court case *Morgan v. Virginia*. In this decision, the court ruled that segregated seating on commercial interstate buses was illegal. This meant that bus companies such as Greyhound could not force blacks to give up their seats to white passengers. In 1955 CORE helped African Americans protest segregated seating on city buses in Montgomery, Alabama, during the Montgomery bus boycott. Some CORE members remained in the South following the boycott.

The Freedom Rides

In the early 1960s, CORE began planning to test another recent Supreme Court decision on bus segregation. In 1960's *Boynton v. Virginia*, the court ruled that it was illegal to segregate blacks and whites in restaurants and restrooms at bus stations where interstate buses stopped along their journeys. The reasoning was that because seating on interstate buses was not supposed to be segregated, the public areas at the bus stations should not be segregated either.

In early 1961, CORE's leaders wanted to find out whether bus stations in the South would follow the decision of *Boynton v. Virginia*. CORE planned its protest in the early months of 1961. The Freedom Rides began on May 4, 1961.

An early CORE protest was the 1947 Journey of Reconciliation. In this event, members of CORE rode on commercial interstate buses to see whether authorities would enforce the decision made in the 1946 US Supreme Court case Morgan v. Virginia. *In this decision, the court ruled that segregated seating on commercial interstate buses was illegal.*

Civil Rights, African American

The first ride The first group of Freedom Riders included seven black and six white Americans. They planned to take two buses from Washington, DC, to New Orleans, Louisiana. Over the next two weeks of the trip, the Freedom Riders attempted to use areas of bus stations that had previously been designated as "whites only."

White citizens protested the 13 Freedom Riders at stops in Virginia, but the group was able to pass through the state unharmed. This was not the case in Rock Hill, South Carolina, where the buses arrived several days later. At a bus station there, African American Freedom Rider John Lewis (1940–) and several others in his party were attacked as soon as they entered a whites-only waiting room. Another Freedom Rider was arrested for using a whites-only restroom. The news media widely covered the incidents.

One of the buses arrived in Anniston, Alabama, on May 14, a few days after the Rock Hill violence. An angry mob met the bus at the station and prevented the passengers from exiting the bus. The mob chased the bus in cars. Someone eventually threw a bomb into the bus, which quickly caught fire. The Freedom Riders were forced to leave the bus and then were beaten by the mob. The second bus traveled to Birmingham, Alabama, that same day. Another angry mob beat the Freedom Riders on that bus.

This violence proved to be too much for CORE's leadership. With the bus drivers now refusing to finish the trip to New Orleans, CORE

Freedom Riders sit on the ground outside the bus after it was set on fire by a group of angry whites who met the bus and its riders on arrival in Anniston, Alabama.
© UNDERWOOD ARCHIVES/ GETTY IMAGES.

canceled the rest of the first Freedom Ride. The Freedom Riders traveled to New Orleans by air instead. The first Freedom Ride had not accomplished what CORE leaders wanted. However, stories of the bus bombing and the violence of the mobs quickly made news throughout the United States and around the world, making people aware of African Americans' struggle for civil rights.

Later rides and federal aid Other CORE leaders refused to be frightened into stopping the rides. Another civil rights group, the Student Nonviolent Coordinating Committee (SNCC; pronounced SNICK), gathered 10 more Freedom Riders. They rode a bus from Nashville, Tennessee, to Birmingham beginning on May 17, 1961. Police arrested all 10 riders upon their arrival at the Birmingham bus station for breaking the state's segregation laws. Again, the riders could not find a driver to take them out of Birmingham, and they had to remain in the city for a few days.

Robert Kennedy (1925–1968), the US attorney general at the time, stepped in to help the Freedom Riders. The attorney general oversees legal matters relating to the US federal government. Kennedy found a driver for the riders' bus. He made sure the Alabama government provided the bus with a state police escort on its journey from Birmingham to Montgomery, which began on May 20. The police left the bus when it reached Montgomery.

The Freedom Riders then attempted to enter the bus station in Montgomery. A mob was waiting for them. The mob beat the riders. Some of the riders suffered health problems for the rest of their lives due to their injuries. More Freedom Riders left Montgomery for Jackson, Mississippi, on May 24, 1961. A group of civil rights supporters met them in Jackson, but police arrested the riders for trying to use whites-only areas in the bus station. The continuing struggle of the riders attracted more African Americans to the Freedom Rides.

End of the Freedom Rides

Although President Kennedy directed the ICC to ban racial segregation in public bus stations, announcing the ban in late May 1961, the ICC was slow to act. Meanwhile, the Freedom Rides became more uncontrollable. Hundreds of young people from across the United States started participating in the rides. Southern jails became crowded with riders who had been arrested for breaking segregation laws.

Civil Rights, African American

Freedom Summer Voter Registration

In the summer of 1964, civil rights groups such as the Congress of Racial Equality (CORE) and the Student Nonviolent Coordinating Committee (SNCC) planned a program called the Mississippi Summer Project. It also was known as the Freedom Summer. The program's purpose was to register African American voters in Mississippi.

Several hundred activists started working on the registrations in Oxford, Mississippi, in mid-June. Most of the activists were white students from the North. They met up with African American activists from Mississippi. As with earlier events of the civil rights movement, Americans who opposed integration efforts interrupted the voter drive. They protested the registration program and threatened the volunteers with violence.

A few days after the Freedom Summer began, three volunteers with the program were reported missing. They were James Earl Chaney (1943–1964), Andrew Goodman (1943–1964), and Michael Henry Schwerner (1939–1964). Chaney was an African American man from Mississippi, while Goodman and Schwerner were both white men from New York City. These disappearances frightened the Freedom Summer volunteers, but they continued the drive.

Chaney, Goodman, and Schwerner had been arrested by police and were later murdered by members of the Ku Klux Klan (KKK), a white supremacist organization. The KKK later buried the men's bodies. Officers of the Federal Bureau of Investigation (FBI) found the bodies in August 1964.

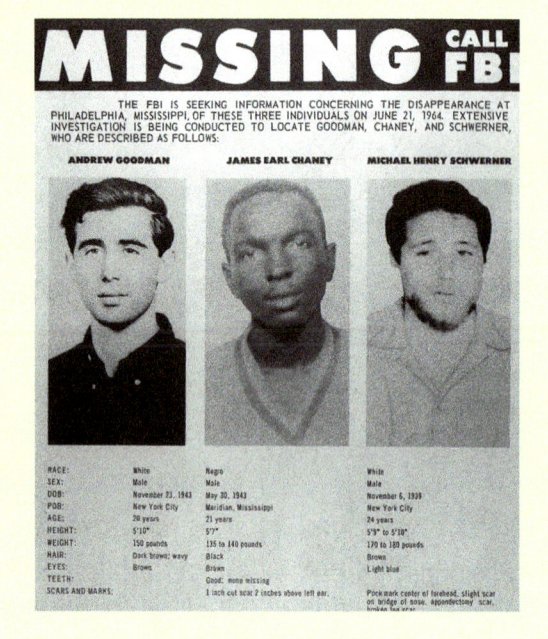

A missing persons poster displays the photographs of civil rights workers Andrew Goodman, James Earl Chaney, and Michael Henry Schwerner after they disappeared in Mississippi. It was later discovered that they were murdered by the Ku Klux Klan. © BETTMAN/GETTY IMAGES.

The murders made African Americans wonder whether they would ever achieve civil rights through peaceful methods such as voting drives. In the end, the Freedom Summer registered about 1,600 black voters. However, about 17,000 had tried to register. Ongoing racial violence in this period motivated the US government to pass the Voting Rights Act of 1965. The act removed barriers that often made it difficult for African Americans to vote.

President Kennedy continued pressuring the ICC to ban segregation on interstate buses and in bus stations. The ICC finally listened on

November 1, 1961. The Freedom Rides had been eye-opening for civil rights activists. They learned that southerners' violence against African Americans and their supporters usually earned media coverage. That coverage, in turn, brought about assistance from the federal government. The desegregation of interstate buses and bus stations was another important step in the ongoing African American civil rights movement.

Lunch Counter Protest, McCrory's

LOCATION: Rock Hill, South Carolina

DATE: January 31, 1961

The lunch counter protest in Rock Hill, South Carolina, in January 1961 was a sit-in by a group of African Americans. Sit-ins are a type of peaceful protest in which activists occupy a place for long periods to call attention to a certain social issue. The activists chose the lunch counter at a McCrory's variety store to challenge the company's refusal to serve African Americans. Lunch counters are eating areas in which customers sit on stools and are served food on the counter in front of them. The activists at the Rock Hill sit-in protested McCrory's policy of serving only white customers. The policy was part of the racial discrimination laws that were common in the American South at the time. The Rock Hill sit-in was part of the larger African American civil rights movement of the 1950s and 1960s.

Sit-ins at lunch counters had become another form of protest against racial discrimination. The first notable sit-in occurred in Greensboro, North Carolina, in February 1960. Four African Americans refused to leave a whites-only lunch counter in the city. That sit-in inspired others across the South, including several in Rock Hill.

Police arrested 10 African Americans at the 1961 Rock Hill sit-in soon after they sat down. They later were charged with trespassing, or entering someone's property without permission. They could pay $100 bail to get out of jail or spend 30 days in a prison work camp. Nine of the 10 men chose the camp and became known as the Friendship Nine, named for Friendship Junior College.

The Rock Hill sit-in helped call attention to the ongoing problem of racial segregation in public places throughout the South. The Civil Rights Act of 1964 finally banned all racial discrimination in public places in the United States.

The sit-in movement

Civil rights activists started staging sit-ins in early 1960. On February 1 of that year, four African American college students staged the first sit-in at the lunch counter of the Woolworth's retail store in Greensboro, North Carolina.

The students knew the lunch counter served food only to white customers. They sat at the counter and tried to order, but they were refused service because they were black. The students did not leave the counter. Instead, they stayed in their seats, waiting to be served. No one ever served them, and the students remained at the counter until Woolworth's closed that night. The students returned to the counter the next day. Students from other nearby colleges joined them. The counter employees again refused to serve them.

Several days later, about 300 African Americans appeared at the Woolworth's lunch counter. It became impossible for the counter to serve anyone. Heavy news coverage quickly spread the story of the sit-in across the United States. This inspired African Americans and activists in other states to stage their own sit-ins at restaurants, libraries, and other segregated public places. Police eventually arrested many of the protesters for trespassing.

African Americans continued the sit-ins in whites-only areas. To keep the protests nonviolent, the activists had to ignore threats and violence from white customers, who sometimes threw food at the activists or physically attacked them. When they were attacked, the activists protected themselves from being hurt but did not fight back.

The sit-ins slowly convinced many restaurants in the South to integrate their seating, or to serve both whites and blacks. Not all restaurants did this. African Americans continued staging sit-ins to protest ongoing segregation in restaurants throughout the South.

The Rock Hill sit-in

Several African American civil rights groups continued to organize sit-ins. One of these was SNCC, which was made up mostly of students from both the North and South. Another group was CORE, which was based

Civil Rights, African American

mostly in the North. These groups helped plan the lunch counter sit-in at Rock Hill, South Carolina.

The sit-in was set to take place on January 31, 1961, at Rock Hill's McCrory's store. This was a five-and-dime, a store where many types of items were sold for low prices. The store also had a lunch counter.

On the scheduled day, a group of African Americans entered McCrory's and sat at the lunch counter. Most of the activists were students from Friendship Junior College in Rock Hill. One activist was a member of CORE. The activists later claimed they had barely sat in their seats when police officers grabbed them roughly from behind, dragged them off their stools, and arrested them for trespassing in a whites-only area. The police took them to jail and held them all in the same cell.

The activists were later charged with trespassing and disturbing the peace. They could pay bail of $100 each to avoid going to jail. However, CORE and other civil rights groups wanted the activists who got arrested to follow a strategy called "jail, no bail." The idea was to save the groups from having to pay bail for the many activists who got arrested. Nine of the activists, who became known as the Friendship Nine, chose to be sent to a prison farm to work for 30 days as punishment. The remaining activist paid the bail and was released.

The civil rights protests at McCrory's actually began in February 1960. Here, activists are shown taking part in that earlier lunch-counter sit-in, which was one of the first of its kind. © AP PHOTO/THE HERALD.

Civil Rights, African American

Desegregation in Birmingham, Alabama

Birmingham, Alabama, remained one of the most segregated cities in the United States into the early 1960s. In 1962 the city closed numerous parks, playgrounds, and pools just so it would not have to obey the US government's order to desegregate its public areas. Tension between whites and blacks was high. Blacks in the city wanted to be given their civil rights. The city government wanted racial segregation to continue.

In the spring of 1963, civil rights leader the Rev. Dr. Martin Luther King Jr. started a series of protests in Birmingham. He hoped to convince the city to desegregate. King and other activists boycotted a number of city businesses that April. The police arrested protesters.

In early May 1963, King began Project C, or Project Confrontation. Project C involved groups of African Americans protesting for civil rights in Birmingham's streets. The police responded with force. Officers sprayed protesters with fire hoses, had police dogs bite them, and physically attacked them.

The Birmingham government finally gave in after several days of violence. It planned to desegregate various public areas, such as lunch counters, pools, restrooms, and drinking fountains. The government did this reluctantly. City officials agreed to desegregate only after it appeared that racial violence in the city was not going to stop.

The activists who had chosen to go to prison were sent to South Carolina's York County Prison Farm. There, they carried blocks of cement, moved piles of sand, and cut weeds. Over the course of the group's time at the prison farm, other African Americans protested segregation throughout Rock Hill. They protested at the farm itself and held sit-ins at bus stations and in churches. At one point, the activists timed a protest to occur while the jailed activists were in solitary confinement. This is a type of imprisonment in which prisoners are placed in cells alone and have almost no contact with other people. Each of the activists had been placed in solitary confinement for singing a song about refusing to be slaves.

Aftermath

The jailed protesters were released from the prison farm on March 2, 1961. After that, civil rights groups stopped staging sit-ins in Rock Hill. Other kinds of protests against segregation continued. CORE leaders knew the lunch counter sit-ins in Rock Hill did not lead directly to the end of racial segregation in the city. The leaders did believe that the sit-ins had helped draw national attention to the fight for civil rights.

In January 2015, 54 years after the Rock Hill sit-in, a judge in South Carolina dismissed the Friendship Nine's trespassing convictions from the 1961 sit-in. Seven of the eight surviving members of the Friendship Nine were present at a Rock Hill courthouse for the public event. City officials there claimed the charges of trespassing in 1961 were wrong and that the activists should be viewed as role models. A diner that had opened at the site of the McCrory's store in Rock Hill kept the original lunch counter. The chairs at the counter had the names of the Friendship Nine engraved on them to remember the event.

March on Washington for Jobs and Freedom

LOCATION: Washington, DC

DATE: August 28, 1963

The 1963 March on Washington for Jobs and Freedom, also called the March on Washington, was the largest African American civil rights protest that had ever been staged to that point. Some 250,000 people met on the National Mall in Washington, DC, on August 28, 1963. They protested racial segregation and other forms of discrimination in the United States. The National Mall is a park in downtown Washington.

Protesters at the march listened to many speakers throughout the day. Civil rights leaders, singers, and politicians appeared at the march to support the civil rights movement. Martin Luther King Jr. was one of the speakers. He closed the march with his "I Have a Dream" speech, which became one of the most famous speeches in American history.

The March on Washington succeeded in its goals. It drew national attention to race issues in the United States. It helped convince the US government that the time for new laws on civil rights issues had come. African Americans finally earned their full civil rights with the Civil Rights Act of 1964 and the Voting Rights Act of 1965. The first act banned racial discrimination in the United States. The second act removed barriers that made it difficult for African Americans to exercise their right to vote.

Origins of the march

The 1963 March on Washington for Jobs and Freedom came about partly because of a similar march that was planned in the early 1940s. African American civil rights leader A. Philip Randolph (1889–1979) thought of the idea for an African American march in Washington, DC, in 1941. At the time, Randolph was the president of the Brotherhood of Sleeping Car Porters. This was an African American labor union. Labor unions are organizations that protect the rights of workers. Porters carry baggage at bus and train stations and hotels.

Randolph wanted African Americans to march against racial discrimination in job hiring in the United States. In the early 1940s, many employers, even the US federal government, refused to hire African Americans. Many white Americans started working in national defense jobs around this time, but not many African Americans did. Randolph suspected that discrimination in the government's hiring practices was to blame.

Randolph wanted 50,000 people to march in Washington, DC, to protest government discrimination against African Americans. President Franklin Roosevelt (1882–1945) did not want the march to happen. To stop it before it began, Roosevelt banned racial discrimination in national defense jobs in 1941. Randolph then called off the Washington march. Within three years, about 2 million African Americans had obtained jobs in national defense.

Before the march

Roosevelt's ban did not end discrimination against blacks everywhere. Many white Americans still treated blacks poorly in other areas of life. For instance, blacks could not use public areas that had been reserved for whites. African Americans began protesting this discrimination in the early 1950s. Their continued protests over the next 15 or so years became known as the civil rights movement.

The movement became more powerful over time. African American protests earned a great deal of attention in the news. By the early 1960s, the protests had helped change some areas of life for African Americans. For example, the Freedom Ride protests of 1961 forced southern states to stop the already illegal practice of segregating interstate buses and bus stations. Segregation still existed in the United States, though, and African Americans continued fighting for change.

Civil Rights, African American

In 1963 Randolph started planning another civil rights march in Washington, DC. Fellow civil rights activist Bayard Rustin (1910–1987) helped him. Randolph and Rustin hoped to gather about 100,000 people for the March on Washington for Jobs and Freedom. Organizing such a large march was challenging. Randolph needed assistance from the many civil rights groups working in the United States at the time. He eventually got help from the National Association for the Advancement of Colored People, Student Nonviolent Coordinating Committee (SNCC), and the Southern Christian Leadership Conference.

Rustin mainly planned the march. He worked throughout 1963 to make sure it succeeded. Rustin had to train people to control the large crowds at the march to prevent anyone from getting hurt. Rustin made sure the microphones and sound system at the march would work so the crowds could hear the speakers and singers.

Leaders of the March on Washington for Jobs and Freedom lock arms as they walk along Constitution Avenue on August 28, 1963. © BETTMAN/GETTY IMAGES.

Civil Rights, African American

John Lewis Recalls the March on Washington

This primary source excerpt is from a speech US Congressional Rep. John Lewis gave at the 50th anniversary of the March on Washington. Lewis, who spoke at the original march, addressed the crowd at the Lincoln Memorial in Washington, DC, on August 28, 2013.

We are standing here in the shadow of Abraham Lincoln 150 years after he issued the Emancipation Proclamation and only 50 years after the historic March on Washington for Jobs and Freedom.

We have come a great distance in this country in the 50 years, but we still have a great distance to go before we fulfill the dream of Martin Luther King, Jr. . . .

In 1963, we could not register to vote simply because of the color of our skin. We had to pay a poll tax, pass a so-called literacy test, count the number of bubbles in a bar of soap or the number of jelly beans in a jar. Hundreds and thousands of people were arrested and jailed throughout the South for trying to participate in the democratic process. Medgar Evers had been killed in Mississippi. And that's why we told President Kennedy we intended to march on Washington, to demonstrate the need for equal justice and equal opportunity in America.

On August 28th, 1963, the nation's capital was in a state of emergency. Thousands of troops surrounded the city. Workers was told to stay home that day, liquor stores were closed, but the march was so orderly, so peaceful, it was filled with dignity and self-respect because we believe in the way of peace, the way of love, the way of

---

Two of the most difficult tasks Rustin faced were gathering marchers and arranging their transportation to Washington. Randolph and Rustin wanted at least 100,000 people to attend the march. To gather this great number of people, Rustin and his staff heavily advertised the march. Rustin then had to help people travel from their home states to the nation's capital. To do this, he asked churches to help raise money to pay for public buses and trains. Rustin then made sure the bus and train schedules were timed correctly so all the marchers were able to get to Washington. By the end of the planning, about 250,000 people were expected at the march. This number included 190,000 blacks and 60,000 whites.

The March on Washington

President John F. Kennedy was concerned about so many people attending the March on Washington. He feared that people would get hurt. He knew that violence at the march might cause the US Congress to stop supporting the civil rights law they were considering passing at the time. Kennedy

Civil Rights, African American

nonviolence. People came that day to that march just like they were on their way to religious service. As Mahalia Jackson sang, how we got over, how we got over, she drew thousands of us together in a strange sense. It seemed like the whole place start rocking. We truly believe that in every human being, even those who—violent—who were violent toward us, there was a spark of the divine.

And no person had the right to scar or destroy that spark. Martin Luther King, Jr. taught us the way of peace, the way of love, the way of nonviolence. He taught us to have the power to forgive, the capacity to be reconciled. He taught us to stand up, to speak up, to speak out, to find a way to get in the way.

People were inspired by that vision of justice and equality, and they were willing to put their bodies on the line for a greater cause greater than themselves. Not one incident of violence was reported that day. A spirit had engulfed the leadership of the movement and all of its participants.

The spirit of Dr. King's words captured the hearts of people not just around America but around the world. On that day, Martin Luther King, Jr. made a speech, but he also delivered a sermon. He transformed these marble steps of the Lincoln Memorial into a modern day pulpit. He changed us forever.

SOURCE: Lewis, John. "Rep. John Lewis's Speech on 50th Anniversary of the March on Washington." *Washington Post* (August 28, 2013). Available online at https://www.washingtonpost.com (accessed October 10, 2017). Courtesy of Washington Post Writers Group.

---

assigned about 6,000 US soldiers to guard the march. The Washington, DC, police department also placed nearly 6,000 local police officers at the event.

The National Mall in Washington, where the march took place, was a busy section of the city. At one end of it was the US Capitol Building. This is where the US Congress meets to make laws. The mall then stretched about 2 miles (3.2 kilometers) to the Lincoln Memorial. This is a large building that honors President Abraham Lincoln (1809–1865). Between the Capitol and the Lincoln Memorial are a large reflecting pool and the Washington Monument. The monument is a tall, narrow, pointed tower that honors President George Washington (1732–1799). The National Mall was often crowded with tourists and other visitors.

On August 28, 1963, the estimated 250,000 marchers appeared on the National Mall and began walking. They held signs calling for civil rights, equal rights for workers, and an end to segregation and police brutality. The crowds were to remain on the mall for an entire day of speeches and performances. Scattered throughout the mall were portable water fountains, restrooms, water trucks, and first-aid stations.

Randolph provided the march's opening remarks. Later, John Lewis of SNCC spoke. Lewis had planned to criticize the US government for failing to pass civil rights laws. Other civil rights activists later convinced him to eliminate much of the anger from his speech so the civil rights movement appeared friendlier. However, Lewis still demanded that the US government begin to recognize African Americans' civil rights immediately. Other civil rights leaders and members of various religious communities spoke later in the day. They called for African Americans to be given the rights promised to all Americans in the Declaration of Independence.

The March on Washington featured musical performances by various singers, including gospel artist Mahalia Jackson (1911–1972). Others were folk trio Peter, Paul and Mary (Peter Yarrow [1938–], N. Paul Stookey [1937–], and Mary Travers [1936–2008]) and folk singers Joan Baez (1941–) and Bob Dylan (1941–). Folk music draws from traditional songs of popular culture. The artists sang songs about freedom, equality, and civil rights. Other celebrities present at the march to show their support for African American civil rights were actors Marlon Brando (1924–2004), Paul Newman (1925–2008), Sidney Poitier (1927–), and Charlton Heston (1923–2008); actor, comedian, and singer Sammy Davis Jr. (1925–1990); author James Baldwin (1924–1987); and baseball player Jackie Robinson (1919–1972). Robinson was the first African American player in Major League Baseball.

Civil rights leader King was the last speaker of the day. He delivered his prepared speech on the steps of the Lincoln Memorial. King encouraged African Americans not to give up fighting for their rights. He reminded them to remain nonviolent in their protests. Toward the end of his speech, King stopped reading from the page in front of him. He started improvising, or speaking without preparation. This style of speaking from the heart went on to make King's speech one of the most famous of the 20th century.

King began repeating the phrase "I have a dream" to tell the crowd about how he hoped that all Americans would be treated equally one day. He wished that whites and blacks would soon live together in peace.

King began repeating the phrase "I have a dream" to tell the crowd about how he hoped that all Americans would be treated equally one day. He wished that whites and blacks would soon live together in peace. King's repetition of the phrase caused it to become known as the "I Have a Dream" speech. King intended to inspire marchers to return to their homes and continue believing that blacks would one day be treated equally to whites.

Results

After the march, the main civil rights leaders met with President Kennedy at the White House to talk about their concerns. King told Kennedy that the US Congress had to agree to support civil rights laws. However, Kennedy was assassinated, or killed for political reasons, in November 1963. Vice President Lyndon B. Johnson then became president.

Johnson worked with Congress to pass the civil rights laws that activists such as King had wanted for so long. The first of these laws was the Civil Rights Act of 1964. It ended segregation and banned employment discrimination throughout the United States. The second was the Voting Rights Act of 1965. It removed barriers that once enabled racial discrimination in voting. These laws together protected African Americans' right to vote and brought equality to black citizens. In 1968 both Martin Luther King Jr. and Robert Kennedy, the late president's brother who was then running for president himself, were assassinated.

For More Information

BOOKS

Arsenault, Raymond. *Freedom Riders: 1961 and the Struggle for Racial Justice.* New York: Oxford University Press, 2011.

Bates, Daisy. *The Long Shadow of Little Rock: A Memoir.* Fayetteville: University of Arkansas Press, 1987.

Bruns, Roger. *Martin Luther King, Jr.: A Biography.* Westport, CT: Greenwood Press, 2006.

Holland, Leslie J. *Dr. Martin Luther King Jr.'s I Have a Dream Speech in Translation: What It Really Means.* Mankato, MN: Capstone Press, 2009.

Parks, Rosa. *Rosa Parks: My Story.* New York: Dial Books, 1992.

Phibbs, Cheryl. *The Montgomery Bus Boycott: A History and Reference Guide.* Santa Barbara, CA: Greenwood, 2009.

Tougas, Shelley. *Little Rock Girl 1957: How a Photograph Changed the Fight for Integration.* Mankato, MN: Compass Point Books, 2012.

PERIODICALS

Cobb, James C. "The Voting Rights Act at 50: How It Changed the World." *Time* (August 6, 2015). Available online at http://time.com/3985479/voting-rights-act-1965-results/ (accessed July 18, 2017).

Cosgrove, Ben. "Brave Hearts: Remembering the Little Rock Nine." *Time* (September 23, 2012). Available online at http://time.com/3874341/little-rock-nine-1957-photos/ (accessed July 18, 2017).

Fessenden, Marissa. "The 'Friendship 9' Who Sat at a White-Only Lunch Counter Have Been Cleared." *Smithsonian* (January 29, 2015). Available online at http://www.smithsonianmag.com/smart-news/friendship-9-who-sat-white-only-lunch-counter-have-been-cleared-180954091/ (accessed July 18, 2017).

Rhodan, Maya. "The Voting Rights Act at 50: How the Law Came to Be." *Time* (August 6, 2015). Available online at http://time.com/3985603/voting-rights-act-1965-history/ (accessed July 18, 2017).

WEBSITES

"Arrested for Sit-In, 'Friendship 9' Convictions to Be Overturned." NBC News, January 28, 2015. http://www.nbcnews.com/news/nbcblk/arrested-sit-in-friendship-9-convictions-be-overturned-n294146 (accessed July 18, 2017).

"The Freedom Riders." Learn NC. http://www.learnnc.org/lp/editions/nchist-postwar/6085 (accessed July 18, 2017).

"Freedom Rides." The Martin Luther King, Jr. Research and Education Institute. http://kingencyclopedia.stanford.edu/encyclopedia/encyclopedia/enc_freedom_rides/ (accessed July 18, 2017).

"The Freedom Rides: CORE Volunteers Put Their Lives on the Road." Congress of Racial Equality (CORE). http://www.core-online.org/History/freedom%20rides.htm (accessed July 18, 2017).

"The History behind the Little Rock Nine." Arkansas.com. https://www.arkansas.com/attractions/central-high/ (accessed July 18, 2017).

"Little Rock Central High School: Crisis Timeline." US National Park Service. https://www.nps.gov/chsc/learn/historyculture/timeline.htm (accessed July 18, 2017).

"March on Washington Fast Facts." CNN, September 1, 2017. http://www.cnn.com/2013/06/05/us/march-on-washington-fast-facts/index.html (accessed July 18, 2017).

"March on Washington for Jobs and Freedom." US National Park Service. https://www.nps.gov/articles/march-on-washington.htm (accessed July 18, 2017).

Pilgrim, David. "What Was Jim Crow." Ferris State University, September 2000. http://www.ferris.edu/jimcrow/what (accessed July 18, 2017).

"Rock Hill, South Carolina, Students Sit-In for US Civil Rights, 1960." Global Nonviolent Action Database at Swarthmore College. http://nvdatabase.swarthmore.edu/content/rock-hill-south-carolina-students-sit-us-civil-rights-1960 (accessed July 18, 2017).

Siemaszko, Corky. "Birmingham Erupted into Chaos in 1963 as Battle for Civil Rights Exploded in South." *New York Daily News*, May 3, 2012. http://www.nydailynews.com/news/national/birmingham-erupted-chaos-1963-battle-civil-rights-exploded-south-article-1.1071793 (accessed July 18, 2017).

3

Civil Rights, Hispanic and Latino

East LA Blowouts 77

A Day without Immigrants 83

Mexican Indignados Movement 90

Over the years, Hispanics and Latinos have struggled to gain civil rights in the United States. Civil rights are guarantees, or promises, that all people are treated fairly and equally under the law. Such rights mean that people cannot be discriminated against due to their race, the language they speak, or the country they come from. Discrimination occurs when people treat others unfairly because they are different. Civil rights can include the right to vote and the right to receive an education. Hispanics and Latinos care about many civil rights issues. Some of the most important issues are immigration, working conditions, crime, and respect for their culture.

The terms *Hispanic* and *Latino* refer to the language a person speaks or to a geographical area. A Hispanic person comes from or has ancestors from a country where Spanish is the main language. Spanish is the language of Spain. Hundreds of years ago, explorers from Spain landed in the Caribbean islands, in Central and South America, and in parts of southern North America. They established colonies and taught Spanish to the native people. Many people in South America speak Spanish. Some speak Spanish in North America, too.

A Latino is a person who comes from or has ancestors from a region known as Latin America. Latin America refers to most areas south of the United States. This includes Mexico, Central America, South America, and most of the islands in the Caribbean. The region is called Latin America because many people in these countries speak Spanish, Portuguese, and/or French. These languages grew out of Latin, which was spoken during the Roman Empire (27 BCE–476 CE). The Roman Empire was one of the largest and most powerful civilizations in history. It ended more than 1,500 years ago. Latin was still spoken for centuries afterward and influenced many cultures.

Civil Rights, Hispanic and Latino

> ## WORDS TO KNOW
>
> **Boycott:** A refusal to buy or use certain items, products, or services as a form of protest.
>
> **Bribery:** Offering someone a gift in return for a favor; often illegal.
>
> **Chicano:** A Mexican American.
>
> **Deport:** To remove immigrants from a nation and send them back to their home country.
>
> **Drug cartel:** A group that produces and sells illegal drugs.
>
> **Hispanic:** A person who is from or who has ancestors from a Spanish-speaking country.
>
> **Latin America:** A region south of the United States that includes Mexico, Central America, South America, and islands in the Caribbean.
>
> **Latino:** A person who is from or who has ancestors from a Latin American country.
>
> **Migrant:** A person who travels often in search of work, usually on farms.
>
> **Unauthorized immigrants:** Immigrants who enter the United States without permission or who stay longer than they are allowed; also referred to as undocumented immigrants.
>
> **Visa:** A government document that allows a person from another country to stay in a certain country.

Brief history

About the 15th century, explorers from Europe sailed west to North, Central, and South America. These explorers called the region the New World. They claimed land for their countries and founded settlements and towns. Explorers from England, France, and the Netherlands claimed land in what is now the United States and Canada. Spain and Portugal's colonies started in the southern United States and Mexico and continued throughout Central and South America.

European conquerors forced the native peoples of the Americas from their lands or defeated them in battle. Many indigenous people got sick and died from diseases common in Europe that they caught from colonists. Native peoples had no immunity to, or ability to resist or fight off, such foreign diseases that were brought to the New World. In North America most native people struggled to adjust to a new way of life after the Europeans arrived. In Latin America the people had trouble as well. However, many people eventually adopted the language of their colonial rulers. They combined their own cultures with some elements from the Europeans to create a new identity.

In the mid-19th century, the population of the United States was growing. People from the eastern parts of the country needed more room.

They then began moving west. The US government bought land from foreign countries, took it from native people, or went to war for it. During the Mexican-American War (1846–1848), the United States and Mexico fought over control of Mexican land. The United States won the war. Mexico was forced to give the United States territory that later became California, Nevada, Utah, Arizona, New Mexico, Colorado, and parts of other states. The US annexation of Texas, which had gained its independence from Mexico in 1836, was no longer disputed. The US government allowed about 100,000 Mexicans living in the region to stay and become US citizens.

Early fight for civil rights

By the early 20th century, the United States was among the richest nations in the world. The expanding farming, mining, and construction industries needed workers. At the time, government officials worried that too many immigrants were coming into the United States from Europe and Asia. These officials put limits on the number of immigrants from many countries. Immigrants from Asian nations were mostly banned from entering the United States. No limits were placed on immigrants from the Western Hemisphere, which included Mexico and other Latin American countries, though. Immigrants from these areas were welcomed at first and filled many open jobs. More than 600,000 Mexicans came to the United States in the first 30 years of the 20th century.

Most immigrants were looking for work or fleeing poverty or violence. Conditions in the United States were better than the situations in many immigrants' homelands. Still, many Hispanic and Latino immigrants faced poor working environments and discrimination. Mexicans and Mexican Americans received especially poor treatment across the South and Southwest. Many were prevented from using the same public spaces as white Americans. Others were denied voting rights or were forced to send their children to Mexican-only schools.

The fight for Hispanic and Latino rights began in the first decades of the 20th century. El Primer Congreso Mexicanista, a political conference, formed in 1911 to protect the rights of Mexicans living in Texas. In 1925 a Mexican American rancher in Arizona won the right in court for his children to attend a school with white children. In the 1920s and 1930s, Latino farm and factory workers made several attempts to organize groups to push for better pay and working conditions.

CRITICAL THINKING QUESTIONS

1. What were some of the main goals of the 1968 East Los Angeles student walkouts? Did the protesters achieve their goals?

2. Why did students think it was important to learn about their culture?

3. What are some reasons a person would choose to leave his or her home country and move to the United States?

4. What effect did the 2006 Day without Immigrants have on the United States?

5. Should undocumented immigrants in the United States be able to become citizens? Explain why or why not.

6. Why do you think the protesters in Mexico believe legalizing drugs would stop violence committed by drug cartels? Explain your reasoning.

7. What would be the impact on Mexico and the United States if drug cartels were left alone?

Changing views on immigration

From 1929 to 1941, people around the world suffered through a period known as the Great Depression. Many people lost the money they had saved in their local banks. They also lost their jobs and struggled to find work to support their families. During this period many Mexicans and Latinos were deported. This means the US government forced them to leave the United States. The government deported more than 500,000 people to Mexico. Sometimes the government even deported Mexican Americans who were US citizens.

In 1941 the United States entered World War II (1939–1945). This war involved almost all of the major countries in the world. More than 16 million Americans left to fight on battlefields in Europe and Asia. To deal with a lack of workers, the United States allowed Mexican immigrants to enter the country for a time as guest workers. The wages they received were lower than what American workers would have made. Still, the pay was higher than what the workers would have earned in Mexico. Millions of immigrants took advantage of the guest worker program, which was known as the Bracero program.

Many Mexicans wanted to work in the United States but some did not want to apply as guest workers. Some of these people simply crossed the border in secret. The government refers to immigrants who enter the country without permission as unauthorized or undocumented immigrants. The number of unauthorized immigrants in the United States grew from about 60,000 in the 1940s to about 450,000 in the 1960s.

Mexican farmworkers are shown topping sugar beets near Stockton, California. COURTESY OF THE LIBRARY OF CONGRESS.

A part of the civil rights movement

The struggles Hispanics and Latinos in the United States faced were similar to those that African Americans endured. All of these groups faced discrimination from the government and from many white citizens. During the 1960s leaders from the African American, Hispanic, and Latino communities stood up and fought for their civil rights. They organized nonviolent marches and protests to call attention to the problems they faced. This was the start of the civil rights movement.

The efforts of African American civil rights leader the Rev. Dr. Martin Luther King Jr. (1929–1968) led to many positive changes in the United States. King and others helped push the US government to pass antidiscrimination legislation. Such laws outlawed discrimination on the basis of skin color, religion, age, sex, or country of birth.

Mexican American labor leader César Chávez (pronounced CHA-vez; 1927–1993) became a hero in the Hispanic and Latino communities. He fought to aid farmworkers across the United States. Chávez and fellow labor activist Dolores Huerta (pronounced WER-tuh; 1930–) helped start a powerful labor union called the National Farm Workers Association in 1962. This led to many improvements in wages and quality of life for both legal and unauthorized immigrants. Chávez's efforts to bring about change

Civil Rights, Hispanic and Latino

inspired many Hispanics and Latinos in the United States. He encouraged Mexican Americans to be proud of their unique culture. This movement, known as the Chicano (pronounced CHEE-ka-no) movement, empowered many Mexican Americans to fight for their rights. For example, Mexican American students in Los Angeles, California, walked out of class in 1968 to push for a better education and respect for their culture.

A powerful voice

In the late 20th and early 21st centuries, the Hispanic and Latino communities in the United States began to grow. By 2002 Hispanics and Latinos had become the largest minority group in the country. In 2015 about 54 million Hispanics and Latinos lived in the United States according to the US Census Bureau. This number represented about 17 percent of the total population. At first, most Hispanic and Latino immigrants lived mainly in California, Texas, and Florida. As the population increased, they began to move to other states across the country.

President Barack Obama presents Dolores Huerta with the Presidential Medal of Freedom at a ceremony at the White House in May 2012. Huerta was acknowledged for her civil rights and women's rights work. © RENA SCHILD/ SHUTTERSTOCK.COM.

Many Hispanics and Latinos came to the United States looking for work. Some came to get an education. Others had family living in the United States. Still more were fleeing violence in their homelands. This was the case for many Mexicans in the early 21st century. The drug trade has caused a high rate of violence in certain parts of Mexico. Drug cartels, which produce and sell illegal drugs, are very powerful and extremely violent in Mexico. The Mexican government has trouble dealing with the violence the cartels cause. Many thousands of people have been killed in Mexico since the government began a major effort to stop the drug trade in 2006. Although some people left the country, others stayed and protested the government's actions. In 2012 Mexicans organized large marches throughout their country. They called on their leaders to find a solution to end the drug cartels' kidnappings and killings.

Protests were not limited to Mexico. In the first decade of the 21st century, Hispanic and Latino immigrants began making their voices

Civil Rights, Hispanic and Latino

heard in American politics. Many Hispanic and Latino immigrants wanted to become US citizens. Among them were about 5.6 million Mexican immigrants living in the United States illegally as of 2016. They pushed for laws to make this process easier. They expressed their opposition to laws aimed at deporting immigrants or limiting their numbers. As Hispanic and Latino immigrant populations grew, they united to show the influence they had on life in the United States.

East LA Blowouts

LOCATION: Los Angeles, California
DATE: March 1–8, 1968

In the late 1960s, Mexican American students in Los Angeles, California, thought their school system was failing to provide them with a quality education. They believed that many of their teachers were treating them unfairly. Their schools were overcrowded and in poor condition. School counselors forced some of the students to take classes they did not want to take. These problems caused many Mexican American students to drop out and not graduate.

In early March 1968, Mexican American students at high schools in East Los Angeles walked out of their classrooms. They wanted to bring attention to their situation. During the next eight days, thousands of students from several East Los Angeles schools joined the protest. The event was known as the East LA Blowouts. *Blowouts* was the word students used to describe the walkouts. Officials from the school district later met with students to listen to their concerns, but little changed.

The walkouts did not have a great effect at the time. However, they did help bring the community together. The event also inspired future students in Los Angeles to stage walkouts to protest other issues. For years after the walkouts, conditions for Mexican American students did not progress. By the 2010s some improvements in education finally had been made. The district became more open to Mexican American needs. For example, the district started allowing schools to offer cultural studies classes. Over time, the number of Mexican American students who graduated from school greatly increased.

Civil Rights, Hispanic and Latino

César Chávez

César Chávez was born into a family of Mexican American farmworkers in Yuma, Arizona. When Chávez was 12, his family moved to California and traveled around the state to work in the fields. His family was very poor. Chávez grew up witnessing the conditions in which migrant workers were forced to live. Farmworkers are sometimes called migrant workers because they migrate, or move, from place to place to find work.

Life for farmworkers in the 20th century was difficult. They worked hard for long hours and received little money for their efforts. Many lived in poor housing conditions. Farm owners often treated them unfairly. Chávez wanted to do something to help improve farmworkers' lives. He thought it was wrong that the people who worked to provide food for American families were going hungry themselves.

Civil rights leaders Mahatma Gandhi (1869–1948) and Dr. Martin Luther King Jr. inspired Chávez. Gandhi led a movement for freedom in his home country of India. King helped African Americans gain civil rights in the United States. Both men made changes in society through peaceful methods.

In 1962 Chávez used his own money to help start the National Farm Workers Association, now known as the United Farm Workers of America. Mexican American labor rights leader Dolores Huerta was a cofounder of this union. The organization's purpose was to improve working conditions for farmworkers. Chávez traveled across California to talk to farmworkers. He asked them to join what he called La Causa, Spanish for "the Cause." Chávez led farmworkers on protest marches and asked people to boycott, or refuse to buy

Mexican American civil rights

The 1960s was a period when many Americans were fighting for civil rights. Much of the focus of the civil rights movement was on the struggles of African Americans. Civil rights leaders such as the Rev. Dr. Martin Luther King Jr. helped organize nonviolent marches and protests that led to many positive changes for African Americans. These successes inspired other groups to begin their own efforts to gain civil rights.

At the time, many Mexican Americans worked on farms in California and in southern states. They often worked long hours for low pay and had little control over their working conditions. In 1962 Mexican American labor leaders César Chávez and Dolores Huerta helped form an organization to improve working conditions for farmworkers in the United States. During the 1960s and 1970s, Chávez and Huerta became leaders in the movement for Mexican American civil rights. Chávez was

Civil Rights, Hispanic and Latino

and use, products from farms that did not treat their workers fairly. He also organized workers to strike in protest of poor working conditions. In a strike, employees refuse to work until their employer agrees to meet their demands.

Through the efforts of Chávez, Huerta, and the union, working conditions and pay for farmworkers improved in the late 1960s and early 1970s. Chávez became a hero in the Mexican American community. In the 1980s he helped raise awareness about how chemicals used in the fields to kill pests were poisoning farmworkers and their children. After Chávez's death in 1993, he was awarded the Presidential Medal of Freedom. This award is the highest honor that a US civilian can receive. As of 2017, his birthday of March 31 is celebrated by many Mexican Americans. César Chávez Day is an official state holiday in California, Colorado, and Texas.

César Chávez in 1979. COURTESY OF THE LIBRARY OF CONGRESS.

considered a hero in the Mexican American community. Like King, he used nonviolent methods to bring about positive change.

The fight for Mexican American civil rights became known as the Chicano movement. *Chicano* comes from the shortened form of the word *Mexicanos*, a term used to describe Mexican people living in the United States. At one time, the term *Chicano* was an insult. By the 1960s Mexican Americans looked at the word differently. Many Mexican Americans did not feel like they belonged to American culture. At the same time, they felt separated from Mexican culture. They began to see the word *Chicano* as a symbol of pride in their unique identity.

Problems with education

During the 1960s, many Mexican American students believed they were being treated unfairly at school. Los Angeles community leaders had been trying to work with the school district to fix the problem for many years, but they were not successful. Mexican American students in the Los Angeles Unified School District thought they were not receiving the same level of education that students of other races were. They thought the lesson plans taught in the schools were designed more for white students and did not meet their needs.

At the time, most of the officials and teachers in Los Angeles schools were white. Many Mexican American students felt their teachers did not understand them or their culture. Although students spoke Spanish at home, they did not learn Spanish in school. Many students believed their teachers did not care about their education and simply passed them from one grade to another. In addition, some students were pushed into vocational, or job-related, classes such as auto shop. They were not encouraged to take courses that could help prepare them for college.

Classrooms were overcrowded, textbooks were out of date, and buildings were in poor condition. The number of Mexican American students who left high school before they graduated was very high. In the late 1960s, about 4 of every 10 Mexican American students from the Los Angeles area dropped out of high school.

Community leaders in East Los Angeles were concerned about the issues Mexican American students faced at school. They expressed their worries to school officials in late 1967. Teacher Sal Castro (1933–2013), student leaders, and activist groups presented a list of demands to the school board asking for reform. The board refused to act on the demands. Castro and the others then decided to try a different method to bring attention to their cause.

Nearly 50 years later, Hispanic and Latino students, as well as black students, still have less access to higher-level math and science classes. © 2018 CENGAGE®.

Black and Latino Students Have Less Access to High-level Math and Science Courses

- 33% of high schools with high black and Latino student enrollment offer calculus, compared to 56% of high schools with low black and Latino student enrollment.
- 48% of high schools with high black and Latino student enrollment offer physics, compared to 67% of high schools with low black and Latino student enrollment.
- 65% of high schools with high black and Latino student enrollment offer chemistry, compared to 78% of high schools with low black and Latino student enrollment.
- 71% of high schools with high black and Latino student enrollment offer Algebra II, compared to 84% of high schools with low black and Latino student enrollment.

SOURCE: 2013-14 Civil Rights Data Collection (CRDC). US Department of Education, Office for Civil Rights, June 7, 2016 (revised October 28, 2016). https://www2.ed.gov/about/offices/list/ocr/docs/2013-14-first-look.pdf.

The blowouts

Castro, students, and activist group leaders began organizing plans for walkouts from schools in East Los Angeles. The blowouts, as the students called them, were planned for early March 1968 in three high schools. At the time, public schools in Los Angeles received money from the government based on the number of students who attended class each day. Staging the walkouts before morning attendance was taken would hurt the schools financially. The protesters hoped this would help them make their point.

In late February the principal at Woodrow Wilson High School canceled a student play that he thought was inappropriate. All of the students in the play were Mexican American. The students were angry that their principal had canceled the play. On March 1, 1968, about 200 students walked out of class in protest. The walkout was not part of the original plan. Castro and the student organizers worried that the events at Woodrow Wilson High would hurt their cause.

On March 5 about 2,000 students at Garfield High School walked out of class. School officials tried to stop the students from leaving and called the police to the school to keep order. This walkout also was not planned. It prompted Castro and the other organizers to move up the date for their main protest to the next day. On March 6 thousands of students from Garfield, Abraham Lincoln, Theodore Roosevelt, and Belmont High Schools walked out of class. School officials called the police in again.

The walkouts continued for the next two days. Students from several other East Los Angeles high schools joined in the protests. The number of students who participated in the walkouts was estimated to be between 10,000 and 15,000. Many students carried signs that read "Chicano Power" and "Education is a right not a privilege." The walkouts were the largest protest by Mexican Americans in the Los Angeles area at the time.

Sonia Salazar, 20, a college student enrolled in Chicano Studies classes and a Belmont High School graduate, joins more than 1,000 people on March 8, 2008, to commemorate the historic East Los Angeles student walkouts that took place 40 years earlier. © ANNIE WELLS/LOS ANGELES TIMES VIA GETTY IMAGES.

Civil Rights, Hispanic and Latino

Supporting the students

Community leaders, parents, and some teachers rallied behind the students. They formed the Educational Issues Coordinating Committee (EICC) to push for school reforms. The school board called a special meeting to address the students' concerns on March 11. At the meeting, the EICC presented a list of 39 demands to the board. The demands included lesson plans that focused on Mexican American culture and needs, education in both Spanish and English, and more Mexican American teachers. The list also called for reducing the number of students per classroom, building new schools, and giving students more say in their education.

The school board held a meeting several weeks later. School officials said they agreed with almost all of the EICC's demands, but the district did not have enough money to carry out the reforms. On March 31, Castro and 12 of the other walkout organizers were arrested and charged with disturbing the peace. School officials suspended Castro from his job. Protesters gathered to support those arrested. Eventually, all charges against them were dropped. Castro was able to return to work in October 1968.

Modern conditions

For many years after the walkouts, conditions for Mexican Americans in Los Angeles schools did not improve much. Many of the student leaders of the 1968 protests believed that school officials had done nothing to bring about change. According to the *Los Angeles Times* (March 7, 1988), the dropout rate for students in East Los Angeles high schools ranged from 30 to 49 percent in 1988. Lesson plans geared toward Mexican Americans had not yet been put into place. Conditions did begin to change toward the end of the 20th century, however.

In the 1990s the Los Angeles Unified School District gave schools the option to offer cultural studies classes to students. Only some schools chose to offer such classes at the time. Students wrote letters to the school board and collected signatures of support from the community to require schools to offer the courses. In 2014 the district made cultural studies classes a requirement for students to graduate. The number of students who dropped out of school early also decreased over time. During the 2015–2016 school year, the Los Angeles Unified School District reported a graduation rate of almost 77 percent for Mexican American students.

The school board called a special meeting to address the students' concerns on March 11. At the meeting, the EICC presented a list of 39 demands to the board. The demands included lesson plans that focused on Mexican American culture and needs, education in both Spanish and English, and more Mexican American teachers.

Civil Rights, Hispanic and Latino

A Day without Immigrants

LOCATION: More than 50 cities across the United States
DATE: May 1, 2006

The United States is a nation of immigrants. Since well before the nation was founded in 1776, millions of people have left their home countries to seek a new life in America. Some left to flee war, poverty, or violence from their governments. Others came because the United States offered an opportunity for them and their families to be successful. In 2015 about 44.7 million immigrants were living in the United States, according to the Pew Research Center. Many of these immigrants came from Latin America. About 27 percent of the immigrants in the United States that year were Mexican. This is likely because the two countries share a border.

The US government has passed various laws that set rules for immigrants who want to enter and stay in the country. Most people from other countries who want to come to the United States must first obtain a visa. A visa is a government document that allows a person to stay in the country. Residents of some nations are allowed to travel to the United States without a visa if they plan to stay for fewer than 90 days. Immigrants who want to become US citizens must meet several conditions and follow certain steps.

Most immigrants follow these guidelines. However, some immigrants do not observe the rules. They enter the United States secretly without getting a visa. Others may stay longer than their visa allows. The government refers to these people as unauthorized or undocumented immigrants. Unauthorized immigrants have broken the law, and government officials can deport them for this. Some undocumented immigrants come into the country illegally because they are fleeing violence, are in desperate need of work, or have family in the United States. Once in the United States, many unauthorized immigrants obey the law. They go to school and find jobs. Many want to become US citizens.

House Resolution 4437

The number of unauthorized immigrants in the United States grew sharply from the late 20th century until 2007. From 1990 to 2007, the

Civil Rights, Hispanic and Latino

The Ybor City Cigar Strike, 1931

In the 1930s many immigrants from the island nation of Cuba worked in cigar factories in the state of Florida. Cigars are rolled-up leaves from tobacco plants that people smoke. People in Cuba have been making them for many years. When Cuban immigrants came to the United States, they brought their cigar-making skills with them.

The workday in a cigar factory was often long and boring. In 1865 workers in Cuba's capital city of Havana began paying people to sit in chairs on the factory floor and read to them. The readers, called lectors, were very popular among factory workers. Sometimes lectors read material that the factory owners did not like. The owners thought some of the material encouraged workers to go on strike. The owners worried that employees might refuse to work until conditions improved at their factories.

Cuban cigar factory workers in the United States also hired lectors to read to them. In 1931 the lector at a cigar factory in Ybor City—a section of Tampa, Florida—read material that the factory owner believed supported Communism. Communism is a system in which property is owned collectively and people are paid according to what they need.

The factory owner made the lector leave, which angered the workers. The employees decided to go on strike and stopped working. The factory owner hired people to beat the strikers to pressure them to return to work. Police arrested some of the workers. The government and media described the workers as possible Communists. For this reason, the public did not support the workers' cause. After several weeks, the factory employees returned to work. When they got back, they discovered that the factory owner had replaced the lector with a radio.

number jumped from 3.2 million to 12.2 million. In 2015 about 11 million undocumented immigrants were in the United States. According to the *New York Times* (March 2, 2017), about 6.2 million came from Mexico; 723,000 came from Guatemala; 465,000 came from El Salvador; and 337,000 came from Honduras. Large numbers of unauthorized immigrants also came from China, India, and Korea. Opponents of undocumented immigration believe that too many people are entering the country illegally. They say that these immigrants should not be allowed to stay in the United States because they broke the law. Critics worry that unauthorized immigrants could take jobs and other benefits intended for American citizens.

In December 2005 Wisconsin politician James Sensenbrenner Jr. (1943–) proposed a new law that would make it harder for undocumented immigrants to remain in the United States. Sensenbrenner was a Republican member of the US House of Representatives. The House and the Senate make up the US Congress. Congress is where the country's

A lector (reader) in a cigar factory in Tampa, Florida. COURTESY OF THE LIBRARY OF CONGRESS.

leaders make laws. Sensenbrenner's bill, known as House Resolution 4437, would have made it a criminal offense, rather than a civil offense, for immigrants to be in the country without proper approval. This was a drastic change in policy. The bill also would have required all employers to make sure that any immigrant workers they hired had documents to prove that they were in the United States legally.

Sensenbrenner and supporters of the bill said it would help control unauthorized immigration. They thought it would improve safety by making every immigrant register with the government. Many immigrants and critics of the bill said it would increase the number of deportations. They believed it would label many hardworking undocumented immigrants as criminals. Opponents worried that many immigrants would stay in the shadows. In other words, they would not go to the hospital for care in an emergency because they would fear being deported. Or they might not report a crime for fear of exposing their undocumented status.

Building a protest movement

The House of Representatives approved Sensenbrenner's bill on December 16, 2005. Before the bill could become law, however, the Senate would have to approve it, and the president would have to sign it. A group of immigrant rights supporters in Los Angeles, California, decided to organize protests against the bill to try to stop its passage. They wanted to raise public awareness about the bill and show how it would affect immigrant communities and businesses across the country.

The organizers were inspired by the farmworker movement of the 1960s led by César Chávez, Dolores Huerta, and many other activists. Movement leaders organized protests, marches, strikes, and boycotts to help improve conditions for immigrant workers on American farms. The 2004 comedy film *A Day without a Mexican* also inspired the protest organizers. In the film, people in California wake up one day to discover that every Mexican has disappeared. As daily life becomes more difficult, people begin to realize how important California's Hispanic and Latino populations are to the state.

The organizers in Los Angeles contacted labor unions, immigrant rights groups, and newspapers and websites that targeted Latinos. They wanted to spread the word about their plans across the country. The organizers held their first protest event on March 10, 2006, in Chicago, Illinois. A crowd of more than 100,000 people marched through the city's downtown area in one of the largest demonstrations for immigrant rights in US history. On March 23, about 30,000 people gathered in the city of Milwaukee, Wisconsin, to voice their opposition to the bill. Parts of Milwaukee were in the district Sensenbrenner represented. Other protests occurred in Los Angeles; Atlanta, Georgia; and other cities around the country.

May Day Protest

Although the protests attracted large crowds, organizers wanted to hold an even bigger single-day event. They believed the event would show people the immigrant community's effect on business in the United States. They chose Monday, May 1, 2006, for the protest. In many countries, May 1 is known as International Workers' Day. The holiday celebrates the rights of the working class. US workers are celebrated on Labor Day, which occurs on the first Monday in September every year.

The protest was called a Day without Immigrants. Both legal and undocumented immigrants were asked to stay home from work and school.

A Day without Latinos

This primary source excerpt is from an interview on CNN conducted by anchor John Roberts with Christine Neumann-Ortiz, who helped organize the Latino immigration protest in Milwaukee, Wisconsin, in March. The interview took place on March 24, 2006.

JOHN ROBERTS, CNN ANCHOR: Latinos in America are showing their anger at an immigration reform bill. Protests are planned for today in Atlanta and tomorrow in Los Angeles. Chicago has already had one. And this demonstration in Milwaukee on Thursday was called "A Day without Latinos." . . .

Christine Neumann-Ortiz helped organize the Milwaukee protest. She's the head of Voces de la Frontera, or the Voices on the Border.

"A Day without Latinos." What was the message you were trying to get across?

CHRISTINE NEUMANN-ORTIZ, RALLY ORGANIZER: Well, we picked a work day and when we knew that it would really have an economic impact, and even if it was for part of the day. So the 30,000 people that marched that day, many of them were low-wage working class families.

And then we also had, by the time we actually had the event, we had over 200 small and medium-sized businesses from the kind of Latino part of Milwaukee and in some of the—you know, about 15 in some of the outlying cities that closed for part or all of the day so that the workers could go and they, the owners themselves, to make that point, that this is—that we contribute economically, despite the rhetoric.

ROBERTS: Now, a lot of people might be wondering across America, why Milwaukee? It's because of the Wisconsin Congressman James Sensenbrenner, whose bill passed the House the other day. What is about that bill that you're opposed to?

NEUMANN-ORTIZ: Well, that's—it is very significant. I think that was part of the significance. But we're—the fact that this bill originated in Wisconsin, we felt it was important that we, as people from Wisconsin, stand up against the kind of politics of hate. . . . And that's really what it is.

ROBERTS: Well, what is it about the bill that you disagree with?

NEUMANN-ORTIZ: Two major things. First of all, that it turns any—all 12 million undocumented people, including the three million children, into aggravated felons, which is equivalent as if you had murdered somebody. Also, any individual or organization that provides any kind of assistance to an undocumented person would also be treated as a felon, because they change the legal definition of smuggler. . . . I think that Congressman Sensenbrenner is trying to blame every social problem on low-wage working class families. This group of low-wage working class families, basically it's a scapegoating. And it's not only that. I think it's justifying the exploitation of, you know, these working class families. And what's disturbing, and should be disturbing for everybody, is how far-reaching and how extremist this proposal is.

SOURCE: Neumann-Ortiz, Christine. Interview by John Roberts. "Latinos Protest Immigration Reform Bill." *American Morning.* CNN (March 24, 2006). Available online at http://www.cnn.com/TRANSCRIPTS/0603/24/ltm.04.html (accessed October 10, 2017). Courtesy of Cable News Network, Inc.

They were told to avoid shopping for the day. At the same time, large marches were planned for major cities across the country. The goal of the event was to cause businesses to shut down for the day because immigrants had not come into work. The organizers hoped that this would make people realize how important immigrants are to the American economy.

More than 1 million people nationwide took part in the event, which also was called the Great American Boycott. One of the largest demonstrations was in Los Angeles, where about 500,000 people protested. Many people waved American flags and flags from their home countries. In addition to demanding the Sensenbrenner bill's defeat, many protesters called for new laws that would make it easier to become a US citizen. In Chicago more than 400,000 people marched in the city's streets. In New York City, more than 12,000 people linked arms to form eight human chains.

About 75,000 people gathered in Denver, Colorado, and more than 50,000 marched in San Francisco, California. Demonstrations were held in more than 50 major cities across the United States. Many stores and restaurants in New York, Chicago, and Los Angeles closed for the day. High schools in areas with large immigrant populations reported lower-than-normal attendance. Some food-processing plants in the Midwest had to shut down. Flower, fruit, and vegetable sellers in California did not

Hispanics and Latinos wave American flags as they protest for immigrant rights as well as illegal immigration reform efforts by the US Congress in Los Angeles, California, on May 1, 2006. © JOSEPH SOHM/ SHUTTERSTOCK.COM.

open their stands. Many farmworkers in California and Arizona skipped work that day, too.

The protesters' mood in most places was one of celebration rather than anger. Employers in some cities even closed their businesses to show support for their immigrant workers. The demonstrations did not bring the nation's businesses to a halt, but they did have an effect in larger cities. The protests showed that the immigrant community had a strong voice.

Effect of movement

The movement gained national attention. Not everyone supported the protesters, though. Some immigrants who owned small businesses said they lost money because of the boycotts. Others said taking the day off from work sent the wrong message. They believed that the protesters could have made a more positive statement if they had worked with their representatives in Congress to reform immigration laws.

The Senate considered House Resolution 4437 but did not vote on it. The Senate decided to propose its own immigration law. That brought an end to Sensenbrenner's bill. Many protesters were happy that the bill did not become law but were disappointed that Congress did not take action to reform US immigration laws.

Some of those who took part in the 2006 demonstrations turned their attention to supporting the Development, Relief, and Education for Alien Minors (DREAM) Act. The DREAM Act was a proposed bill that would allow undocumented immigrants under age 16 to become US citizens if they finished two years of high school, college, or military service. They also would have to meet several other conditions. Several protests were staged across the United States in support of the DREAM Act. As of late 2017, the proposal had yet to become law.

On February 16, 2017, US immigrants staged another protest called a Day without Immigrants. This time the protest targeted the immigration policies of President Donald Trump (1946–). Trump took office in January 2017 and promised tougher immigration laws. He said he would build a wall along the US-Mexico border to keep undocumented immigrants from entering the country. He promised more deportations. Many restaurants, shops, and businesses in cities across the nation closed for the day as workers stayed home. Schools in immigrant communities had lower attendance rates. Thousands of demonstrators gathered to protest the president's policies.

Civil Rights, Hispanic and Latino

Mexican Indignados Movement

LOCATION: Multiple cities across Mexico

DATE: Beginning in 2011

In early 2011 people in the Middle East staged a series of protests against unjust treatment by their governments. These protests became known as the Arab Spring. The demonstrations forced some leaders from power. They also inspired people around the world to try to change conditions in their own nations. In many cases, protesters wanted to make positive social changes. They focused on issues such as poverty, unemployment, and unfair economic systems.

The Arab Spring influenced the 15-M movement in Spain. This movement focused on Spain's economic problems. The 15-M movement then encouraged citizens in Mexico to protest various economic, political, and social issues. In particular, many people had concerns about the violence that resulted from the country's drug trade.

In 2006 the Mexican government began a major effort to stop the selling and transportation of illegal drugs in the country. The government used the military in its attempt to stop the groups of drug suppliers, called cartels. Massive violence occurred as a result. Thousands of people were killed or injured in the effort to stop the drug trade. Many Mexicans were angry about the surge in violence. They blamed the cartels for the violence, but some believed the government's response only made matters worse.

The protests against the violence were part of the Mexican Indignados movement. The word *indignados* (pronounced in-DIG-na-dos) means "the outraged" in Spanish. Poet Javier Sicilia (1956–) inspired the movement. Cartel members killed his son in March 2011. Small protests grew into a nationwide event as Sicilia led thousands of people on marches throughout Mexico in 2011. He brought the protests to several cities in the United States a year later. Public anger increased following the 2014 disappearance and suspected killing of 43 college students by a cartel. The incident led to several additional protests and more calls to stop the violence.

Raul Vera (left), bishop of Saltillo, and Javier Sicilia (center) walk to the start of a march for peace, which began in Cuernavaca. Participants of the march demanded a halt to the violence affecting civilians. © GUSTAVO GRAF/LATINCONTENT/GETTY IMAGES.

Mexico's war on drugs

Mexico is a key part of the illegal drug trade. Mexican cartels make tens of billions of dollars a year by selling drugs in the United States. Many of the illegal drugs are produced in Mexico. Other drugs are made in South American countries and then transported north through Mexico on their way to US markets. For many years the cartels used the profits they made from selling drugs to bribe Mexican police officers, judges, and politicians. The bribes, or illegal gifts, ensured that the officials would not try to stop the cartels.

In 2006 Felipe Calderón (1962–) was elected president of Mexico. Calderón promised to take action against the illegal drug trade and declared war on the cartels. Calderón knew the cartels had bribed many local police forces. He sent in thousands of military troops to replace the police. The troops tracked down and killed the leaders of many cartels. With their leaders gone, the powerful cartels split up and formed several new groups. These groups fought with one another to control the drug trade in Mexico.

Violence in Mexico increased as rival gangs fought one another and the government tried to stop the drug trade. Kidnappings and killings were common. Politicians, journalists, and average citizens who spoke out against drug cartels were often found dead. Many others died when they became caught in fighting between rival gangs. In 2011 the homicide rate in Mexico was about three times what it had been in 2007, according to the

Civil Rights, Hispanic and Latino

Javier Sicilia's Open Letter

This primary source excerpt comes from poet Javier Sicilia's open letter to the Mexican government and the drug cartels. Published in early April 2011, the letter was written after Sicilia's son was murdered. In it, he calls for the violence to end.

The brutal assassination of my son, Juan Francisco, of Julio César Romero Jaime, of Luis Antonio Romero Jaime, and of Gabriel Anejo Escalera, is added to so many other boys and girls who have been assassinated just the same throughout the country, not only because of the war unleashed by the government of Calderón against organized crime, but also the rotting of the heart that has been wrought by the poorly labeled political class and the criminal class, which has broken its own codes of honor. . . .

We have had it up to here with you, politicians—and when I say politicians I do not refer to any in particular, but, rather, a good part of you, including those who make up the political parties—because in your fight for power you have shamed the fabric of the nation. Because in middle of this badly proposed, badly made, badly led war, of this war that has put the country in a state of emergency, you have been incapable—due to your cruelties, your fights, your miserable screaming, your struggle for power—of creating the consensus that the nation needs to find the unity without which this country will not be able to escape. . . . We have had it up to here because you only have imagination for violence, for weapons, for insults and, with that, a profound scorn for education, culture, and opportunities for honorable work, which is what good nations do. We have had it up to here because your short imagination is permitting that our kids, our children, are not only assassinated, but, later,

Council on Foreign Relations. As of 2016 more than 100,000 people had been killed in drug-related violence since the start of Mexico's drug war.

Grieving poet starts movement

People staged demonstrations against drug violence in Mexico several times before 2011. These efforts had little effect. On March 28, 2011, gang members killed the 24-year-old son of well-known author and poet Javier Sicilia. The bodies of Juan Francisco Sicilia and six others were found in a car in Cuernavaca (pronounced kwer-NA-va-ka), a town south of Mexico City. Not long before this, Juan Francisco's friend had reported a robbery to local police. A cartel member had committed the crime. Juan Francisco and his friends were killed in an act of revenge.

Sicilia blamed President Calderón's war on drugs for creating the violence that killed his son and many others. Because Sicilia was a famous figure, his son's death attracted much media attention. Sicilia decided to use the attention to unite people and call for an end to the violence.

criminalized, made falsely guilty to satisfy that imagination. We have had it up to here because others of our children, due to the absence of a good government plan, do not have opportunities to educate themselves, to find dignified work and spit out onto the sidelines become possible recruits for organized crime and violence. . . .

As for you, the criminals, we have had it up to here with your violence, with your loss of honor, your cruelty and senselessness. In days of old you had codes of honor. You were not so cruel in your paybacks and you did not touch the citizens nor their families. Now you do not distinguish. Your violence already can't be named because, like the pain and suffering that you provoke, it has no name nor sense. You have lost even the dignity to kill. You have become cowards like the miserable Nazi sonderkommandos [prisoners who were forced to help run the gas chambers] who kill children, boys, girls, women, men and elders without any human sense. . . .

There is no life, [French philosopher] Albert Camus wrote, without persuasion and without peace, and the history of Mexico today only knows intimidation, suffering, distrust and the fear that one day another son or daughter of another family will be debased and massacred. . . .

Additionally, I opine that we must return dignity to this nation.

SOURCE: Sicilia, Javier. "Javier Sicilia's Open Letter to Mexico's Politicians and Criminals." Translated by Al Giordano. *Narco News Bulletin* (April 4, 2011). First published in *Proceso* (April 3, 2011) in Spanish. Available online in English at http://narconews.com/Issue67/article4346.html and in Spanish at http://www.proceso.com.mx/266990/javier-sicilia-carta-abierta-a-politicos-y-criminales (accessed October 11, 2017). Courtesy of *Narco News Bulletin* and *Proceso*.

In early April 2011, Sicilia published an open letter to the government and the drug cartels. He called on President Calderón and Mexico's politicians to stop the military involvement in the drug war. He asked them to try to make a deal with the cartels to end the violence. Sicilia also pleaded with the drug gangs to stop targeting ordinary citizens. In the letter he used the phrase *Estamos hasta la madre!* The term is Mexican slang for "We've had it up to here!" The phrase became the unofficial motto of Sicilia's Movement for Peace with Justice and Dignity.

Protests begin

Sicilia called for demonstrations across Mexico. On April 6 protesters in more than 40 cities gathered to march against drug violence. More than 20,000 people demonstrated in the nation's capital, Mexico City. About 50,000 people marched in Cuernavaca, the town where Sicilia's son was

Civil Rights, Hispanic and Latino

1968 Tlatelolco Massacre

During the late 1960s, high school and college students in many parts of the world took part in various protests. In the United States many people were unhappy about the nation's involvement in the Vietnam War (1954–1975). In Mexico students were upset about police and government violence.

In 1968 a fight among students broke out at the end of a soccer game in Mexico City. Police tried to break up the fight. The students believed the police used too much force to stop the fight and challenged law enforcement. The protest grew larger. The Mexican government sent in the army to handle the situation. The protests ended when the army fired a rocket-propelled explosive into a building where the students were demonstrating. Several students were killed.

In the weeks after the incident, students across Mexico organized rallies against police and government violence. Government leaders responded by sending the army to take over two universities where students were protesting. On October 2, 1968, thousands of students attended a rally at a square in the Tlatelolco (pronounced tla-TEE-lo-ko) section of Mexico City. As the event ended, the army arrived to arrest the leaders of the protest movement.

Suddenly, shots were heard. The soldiers believed that students were firing at them, so they began shooting into the crowd. As the students ran, the army sent in tanks to end the protests. For many years, the Mexican government claimed that four people died in the incident. People at the rally, however, said hundreds had been killed.

In the 21st century, the government tried to discover the truth about the Tlatelolco massacre. Much of the evidence had been lost. The government did determine that officials in 1968 had ordered hidden gunmen to fire at the soldiers. This made the soldiers think the students were shooting at them. In the end, the government concluded that 40 students had been killed during the event.

killed. Protesters held signs that read "No more blood!" and "We are fed up!" Many of the marchers called for President Calderón to resign.

On May 5 Sicilia led a 60-mile (96-kilometer) march from Cuernavaca to Mexico City. The protest started with about 200 people. Thousands of people joined the march in the two days it took to reach the capital. The main demonstration grew to include more than 100,000 people in Mexico City. Family members of other victims joined Sicilia to speak at the rally. Some held up pictures of loved ones killed in the violence. Protests were held in more than 30 cities across the country.

Sicilia continued his effort in the summer of 2011, leading a 14-bus protest tour to 12 Mexican cities. His effort caught the attention of President Calderón, who agreed to meet with Sicilia and family members of other victims. The meetings were shown live on national television.

Calderón said he understood the protesters' point of view. However, he believed stopping the war on illegal drugs would send the message that the cartels had won. In 2012 Sicilia brought his bus tour to several cities in the United States. He called for an end to the war on drugs. Sicilia supported making drugs legal in Mexico and the United States. He believed legalizing drugs would reduce the amount of money and power the cartels gained by selling illegal drugs.

Missing students spark anger

The president of Mexico is elected to a six-year term and cannot run for reelection. When Calderón's time in office ended in 2012, Enrique Peña Nieto (1966–) replaced him. Peña Nieto promised to turn his attention to reducing violence against citizens and businesses. He said he would stop targeting the drug kingpins. The homicide rate fell during his first years in office. Nevertheless, it was still twice as high as it had been before the war on drugs began.

In September 2014 a group of college students was trying to attend a demonstration in honor of the victims of the 1968 Tlatelolco massacre. Tlatelolco is a section of Mexico City. In 1968 about 40 people died when government troops opened fire on a crowd of protesters. The college students in 2014 took over several buses in the city of Iguala (pronounced ig-WAL-la) and forced the drivers to take them to the site of

The disappearance of 43 students in Mexico has angered many citizens. Here, student teachers from Ayotzinapa clash with riot police along a highway in Guerrero State in 2015. The 43 students had been missing for about a year at that time. © URI CORTEZ/AFP/ GETTY IMAGES.

the demonstration. Along the route, local police stopped the buses and began shooting. Several people were killed.

Many of the remaining students tried to escape. Police caught up with 43 of the students and captured them. The students disappeared. In the weeks after the incident, the government said that the mayor of Iguala had ordered the police to round up the students. The police handed the students over to the local drug cartel. Supposedly, the cartel killed the students. Both the mayor and the police apparently took bribes from the cartel. Government officials arrested more than 130 people involved in the incident, including the mayor and his wife.

The students' disappearance led to a series of angry protests beginning in October 2014. Groups of people ranging from a few hundred to more than 100,000 marched in cities across the nation. Many people carried pictures of the missing students. They again called for an end to the violence. Protesters criticized the government's response to the case. They claimed the official story was a lie and that President Peña Nieto and government officials were hiding the truth to protect themselves. Public anger and protests continued for more than two years. Larger demonstrations were held on the anniversary of the students' disappearance in 2015 and 2016. Protests were also held outside Mexico in the United States and other nations.

In 2016 a special group of investigators said that the government's explanation of the students' disappearance had many problems. The group said the evidence in the case told a different story. The investigators claimed that government officials had tried to interfere in the investigation. As of 2017, the truth about the missing students remained unknown and continued to anger the Mexican people.

For More Information

BOOKS

García, Mario T., and Sal Castro. *Blowout!: Sal Castro and the Chicano Struggle for Educational Justice.* Chapel Hill: University of North Carolina Press, 2011.

Hunter, Miranda. *Story of Latino Civil Rights: Fighting for Justice.* Philadelphia: Mason Crest, 2006.

Mize, Ronald L., and Grace Peña Delgado. *Latino Immigrants in the United States.* Cambridge, UK: Polity Press, 2012.

Tinajero, Araceli. *El Lector: A History of the Cigar Factory Reader.* Translated by Judith E. Grasberg. Austin: University of Texas Press, 2010.

PERIODICALS

Archibold, Randal C. "Immigrants Take to U.S. Streets in Show of Strength." *New York Times* (May 2, 2006). Available online at http://www.nytimes.com/2006/05/02/us/02immig.html (accessed July 17, 2017).

Ellingwood, Ken. "In Mexico City, Crowds Protest Drug Violence." *Los Angeles Times* (May 8, 2011). Available online at http://articles.latimes.com/2011/may/08/world/la-fg-mexican-violence-protest-20110509 (accessed July 18, 2017).

Glaister, Dan, and Ewen MacAskill. "US Counts Cost of Day without Immigrants." *Guardian* (May 1, 2006). Available online at https://www.theguardian.com/world/2006/may/02/usa.topstories3 (accessed July 17, 2017).

"Invisible No More: The Latino Struggle for Civil Rights." *Focus On* (December 2010). Available online at http://www.nea.org/assets/docs/HE/Hispanicsfocus10.pdf (accessed July 20, 2017).

Padgett, Tim. "Why I Protest: Javier Sicilia of Mexico." *Time* (December 14, 2011). Available online at http://content.time.com/time/specials/packages/article/0,28804,2101745_2102138_2102238,00.html (accessed July 18, 2017).

Wilkinson, Tracy. "New Report Raises Chilling Possibility That Mystery of 43 Mexican Students' Disappearance Will Never Be Solved." *Los Angeles Times* (April 25, 2016). Available online at http://www.latimes.com/world/mexico-americas/la-fg-mexico-students-20160425-story.html (accessed July 18, 2017).

Woo, Elaine. "'60s 'Blowouts': Leaders of Latino School Protest See Little Change." *Los Angeles Times* (March 7, 1988). Available online at http://articles.latimes.com/1988-03-07/local/me-488_1_lincoln-high-school-graduate (accessed July 13, 2017).

Yee, Vivian, Kenan Davis, and Jugal K. Patel. "Here's the Reality about Illegal Immigrants in the United States." *New York Times* (March 2, 2017). Available online at https://www.nytimes.com/interactive/2017/03/06/us/politics/undocumented-illegal-immigrants.html (accessed July 19, 2017).

WEBSITES

"Hispanics in the US Fast Facts." CNN, March 31, 2017. http://www.cnn.com/2013/09/20/us/hispanics-in-the-u-s-/index.html (accessed July 27, 2017).

"How the United States Immigration System Works." American Immigration Council, August 12, 2016. https://www.americanimmigrationcouncil.org/research/how-united-states-immigration-system-works (accessed July 19, 2017).

Lee, Brianna, and Danielle Renwick. "Mexico's Drug War." Council on Foreign Relations, May 25, 2017. https://www.cfr.org/backgrounder/mexicos-drug-war (accessed July 18, 2017).

López, Gustavo, and Kristen Bialik. "Key Findings about U.S. Immigrants." Pew Research Center, May 3, 2017. http://www.pewresearch.org/fact-tank/2017/05/03/key-findings-about-u-s-immigrants/ (accessed July 17, 2017).

"Mexico's 1968 Massacre: What Really Happened?" National Public Radio, December 1, 2008. http://www.npr.org/templates/story/story.php?storyId=97546687 (accessed July 19, 2017).

Pao, Maureen. "Cesar Chavez: The Life behind a Legacy of Farm Labor Rights." National Public Radio, August 12, 2016. http://www.npr.org/2016/08/02/488428577/cesar-chavez-the-life-behind-a-legacy-of-farm-labor-rights (accessed July 14, 2017).

Simpson, Kelly. "East L.A. Blowouts: Walking Out for Justice in the Classrooms." KCET, March 7, 2012. https://www.kcet.org/shows/departures/east-la-blowouts-walking-out-for-justice-in-the-classrooms (accessed July 13, 2017).

Yu, Titi. "A New Documentary Celebrates the Life and Work of Dolores Huerta." Moyers & Company, October 6, 2017. http://billmoyers.com/story/dolores-huerta-documentary/ (accessed October 15, 2017).

OTHER

A Day without a Mexican. DVD. Directed by Sergio Arau. Los Angeles: Altavista Films, 2004.

4

Economic Discontent

Secret Document of the Farmers of Xiaogang **105**

Porkulus Protests, Tea Party **111**

15-M Movement **116**

Brexit **122**

Throughout time, people have been divided into economic classes. These classes include the wealthy, the middle class, and the poor. In many cases, powerful people have gained wealth by using the poor for labor. For example, wealthy landowners in Europe used to allow poor people to farm on their large estates. The owners then collected much of the harvest as payment for the use of their land. This left the poor farmers with very little for themselves.

Over the years, economic inequality has led to popular revolts and protests. Economic inequality is the large difference between the poor and the wealthy. Protests often occur when ordinary people have little hope that their lives will improve. Some protest when they do not have enough money or resources to feed their children or themselves. When people protest, they gather together to try to change something they feel is wrong.

Economic protests have occurred throughout history. Taxes on tea imported to the British colonies led to the Boston Tea Party in 1773. This event helped spark the American Revolution (1775–1783), which created the United States as the colonies were freed from British control. Such revolts continued over the centuries. French workers joined the July Revolution in 1830, which led to a new king taking the throne. Russians marched against their wealthy rulers to start the Russian Revolution of 1905. Low wages and poor working conditions have also inspired workers in many countries to form unions and demand better treatment from their employers.

Income inequality remained an important issue in the late 20th and early 21st centuries. The economy shifted a great deal in the latter half of the 20th century. The inequality in the distribution of wealth expanded, creating an even larger gap between the wealthy and the poor. Modern studies have found that the richest members of a nation often hold a large percentage of the wealth. In 2011 the top 20 percent of US households held more than 84 percent of the nation's wealth, according to an article by

Economic Discontent

> ### WORDS TO KNOW
>
> **Austerity:** Conditions of extreme spending cuts at a national level.
>
> **Capitalism:** An economic system defined by private enterprise for profit.
>
> **Conservative:** A person who holds traditional beliefs concerning social issues and favors limited government spending.
>
> **Developing countries:** A country that has a low standard of living, including low average annual income per person, high infant mortality rates, widespread poverty, and an underdeveloped economy. Most of these countries are located in Africa, Asia, and Latin America.
>
> **Dictator:** Ruler who has total power over a country.
>
> **Dynasty:** A line of hereditary rulers or a family in which members hold a great deal of power in fields such as business and politics.
>
> **Economic inequality:** A large difference in income between the poor and the wealthy.
>
> **Fiscal responsibility:** When the government taxes just enough to pay for necessary expenses.
>
> **Housing bubble:** An increase in housing prices caused by high demand that eventually decreases, causing values of properties to decline sharply.
>
> **Impoverished:** Extremely poor.
>
> **Market economy:** An economic system of free competition in which prices are determined by supply and demand.
>
> **Mortgage:** Payments made on a loan from a bank to help pay for the purchase of a home.
>
> **Pork barrel spending:** Funds attached to laws for projects that benefit a lawmaker's home district.
>
> **Recession:** A period when trade and economic production slows.
>
> **Stimulus:** An action that causes another action to take place.

Nicholas Fitz in *Scientific American*. The bottom 40 percent of households held just 0.3 percent.

In *Scientific American,* Fitz also noted that the ratio of chief executive officer (CEO) pay to worker income was about 20 to 1 in 1965. (CEOs are the heads their companies, often responsible for making difficult business decisions.) This large difference in pay meant that CEOs earned about $20 for every $1 the average worker earned. This ratio increased steadily over the years. By 2016 the CEO-to-worker ratio was 347 to 1. Income inequality like this is found all around the world.

In 2017 Oxfam, a group of charities that work together to stop poverty, reported that just eight billionaires held as much wealth as the poorest half of the global population (3.6 billion people). Average citizens can become discontented, or upset, when so few people control such a large share of the world's wealth. This unhappiness can lead people to take action.

Effects of poverty

Experts link poverty to many social problems. In poor areas, schools often do not have enough money. Students sometimes drop out to find work to help their families. Some low-income students may also believe that an education will not help them because they cannot afford to go to college. Studies have found that the US high school dropout rate is higher in states with greater income inequality. Violent crime is also more common in low-income communities. Homicide rates, or murder rates, are higher in states with greater income inequality as well. Studies have also found similar results in Canada.

Research shows that children's well-being is better in countries with more income equality. Such countries include Finland, the Netherlands, and Sweden. Other benefits of income equality include longer life expectancy. Countries where income is more equal also have fewer suicides and lower rates of teen pregnancy.

Health and safety

According to the World Health Organization (WHO), about 1.2 billion people in the world live on less than $1 a day. This is known as extreme poverty. Poverty causes health problems for a number of reasons. Low-income communities often have little access to health care and healthful foods, such as fresh fruits and vegetables. Some people do not even have access to clean water, proper shelter, or sanitary facilities (toilets). People can develop serious illnesses when they do not have access to these basic necessities of healthy living.

People in low-income areas may also have difficulty finding work. Those who do not graduate from high school are even less likely to find gainful employment. The jobs available to them may be dangerous. Other jobs might not pay enough for people to support their families. In some cases, citizens in these communities may need to work two or three jobs to make ends meet. Even people who have steady employment may not have benefits, such as sick days or health insurance. This means that they must go to work even when they are sick just so they can make enough money to survive.

Human development

Poverty is an issue of wealth, but it is also an issue of human development. Human development has to do with people's well-being. It also involves the opportunities people have to improve their quality of life. The United

CRITICAL THINKING QUESTIONS

1. Why does income inequality lead to protests? Do you think protests are a good way to address the issue? Why or why not?

2. Why did Chinese officials allow the farming methods used by the people of Xiaogang to continue even though they were illegal?

3. What were some measures the Spanish government took to fix problems caused by the global recession of 2008?

4. What was the main historical event that inspired the name of the Tea Party movement? Why was this event significant to the ideas expressed by the 21st-century movement?

5. Why did some British citizens want to leave the European Union? Why did others want to stay?

6. How does economic discontent impact a country?

Nations (UN) measures human development in three areas: life expectancy, years of education, and gross national income per capita. Income per capita refers to the amount of money an average person earns in a particular country or region. The UN uses information in these three areas to determine a country's human development index (HDI). The organization also measures weaknesses in these areas in the human poverty index (HPI).

The HDI and HPI were created to view the development of countries from a human perspective. Rather than focus on the economies of countries, the HDI weighs the people and their achievements instead. The UN has found that countries that rank low in human development rank high on the poverty scale. In a well-balanced society, human development should be high and human poverty should be low.

Political discontent

In many countries, people's feelings about their government are related to their beliefs about the economy. People often blame government officials when the economy is doing poorly. In democratic nations, most people have the opportunity to vote out officials they feel are doing a bad job of managing national wealth. Yet, this is not the case in other countries around the world.

In some countries, a political party is so powerful that it cannot be challenged. In China, the Communist Party has been in power for decades. Chinese citizens have no real choice in voting. People may express their dislike for the government or its leaders, but they are prohibited from organizing protests or demonstrations. Voters in China elect local officials of the ruling party. These local leaders then vote for people in more powerful positions. In this way, average citizens seem to have a choice. However, people can only vote for members of the ruling party. This means they may not be free to choose leaders whose ideas they truly support.

Still, even such strict government controls have not stopped people from rebelling against a system that keeps them poor. This was the case in 1978 when families in Xiaogang (pronounced sh-OW-gang), China, were starving because they did not have enough food. Under the Communist system, the people of Xiaogang worked on a collective farm. They handed over much of what they grew to the government. There was usually not enough food for everyone. This was because the farmers were not motivated to work hard. This changed when the farmers made a secret agreement to keep some of what they grew for their families. Their rebellion was an act of desperation, but their success changed China's economy and helped millions of people.

Ballot box power

People may become unhappy with their government's leadership even in countries where they have political freedom. Voters may disagree with a decision that affects them and their families. In 2016 the people of the United Kingdom voted on a major issue. They had to decide whether the country should leave the European Union (EU), an organization of many countries with a shared economy. The United Kingdom had joined the forerunner to the EU in 1973. More than half the country voted to leave the EU in 2016.

Many young adults in the United Kingdom were upset with the vote. They had spent their whole lives as members of the European community. They felt this change would hurt their future opportunities. Many protested the decision and demanded another vote, but the decision was already final. The United Kingdom went forward and began planning to leave the EU. This angered even more people, who organized larger demonstrations and marches.

Anger about political decisions has led to political action in the United States over the

Many in the United Kingdom were unhappy with the results of the vote to leave the European Union. Some took to the streets to show that they wanted to remain part of the European Union. © MICHAELPUCHE/ SHUTTERSTOCK.COM.

Economic Discontent

years as well. Around 2009, some citizens disagreed with economic plans meant to stabilize the economy following a major recession that began in 2008. A recession is a time when trade and production slow down. Many people lost their jobs during this period. The government made plans to give them more benefits. Lawmakers also voted to assist some big industries, such as banks, that were failing because of debt, or money owed. Many Americans lost their homes because they could not afford their mortgage, which is the monthly payment they make on a home loan from a bank. When a borrower cannot pay his or her mortgage, the holder of the mortgage can take possession of the property in a process called foreclosure and then sell it. About 8 million foreclosures occurred in the United States from 2008 to 2010. The government also tried to help these people.

Some conservative voters did not want the government to use money for these purposes. Conservatives often hold traditional beliefs concerning social issues and favor limited spending by the government. A group of conservatives came together to form the Tea Party movement to express their concerns. They organized protests and supported political candidates who were also against the government's plans. The Tea Party managed to get some of these candidates elected. These actions moved the Republican Party to take on more conservative ideas.

Effects of the recession

The 2008 recession affected people around the globe. In Spain, people were dealing with high rates of unemployment. As in the United States, many Spanish banks were in danger of failing. People were losing their homes because they could not afford to make payments. Spanish citizens organized protests in public squares and marches in the streets throughout the country in 2011. They wanted to express their dissatisfaction with the economy.

People on social media helped organize the demonstrations. Many groups worked together even though they may not have had the same goals and ideas. This movement became known as the 15-M movement. Members of the movement wanted to speak out about issues such as rising unemployment and government corruption, which is dishonest or illegal behavior by politicians.

Spanish citizens' anger with their government matched the feelings of many people around the world. A 2014 Pew Research Center global

---

A group of conservatives came together to form the Tea Party movement to express their concerns. They organized protests and supported political candidates who were also against the government's plans. The Tea Party managed to get some of these candidates elected.

survey found that most people in developed nations believed that higher-income citizens had too much political power. They felt that wealthy people could influence the government. They also believed poor people had much less political power. Movements around the world reflected these findings. People hurt by failing economies continued to organize and demand change.

Secret Document of the Farmers of Xiaogang

LOCATION: Xiaogang, China

DATE: 1978

China is controlled by the Chinese Communist Party (CCP). With more than 85 million members, the CCP is the world's largest political party. For much of the 20th century, the country operated like a traditional Communist country. All businesses and properties in the country were collectively owned by the government. Farmers did not own their fields. Factory operators did not own their production facilities, products, or raw materials.

During the 1970s, farmers in Xiaogang, China, were struggling. The government ordered them to grow food on a collective farm. The government took most of the crops but gave some food to the farmers and their families. However, the harvests were often poor because the farmers were not motivated to work hard when the government took most of their food. Because of this, many people in the village were starving.

Some of the farmers met in secret and agreed to save some food for themselves. They worked very hard because they knew they would be helping their families by having a good harvest. This secret agreement was against the law in the Communist country. Yet, when the government found out about the agreement, its reaction was not what the farmers had expected.

The Road to Communism

China was closed to most outsiders for centuries. Emperors of various dynasties ruled the country. These leaders only allowed outsiders to trade at certain ports. At the end of the 19th century, the ruling Qing (pronounced

Economic Discontent

1971 *Cacerolazo* Protests in Chile

In 1970 Salvador Allende (1908–1973) was elected president of the South American nation of Chile. Allende was a Socialist. In this type of system, people do not own property, land, or businesses. The government owns everything and shares it among the people. Allende also took some positions that were popular with the Communist Party in Chile. Before 1970, many American businesses were operating in Chile. When Allende was elected, the government began to take control of the businesses. The profits were distributed among the population.

Communism was considered by several other nations in Central and South America. However, it was not popular among all people. The United States was against Communism and tried to stop countries from installing Communist governments. The change to a Communist government could cause problems with a country's economy. In 1971 the people of Chile were facing many economic problems, including higher prices and food shortages.

On December 1, 1971, a group of about 5,000 women marched to the palace of President Allende in the capital of Santiago. They were angry about the rise in hunger among the people. The women were also concerned about Fidel Castro's (1926–2016) visit to their country. Castro was the president of Cuba. He was one of the most famous Communist leaders in the world at that time. As the women protested, they made noise by banging on pots and pans. This type of demonstration became known as a *cacerolazo*

CHing) dynasty was struggling with the loss of territories and power following several wars. These conflicts continued into the early 20th century.

The Qing rulers made changes to the government to try to hold on to power. Leaders abandoned civil service examination tests used to control who qualified for jobs to make sure only the wealthiest and well-educated people held power. They invested in the military to make it stronger and set up some elected governmental bodies. This system of self-government allowed the Chinese people to elect candidates to assemblies but limited the power of these local government officials. The central government still gave the orders. Local officials enforced these laws in the provinces.

Many battles took place in China during the early 20th century. A small revolt in Wuchang (pronounced WU-chang) in 1911 turned into widespread fighting. This marked the start of the Chinese Revolution of 1911. Qing leadership agreed to make some changes, but those revolting rejected these ideas. The provinces sent representatives to a national assembly in Nanjing (pronounced NON-jing) in what they were calling (pronounced KA-sero-lazo) protest from the Spanish word for "casserole."

Women of all ages banged their pots and pans. They chanted slogans such as "In Chile there is hunger!" and "We do not want Castro here!" Police fired tear gas into the crowd. Tear gas is a chemical substance that can cause burning in the eyes and difficulty breathing. Pro-Communist protesters also attacked the marchers. The women continued to march. Eventually, police used more tear gas and powerful water hoses to clear the streets of protesters. About 88 people were hurt in the demonstrations.

In 1973 Allende was overthrown in a military coup and committed suicide. Following its first use in Chile, the noisy cacerolazo style of protest became common in many South American countries. It continues to be used by demonstrators in the 21st century.

A monument to Salvador Allende is shown in Santiago in Chile. © ANTON_IVANOV/SHUTTERSTOCK.COM.

the Republic of China. These representatives elected Sun Yat-sen (1866–1925) as temporary president. In 1912 the emperor's family gave up all claims to power.

The revolutionaries did not get everything they wanted, though. China is a large country, and citizens in some regions did not accept the new government. People in certain areas took power for themselves. Instead of making changes, the central government then had to focus on uniting China. The CCP and the Nationalist Party, or Kuomintang (KMT), eventually worked together to bring these rebelling leaders under control in the 1920s. In the mid-1940s, fights between the CCP and KMT led to a civil war.

The CCP had been gaining power and popularity, especially in rural areas. The party eventually defeated the KMT in the Chinese Revolution of 1949. CCP leader Mao Zedong (pronounced Mou ZA-dong; 1893–1976) announced that China would be a Communist country called the People's Republic of China (PRC). Under Communist rule, the country remained largely isolated from outside influence for many years.

Cultural Revolution

As the leader of China, Mao ordered new policies, such as collective agriculture. In this system, farmers worked to produce food for the whole country rather than just for the people in their communities. The government tried to control farming from a distance. The government told farmers what to plant instead of allowing them to plant crops that grew well in their regions. Even though farmers were growing crops, the food did not get to the people who needed it. Between 1959 and 1962, at least 30 million Chinese people died of starvation under this system.

Mao saw his position weakening. To stay in power, he called on young Chinese people to join him in a Cultural Revolution in 1966. He wanted to remove power from party leaders and government officials. Mao closed all the schools. He encouraged young people to form unofficial groups called the Red Guards. These groups attacked older Chinese citizens and scholars across China. The Red Guards saw educated people as the enemy.

The Cultural Revolution greatly affected the economy. Industries produced fewer goods, and people suffered. In 1971 Mao worked with Premier Zhou Enlai (pronounced chew EN-lie; 1898–1976) to hold on to power. Zhou reopened schools and worked to strengthen the country's leadership structure. Both Mao and Zhou died in 1976. Leadership of China passed to Deng Xiaoping (pronounced deng CHOW-ping; 1904–1997) in late 1978. Deng did not fully embrace capitalism, or private enterprise for profit. He understood the importance of a strong economy, though. Deng rejected some of the ideas of earlier Communist leaders. He supported the development of a market economy, or a system of free competition. Over time, people were less impoverished, or extremely poor, and had more food. Deng helped the economy improve to benefit the people of China. This progress helped him remain in power.

Secret agreement

Twenty families lived in the Xiaogang village in 1978. Deng's changes and policies had not yet begun. Food shortages were common and widespread. Under Mao, the family farms had been combined to form a collective farm that was worked by all the village residents. Many people in Xiaogang had already starved to death because of this change. People were discouraged. Even if they worked hard, the crops did not belong to them. The farms also did not provide enough food for their families.

This 2008 sculpture depicts the signing of the original contract by the farmers in Xiaogang in 1978. They entered a pact to carry out a bold economic experiment and became heroes of reform. © STR/AFP/GETTY IMAGES.

The government sent grain to the village for years, but it was not enough. The village team leader rang bells and blew whistles to call people to work the fields, but few answered the signals. Much of the ground was not cleared and was unprepared for planting. Many people left the village for months at a time to travel to larger communities, where they begged for food and money. People in villages all over China faced the same kinds of problems. However, conditions in 1978 were even worse than usual. A severe drought caused the harvest to be even smaller than it had been in years past.

The heads of the families of Xiaogang came up with a plan to make their lives better. They met in a mud hut and divided the land that was available for farming. They assigned portions to every family. The families would work their fields and turn over a certain amount to the collective. If they produced more than that amount, they could keep a part of the harvest for themselves. The leaders wrote up an agreement that

Economic Discontent

explained the plan. The head of every family signed it with a thumbprint. The members also made a plan of what they would do if government officials arrested them. They agreed that the rest of the village would take care of their children if this happened. The members knew government officials could arrest and kill them if they found out what was happening in the village.

Instant change

The people of Xiaogang got to work right away. They were now motivated to help their families. The team leader was surprised to find people working in the fields before dawn. The families planted grain on almost twice as much land as they had the year before. Some families competed against one another to see how much food they could grow. The first harvest under the new system produced more grain than the previous five years combined.

Other villages nearby were a part of the same area commune, or working group. The people in these villages found out what the Xiaogang families were doing. They tried to divide the farmland so they could keep any extra food, too. The commune leaders learned about the Xiaogang families' plans and tried to stop them. The leaders also stopped sending supplies such as seeds and fertilizer to Xiaogang to punish the farmers for not obeying the government. However, CCP officials noticed that Xiaogang was producing much more food than it had in the past. The government also observed that Xiaogang was growing more food than other villages in the commune were. The farmers' plan had been discovered, but they were not arrested as they had feared.

The members made a plan of what they would do if government officials arrested them. They agreed that the rest of the village would take care of their children if this happened. The members knew government officials could arrest and kill them if they found out what was happening in the village.

Instead, a local official visited the village and said the farmers' experiment was worth a try. The Anhui Province party leader also visited. He supported the plan, even though the CCP still demanded that workers support communal farming. Communes around China began breaking up the collective farms. Xiaogang's grain harvests grew year after year.

In 1980 Deng said he approved of the change in farming practices. Within four years, all the communes across China were gone. In 1985 Deng put new economic plans in place. He encouraged private enterprise. He allowed people to work for their own profit. This change improved China's economy quickly. Hundreds of millions of people escaped poverty over the next three decades. In 2017 the World Economic

Forum ranked China's economy second in the world. Even with this success, not all businesses in China became privately owned. The government still owned the banks and the media, such as television stations. The land also belonged to China, but people could buy houses and other property. The Xiaogang farmers who feared being killed if their plan was discovered became national heroes instead.

Porkulus Protests, Tea Party

LOCATION: United States

DATE: 2009–2010

Porkulus protests, or pork protests, were the first wave of a conservative American political effort that eventually became known as the Tea Party movement. *Pork* refers to pork barrel spending, or federal money that members of Congress tack onto laws to benefit projects in their home states. Leaders of the movement were against this type of spending. They also supported the free market, fiscal responsibility, and smaller government. A free market is an economic system in which privately owned businesses are not restricted and prices are set by competition. Fiscal responsibility means the government sets enough taxes to pay needed expenses and uses public money wisely.

Some organizers said the name Tea Party came from the phrase "Taxed enough already." The organization described itself as a grassroots movement, meaning it was made up of and directed by members rather than a political party or other group. However, powerful individuals such as billionaire brothers David Koch (pronounced coke; 1940–) and Charles Koch (1935–) helped fund the group. The Kochs and their Citizens for a Sound Economy political group even created a Tea Party website in 2002. This was years before the movement began organizing protests.

The name Tea Party is also tied to US history. American colonists protested high British taxes and other issues in 1773. A group called the Sons of Liberty sneaked onto ships that were delivering goods in Boston Harbor in Massachusetts on December 16. During the night, the Sons of Liberty dumped the ships' products, including hundreds of crates of tea, into the harbor. This protest against taxation became known as the

Boston Tea Party. Following the protest, Britain responded with even more rules to punish the colonists. A few years later, both sides clashed in the American Revolution, as the colonists fought for independence from Great Britain.

Countdown to financial trouble

A worldwide global recession affected the United States in 2008. The recession involved many factors, including a credit bubble. In economics, a bubble occurs when the trade for something is greater than its actual value. As the price of the product or service goes up, fewer people are able to afford it. Eventually, the bubble bursts because there are no more investors.

When people buy homes, they usually do not have the money to pay for the house. They apply for a loan from a lender, such as a bank. Mortgages are the loans that help people purchase homes. Before agreeing to a mortgage, the lender has to be sure the borrower can afford to pay back the loan. If the borrower cannot make the payments, the bank may take possession of the house. Lenders set standards that they use to decide if they will offer particular people loans.

Many lenders loosened their standards before 2008. Banks gave loans to people who might not be able to repay them. Some banks allowed people to take loans for 100 percent or more of the value of the homes they bought. When the recession hit, many people lost their jobs. Some of these people were unable to pay their high mortgages. Many banks had sold parts of these risky loans to other lenders, which made things even worse. The problem quickly spread throughout the housing market and the banking industry. Other businesses were soon affected as well.

In late 2008, the government under President George W. Bush (1946–), a Republican, set up new programs to try to save the banks and other businesses. Officials believed the economy would collapse if these companies failed. One of these programs was the Emergency Economic Stabilization Act of 2008. Government departments made and guaranteed loans and bought bank stocks through these laws. Some of the money helped homeowners change their mortgages, so they could keep making payments. However, others did not receive assistance and lost their homes. The government also enacted the Troubled Asset Relief Program (TARP). TARP helped save three major American auto manufacturers and some large banks from going out of business.

President Obama's plan

The US presidential election took place in the midst of this economic crisis. Barack Obama (1961–) won the election on November 4, 2008. After he took the oath of office on January 20, 2009, he immediately set to work to reverse the economic slide. A month after taking office, the Democratic president signed into law the American Recovery and Reinvestment Act (ARRA), a $787 billion spending bill. It was commonly called a stimulus package because it was meant to fuel the economy by having people spend money. The ARRA provided many tax cuts for American families that allowed them to keep more of their earnings. The act also increased unemployment funding for people who lost their jobs and were unable to find work. It funded road and bridge projects and helped school districts pay for teachers.

This stimulus did not have an immediate effect. During the first three months of 2009, the US job market lost another 2 million jobs. By the middle of the year, the economy was improving. The economy finally saw job growth in late 2010.

The stimulus was not popular with everyone, though. When Obama was selling his plan to the public and Congress during his first month in office, many Republican leaders said the cost of the spending bill was too high. Many conservatives were angry that the government was using taxpayers' money to bail out lenders and big businesses. Some activists began sending tea bags in the mail to their representatives in Washington, DC, with letters complaining about high taxes. The tea bags were a reference to the Boston Tea Party. The activists soon began talking about holding rallies and protests against the stimulus.

First Tea Party events

On February 19, 2009, a television analyst on the cable news network CNBC made comments about the state of the economy. Rick Santelli (1953–) expressed anger that the government would help people who could not afford to pay their mortgages. He said that paying this debt was a personal responsibility and the government should not provide assistance. Santelli argued that it was time for the United States to hold a modern-day Tea Party as a protest against the mortgage relief plan.

Some conservatives who were listening began discussing what Santelli said on social media. They used Twitter to organize the first of many conference calls for the following day. This led to 50 conservative activists

Some activists began sending tea bags in the mail to their representatives in Washington, DC, with letters complaining about high taxes. The tea bags were a reference to the Boston Tea Party.

Economic Discontent

A man dressed as an old-fashioned town crier arrives at a tax day Tea Party protest in Fort Myers, Florida, in 2009.
© PERRY CORRELL/SHUTTERSTOCK.COM.

organizing as the Nationwide Tea Party Coalition. They agreed to sponsor Tea Party protests in 51 cities on February 27. Nearly 100 people helped to organize these events in seven days. The group claimed that 30,000 participants turned out for these protests.

The coalition then set up a website and began organizing a Tax Day Tea Party protest on April 15, which is the deadline for filing individual income tax returns. Organizers later reported that more than a million protesters had participated in rallies in more than 900 cities. Outside sources put the number of participants at close to 250,000. Many people used social media, including Facebook, to set up local Tea Party chapters and organize protests. During the summer of 2009, a cross-country tour called the Tea Party Express visited more than 30 cities, where rallies also took place.

Tea Party members

A 2012 CBS News/*New York Times* poll found that 18 percent of Americans supported the Tea Party. Most (89 percent) of the supporters were white, and only 1 percent was black. Men made up 59 percent of the party, and those aged 45 or older made up 75 percent of supporters. About 36 percent of supporters lived in the South. Nearly half (48 percent) said they usually voted for Republican candidates. The top issue that angered

Tea Party members was President Obama's health-care reform bill. They also felt that the government did not represent the American people and were upset with government spending.

Impact

The Tea Party quickly targeted a number of politicians who were up for reelection in the November 2010 midterms. Midterms are congressional elections held in the middle of a president's term. When President Obama took office, his Democratic Party had the most seats in the House of Representatives. The Tea Party supported many Republican candidates in the midterm elections. The Republicans won enough seats to take control over the House. Republicans also won many seats in the Senate. Tea Party–endorsed Republican candidates who won Senate seats included Rand Paul (1963–) from Kentucky and Marco Rubio (1971–) from Florida.

The Tea Party's influence stretched beyond the ballot box. Many observers said the movement forced Republican lawmakers further to the right. This meant that many Republican politicians took a more conservative stand on issues because they believed this is what voters wanted. During the 2012 Senate election, the Tea Party again threw its support behind conservative candidates, including Ted Cruz (1970–), who won the Senate race in Texas.

The Tea Party was not as successful in the elections in 2014. Many Tea Party–supported candidates lost in the primary elections. Primaries decide who will represent each party in the November elections. Still, many Republican candidates who supported Tea Party ideas won their races. The midterms helped Republicans gain control of both houses of Congress as the party continued to shift to the right.

In 2015 Republican Party leadership and Tea Party supporters were in a struggle for control. House Speaker John Boehner (1949–) resigned when he was unable to resolve differences within the Republican Party. The Tea Party supported Congressman Paul Ryan (1970–) of Wisconsin as the new Speaker of the House. The Speaker is the leader of the majority party in the House of Representatives. The following year, Tea Party-backed candidates for president lost in the Republican primary to political newcomer Donald Trump (1946–).

Trump won the presidential election in late 2016. Tea Party supporters once again called for conservative policies from the new Republican government. Senator Paul was among the political leaders backing a conservative agenda. Tea Party members reached out to Trump's administration to encourage support for conservative Republican leaders and small-government ideas.

15-M Movement

LOCATION: Spain
DATE: 2011

A protest movement began in Spain in the early 2010s. After two years of economic crisis, the Spanish people were angry that the government was trying to address the issue by cutting back on spending. These actions, known as austerity measures, caused the Spanish people a great deal of economic hardship.

In 2011 the unemployment rate in Spain stood at more than 20 percent, according to the World Bank. About 30 percent of young people were unemployed. In addition, the high cost of housing and political division left people feeling hopeless. Many Spanish citizens believed politicians were unable or unwilling to work together to solve these problems.

On May 15, 2011, in Madrid, Spain, the 15-M movement began. It was organized mostly online. The movement included a series of protests and meetings where people discussed economic and political problems to try to find solutions. More than 80,000 people across Spain reportedly participated in the protests, which the citizens' organization Democracia Real Ya (DRY) helped plan. Smaller groups joined the 15-M movement to work toward similar goals regarding changing the economy and the government. Eventually, the movement led to the formation of a new political party in Spain. It also inspired movements in other parts of the world, such as in Greece.

Global recession

The financial crisis of 2008 hit many countries around the world very hard. Spain was one of those countries. Before the recession, Spain had a strong economy and the government made sound decisions about finances. The city of Madrid spent less than it collected in tax revenue. This helped the city pay off debt. However, Spain experienced a housing bubble. This occurred because housing prices increased due to high demand. Eventually, the supply of houses was much greater than the demand, so property prices fell sharply.

Spain is a member of the European Union (EU). The EU is a political and economic union of mostly European nations. In 1999 the EU introduced the euro, a common form of currency that could be used in member nations. Between 1996 and 2007, property prices in Spain tripled. Spanish investors, including banks, bought large amounts of property during this time in an effort to resell these properties for a profit. When the recession hit, property prices fell and the housing bubble burst.

The downturn in the housing market affected other businesses, such as the construction industry. People could no longer afford to build houses. Hundreds of thousands of construction workers then lost their jobs. Banks were left holding many properties because homeowners could no longer pay their mortgages. An estimated 600,000 people lost their homes between 2007 and 2014, according to teleSUR, a multimedia service in Latin America. People cut back on other spending. This decrease in spending rippled through the economy.

At the same time, Spain experienced a labor bubble. When business was good, wages rose rapidly. Yet, jobs disappeared just as quickly when the recession hit. People who lost their jobs were no longer paying income taxes. Income taxes are an important source of revenue for many public services. The government then had to borrow and spend to keep the economy from collapsing. In addition to losing money from income taxes, many out-of-work citizens were collecting government benefits. This added to the strain on the Spanish economy.

Continuing economic trouble

Even after the recession ended around 2010, Spain experienced further economic troubles. The government announced more austerity measures to improve the economy. In early 2011, officials revealed a plan for pension reform, which raised the retirement age in Spain from 65 to 67. This meant people would have to work longer before they could retire and receive the benefits they had earned. People were angry about this change and other actions the government was taking.

In 2011 Spain entered its second year under austerity programs. Many people were becoming increasingly unhappy. The unemployment rate was at 21 percent. People feared the government would put even

People who lost their jobs were no longer paying income taxes. Income taxes are an important source of revenue for many public services. The government then had to borrow and spend to keep the economy from collapsing.

Economic Discontent

French Protests of May 1968

Students have protested many issues throughout the years. In the 1960s young people were speaking out about various social problems. In France many students were unhappy with the way President Charles de Gaulle (pronounced de GOL; 1890–1970) ran the country. They were upset about the out-of-date university system, a lack of job opportunities, and the strict rules of traditional French society.

On May 3, 1968, police broke up a student protest at the Sorbonne. This famous school was part of the University of Paris. Many students were injured and hundreds more were arrested. After the protest, the university canceled classes at the Sorbonne. Angry students took to the streets for several days to stage more demonstrations. On the night of May 10, about 20,000 students protested around the university. The police told them to leave, but they refused.

The students overturned cars to create barriers between themselves and the police. As the riots continued, the police worked to remove the students so the streets could be reopened for traffic. Throughout the night, police and students battled in violent clashes. Students threw explosive devices at the police. The police attacked and beat many of the students. No one was killed but between 300 and 400 people were injured.

In the days after the rioting, students at other French universities joined in the demonstrations. Students took over the Sorbonne. Some groups wanted to overthrow President de Gaulle and start a new government. French workers called for nationwide strikes, or refusals to work, in support of the student protesters. Millions of workers walked off their jobs. Some even took over the factories where they worked. These actions forced many French businesses and public services to close.

By May 30, President de Gaulle warned that he would use military force to stop the protests. He called for new elections and organized marches against the protesters. In June, de Gaulle banned

more austerity plans in place. Groups online began organizing a protest. They chose May 15 as the day to demonstrate. The date was one week before the local and regional elections on May 22.

Like-minded individuals join forces

Tens of thousands of people in Madrid, Barcelona, and other Spanish cities participated in demonstrations against the austerity programs during the first day of protests. Some took part in sit-ins, or protests in which participants refuse to leave a location. People set up tents and created protest camps in the centers of many cities. Most protesters were young people, but all ages demonstrated. Many people said they were disappointed with the major political parties and felt the people in power were

Economic Discontent

any further protests and forced the students from the Sorbonne. The protests eventually stopped, but the government did grant workers higher wages and better working conditions. Officials also passed a law to improve the education system and modernize schools.

A scene from one of the May 1968 protests in Paris, France. © REPORTERS ASSOCIES/GAMMA-RAPHO VIA GETTY IMAGES.

dishonest. Protesters believed their government was not a true democracy because it did not represent the people.

Hundreds of people occupied the tent city in Puerta del Sol square in Madrid. It eventually expanded to include a garden, a library, a market, and a pharmacy. People set up information booths to share their ideas. Others hung posters on street lampposts and other structures. Thousands of people continued to demonstrate across Spain every day for a week. Crowds of protesters filled the streets of Madrid every evening.

In the May 22 elections, the conservative Popular Party won the most seats in the local and regional elections. The protesters agreed to end the tent camp the following month. However, organizers planned other protests in the weeks that followed. On June 19, about 37,000 people marched in Madrid, while thousands more marched in 55 other Spanish cities. Most protests were peaceful, although police made some arrests.

As the protests continued, smaller groups joined forces to work with DRY. DRY wanted to model the movement on two protests in Iceland and several Arab countries. Icelandic activists had worked to get people who had damaged the country's financial footing arrested. The pro-democracy Arab revolutions, called the Arab Spring, involved efforts to overthrow governments and demand fair and equal treatment. The 15-M movement was not as political. Instead, Spanish activists met in public places to have face-to-face discussions about specific problems or issues. People offered suggestions and voted on a plan of action, which included holding protests at a specific location. The 15-M protesters organized events they felt would help them solve the problem.

Helping with housing concerns

Although various protest groups in Spain had different goals, they had much in common. The Platform for People Affected by Mortgages (PAH), for instance, was a group of activists who were angry about the effects of the housing market collapse. Activists met in front of properties that the banks were going to take back from homeowners who could not pay their mortgages. The banks were evicting people, or throwing them out of their homes. They protested and prevented law enforcement from taking possession of the properties. The newly organized 15-M movement supported the PAH, which had been active for about two years at that time. Together they pressed lawmakers to focus on the issue and address mortgage protection.

The partnership with 15-M helped the PAH by raising awareness. Soon, more people formed PAH groups. Attendance at the PAH anti-eviction protests eventually increased from about 50 members to hundreds. This was 15-M's first effort at influencing politics, and it was successful. In 2012 the government ordered banks to freeze mortgage evictions. The PAH continued to fight against banks taking back properties by staging demonstrations and trying to find ways for people to keep their homes.

Political efforts

Many people blamed the Spanish Socialist Workers' Party (PSOE) for the poor economy and resented its role in setting up the extremely unpopular austerity measures. In November 2011, Spain held its general elections.

Thousands of people gather to protest for economic equality in Puerta del Sol square in Madrid on May 15, 2011. © PEDRO RUFO/SHUTTERSTOCK.COM

The Popular Party won a majority of seats in parliament, the national governing body. The following month, the government announced more austerity measures for 2011 and higher taxes for wealthy Spaniards. At the time, the unemployment rate was almost 23 percent.

In March 2012, the government announced taxes on businesses, stopped raises for government employees, and cut spending. These changes were not enough to keep the Spanish economy from slipping into another recession. Many people marched in protests against the new government cuts. The change in government had not done away with the austerity programs. The conservative government's actions made people more angry. Soon after, the government tried to fix the struggling banking industry and was forced to accept the EU's offer of a loan.

Podemos founded

Despite the government's actions, activists were encouraged by their success with the PAH. Pablo Iglesias (pronounced eg-les-ee-as; 1978–),

Economic Discontent

a political science lecturer, had spent several years working with student protesters and fellow scholars to fight global capitalism. Iglesias and his students launched a new political party called Podemos on January 17, 2014. Groups formed other political parties in response to the austerity programs, but Podemos thrived. In 2015 Iglesias spoke to a crowd of 150,000 in Puerta del Sol. Within months, polls found Podemos represented 22 percent of Spanish citizens. Many Podemos candidates won races for political office in local elections in 2015. The people of Barcelona even elected a new mayor who was an activist in the anti-eviction movement.

In national elections in late 2015, four parties split the vote. No party had enough seats to hold an overall majority. Instead, members of various parties held talks to see if they could form a coalition, or partnership, to lead the government. The power shift took away some of the influence of the two longest-running parties. Spain was forced to hold general elections again in June 2016. Once again, the conservative Popular Party won the most seats but not enough for an overall majority. Podemos came in third place in the elections.

Ongoing efforts

Protests continued in Spain in the latter 2010s. Demonstrators continued to meet in public squares on May 15. Tens of thousands of people marched in Madrid in 2017. Trade unions and liberal groups joined the protests as well.

The movement led to many changes in Spain. More young people became politically active. The 15-M movement forced the government to be more transparent, or open about its activities. Experts saw real changes from these actions in the economy. In the first quarter of 2017, unemployment was still high but fell to 18.7 percent.

Brexit

LOCATION: United Kingdom
DATE: 2015–2017

Brexit is the name given to the decision made by the United Kingdom to leave the European Union (EU). The word comes from a combination of the words *Britain* and *exit*. The United Kingdom was a member of the EU, which is an economic and political partnership of countries. The United Kingdom includes England, Wales, Scotland, and Northern Ireland. On June 23, 2016, the majority of people in England and Wales voted to leave the EU. Brexit passed with the majority vote.

EU history

The European Economic Community (EEC) began after World War II (1939–1945). This organization of just a few European nations became the European Union in 1993. Before this change, the EEC helped its member nations recover from the war by establishing an economic union. The United Kingdom joined the EEC in 1973. Many countries later followed. In 1985 member nations signed the Schengen Agreement. This treaty allows citizens of countries that signed the agreement to move freely among member nations without showing passports. After the EEC became the EU, most member nations also adopted a common form of currency known as the euro.

Beginning around 2008, several economic crises hit Europe. At the same time, many Middle Eastern countries were coping with civil wars, terrorism, and economic hardship. Refugees began flooding into Europe. EU countries then had to make decisions about how to help these refugees. Some EU countries refused to take refugees, and others limited the number they would accept.

Earlier in the 21st century, terrorists began attacking citizens in the United Kingdom. One of the first major events occurred on July 7, 2005, when Islamist extremist suicide bombers conducted four attacks in London. Other attacks followed. These events made some UK citizens nervous about accepting refugees from the Middle East into their country. However, most of the early attacks were committed by British citizens or immigrants who had spent most of their lives in the United Kingdom.

Some citizens believed that membership in the EU allowed people to enter the United Kingdom too easily. Many politicians began discussing whether the United Kingdom should leave the EU and how to do this. They believed that leaving the EU would give them more control over immigration and keep out people who meant British citizens harm. Talk about leaving the EU was not new. Some people were against the United Kingdom joining the EEC in the first place, and the debate continued for more than 40 years.

Many politicians began discussing whether the United Kingdom should leave the EU and how to do this. They believed that leaving the EU would give them more control over immigration and keep out people who meant British citizens harm.

Economic Discontent

Protesters with the Vote Leave Campaign gather to make a case for Brexit in London about a week before the vote.
© MIKE KEMP/IN PICTURES VIA GETTY IMAGES.

The referendum

UK Prime Minister David Cameron (1966–) tried to change the United Kingdom's relationship with the EU. He said in 2013 that if this effort failed, the British people would be able to vote on the issue of staying or leaving the EU. Despite Cameron's efforts, Parliament, the UK's governing body, took steps to move forward with the European Union Referendum Act in 2015. This act allowed the government to hold a nationwide vote on the issue.

Cameron continued to hold discussions with EU representatives. Later in 2015, various EU branches met about the United Kingdom. The European Council (EC), the governing body of the EU, offered the United Kingdom a new deal in February 2016. Many British leaders said they wanted more than what was offered, though. Cameron, who campaigned for the Remain side, or the side to remain part of the EU, managed to gain more from the council. Nevertheless, critics said the agreement did not address limits to immigration. By the end of the month, political leaders began choosing sides. Cameron then set the date for the referendum, or vote, on leaving the EU.

In addition to immigration issues, many Britons were also concerned about the free market of labor. This allowed workers from other EU countries to work in the United Kingdom. Many people believed that such an open system made it more difficult for British citizens to find jobs.

Experts raised concerns about economic issues as well. The independent National Institute of Economic and Social Research released a study that looked at the effects of the United Kingdom leaving the EU. The study found that the United Kingdom would save money by not having to contribute to the EU budget, but it faced increased costs by leaving the EU trade system. This research showed that the United Kingdom would lose money and poor British families would struggle more. Other families would suffer as well because the country would not trade as often with the rest of Europe and people might earn less.

Vote and aftermath

The Brexit vote was held on June 23, 2016. Many Britons said they were still unhappy about large numbers of migrants entering Europe, and many voters wanted to be free of EU rules. The UK Independence Party (UKIP), a political group led by Nigel Farage (1964–), wanted to leave the EU. Farage had led a Leave movement called Euroscepticism for about 20 years. Although researchers said the Remain side had a slight lead just before the vote, the result was 48.1 percent for Remain and 51.9 percent for Leave.

The pro-Brexit decision set in motion a complex series of negotiations. The United Kingdom could not simply leave the EU. When it had joined, the country agreed to a series of rules it would have to follow to separate from the EU community. According to Article 50 of the Lisbon Treaty, the country is first required to notify the EC of its plan to leave the EU. The country then cannot withdraw from the EU for another two years. Many problems had to be solved, such as how trade would continue. Cameron announced his resignation after the vote. Negotiations then passed to the next prime minister, Theresa May (1956–).

Like Cameron, May was in favor of remaining in the EU. She took some time before triggering Article 50. May felt the United Kingdom needed to agree on its goals before the country began talks with the EU. Many people protested in favor of and against Brexit. Even after the vote, people continued to march in protest of the result.

Protests and reactions The UK economy immediately suffered after the referendum. The pound, the currency of the United Kingdom, lost value in its biggest one-day fall against the US dollar on record. Within a week, many Britons who had voted to leave the EU said they wished they had voted to stay. More than 4 million people signed a petition calling for another EU referendum. The government rejected that request. Many voters said they had voted Leave but were still shocked to see the results. Soon protesters began marching against the Leave decision. A rally was organized in Trafalgar Square in London but was canceled because of heavy rain. Tens of thousands of people went anyway.

On July 2 an estimated 30,000 to 50,000 people demonstrated in the streets of London, a city that voted at 60 percent to remain. Most protesters were young adults who were born after the United Kingdom joined the EU. They opposed the decision because they felt it would affect their lives. Some carried banners with slogans such as "Our future has been stolen" and "My generation will Remain." The demonstration began in Park Lane and wound its way to Parliament Square. The

Economic Discontent

Japanese Rice Riots of 1918

Many countries suffered economic problems following the world wars. After World War I (1914–1918), conditions in Japan were difficult. Japan had fought on the side of the Allies (the United Kingdom, France, the United States, and other nations). The Allies won the war, but the economy in Japan suffered. War debt and other issues caused inflation, meaning prices on everyday goods and items rose as the value of the country's currency fell. Over a few months in 1918, the cost of rice doubled.

Rice is very important to the Japanese people. It is one of the nation's more popular foods and has a special place in Japanese culture. With prices rising as fast as they did in 1918, many people had trouble buying food. Most people did not make enough money to keep up with higher costs. Many people blamed the government, rice sellers, and wealthy people for driving up prices.

Many people in the coastal Toyama section of Japan worked at the docks, where ships loaded and unloaded goods. In July 1918 several women began organizing boycotts of ships that exported rice. Women also began holding sit-ins, strikes, and marches in protest of the high cost of rice. During a boycott, people refuse to buy goods from a company or use its services. A strike is a refusal to work until employers meet certain demands. As the women's efforts gained attention, other people began joining the protests. Eventually people began rioting, looting, and burning property. About 25,000 people were arrested.

The rioting soon spread to other areas of Japan. In early August, more than 100,000

march itself lasted nearly four hours. The closing rally filled Parliament Square, with an estimated 30,000 people.

Over the months that followed the referendum, a number of people participated in demonstrations against Brexit. In February 2017, demonstrators set up a mock checkpoint, or station where people traveling between countries must stop to be approved. They did this on a road between Northern Ireland and the Republic of Ireland. The Republic of Ireland is an independent sovereign state, meaning it is not a part of the United Kingdom. Northern Ireland is one of the countries that make up the United Kingdom. Northern Ireland was included in Brexit, while the Republic of Ireland was to remain in the EU. People in both countries on the island of Ireland were worried about how Brexit would affect them, including travel restrictions and trade issues. The mock checkpoint was meant to remind people, and governments, of how Brexit could divide the Irish people. The Irish government, which was awaiting news as to how Brexit would affect the countries, was exploring places that checkpoints could be established.

people rioted in the city of Nagoya. The rioters attacked police and rice sellers and destroyed many buildings. By mid-August, violent protests were held in more than 30 cities, including the capital of Tokyo. In the city of Kobe, demonstrators burned the police station and newspaper offices. In Osaka more than 230,000 people rioted.

The rice riots inspired other movements across Japan. Tens of thousands of workers walked off their jobs to protest low wages and poor working conditions. In response, the government called on the army to deal with the protests. By September the military had most of the riots and strikes under control. In 1918 Japan was the site of about 400 protests and demonstrations. As a result, Japan's prime minister, Terauchi Masatake (1852–1919), resigned.

The rice riots caused Terauchi Masatake to resign from office. © CULTURE CLUB/GETTY IMAGES.

EU anniversary demonstration March 25, 2017, was the 60th anniversary of the signing of the Treaty of Rome. This treaty established the EEC and eventually led to the founding of the EU. Many Britons observed the day with a Unite for Europe march in London. The crowd was reported to be in the tens of thousands. More than 1,000 people also marched on the Scottish Parliament in Edinburgh, Scotland, in a demonstration organized by the Young European Movement. Some Britons living in Italy and Spain also participated in Brexit protests. Protesters from both sides of the issue attended these events. The timing of these protests was important, as Prime Minister May was set to trigger Article 50 a few days later.

Many foreigners living in the United Kingdom also attended protests. These people feared for their future. Some said others had told them they would have to leave the United Kingdom and return to their homelands, despite having lived in England for decades. Some foreigners had established businesses in the United Kingdom. They

Economic Discontent

British Prime Minister Theresa May Speaks about Brexit

This primary source excerpt is from a speech that British Prime Minister Theresa May gave on January 17, 2017. In the speech, May lays out a plan for what kind of relationship the United Kingdom will have with the European Union after Brexit.

A little over six months ago, the British people voted for change.

They voted to shape a brighter future for our country.

They voted to leave the European Union and embrace the world.

And they did so with their eyes open: accepting that the road ahead will be uncertain at times, but believing that it leads towards a brighter future for their children—and their grandchildren too.

And it is the job of this Government to deliver it. That means more than negotiating our new relationship with the EU. It means taking the opportunity of this great moment of national change to step back and ask ourselves what kind of country we want to be.

My answer is clear. I want this United Kingdom to emerge from this period of change stronger, fairer, more united and more outward-looking than ever before. I want us to be a secure, prosperous, tolerant country—a magnet for international talent and a home to the pioneers and innovators who will shape the world ahead. I want us to be a truly Global Britain—the best friend and neighbour to our European partners, but a country that reaches beyond the borders of Europe too. A country that gets out into the world to

---

wondered what they would do if they had to leave the country. Many had married British citizens and worried about what would happen to their spouses and children if they had to leave. On March 29, 2017, May delivered the letter triggering Article 50 to the European Council. Brexit talks between the United Kingdom and the EU started on June 19, 2017.

Post–Article 50 effects The UK economy continued to struggle. A year after the referendum, the pound was still about 14 percent below its level on June 23, 2016. Imports, or goods brought in from other countries, were much more expensive. Businesses were reluctant to invest in the United Kingdom because they did not know how Brexit would affect them. Experts predicted business investment would remain low for several years. Sales fell off in the first few months of 2017 as shoppers began to cut back on spending. A number of major banks also planned to move staff from London to other cities, such as Paris.

build relationships with old friends and new allies alike.

I want Britain to be what we have the potential, talent and ambition to be. A great, global trading nation that is respected around the world and strong, confident and united at home. . . .

That is why this Government has a Plan for Britain. One that gets us the right deal abroad but also ensures we get a better deal for ordinary working people at home.

It's why that plan sets out how we will use this moment of change to build a stronger economy and a fairer society by embracing genuine economic and social reform.

Why our new Modern Industrial Strategy is being developed, to ensure every nation and area of the United Kingdom can make the most of the opportunities ahead. Why we will go further to reform our schools to ensure every child has the knowledge and the skills they need to thrive in post-Brexit Britain. Why as we continue to bring the deficit down, we will take a balanced approach by investing in our economic infrastructure—because it can transform the growth potential of our economy, and improve the quality of people's lives across the whole country.

It's why we will put the preservation of our precious Union at the heart of everything we do. Because it is only by coming together as one great union of nations and people that we can make the most of the opportunities ahead.

SOURCE: May, Theresa. "Theresa May's Speech Laying Out the U.K's Plan for Brexit." *Time* (January 17, 2017). Available online at http://time.com/4636141/theresa-may-brexit-speech-transcript/ (accessed October 11, 2017). Courtesy of Time Inc.

Many manufacturers were closely following Brexit talks. Automakers, for example, worried about trade deals with the EU that could add high fees to cars made in the United Kingdom. Food and drink suppliers, construction companies, and many other industries also worried about the increasing cost of doing business in mainland Europe due to Brexit. As of late 2017, May and other British leaders continued to work on the details concerning Britain's exit from the EU.

For More Information

BOOKS

Dillon, Patrick. *Story of Britain from the Norman Conquest to the European Union.* Somerville, MA: Candlewick Press, 2010.

Parker, Christopher S., and Matt A. Barreto. *Change They Can't Believe In: The Tea Party and Reactionary Politics in America.* 2nd ed. Princeton, NJ: Princeton University Press, 2013.

Skocpol, Theda, and Vanessa Williamson. *The Tea Party and the Remaking of Republican Conservatism.* Oxford: Oxford University Press, 2012.

PERIODICALS

"A Background Guide to 'Brexit' from the European Union." *Economist* (February 24, 2016). Available online at https://www.economist.com/blogs/graphicdetail/2016/02/graphics-britain-s-referendum-eu-membership (accessed July 24, 2017).

Eckholm, Erik. "Xiaogang Journal; Village of Small Farmers Marks Own Great Leap." *New York Times* (September 19, 1998). Available online at http://www.nytimes.com/1998/09/19/world/xiaogang-journal-village-of-small-farmers-marks-own-great-leap.html (accessed July 24, 2017).

Fitz, Nicholas. "Economic Inequality: It's Far Worse Than You Think." *Scientific American* (March 31, 2015). Available online at https://www.scientificamerican.com/article/economic-inequality-it-s-far-worse-than-you-think/ (accessed July 28, 2017).

Flock, Elizabeth. "Spanish 'Revolution': Thousands Gather in Madrid's Puerta del Sol Square." Washington Post (May 18, 2011). Available online at https://www.washingtonpost.com/blogs/blogpost/post/spanish-revolution-thousands-gather-in-madrids-puerta-del-sol-square/2011/05/18/AFLzpZ6G_blog.html?utm_term=.40c473d34d92 (accessed November 12, 2017).

Steinfels, Peter. "Paris, May 1968: The Revolution That Never Was." *New York Times* (May 11, 2008). Available online at http://www.nytimes.com/2008/05/11/world/europe/11iht-paris.4.12777919.html (accessed July 24, 2017).

Stone, Jon, and Katie Forster. "Brexit Protest: Tens of Thousands March through London Calling for UK to Remain in EU." *Independent* (July 2, 2016). Available online at http://www.independent.co.uk/news/uk/home-news/brexit-eu-referendum-protest-march-30000-anti-saturday-2-july-anger-banners-leave-vote-central-a7115646.html (accessed July 24, 2017).

WEBSITES

"Discontent with Politics Common in Many Emerging and Developing Nations." Pew Research Center, February 12, 2015. http://www.pewglobal.org/2015/02/12/discontent-with-politics-common-in-many-emerging-and-developing-nations/ (accessed July 21, 2017).

"Episode 337: The Secret Document That Transformed China." *Planet Money*, National Public Radio, May 14, 2014. http://www.npr.org/sections/money/2014/05/14/312488659/episode-337-the-secret-document-that-transformed-china (accessed July 19, 2017).

"How China Is Ruled: Communist Party." BBC News, October 8, 2012. http://www.bbc.com/news/world-asia-pacific-13904437 (accessed July 19, 2017).

"Just 8 Men Own Same Wealth as Half the World." Oxfam, January 16, 2017. https://www.oxfam.org/en/pressroom/pressreleases/2017-01-16/just-8-men-own-same-wealth-half-world (accessed October 6, 2017).

Montopoli, Brian. "Tea Party Supporters: Who They Are and What They Believe." CBS News, December 14, 2012. http://www.cbsnews.com/news/tea-party-supporters-who-they-are-and-what-they-believe/ (accessed July 17, 2017).

Pasion, Adam. "Rice Riots." Japan Daily, August 26, 2015. https://japandaily.jp/rice-riots-1693/ (accessed July 24, 2017).

"Poverty and Health." World Health Organization, 2017. http://www.who.int/hdp/poverty/en/ (accessed October 6, 2017).

"Spain's 15-M Movement: Anti-austerity from the Streets to the Parliament." teleSUR. http://www.telesurtv.net/english/news/15-M-Movement-Anniversary-20160514-0030.html (accessed July 18, 2017).

"Spain's Indignados Protest Here to Stay." BBC News, May 15, 2012. http://www.bbc.com/news/world-europe-18070246 (accessed July 18, 2017).

5

Environment

Forward on Climate Rally **139**

Copenhagen Protests **144**

Global Frackdown **151**

Pacific Climate Warriors Blockade **157**

March for Science **163**

The environment is the natural world around us. The air we breathe, the water we drink, and the land we live on are all part of our environment. Environmentalism is a movement that seeks to improve and protect the environment. Environmentalists are people who want to limit human activities that harm the environment, such as pollution and the burning of fossil fuels, which releases harmful gases into the air.

Environmentalists often subscribe to the slogan "Think globally, act locally." This means that people can have a positive influence on our world by making changes at the local level—where we live. Environmentalists believe that all people on Earth are connected because protecting the planet is a community effort involving everyone on the planet. Actions taken to help the environment, such as recycling, are described as being "green."

History of the environmental movement

Beginning in the 19th century, people began to notice how their activities affected the environment. Because of human actions, some species of animals, such as the dodo bird and the passenger pigeon, became extinct, or died off. Rivers, lakes, and other water sources became dirty and undrinkable. People became sick from the changes in the environment.

One of the first people in the United States to write about the growing human effect on the natural world was Henry David Thoreau (1817–1862). Thoreau was a famous writer who spent much of his time outdoors appreciating nature. He believed that humans were capable of living within their environment without damaging it. Many environmentalists have adopted his ideas.

However, people's relationship with the environment increasingly changed toward the middle to the end of the 19th century. The Industrial

Environment

> ### WORDS TO KNOW
>
> **Acid rain:** Precipitation that contains a high level of acidity that is caused by pollutants in the environment.
>
> **Civil disobedience:** A nonviolent method of protesting.
>
> **Climate change:** Long-term, significant, measured change in the climate as seen in temperature, wind patterns, precipitation, and other factors. The term is often used today to describe any changes to global weather patterns that result from human practices.
>
> **Climate refugee:** Any person who has been forced to leave his or her home as a direct result of changes to the environment.
>
> **Compost:** To change once-living matter into decayed material that can be used to fertilize soil.
>
> **Deforestation:** The clear-cutting of forests for such human purposes as homes, businesses, and farms.
>
> **Desertification:** A process in which land becomes increasingly dry and unusable due to climate change.
>
> **Developing countries:** A country that has a low standard of living, including low average annual income per person, high infant mortality rates, widespread poverty, and an underdeveloped economy. Most of these countries are located in Africa, Asia, and Latin America.
>
> **Environmentalism:** The idea that people must actively take part in political and social movements to bring about positive changes that improve the health of the planet.
>
> **Fossil fuels:** Energy sources such as gas, oil, and coal that result from millions of years of natural processes, such as the decay of ancient plants and animals.
>
> **Fracking:** A method of getting natural gas and oil from rock by injecting water and chemicals at high pressure into the ground.
>
> **Global warming:** Rising temperature of Earth's atmosphere caused by an increase of greenhouse gases.
>
> **Greenhouse gases:** Gases that collect in the upper atmosphere of Earth and are believed to be responsible for changes to the planet's climate and weather patterns.
>
> **Renewable energy:** Sources of energy that can be naturally replaced by the environment and include solar, wind, and water.
>
> **Sustainable:** A method of using natural resources without depleting them or damaging them permanently.

Revolution (c. 1760–1840) brought about many of these changes. This was a time of rapid change in which machines and power-driven tools were used to mass-produce products. People began to use new methods that made the production of goods much easier. More people moved to cities to find better-paying jobs in factories. Cities grew very quickly, and people often had a better standard of living as a result.

At the same time, pollution started to become a problem. Although the growing number of factories resulted in many advances that benefited people, the cities where these factories were located became very dirty. Toxic runoff and smoke pollution from these businesses severely damaged the environment. By the 1890s, the first organizations devoted to preserving the environment were founded.

Changes in the 20th century

In the United States, one of the most important early environmentalists was Scottish American naturalist John Muir (1838–1914). In 1892 he founded the Sierra Club, a group dedicated to protecting natural places around the world. Thanks in part to Muir and the Sierra Club's efforts, in 1916 the US government created the National Park Service (NPS). The NPS is responsible for managing all national parks and monuments in the United States. These parks include Yosemite National Park in California; Yellowstone National Park in Wyoming, Montana, and Idaho; and Everglades National Park in Florida.

President Theodore Roosevelt and John Muir on Glacier Point, Yosemite Valley, California, in 1903. COURTESY OF THE LIBRARY OF CONGRESS.

Environmentalists later worked to protect animals in addition to land. In 1940 Congress passed the Bald and Golden Eagle Protection Act to prevent the national symbol of the United States from becoming extinct. In the 1960s scientists discovered that DDT, a pesticide once used to kill insects, was thinning the egg shells of bald eagles and some other birds. This caused the eggs to break when adult birds sat on them to keep them warm. In 1962 American scientist Rachel Carson (1907–1964) wrote a book called *Silent Spring*. The book discusses the threats that pesticides such as DDT pose to eagles and other animals, humans, and the environment. Thanks to this early environmental effort, the United States banned DDT in the early 1970s. Carson's book also helped bring the idea of environmentalism to many people's attention.

In June 1969 the Cuyahoga River outside Cleveland, Ohio, caught fire. The river had caught fire nine times before, but this time it attracted national attention. Some credit the event with helping to strengthen Americans' resolve to protect their natural resources. The Cuyahoga was in a region with many factories that pumped waste into the river.

Environment

For Americans, the idea that a polluted river could catch fire was terrifying. Many organizations responded to the situation by planning an event to highlight the growing threats to the planet. These groups established Earth Day, which was held for the first time on April 22, 1970. On Earth Day more than 20 million Americans gathered at local events to raise awareness about pollution and discuss ways to protect the environment. It was one of the largest organized demonstrations in US history and is still held each year.

In the United States the publicity from these events resulted in the federal government creating new environmental agencies. These included the Environmental Protection Agency (EPA) and the National Oceanic and Atmospheric Administration (NOAA). In addition, Congress passed the Endangered Species Act and the Marine Mammal Protection Act to protect at-risk animal species.

Other environmental disasters showed the need for continuing efforts. At Love Canal in New York, toxic waste forced residents to abandon their homes in 1978. A disaster in Bhopal, India, in 1984 killed 10,000 people when a gas leak at a Union Carbide plant spread poisonous fumes throughout the town while people slept. Thousands more died and others went blind in the aftermath of the world's worst industrial disaster.

Perhaps most frightening was the 1986 Chernobyl (pronounced cher-NO-bull) nuclear disaster in the Soviet Union (now located in

In 2010 victims of the largest industrial disaster in history protest near the Bhopal Mother Statue during a torch rally marking the 26th anniversary of the incident in India.
© ARINDAMBANERJEE/ SHUTTERSTOCK.

Ukraine). The accident occurred when a nuclear reactor exploded and spread harmful chemicals through the air. Nuclear reactors make nuclear power, a type of energy created by the splitting of atoms.

These events prompted global organizations such as the United Nations (UN) to become more active in protecting the environment from pollution and other threats. In 1988 the UN created the Intergovernmental Panel on Climate Change (IPCC). This group examines the effects of climate change on global weather patterns. In 1992 more than 160 nations signed the United Nations Framework Convention on Climate Change (UNFCCC) to try to limit the amount of greenhouse gases released into the air. Greenhouse gases trap heat in Earth's atmosphere, causing the planet to warm.

Although climate change does occur naturally, scientists believe that these large amounts of greenhouse gases are causing climate change to occur more rapidly and in some cases, more intensely. Today when most people use the term *climate change* they are referring to weather changes due to human activity. Without changes to human habits, the greenhouse gases will cause sea levels to rise and could continue to increase temperatures to levels that cannot support life on the planet.

Environmental concerns in the 21st century

In the 21st century environmentalists continue to seek solutions to the threats Earth faces. Environmental groups ask people to use green sources of energy, such as solar power, that do not have a negative effect on the planet. In 2006 former Vice President Al Gore (1948–) produced a documentary called *An Inconvenient Truth*, which highlights the dangers of climate change. For his efforts, Gore shared the 2007 Nobel Peace Prize with the IPCC. Although such recognition has helped motivate environmentalists, much of the world still relies on fossil fuels such as gas, oil, and coal. Fossil fuels are energy sources that when burned produce carbon dioxide (CO_2), a greenhouse gas linked to climate change. In addition, environmental crises continue to raise awareness about continuing threats to the world's health.

Human activities have a major effect on Earth. Many places around the world have experienced dramatic changes in normal weather patterns. These changes have resulted in more severe storms, droughts, floods, and temperature shifts. In coastal areas higher tides and rising ocean levels caused by melting polar ice threaten people's lives and livelihoods. If water levels continue to rise, some islands (and even some island nations) may disappear entirely.

Environment

> **CRITICAL THINKING QUESTIONS**
>
> 1. How do you think human beings have affected Earth, both positively and negatively?
> 2. Why do environmentalists think it is so important to protect the planet?
> 3. Which sorts of goals do environmental activists hope to achieve through protesting? Do you think they have been successful? Why or why not?
> 4. Which forms of activism might be effective ways to create positive changes to the environment?
> 5. What effect has the environmental movement had on national laws?
> 6. Are some groups of people more affected by changes to the environment than others? In what ways are these groups affected?
> 7. What are some ways that an individual person can help the environment?

In places such as the Sahara Desert in northern Africa, increasing droughts are leading to a process called desertification. This occurs when land becomes dry and barren. The land then becomes unable to support any life. Problems with desertification usually occur in poorer countries in Africa and Asia. Environmental problems often have a greater effect on poorer communities. This is due in part to the ability of wealthy nations to spend money to fix problems.

Many other environmental problems continue to threaten the planet in the 21st century. Deforestation occurs when trees are cut down in large numbers. Soil erosion is a problem in which soil becomes unsuitable for growing crops. Pollution threatens the health of people, plants, and animals. Environmentalists are actively seeking to resolve these problems.

Methods for making an environmental impact

Environmentalists use various methods to bring about change. Their long-term goal is to protect the environment from additional damage. Such efforts may require different approaches. For instance, environmentalists hoping to alter or create laws to protect the animals and Earth often personally appeal to people who have the ability to make changes. These people may be business leaders, local officials, or national politicians. Environmental organizers typically ask their supporters to contact these influential people to show the high level of concern their causes generate.

Environmental groups may hire people called lobbyists who have experience in convincing politicians to make policy changes. Lobbyists attempt to sway opinions toward a particular cause. The efforts of lobbyists in the United States led to the creation of many laws that benefit the environment, including the Clean Air Act of 1963. This law helped establish national guidelines to control air pollution.

Sometimes these methods are not effective. In such cases, environmental groups may seek more direct action. They will sometimes engage in civil disobedience, which is a nonviolent form of protesting. Civil disobedience may include rallies, marches, sit-ins, and hunger strikes. During such protests, police may arrest demonstrators. However, some protesters feel that their arrests bring extra attention to their cause.

Environmentalism may be expressed through individual choices. What people buy, how they live, and how they impact the environment can all affect the planet. The decision to recycle, compost materials, reduce energy use, walk instead of drive, or eat a vegetarian diet can express a person's desire to live a green lifestyle.

Forward on Climate Rally

LOCATION: Washington, DC

DATE: February 17, 2013

The Forward on Climate rally was a protest in which environmentalists marched to the White House on February 17, 2013. The goal was to show their opposition to an oil pipeline that was set to be expanded. This pipeline, a system for transporting oil and gas, is called the Keystone XL project. The rally drew about 40,000 people. It was one of the largest climate rallies in US history.

The marchers hoped to show the government how many people opposed this potentially damaging project. More than 90 organizations participated, including the Sierra Club and the Natural Resources Defense Council (NRDC). Typically, these two groups do not participate in physical activism such as marches. Rather, they traditionally seek political solutions to environmental problems. The rally had some success. The Keystone XL pipeline expansion was suspended temporarily in 2015 under President Barack Obama (1961–), a Democrat. However, newly installed President Donald Trump (1946–), a Republican, approved it in 2017.

Environment

Background

The Forward on Climate rally was organized with the goal of preventing further construction of the Keystone XL pipeline. This project is part of a wider system that transports oil between Canada and the United States. It requires the construction of a series of aboveground pipes through which oil will move. Upon completion of the 1,179-mile (1,897-kilometer) project, between 570,000 and 830,000 barrels of unprocessed crude oil will be transported through the pipeline each day. The Keystone XL will be part of an existing pipeline that stretches 2,925 miles (4,707 kilometers) throughout the central portions of Canada and the United States. Because the northern Keystone XL portion crosses a national border, it requires a federal permit. Other parts of the pipeline located solely within the United States were completed with only state input.

The project is owned by TransCanada, an oil production company in Canada. Many groups support its completion. Oil companies in both Canada and the United States will be able to transport and process oil extracted in North America more easily. This could help lower fuel prices. The project itself will create short-term construction jobs during its assembly and then long-term oil-production positions after its completion. Supporters of the project suggest that the pipeline may create as many as 100,000 jobs. A US State Department study, however, argues that the pipeline will bring 1,950 new jobs over a two-year period and then only 50 jobs after that. Many US politicians support its construction because it will contribute $3.4 billion to the economy. In addition, TransCanada threatened to sell its crude oil to China rather than to the United States if the pipeline is not constructed. Opponents of the project argue that even if the pipeline is constructed, the Canadian oil that is transported through it could still be sold to overseas markets and not benefit US consumers.

The greatest opposition to the Keystone XL project has come from environmental groups, however. They argue that the risk of an oil leak could harm the region.

Many groups oppose the Keystone XL project. These include landowners who fear the project might harm their properties. Native Americans in both the United States and Canada fear that the pipeline could damage their land. They worry particularly about oil leaks. Leaks have occurred in other pipelines, including another section of the Keystone. Some of the proposed routes for the Keystone XL and the related Dakota Access Pipeline (DAPL) cross lands that many Native American groups consider sacred.

The greatest opposition to the Keystone XL project has come from environmental groups, however. They argue that the risk of an oil leak could harm the region. The method that TransCanada uses to remove oil from sands relies on a system more like mining than drilling. According to Juliet Eilperin in the *Washington Post*, this method releases up to 15 percent more greenhouse gases than traditional drilling. Greenhouse gases collect in Earth's atmosphere. An excess amount of these gases is believed to contribute to the weather pattern shifts associated with climate change. An increase in the release of such gases by the Keystone project could speed up climate change.

Environmental groups suggest that the project will increase the US dependency on fossil fuels. In addition, the Keystone XL project will cross the environmentally fragile region of both the Sandhills and the Ogallala Aquifer in Nebraska. The pipeline is expected to cross the living areas of 12 endangered species of animals, including whooping cranes, the greater sage-grouse, piping plovers, and black-footed ferrets. The Sandhills is an important stop on the migration routes of many bird species. The Ogallala Aquifer is believed to contain one of the largest reserves of untapped freshwater in the world. A major oil spill in either area could be a disaster.

The Forward on Climate rally

Many environmental groups promoted the Forward on Climate rally to bring attention to the Keystone XL project. Several groups took the lead in organizing the event. These groups included 350.org, the Sierra Club, and the Hip Hop Caucus. Opposition to the Keystone XL project was the driving force behind the rally. Still, organizers hoped to raise awareness of other problems as well. They sought to highlight problems such as harmful carbon dioxide (CO_2) levels in the atmosphere. They also wanted to promote alternatives to fossil fuels. Organizers hoped to push the federal government to create plans that account for climate change.

On February 17, 2013, activists gathered at the Washington Monument in Washington, DC. From there, they marched to the White House for a rally. Organizers said about 40,000 people participated in some aspect of the event. The protesters specifically targeted President Obama in their message. They believed Obama had the ability to block further expansion of the Keystone XL pipeline. The event's title, Forward on Climate, was intended to echo Obama's 2012 campaign motto of "Forward." The rally was held on Presidents' Day in another nod to its intended audience.

Environment

Marchers take part in the Forward on Climate rally on February 17, 2013. At that time, it was the largest climate rally in US history. © RENA SCHILD/SHUTTERSTOCK.COM.

The weather on the day of the rally was very cold. Despite this, thousands of people came to show their support. Many demonstrators wore costumes. Attendees received free polar bear hats, a reference to the threat polar bears face from climate change. The rally featured a number of speakers. Among the presenters were Senator Sheldon Whitehouse (1955–) of Rhode Island, 350.org founder Bill McKibben (1960–), Sierra Club chairman Michael Brune (1971–), Chief Jacqueline Thomas of the Saik'uz First Nations people of British Columbia, and Hip Hop Caucus president Lennox Yearwood Jr. (1969–). Other rallies were held in connection with the Washington, DC, event. In Los Angeles, Congressman Henry Waxman (1939–) and actor Ed Begley Jr. (1949–) were among the best-known participants.

Aftermath

The Forward on Climate rally was successful in raising awareness about the dangers of oil pipelines. On March 29, 2013, an oil spill from a pipeline in Mayflower, Arkansas, raised fears among the public about the Keystone XL project. The Obama White House continued to voice its opposition to the Keystone extension. Various members of Congress, however, supported the project. Many Republicans argued that the pipeline would reduce US dependence on foreign nations for oil supplies. Representatives felt this was important because many of these countries do not share the United States' democratic ideals.

Love Canal Protests

Love Canal was an area of Niagara Falls, New York, named for William T. Love, a 19th-century businessman who dug a canal between the branches of the Niagara River. Love hoped to use the area to create a waterfall that could be used as an energy source. The project was never finished. Instead, Love left behind a deep canal, known as Love Canal. In 1920 the canal became a chemical waste disposal site used to dump garbage and dangerous materials.

In 1953 the site was covered with dirt and sold to a local school district for $1. The school district built an elementary school on the site, despite the dangerous chemicals that were buried underground. A construction company bought the remaining land and built 800 homes and 240 apartments on it. The unsuspecting homeowners began complaining about smells and unusual substances coming to the surface in their basements and yards. Studies showed that toxic fumes were in the air. Despite these warning signs, the city took little action. In 1978 the state of New York began investigating in response to complaints from the neighborhood's residents. By August 1978 the residents of the area had formed several organizations, including the Love Canal Parents Movement and the Love Canal Homeowners' Association to look out for their interests.

Residents increasingly became sick. The state ordered the school to close and removed pregnant women and small children from the area. New York agreed to buy 239 homes but left the rest of the community intact. Residents of the area were furious. They began a campaign to bring attention to their health problems. They marched to the state capitol, held vigils, and gave interviews to the press. Children continued to get sick. Because of the toxic nature of the land, residents were unable to sell their homes and move.

Children who live in the area of the Love Canal neighborhood, a former dump for dangerous chemicals, stage a silent protest using homemade signs. They are concerned about the lack of immediate relief for 37 families who were advised to leave their homes because the chemicals were leaching to the surface of the ground. © AP IMAGES/DS.

The residents continued to protest and generate bad publicity for New York State officials, whom many people felt were not doing enough to help with the situation. In October 1980 US President Jimmy Carter (1924–) finally ordered Love Canal to be abandoned. The government paid residents for their homes. Later, Congress passed the Comprehensive Environmental Response, Compensation, and Liability Act (CERCLA). The act is responsible for identifying and cleaning areas where toxic leaks have been located.

In 2015 Congress passed a bill to move forward with the project. On February 24, 2015, Obama vetoed the bill, which prevented it from passing into law. Congress was unable to gain the two-thirds vote necessary to override the president's veto. Finally, on November 6, 2015, Obama stopped the construction of the Keystone XL pipeline.

Native American groups continued to be among the most vocal opponents of the Keystone XL and DAPL. Some of these groups gathered with their supporters near the Standing Rock Indian Reservation located in North and South Dakota to oppose the construction of the DAPL. Activists also sought help from the legal system through a series of lawsuits and used civil disobedience. Protesters of the DAPL occupied one site and refused to move. Some groups even damaged construction equipment. Conflicts between DAPL protesters and police occasionally grew violent. Numerous activists demonstrating near the Standing Rock Indian Reservation were arrested. The news media showed images of police firing water cannons at people. On December 4, 2016, Obama blocked further work on the DAPL.

One of Donald Trump's first acts when he became president in January 2017 was to revisit the Keystone XL and DAPL. He signed presidential orders allowing construction on both pipelines to continue. By 2017, however, support for these projects had dropped from their highs in 2013. In 2017 the Pew Research Center, a think tank (body of experts) that polls people about various issues, found that 48 percent of Americans did not support the construction of the two pipelines. Only 42 percent of the people polled approved of the projects. In comparison, 66 percent favored the completion of the pipelines in 2013, and only 23 percent opposed the projects. The changes in the public's opinions about these projects were due, in part, to the publicity that the Forward on Climate rally and the DAPL protests created. As of October 2017, the DAPL was in operation but work on the Keystone XL was still stalled.

Copenhagen Protests

LOCATION: Copenhagen, Denmark

DATE: December 2009

In December 2009 representatives from many countries gathered in Copenhagen, Denmark, for the United Nations Climate Change Conference. This meeting was known as COP 15. The nations in attendance hoped to create new rules to reduce the effects of climate change. Several thousand protesters disrupted the COP 15 meetings. They were part of the Reclaim Power protest organized and led by a group known as Climate Justice Action (CJA). More than 1,700 people were arrested during the 12-day conference, with protests reaching their peak on December 16.

Large groups of protesters demonstrated at Copenhagen's Bella Center, where COP 15 was taking place. The protesters were angry because they believed that delegates at the conference were not doing enough to combat threats from climate change. By gathering outside the conference in large numbers, protesters hoped to influence national governments to push for tougher rules to protect the planet. Despite protesters' efforts, the conference closed with little progress.

Background

The United Nations (UN) is an organization that brings different countries together to work on international issues. The UN has been a leader in worldwide efforts to reduce the effects of climate change. In 1992 members of the UN passed a treaty called the United Nations Framework Convention on Climate Change (UNFCCC). This agreement created a set of rules for all nations to follow. The goal was to reduce greenhouse gases in Earth's atmosphere.

Greenhouse gases absorb and release solar energy that helps heat the planet. Without these gases, Earth would be much colder. However, certain human actions, such as the burning of fossil fuels, have trapped more of these gases in the atmosphere. The increase in these gases is responsible for many changes to normal weather patterns. In particular, increased greenhouse gases make Earth warmer. This is known as global warming. Global warming can cause the ice caps in the Arctic and Antarctica to melt. As a result, oceans may rise. Higher temperatures can lead to many other environmental problems.

The international community has tried to make changes to prevent further damage to Earth. For example, countries have signed treaties in which they agree to follow certain guidelines. The UNFCCC is among the most powerful of these treaties because 197 parties entered into the agreement. Almost every nation on Earth is a member of the UNFCCC. The members meet every year to discuss ways to help control the release of more greenhouse gases. These annual meetings are called the Conference

The protesters were angry because they believed that delegates at the conference were not doing enough to combat threats from climate change. By gathering outside the conference in large numbers, protesters hoped to influence national governments to push for tougher rules to protect the planet.

Environment

Climate Challenge!

1. Imagine that last summer was much hotter than usual where you live. Is this a sign of climate change? Yes or no?

   Answer: No. The weather naturally varies from year to year, and some years are hotter than others.

2. Imagine that almost every summer for the past decade has been hotter than usual. Is this a sign of climate change? Yes or no?

   Answer: Yes. Climate change occurs over many years, so a pattern of many hotter summers could be a sign of climate change. This is especially true if the same pattern is happening in many places around the world.

SOURCE: "A Student's Guide to Global Climate Change." US Environmental Protection Agency, 2016.

of the Parties, or COP. The 2009 meeting in Copenhagen was the 15th such meeting, making it COP 15. The primary goal of COP 15 was to update the 1997 Kyoto Protocol. The Kyoto Protocol was named after the Japanese city in which it was created. The treaty acknowledged that humans were responsible for global warming. It outlined the first set of objectives to reduce greenhouse gases.

Entering COP 15, officials from various countries hoped for different results. A group called the Alliance of Small Island States (AOSIS) wanted to create legal provisions to reduce levels of greenhouse gases. They are concerned that melting ice caps will contribute to sea-level rise, which will flood their island nations. A few African nations known as the African bloc supported the AOSIS. A collection of indigenous peoples also aided the group. Indigenous peoples are the original residents of a place. Many of the protesters who gathered outside the conference supported this collection of groups and their desire for strong laws regarding climate change. The countries that produce the most greenhouse gases hoped to pass rules that were not as tough as those sought by the AOSIS and its allies.

Protesters from several environmental nongovernmental organizations (ENGOs) gathered at COP 15. ENGOs are not connected to governments. At previous UNFCCC gatherings, the Climate Action Network (CAN) had represented these ENGOs in meetings. After COP 13 in 2007, however, some ENGOs had grown discouraged. They believed that CAN supported the positions of companies and powerful nations rather than backing all countries and people equally. The ENGOs formed two new separate groups called Climate Justice Action (CJA) and Climate Justice Now. These two networks of ENGOs joined forces at COP 15. They decided to name their protest effort Reclaim Power.

COP 15

Protest groups agreed ahead of COP 15 to use an "inside-outside" plan. With this approach, protesters planned to cooperate with groups that were direct participants in the conference. The protesters targeted December 16 as the height of their campaign. On this day, supporters of the movement inside the conference planned to walk out of the Bella Center as a group in protest. They would join with members of ENGOs outside. Together, they would hold what they called a People's Assembly within the UN area. The protest would feature speeches, marches, and chants. They hoped it would draw media attention and put pressure on the delegates still inside to listen to their concerns.

COP 15 began on December 7, 2009. Representatives from member countries gathered in the hope of creating solutions to the problems of greenhouse gases and global warming. Talks lasted for several days with little progress. Over the course of these debates, the small island nation of Tuvalu (pronounced too-VA-loo) tried to get the assembly to consider its plan to create a set of rules that all nations would have to follow. However, Tuvalu had trouble getting other nations to review its plan. This was disappointing for Tuvalu and its supporters in the African bloc, the AOSIS, and groups representing indigenous peoples. Protesters regarded people from these groups to be vulnerable, or at risk. People, governments, and companies with more money and power could easily harm these nations by taking actions that went against the countries' best interests.

Protesters wanted to help these groups. Each day included a different form of protest. On December 11, protesters targeted all corporations that were participants in the conference. The next day protesters spread throughout Copenhagen to participate in smaller individual campaigns. On December 14, they hoped to block the Copenhagen harbor and shut down shipping companies for the day. The goal was to emphasize international companies' role in affecting climate change. On December 15, protesters created plans to highlight the struggles of people who had lost their homes to climate change. They also wanted to point out the negative effects of global warming on agriculture.

Danish police blocked the protesters' plans during each campaign. A force of 9,000 Danish officers began to actively stop protesters' plans. The Danish government and the UN had set aside a space for protest groups. On December 9, police raided this facility and arrested 200 people. The Danish government quickly passed a series of laws to increase police powers. These laws gave police officers the power to arrest protesters whom they believed might break laws in the future. The

Environment

Al Gore Nobel Peace Prize Lecture, 2007

This primary source excerpt is from the speech that former Vice President Al Gore gave when he won the Nobel Peace Prize in 2007. He was a joint-recipient of the prize with the Intergovernmental Panel on Climate Change. They were honored for their work to raise awareness of the role humans play in climate change and its effects.

We, the human species, are confronting a planetary emergency—a threat to the survival of our civilization that is gathering ominous and destructive potential even as we gather here. But there is hopeful news as well: we have the ability to solve this crisis and avoid the worst—though not all—of its consequences, if we act boldly, decisively and quickly. . . .

So today, we dumped another 70 million tons of global-warming pollution into the thin shell of atmosphere surrounding our planet, as if it were an open sewer. And tomorrow, we will dump a slightly larger amount, with the cumulative concentrations now trapping more and more heat from the sun.

As a result, the earth has a fever. And the fever is rising. The experts have told us it is not a passing affliction that will heal by itself. We asked for a second opinion. And a third. And a fourth. And the consistent conclusion, restated with increasing alarm, is that something basic is wrong.

We are what is wrong, and we must make it right. . . .

In the years since this prize was first awarded, the entire relationship between humankind and the earth has been radically transformed. And still, we have remained largely oblivious to the impact of our cumulative actions.

UN followed suit and suspended several environmental groups that were participating in the conference. Several activists were removed from the protesters' building. Among them was prominent Nigerian author and environmentalist Nnimmo Bassey (1958–). Finally, on December 15, Danish undercover police arrested several protesters, including three spokespeople for the CJA.

Protesters clash with police

The surprise arrests raised concerns among activists that the police would try to stop their peaceful protest and assembly set for December 16. In response, the ENGOs decided to split into four blocs. The blue bloc included groups that had previously received permission from the Danish government for a December 16 march. The yellow bloc was a collection of ENGOs that had been refused entry into the Bella Center. There were also the green and autonomous (pronounced aw-TAWN-uh-muhs, meaning that they were

> Indeed, without realizing it, we have begun to wage war on the earth itself. Now, we and the earth's climate are locked in a relationship familiar to war planners: "Mutually assured destruction."...
>
> Now science is warning us that if we do not quickly reduce the global warming pollution that is trapping so much of the heat our planet normally radiates back out of the atmosphere, we are in danger of creating a permanent "carbon summer."
>
> As the American poet Robert Frost wrote, "Some say the world will end in fire; some say in ice." Either, he notes, "would suffice."
>
> But neither need be our fate. It is time to make peace with the planet.
>
> We must quickly mobilize our civilization with the urgency and resolve that has previously been seen only when nations mobilized for war. These prior struggles for survival were won when leaders found words at the 11th hour that released a mighty surge of courage, hope and readiness to sacrifice for a protracted and mortal challenge....
>
> The future is knocking at our door right now. Make no mistake, the next generation will ask us one of two questions. Either they will ask: "What were you thinking; why didn't you act?"
>
> Or they will ask instead: "How did you find the moral courage to rise and successfully resolve a crisis that so many said was impossible to solve?"
>
> **SOURCE:** Gore, Al. "Al Gore—Nobel Lecture." Nobelprize.org (December 10, 2007). Available online at http://www.nobelprize.org/nobel_prizes/peace/laureates/2007/gore-lecture_en.html (accessed October 11, 2017). Courtesy of Nobelprize.org

not connected to a particular organization) blocs. The blue and yellow blocs would try to meet within the grounds of the UN conference. The green and autonomous blocs would use various forms of civil disobedience. Protesters at COP 15 who intended to use this approach were expected to try to enter the grounds of the conference by climbing fences or through other methods. All four blocs would attempt to gather in the same area and hold their People's Assembly.

On December 16 indigenous leaders began a walkout from the Bella Center as planned. Members of the other three blocs began their protest with a 4-mile (6-kilometer) march across Copenhagen. Participants banged drums and wore colorful outfits, including panda bear costumes. Before the protesters could reach the Bella Center, however, UN and Danish forces stopped them. The protests grew violent. Police assaulted many activists with pepper spray and tear gas. Some were beaten. Officers arrested more than 1,000 people in a single day. The Danish government insisted that these clashes occurred only after protesters began to throw

Environment

Some 100,000 participants and marchers join the protest of COP 15 in Copenhagen in 2009. © RICARDO ESPLANA BABOR/SHUTTERSTOCK.COM.

bricks and damage property in the city's center. For their part, activists claimed they were victims of unfair attacks and arrests.

Aftermath

Experts noted that the conference had few lasting results. No legally binding rules were passed. Many countries decided to focus instead on setting loose goals to reduce the release of greenhouse gases. While member nations recognized the need to reduce the amount of greenhouse gases, they decided to have countries review their own activities. They were asked to report their efforts to the UN every two years. Some financial assistance was offered to developing countries such as Tuvalu to help them deal with problems from climate change. Developing countries are poor nations that are looking to advance economically and socially. Activists argued that the agreement reached at COP 15 would do little to affect climate change.

Activist leaders were very angry about their treatment at COP 15. They believed they had been unfairly banned from participating in the conference. When they tried to express their voices in other ways, they were arrested. While most of those who had been arrested were quickly released, 16 protest leaders remained in jail for several weeks. To show support for these people, fellow activists held protests in locations around the world. They also held their own set of meetings during the following year to bring attention to what they saw as the growing crisis of climate change.

Global Frackdown

LOCATION: Worldwide

DATE: October 11, 2014

The Global Frackdown is an annual event intended to highlight the possible dangers of hydraulic fracturing, or fracking. Fracking is a method of removing oil products from certain types of rock found deep in the ground. During fracking, a mixture of liquids containing water, chemicals, and other materials is injected at high pressure into the ground. Many people are concerned about the environmental threats that stem from fracking. Some worry that it pollutes both the immediate site and neighboring groundwater. Evidence also suggests that fracking creates small earthquakes.

The first Global Frackdown occurred in 2012. The event has grown to include hundreds of corresponding activities in more than 30 nations. The goal of the Global Frackdown is to establish a complete ban on fracking. Participants have tried to push elected officials to move away from relying on fossils fuels such as oil, gas, and coal for energy. Instead, participants hope to encourage investments in renewable energy sources such as solar and wind. Renewable energy comes from resources that cannot become exhausted.

Fracking

Fracking involves shooting high-powered bursts of liquid into a type of rock called shale. Shale is composed of hard mud and other particles. Some types of shale, often called oil shale, contain organic matter that can be processed to make a type of oil called shale oil. Shale oil can be used in the same ways that other petroleum products are used.

Fracking involves drilling a hole several thousand feet into the ground. Workers keep drilling until they reach veins of oil shale that usually run parallel to the ground surface. The hole is filled with steel

Environment

Julia "Butterfly" Hill's 738-Day Tree Sitting Protest

Environmentalists take on a variety of causes. Activist Julia "Butterfly" Hill (1974–) saved a giant California redwood tree by living in its branches for more than two years. Born in Missouri and raised in Arkansas, Hill earned the nickname "Butterfly" while hiking as a child. A butterfly landed on her hand and stayed there the entire hike. When Hill was 22, she was seriously injured in a car accident. After a year of medical treatment and therapy, she made a full recovery and began a new direction in life. She decided she wanted to have a positive influence on the future of the planet.

Hill moved to California, where the size and age of California redwood trees amazed her. She immediately became involved in a campaign to prevent the Pacific Lumber Company's removal of these trees. She joined a group of people who physically sat in these trees to prevent them from being cut down. Hill chose a redwood tree that was estimated to be 1,500 years old. She named the tree Luna. Hill climbed onto a pair of six-by-six-foot prepared platforms nestled into the trees' branches. Her first attempt at living in the tree lasted only six days. In December 1997 she once again climbed into the tree's branches and stayed there for two years.

Her time in the tree was difficult. Protesters, helicopters, security forces, and tree cutters harassed her. The winter weather was harsh. Heavy rains, wind, and cold temperatures tested her. Hill relied on a wood stove and donations from people who supported her cause. Her protest gained widespread media attention. She stayed in the tree for 738 days. Hill came down in December 1999 only after Pacific Lumber agreed to spare old-growth trees such as Luna. The company also agreed to explore sustainable methods of cutting down trees so the health of forests would not be affected.

---

pipes that are sunk into the ground, usually through layers called aquifers. Aquifers are types of rock that contain water. Once the vein of shale rock is reached, a hole is dug horizontally through this layer. The hole allows the drillers to create new routes for the oil to move from the rock into pipes. When completed, the series of pipes often forms an L shape.

A device called a perforation gun is lowered into the horizontal pipe. Small explosive charges are placed through the vein of rock. They create a series of small cracks in the shale. A liquid mixture called fracking fluid is then shot at great pressure into the pipes. This results in newly made cracks in the earth. Fracking fluid consists of water and other chemicals. It also contains other materials such as sand or ceramic balls. These keep the fractures in the earth open, allowing oil and gas to move freely out of the rock.

This process frees any oil or gas that is trapped within the rock. At this point, workers stop the pumping of liquids. A flow of oil and gas, plus some of the fracking fluid and chemicals, begins to run through

Julia "Butterfly" Hill spent 738 days living in Luna, a massive old growth redwood tree, in order to save it from loggers. © GERARD BURKHAR/GETTY IMAGES.

the pipes toward the surface. The combination of materials may contain "produced water." This is a type of fluid sometimes found in these layers. Produced water may be filled with other agents, such as toxic chemicals, salts, and other harmful products naturally found in shale rock. Sometimes produced water is reused as part of the water in fracking fluid. Much of it must be treated and stored as wastewater, a by-product of fracking. This wastewater is toxic to people. The released oil and gas are then transported to processing centers that change them into usable petroleum products.

Origins of fracking Fracking dates to the 19th century when it saw limited use in the United States. The modern era of fracking began in the 1990s. Oil is an extremely valuable resource, but the most profitable oil fields are in foreign countries. In the 1990s American oil companies tried to find new ways to produce oil in the United States. Drilling for oil in the nation was usually more expensive due to higher labor costs and oil deposits that were hard to access. American businessman George P. Mitchell (1919–2013) created a method that combined older methods of fracking with horizontal drilling. Horizontal drilling is a nontraditional form of accessing oil that involves drills that are parallel to the ground. The resulting process made fracking in the United States less expensive. When foreign oil prices reached higher levels, fracking suddenly became a highly profitable form of acquiring oil and gas in the United States.

Background to Global Frackdown 2014

Many activists do not see fracking as environmentally friendly. Fracking requires massive amounts of water, which is itself an increasingly endangered resource. The lack of water is a problem in many parts of the world. In the United States, parts of California, Kansas, and Texas suffer from a lack of available groundwater. Environmentalists consider the use of water for fracking to be an enormous waste of a valuable resource.

The water used in fracking becomes heavily polluted. It must be stored so that people are not exposed to it. Although oil companies are willing to keep wastewater that comes to the surface away from the public, a large amount of tainted water remains underground. There, it runs the risk of contaminating natural aquifers running nearby. If wastewater meets with these aquifers, the groundwater could become unusable. Fracking may further lead to the release of gases into nearby drinking wells. In the documentary *Gasland* (2010), a man shows the impact of gas on his household water. He holds up a lighter to the water coming from his kitchen faucet and it bursts into flames. Fracking machinery and damage to the fracked areas can leave lasting environmental damage.

Fracking relies on disrupting the geology of the ground. In places such as Oklahoma, where fracking occurs regularly, this practice has been linked to small tremors, or shaking of the ground. Environmentalists maintain that practices such as fracking that damage the environment and increase dependence on fossil fuels should be stopped. They believe companies should seek out sources of renewable energy that do not contribute to climate change.

Industry executives say that fracking creates fewer carbon emissions (releases of the greenhouse gas carbon dioxide) than coal. Fracking is also better for the environment than coal. The fracking industry is responsible for thousands of jobs in the United States.

Fracking helps the country be less dependent on foreign nations for oil, which helps keep prices lower. According to the US Energy Information Administration (EIA), natural gas prices had fallen to their lowest point in a decade by 2016. Fracking can have other positive economic benefits. According to the International Energy Agency (IEA), by 2013 the United States had become the biggest producer of natural gas in the world.

Global Frackdown 2014

Global Frackdown 2014 marked the third staging of this event. Food & Water Watch, an environmental group founded in 2005, first launched the Frackdown campaign in 2012. The first event involved 200 related events in 20 countries around the world, including large marches in France and South Africa. By 2013 the Global Frackdown had grown to 250 events worldwide. The 2014 event proved to be the biggest version of the

Anti-fracking protesters participate in a global day of action in 2014 in London, UK. © GUY BELL / ALAMY STOCK PHOTO.

Global Frackdown to date. Global Frackdown 2014 followed quickly behind the People's Climate March on September 21, 2014. This event drew 400,000 participants. Before the Global Frackdown, 250 groups from 40 nations sent a letter to the United Nations asking its leadership to issue a ban on fracking around the world.

For Global Frackdown 2014, some 200 organizations participated by planning individual events. More than 300 events in countries from five continents occurred on October 11, 2014. In the United States, 34 states and territories had scheduled events. Although none of these individual events saw participation on the level of the People's Climate March, several Frackdown events drew crowds in the thousands.

Most events consisted of marches, protests, and rallies. In Oakland, California, college students protested the use of fracking in 10 California counties. They listened to speakers who detailed the environmental effects of fracking and devised plans to make their efforts more effective. In Wales, which is part of the United Kingdom, hundreds of activists marched to the Welsh government's headquarters to demand a permanent ban on fracking. To highlight their support from the public, the Welsh activists delivered thousands of signed postcards from people opposed to fracking. Several Welsh politicians participated in a rally on the steps of the Parliament building. Other global events included meetings sponsored by local governments, concerts intended to publicize the dangers of fracking, and conferences featuring presentations from climate specialists.

Aftermath

Organizers of the Global Frackdown credit their movement and the resulting publicity for several achievements. In the United States fracking has been banned in New York since 2014. Maryland banned the practice as of 2017. In Europe bans on fracking have been upheld in both Bulgaria and France. In Romania local officials have been granted the ability to prevent fracking in their regions. The European Parliament gave local communities in Europe the right to be included in any decisions about fracking in their areas. Plans for fracking in South Africa were delayed until further reviews could be conducted.

Since the 2014 event, organizers have opted to spread Global Frackdown activities over several weeks rather than focusing on a single day. This has allowed for greater flexibility in creating events. It further allows organizations to increase publicity by having multiple days dedicated to corresponding activities.

Organizers of the Global Frackdown credit their movement and the resulting publicity for several achievements. In the United States fracking has been banned in New York since 2014. Maryland banned the practice as of 2017.

Environment

Pacific Climate Warriors Blockade

LOCATION: New South Wales, Australia

DATE: October 17, 2014

On October 17, 2014, a group called the Pacific Climate Warriors blocked the Port of Newcastle in New South Wales, Australia. The goal was to use nonviolent methods to prevent coal ships from leaving the port. The activists were organized by 350.org, an international environmental group concerned with reducing greenhouse gases. Much of the greenhouse gases produced by humans are created by the use of fossils fuels. The greenhouse gases become trapped in Earth's atmosphere. Many scientists believe an excess amount of these gases is responsible for changes in the planet's climate.

The Pacific Climate Warriors consist of activists from 13 Pacific island nations. For the protest, the group used traditional canoes like those their ancestors built centuries ago. The sight of tiny canoes stopping massive coal ships resulted in enormous publicity for the Pacific Climate Warriors' cause in Australia and internationally. Both sides had assistance. Hundreds of Australians paddled out in kayaks to join the Pacific Climate Warriors. A large police force accompanied the coal ships.

The demonstration brought attention to the battle over climate change. Before the group's protest, most people focused on the possible effects of warmer temperatures and changes to the weather. The Pacific Climate Warriors promoted the fact that global warming threatens their islands' future and their peoples' cultural history.

Background

Members of the Pacific Climate Warriors are primarily people who are the native, or indigenous, residents of small island nations. Climate change has affected their countries more than many other places around the world. Climate change has been linked to rising temperatures that melt polar ice caps in the Arctic and Antarctic regions. As these ice caps melt, the excess water causes Earth's sea levels in the oceans to rise. Rising oceans affect the populations of small island nations. Island residents have nowhere else to go when ocean tides rise. In some places

Environment

The Reasons Why a Blockade Is Needed

This primary source excerpt is from an article written by Milañ Loeak, a Pacific Climate Warrior, for the Guardian *in October 2014. She is the daughter of Christopher Loeak, who was president of the Marshall Islands.*

What would you do if your neighbour demolished your home, and then sold your land to the highest bidder? You would likely call the police, the property ombudsman, or whoever had the power to stop it. Unfortunately for those of us in the Pacific, the people with the power to stop this happening don't see our rights as a priority.

We've spent the last 20 years arguing for international action on climate change with very little effect and now we're down to our last line of defence. This is why we've been compelled to take action and block Australia's largest coal port in Newcastle today. Some will call us eco-terrorists and claim that we are just here causing trouble, but wouldn't you do the same if it was your country ... under threat?

The Marshall Islands, where I was born and call home, is one of the most remote places in the world. We are a collection of 24 tiny atoll islands located halfway between Papua New Guinea and Hawaii.

As island people, we've traditionally enjoyed a close relationship with the sea. But lately the sea has become a source of fear. We have suffered through droughts and continue to be threatened by sea level rise. Earlier this year over 1,000 people were forced to be evacuated after king tides rose across our homes. Just last week king tides hit the islands again, destroying homes, businesses and infrastructure across the country. . . .

Yet we won't give up our homes so easily. We have chosen to fight and not to drown. This is why I've chosen to come to Australia, along with several of my brothers and sisters from 11 other Pacific island nations, to confront the neighbour that is profiting from the destruction of our homes. We're blockading the world's largest coal port in Newcastle to show that elsewhere in the world, whole nations are paying the price for Australia's coal and gas wealth. . . .

Blocking the Newcastle port may not, in the end, make even the slightest bit of difference to the mining companies of the world, but our aim is to send a message to the organisations that profit from the extraction of fossil fuels: they can no longer distance themselves from the impacts of their actions.

We're calling on the Australian public to come and join us in saying no to the building of new coal and gas infrastructure. We're imploring you to stand with us, canoe against coal ship, and help us defend our homes against those who would seek to destroy it.

SOURCE: Loeak, Milañ. "We Won't Stand by While Coal Companies Destroy Our Marshall Islands Homes." *Guardian* (October 16, 2014). Available online at https://www.theguardian.com/commentisfree/2014/oct/17/we-wont-stand-by-while-coal-companies-destroy-our-marshall-islands-homes (accessed October 12, 2017). Courtesy of Guardian Media.

the entire island becomes covered with water. In time these countries could disappear entirely if the sea level continues to rise.

Islands are home to more than 40 million people worldwide. Rising sea levels are a great threat to their long-term survival. Waves from storms and increasing high tides already have led to repeated instances of flooding. Higher sea levels have increased threats to islands' fisheries, freshwater supplies, and food production. Some people from places such as the Isle de Jean Charles in Louisiana and Kivalina, Alaska, and from islands in the countries of Tuvalu and the Solomon Islands have been forced to leave their homes due to rising ocean levels. The South Pacific island nations of Kiribati (pronounced KEER-uh-bass), the Maldives (pronounced MOL-deevz), and Vanuatu (pronounced van-wah-TOO) face similar risks.

People who have been forced to leave their homes due to environmental changes are called climate refugees. Refugees are people who have to flee their homes to escape danger. According to research from Cornell University, 2 billion people could be forced to leave their homes because of rising sea levels by 2100. Roughly one-fifth of the world's population could become climate refugees because of sea-level rise.

One of the leading contributors to global warming is the use of fossil fuels. Coal is among the most damaging types of these fuels. Mining coal is very destructive. Surface mining requires explosives to loosen coal from the seams where it is located. This form of mining can be very harmful to the environment. In addition to the destruction of the land, pollutants are often scattered into the surrounding environment. Pollutants can be picked up by the wind or drift into water supplies. Sixty-six percent of all mining in the United States in 2015 was through surface mining.

Underground mines are less harmful. Even so, pollutants can still leak from underground mines despite their great depths. Underground mining also creates great risks to the health and safety of miners. Methane gas that builds up in mines can explode, tunnels may collapse, and miners often breathe in pollutants that have been linked to cancer.

The release of methane gas is the most damaging environmental effect of coal mining. Problems linked to acid rain, smog, haze, and disease all result from burning coal. According to the US Energy Information Administration, up to 10 percent of methane emissions and 1 percent of greenhouse gases in the United States come from coal mining. Burning coal creates more greenhouse gases. Coal was responsible for 24.5 percent of all greenhouse gases released in the United States in 2012. It has the highest carbon content of any fossil fuel.

Environment

Nuclear Energy Protests Following Meltdown in Fukushima, Japan

Nuclear power became the subject of protests after a magnitude 9.0 earthquake struck off the coast of Japan in 2011. It caused a series of massive tidal waves (or tsunamis, pronounced su-NAW-meez) to strike Japan's coast. Almost 19,000 people died. At the Fukushima Daiichi (pronounced fu-KUU-shih-muh die-EET-chi) Nuclear Power Plant, three of the reactors failed over several days. A wave 43 feet (13 meters) high had damaged the reactors. The seawall intended to protect the plant from such an event was only 33 feet (10 meters) high.

As a result, the reactors had nuclear meltdowns. This occurs when the cores of these devices experience damage from overheating. The meltdowns released nuclear material into the surrounding area. This is harmful to people so they fled the city where the plant was located and several other neighboring communities. Up to 170,000 people were forced to leave. By 2017 approximately 80,000 of these residents had not returned to their homes.

The people who were forced to leave were worried about their health. They wondered whether they would ever be allowed back into their homes. Investigations of the power plant showed that the accident had been preventable. This made many Japanese people very angry and concerned about the safety of other nuclear plants. Beginning in March 2012, up to 200,000 people attended rallies every Friday in front of the prime minister's house. The Metropolitan Coalition against Nukes organized these events. The group held the Tokyo Big March in Japan's capital on March 11, 2012, in which people formed a human chain around the Japanese parliament.

In response, the government promised to end the country's reliance on nuclear power by 2030. However, the Japanese Liberal Democratic Party (LDP), which supported the use of nuclear power, returned to power in December 2012. The LDP decided to ignore the previous plan to abolish nuclear power. Many Japanese people grew discouraged by the lack of response to their worries. As a result, the number of protests and activists fell in the following years. By 2017 protests were drawing an average of only 1,000 people. Antinuclear groups still expressed hopes for creating long-term changes to Japan's nuclear policies.

Pacific Climate Warriors blockade

The Port of Newcastle is the largest coal port in the world. It is found in the state of New South Wales on Australia's southeastern coast. Due to its broad coal and gas operations, Australia is one of the world's biggest producers of greenhouse gases per capita. Per capita is a measure of a quantity per person. In 2014 Australia revealed plans to further expand the Newcastle harbor and its coal industry. The Pacific Climate Warriors hoped to send a message to Australian authorities. They wanted to warn officials about the threats to their island nations from the greenhouse

Environment

The Fukushima plant meltdown drew protests in other countries, including Germany. The country decided to shut down its nuclear reactors by 2022, some 14 years earlier than planned. German Chancellor Angela Merkel (1954–) made the announcement about closing the country's 17 nuclear reactors.

Just over a month after the Fukushima nuclear disaster, Germans protest against the use of nuclear power in their country. As shown here, the demonstrators carry a banner that refers to the nuclear disaster in Fukushima but also the massive nuclear meltdown in Chernobyl, then part of the Soviet Union, in 1986. © S. KUELCUE/SHUTTERSTOCK.COM.

gas–driven rise in sea levels. The Warriors' slogan was, "We are not drowning, we are fighting!"

Supported by 350.org, the activists spent 18 months organizing their protest. They built five traditional canoes. They enlisted the support of hundreds of other volunteers to follow them into the harbor in small boats. Their goal was to block as many coal ships as possible from leaving the harbor. In the past, Australian environmental groups tried to block the Newcastle harbor. However, the 2014 event marked the first participation of the Pacific Climate Warriors.

Environment

Protesters representing various Pacific Island nations pose with a banner as they announce an official campaign against the coal industry in front of the Sydney Opera House in 2014. The group, known as the Pacific Climate Warriors, led a protest of the world's largest coal port in Newcastle, Australia. © PETER PARKS/AFP/GETTY IMAGES.

Before the event, protesters participated in Polynesian (pronounced paw-luh-NEE-zhen) war dances. Protesters dressed in traditional costumes and carried both national and indigenous flags. Members of the Pacific Climate Warriors then filled five canoes and tried to block coal ships from leaving the harbor. The group included activists from the Pacific island nations of Fiji, the Marshall Islands, Papua New Guinea (pronounced PAW-pyu-uh NU GI-nee), the Solomon Islands, Tokelau (pronounced TOE-kuh-lau), and Vanuatu. Supporters in kayaks, dinghies, and other small boats quickly followed them. Protesters in the boats linked together to prevent ships from leaving. Police in motorboats and on jet skis tried to clear paths through the protesters to allow the ships to leave.

According to protesters, police tried to take their paddles away. Some members of the police force were accused of knocking over kayakers and damaging a canoe from Vanuatu by ramming it repeatedly. Upon returning to shore, several protesters were held by police. None of the demonstrators faced charges, and no one was arrested. The police expressed concern that the blockade members, particularly those in very small boats that could tip easily, were endangering their own lives by moving in front of large ships. In the end, the members of the Pacific Climate Warriors were successful in blocking 8 of 12 ships from leaving the harbor.

Aftermath

After the protest ended, the Pacific Climate Warriors continued their campaign against climate change. They participated in five nonviolent protests of Australian fossil fuel companies over the course of one week. The largest of these protests occurred at the Melbourne, Australia, headquarters of ANZ, the primary producer of fossil fuels in the country. Since the blockade of the Newcastle harbor, the Pacific Climate Warriors have looked for other ways to support indigenous people who are threatened by environmental issues. In May 2017 they joined a protest in Canada that sought to prevent the opening of a new fossil fuel site.

For the members of the Pacific Climate Warriors, the blockade of Newcastle harbor enabled them to take direct action in helping to save their islands. The construction of the canoes helped bring communities together in traditional activities. The vessel built by members of the Tokelau nation, for instance, marked the first time the islanders had constructed a canoe using traditional methods in more than 80 years. The demonstration further helped link members of various nations and different tribes together in a single action.

March for Science

LOCATION: Worldwide

DATE: April 22, 2017

The March for Science was a collection of more than 600 linked events in cities around the world. The event had more than 1 million participants globally. The goal was to highlight the political threats to evidence-based policies in the United States and worldwide. Evidence-based policies are national policy decisions and laws based on facts that have been backed by research. For instance, when researchers found that the use of seat belts helped save lives, many US states adopted laws that required drivers and their passengers to wear seat belts. Supporters of evidence-based research have become increasingly concerned that lawmakers are ignoring science.

Environment

US Adults in 2016 Believe Climate Change Is Caused By:

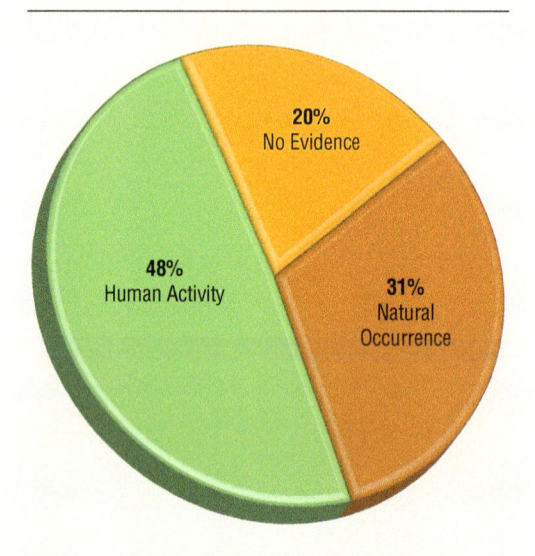

- 48% Human Activity
- 31% Natural Occurrence
- 20% No Evidence

Note: Respondents include those who believe in a certain position or lean in that direction. The percentages do not total 100 due to rounding.

SOURCE: Adapted from Funk, Cary, and Brian Kennedy. "Public Views on Climate Change and Climate Scientists," *The Politics of Climate*. Pew Research Center, October 4, 2016. http://assets.pewresearch.org/wp-content/uploads/sites/14/2016/10/14080900/PS_2016.10.04_Politics-of-Climate_FINAL.pdf.

Despite scientific consensus that climate change is linked to human activity, only half of US adults believed that in 2016.
© 2018 CENGAGE®.

They believe that some policy makers have tried to reduce the amount of influence that science and fact-based studies have on decision-making.

Activists argue that some lawmakers have tried to disprove theories that do not support politicians' personal beliefs. They call this part of a "war on science." These activists say that proven science regarding climate change has been particularly challenged. The March for Science was organized to emphasize the challenges and lack of financial support for what activists regard as reliable scientific studies. Organizers estimate that on April 22, 2017, up to 1.3 million people gathered at events around the world to demonstrate their support for evidence-based policies and proven scientific studies. One of the largest of these events was held in Washington, DC.

Background

The debate over the role of science in lawmaking increased in the 21st century. In particular, questions about climate change have especially driven this debate in the United States. Some politicians have expressed doubt that Earth is undergoing a shift in weather patterns or that a global trend toward warmer temperatures exists. Scientists argue that numerous studies show that the threat of climate change is real and must be addressed.

March for Science

Organizers of the March for Science chose April 22, 2017, to correspond with the celebration of the 47th annual Earth Day. Earth Day is observed every year to recognize the need for environmental protections. The organizers selected Earth Day because they wanted to emphasize the connection between scientific study and the need for changes to environmental policies.

Critics believe that such politicians are driven by self-interest. Environmentalists claim that special interest groups that do not want stronger

Environment

environmental laws push politicians to doubt the science behind climate change. Critics say this allows companies to earn greater profits by dealing with fewer rules and laws that protect the environment.

People who mistrust the science behind climate change argue that agreement about its existence is not strong. They say this despite the fact that 97 percent of climate scientists say otherwise. They note that some scientists have conducted research that shows changes to weather and temperatures may be overstated. Some business groups have argued that patterns of possible global warming are within acceptable limits, so no changes to environmental policies are necessary. Those who reject the idea of climate change are often referred to as "climate deniers."

Under President Donald Trump activists began to worry that the broad scientific agreement about climate change was being ignored.

Bill Nye the Science Guy (center) leads a group of activists and protesters as part of the March for Science in Washington, DC.
© JOSEPH GRUBER/SHUTTERSTOCK.COM.

Environment

Adam Savage at the March for Science

This primary source excerpt is from a speech that Mythbuster Adam Savage gave at the March for Science in San Francisco, California, on April 22, 2017. It was posted on Adam Savage's Tested website.

I speak today not just to those who agree with me, to the choir, but also to those who don't. I'm assuming we begin from the same basic principles. We may differ in terms of the method, but I think we can agree on the goal: that we all want to leave a better world and life for our children, our loved ones, our communities. Science is the key way to achieve that. . . .

Claude Levi-Strauss said, "The scientist is not the person who gives the right answers, they're the one who asks the right questions." Science does not require a scientist in order to happen. It is in fact one of the oldest of human drives to explore. We are moved, we are driven, inspired to better understand our universe and ourselves.

We push ourselves to the edge of what is known and we seek to know more. We are as a singular species tinkerers, explorers, problem solvers. We are social, we are storytellers, we are question askers, we are scientists. You are all scientists. . . .

Why are we marching today for science? Because science has an enemy. Our enemy is strong and it fights dirty. But science's enemy is not a person, a political party, an ideology, it is not a behavior, a budget or a law.

If science is about exploring and understanding our world, clearly then the enemy is our own

Scientists do not usually engage in political activity as an organized group. In the lead-up to the March for Science, however, organizers enlisted both environmental and scientific organizations. This spirit of cooperation came from concerns that arose during the 2016 US presidential election. While running as the Republican candidate for president and even before the election, Trump expressed doubts about climate change.

Once elected, Trump appointed officials who did not accept environmental policies designed to limit climate change. Trump proposed making large cuts to scientific agencies under the federal government's control. These cuts would affect departments such as the National Institutes of Health (NIH) and the Environmental Protection Agency. The Trump administration even removed a lot of climate information from the government's websites. Scientists thought the Trump administration might try to silence studies that went against the interests of companies that pollute the environment. Under Trump, officials proclivity as individuals and as communities to stay inside a bubble and see the world not as it is but how we wish it to be. This is called bias. Bias is the enemy of science. . . .

Bias is strong. It is in us, in our families, in our communities. It is in our institutions. It feels safe, but bias is very dangerous. It cannot only skew the results of a test, it can undermine our conclusions and the policies we make based upon those conclusions. It is imperative that each one of us confront our own personal as well as institutional bias and prejudice. . . .

The hundreds of thousands of us on the streets in the United States and around the world are a confluence, a galaxy. We are a constituency. We are agents of change. More accurately, we are reagents. Each of us is a molecule, a precise geometry of atoms bonded together under unique rules and conditions. Individually on our own no single one of us can bring enough energy to an equation to accomplish something significant.

But when we band together, when we find our sisters and brothers, when we participate in our democracy, when we speak clearly to those in power from our hearts and with our votes, when we make our collective voices be heard, we can move worlds. So let us, all of us, molecules, reagents, scientists, humans, let us march to start a proper chain reaction. Let us bring about change and let's move this world.

SOURCE: Savage, Adam. "Adam Savage's March for Science Speech." Tested, April 22, 2017. http://www.tested.com/science/609291-adam-savages-march-science-speech/ (accessed October 12, 2017). Courtesy of Adam Savage's Tested.

without scientific degrees were appointed to head scientific agencies. These changes concerned many scientists. In addition, environmentalists worried that these approaches would lead to the weakening of laws designed to protect the water, the air, and other parts of the environment.

While the largest part of the March for Science was held in Washington, DC, more than 600 associated events were held around the world. The Washington march drew between 100,000 and 150,000 people. Many people carried signs, often with puns that used mathematical equations, chemical abbreviations, and references to scientific in-jokes. The crowd gathered at the National Mall near the Washington Monument to listen to speakers. Participants then marched down Constitution Avenue to the Capitol building.

The march did not intend to target President Trump specifically, but speakers and activists nevertheless referenced him. Speakers demanded that politicians be held responsible for their actions, particularly concerning policy decisions. Many speeches called for stronger rules for climate change, increased conservation efforts, and updated educational materials for students.

Other events around the world featured speakers, rallies, and marches. The Boston march included a brass band. In Oklahoma protesters demanded changes to fracking, a form of oil drilling that has been linked to small earthquakes and poisoned groundwater. For many protesters the March for Science marked the first time they had participated in an event of this nature.

Aftermath

The March for Science was credited with increasing scientists' interest in activism. In the past, scientists have tended to shy away from interference in policy making. Changes within the federal government, however, have motivated scientists to take a stand in support of policies backed by sound science. Scientists realized that science may be ignored in future policy making and became more involved in activism. For instance, membership in the Union for Concerned Scientists (UCS) grew by 20 percent after the March for Science. The organization was founded in 1969 by scientists at the Massachusetts Institute of Technology who were discouraged by the government's misuse of science. The UCS continues its efforts in the 21st century by getting scientists involved in policy making. The organization began a program called Science Champions in July 2017 that has recruited 500 scientists to participate in efforts to support science in government policy.

Despite the efforts of the participants of the March for Science, the Trump administration continued with its stated pro-business agenda. In June 2017 Trump withdrew from the Paris Agreement. This international treaty aims to reduce the amount of greenhouse gases released on an annual basis. As of November 2017, the agreement had been approved by 169 nations. Prior to Trump's withdrawal, the United States had been one of the nations that agreed to participate.

In July 2017 Trump announced Sam Clovis (1949–), a nonscientist and a noted critic of scientific studies supporting climate change, as his nominee to be the chief scientist with the US Department of Agriculture. (Clovis withdrew his name from consideration in November 2017 amid a political controversy.) The organizers of the March for Science continued to pressure politicians to assign greater importance to science in the future.

In the past, scientists have tended to shy away from interference in policy making. Changes within the federal government, however, have motivated scientists to take a stand in support of policies backed by sound science.

For More Information

BOOKS

Anderson, Joan. *Earth Keepers*. New York: Harcourt Brace, 1993.

Bledsoe, Karen E. *Consumption and Waste*. New York: Bloomsbury, 2014.

David, Laurie, and Cambria Gordon. *The Down-to-Earth Guide to Global Warming*. New York: Scholastic, 2007.

Felix, Rebecca. *12 Things to Know about Fracking*. Mankato, MN: Black Rabbit Books, 2015.

Kallio, Jamie. *12 Things to Know about Climate Change*. Mankato, MN: Black Rabbit Books, 2015.

PERIODICALS

Davidson, Helen. "Pacific Islanders Blockade Newcastle Coal Port to Protest Rising Sea Levels." *Guardian* (October 17, 2014). Available online at https://www.theguardian.com/environment/2014/oct/17/pacific-islanders-blockade-newcastle-coal-port-to-protest-rising-sea-levels (accessed July 22, 2017).

Eilperin, Juliet. "The Keystone XL Pipeline and Its Politics, Explained." *Washington Post* (February 4, 2014). Available online at https://www.washingtonpost.com/news/the-fix/wp/2013/04/03/the-keystone-xl-pipeline-and-its-politics-explained/?utm_term=.2b02fc9a65c7 (accessed July 22, 2017).

Gray, Louise. "Copenhagen Climate Summit: Protests Threaten to Shut Down Talks." *Telegraph* (December 16, 2009). Available online at http://www.telegraph.co.uk/news/earth/copenhagen-climate-change-confe/6824890/Copenhagen-climate-summit-protests-threaten-to-shut-down-talks.html (accessed July 22, 2017).

Mooney, Chris. "Scientists Say the Pace of Sea Level Rise Has Nearly Tripled since 1990." *Washington Post* (May 22, 2017). Available online at https://www.washingtonpost.com/news/energy-environment/wp/2017/05/22/scientists-say-the-rate-of-sea-level-rise-has-nearly-tripled-since-1990/?utm_term=.12d6f04f66c0 (accessed July 22, 2017).

St. Fleur, Nicholas. "Scientists, Feeling under Siege, March against Trump Policies." *New York Times* (April 22, 2017). Available online at https://www.nytimes.com/2017/04/22/science/march-for-science.html (accessed July 22, 2017).

van der Zee, Bibi. "High-Profile Activist's Arrest Fuels Fears of Police Crackdown in Copenhagen." *Guardian* (December 15, 2009). Available online at https://www.theguardian.com/environment/2009/dec/15/danish-police-mass-protest-copenhagen (accessed July 22, 2017).

Yong, Ed. "How the March for Science Finally Found Its Voice." *Atlantic* (April 23, 2017). Available online at https://www.theatlantic.com/science/archive/2017/04/how-the-march-for-science-finally-found-its-voice/524022/ (accessed July 22, 2017).

Zornick, George. "'Forward on Climate' Rally Sends a Message to Obama: No Keystone." *Nation* (February 17, 2013). Available online at https://www.xthenation.com/article/forward-climate-rally-sends-message-obama-no-keystone/ (accessed July 22, 2017).

WEBSITES

Black, Richard. "Copenhagen Climate Accord: Key Issues" BBC News, December 19, 2009. http://news.bbc.co.uk/2/hi/science/nature/8422186.stm (accessed July 22, 2017).

"Coal Explained: Coal and the Environment." US Energy Information Administration (EIA), February 1, 2017. https://www.eia.gov/energyexplained/?page=coal_environment (accessed July 22, 2017).

Gibbs, Lois Marie. "History: Love Canal: The Start of a Movement." Boston University School of Public Health, 2008. https://www.bu.edu/lovecanal/canal/ (accessed July 22, 2017).

Manfreda, John. "The Real History of Fracking." Oil Price, April 13, 2015. http://oilprice.com/Energy/Crude-Oil/The-Real-History-Of-Fracking.html (accessed July 22, 2017).

"March for Science." EarthDay.org, April 22, 2017. http://www.earthday.org/marchforscience/ (accessed July 22, 2017).

Mellino, Cole. "Climate Refugees: Meet the First Climate Refugees." EcoWatch, January 5, 2016. https://www.ecowatch.com/meet-the-worlds-first-climate-refugees-1882143026.html (accessed July 22, 2017).

"Rising Seas Could Result in 2 Billion Refugees by 2100." Science Daily, June 26, 2017. https://www.sciencedaily.com/releases/2017/06/170626105746.htm (accessed July 22, 2017).

Smith-Spark, Laura. "March for Science: Protesters Gather Worldwide to Support 'Evidence.'" CNN, April 22, 2017. http://www.cnn.com/2017/04/22/health/global-march-for-science/ (accessed July 22, 2017).

Suls, Rob. "Public Divided over Keystone XL, Dakota Pipelines; Democrats Turn Decisively against Keystone." Pew Research Center, February 21, 2017. http://www.pewresearch.org/fact-tank/2017/02/21/public-divided-over-keystone-xl-dakota-pipelines-democrats-turn-decisively-against-keystone/ (accessed July 22, 2017).

"What Is Fracking and Why Is It Controversial?" BBC News, December 16, 2015. http://www.bbc.com/news/uk-14432401 (accessed July 22, 2017).

OTHER

Gasland. Documentary. Directed by Josh Fox. Brooklyn, NY: International WOW Company, 2010.

An Inconvenient Sequel: Truth to Power. Documentary. Directed by Bonni Cohen and Jon Shenk. San Francisco: Actual Films, 2017.

An Inconvenient Truth. DVD. Directed by Davis Guggenheim. Los Angeles: Paramount Pictures, 2006.

6

Free Speech

Freedom of speech is the right to express oneself without fear of punishment. The idea of free speech is one of the most important elements of democracy. It gives all people the right to express their thoughts and ideas freely. At the same time, there are many questions about the limits of free speech and whether all types of speech should be protected. Many people, for example, disagree over whether hate speech or the use of offensive language should be considered free speech. Because of questions like these, the meaning of free speech has changed, and continues to change, over time.

Freedom of speech is often seen as a key principle of American democracy. It is a major part of the American way of life. Freedom of speech is so important to Americans that it is a guaranteed right in the US Constitution. Although free speech is highly valued in the United States, many questions about the limits of free speech exist. Throughout US history, these questions have led to arguments concerning free speech and whether the Constitution protects activities such as anti-war protests and flag burning.

While many countries around the world have laws protecting free speech, other nations place stricter limits on what people can say or write. Countries such as Iran and China, for example, have laws that restrict freedom of speech through censorship. Censorship is the act of removing anything considered harmful or offensive from books, magazines, newspapers, the Internet, or other forms of media. In such places, freedom of speech is threatened, and sometimes it is not protected at all.

Harry Potter Book Burning **177**

Muslim Protests of Danish Cartoons **183**

"Je Suis Charlie" Protests **189**

Yale Student Protests on Free Speech **194**

History of free speech

The idea of free speech dates back practically to the beginning of spoken languages. Historians believe the first spoken languages may have originated

Free Speech

WORDS TO KNOW

Amendment: A change in the wording of a law or bill.

Censorship: The act of removing material that government, church, or other leaders have judged to be objectionable in books, newspapers, or other media.

Embassy: The office in one country where a representative of another country lives and works.

Heresy: A belief or opinion that does not agree with the official beliefs or opinions of a particular religion.

Idol worship: The worship of a false god.

Obscene: Something that is shockingly offensive.

Occult: Matters that deal with the supernatural or magic.

Political correctness: The act of avoiding certain language or activities that could offend a particular person or group of people.

Prophet: A messenger of God.

Racial diversity: To include people from various racial backgrounds.

Racial insensitivity: A lack of understanding of the experiences of people of other races.

Racism: Unfair treatment of people of different races, usually based on the idea that one's own race or culture is better.

Radical: Someone who favors extreme measures to make a point or bring about change.

Terrorism: The use of fear and violence to achieve political goals.

---

more than 1 million years ago. The earliest written languages did not begin until the 4th millennium BCE. As different spoken and written languages developed in ancient civilizations, people began to develop new ideas about the use of these languages, including the idea of free speech.

The principle of free speech began with the ancient Greeks. As Greek society developed over time, two ways of thinking about free speech arose. While many Greek writers wanted the freedom to express themselves through their works as they chose, members of the ruling class wanted to control this freedom to protect their own power. In the Greek city-state of Athens, freedom of speech became one of the defining features of the world's first democracy.

Despite the example set in Athens, freedom of speech was not widely accepted until many centuries later. During the Middle Ages (c. 500–c. 1500), the powerful rulers of Europe did not allow people to question their authority. The rulers dealt harshly with citizens who dared to do so. After German inventor Johannes Gutenberg (c. 1398–c. 1468) built the first printing press in the 15th century, these rulers created even stricter limits on freedom of speech.

During this time, the Catholic Church frequently used censorship to limit speech. The church was mainly concerned with banning books for heresy (pronounced HAIR-a-see), which included opinions that did not agree with church teachings. Books that disagreed with the church's official position on scientific matters were among the most commonly banned works. The works of Polish mathematician and astronomer Nicolaus Copernicus (1473–1543), who often wrote about the sun as the center of the universe, were often banned.

In the 16th and 17th centuries, Christians across Europe who were unhappy with the Catholic Church began to break away during what was called the Protestant Reformation. In many of the countries that split from the church, rulers soon found it necessary to censor free speech. One of these leaders was English King Henry VIII (1491–1547), who established the Church of England. Henry VIII and his daughter Elizabeth I (1533–1603) both banned books that were critical of the Church of England. They formed the Court of Star Chamber as a way to control slander, which is false speech about a person. These restrictions on free speech continued even after the Stuarts, who were Catholic, came to power following Elizabeth's death. After the English Civil War later in the 17th century, Parliament ended the Star Chamber but used the Licensing Order of 1643 to continue controlling what people were allowed to publish.

The spread of free speech True freedom of speech like that known in the 21st century began after English ruler James II (1633–1701) was overthrown during the Glorious Revolution of 1688. James II was succeeded by William III (1650–1702) and Mary II (1662–1694). Shortly after taking power, William and Mary agreed to accept the newly written Bill of Rights. The Bill of Rights established freedom of the press for the first time in England. The king and queen still held certain censorship powers.

In the century that followed the signing of the English Bill of Rights, the ideas of free speech and freedom of the press became more popular across Europe. Sweden ended censorship in 1766. Denmark and Norway did the same a few years later. In 1789 France's National Assembly passed the Declaration of the Rights of Man and of the Citizen. This important human rights document supported freedom of speech and the right to own a printing press.

As Europe moved away from its long tradition of censorship, another major effort to support freedom of speech was beginning in the newly

CRITICAL THINKING QUESTIONS

1. Do you think burning books is an effective form of censorship? Why or why not?

2. Do you think people should consider the feelings of people from other backgrounds when speaking or writing? Do you think this limits free speech? Why or why not?

3. Do you think that people should have to put sensitivity to others' beliefs ahead of their own right to freedom of speech? Why or why not?

4. Should free speech be unlimited? Is it right to use free speech to offend others? Explain.

5. Does *Charlie Hebdo* have the right to publish religious cartoons without fear of being attacked? Why or why not?

---

formed United States of America. After winning independence from Britain, early American leaders worked to gain certain freedoms. They wanted to turn the former colonies into a country where citizens would enjoy more freedoms than ever before. That effort led to one of the most important political documents ever created, the US Constitution.

1st Amendment The debate over how the new American government should work was divided between two groups of people: Federalists and Anti-Federalists. The Federalists wanted a strong central (or federal) government. The Anti-Federalists believed that states should hold the most government power. As the Constitution developed, it came to favor the Federalist position. To get enough support from Anti-Federalists for adoption of the Constitution, the Federalists had to offer a compromise. Their solution was to promise the Anti-Federalists the addition of a Bill of Rights once the Constitution passed. The Anti-Federalists were satisfied with this promise and allowed the Constitution to become law.

The Bill of Rights was a series of 10 amendments, or changes to the Constitution. It outlined the personal liberties granted to all Americans. The first of these amendments guaranteed freedom of religion, freedom of speech, freedom of the press, and the right to assemble.

From the time the Bill of Rights took effect in 1791, the 1st Amendment set a new standard for free speech. With the protections the 1st Amendment offered, the United States became one of the freest countries in the world. Nowhere else were people safer from the threat of censorship than in the United States.

The challenge of free speech

Even with the 1st Amendment in place, the US government faced a big task in determining the limits of free speech over time. On many occasions, the US Supreme Court has had the responsibility of defining 1st Amendment rights. The court has continually had to determine whether the 1st Amendment protects certain types of speech. The court's decisions in such cases have played an important role in further defining the meaning of free speech in the United States.

In hearing 1st Amendment cases, the Supreme Court has done much to explain exactly which types of speech the Constitution protects. Over the years, the court has decided that free speech includes the right to use offensive language in political messages. It includes the right to give money to political campaigns and to take part in symbolic forms of speech, such as burning a flag in protest. In the 1940s the court decided that the 1st Amendment gave people the right to choose not to speak in some circumstances, such as by refusing to salute the flag.

The Supreme Court has ruled on which types of speech are not protected by the 1st Amendment, too. In one famous cased decided in 1919, the court ruled that speech designed to provoke a response that might be harmful to others, such as yelling "fire" in a crowded theater, is not protected. In 1957 the court decided that the 1st Amendment does not give citizens the right to make or distribute certain types of obscene materials. At the height of the Vietnam War (1954–1975) in the 1960s, the court decided that burning draft cards to protest the war was not a protected form of speech. All of these decisions helped to better define free speech as guaranteed by the Constitution.

Free speech in the 21st century

In the United States and around the world, people continue to debate the limits of free speech. One of the longest-running debates concerns the publication of books. When a certain group finds a particular book to be offensive in some way, members of that group sometimes choose to burn copies of the book in protest. In 2001 members of New Mexico's Christ Community Church burned copies of books from author J. K. Rowling's (1965–) Harry Potter series claiming that the books promoted satanism, or worship of the devil.

Some questions about the limits of free speech consider whether freedom of speech should be viewed as more important than other social issues. In 2015 Yale University was the scene of protests over free speech and racial insensitivity, a lack of understanding of the experiences of people of other races. After a series of racial incidents at the school, people debated whether efforts to promote racial understanding ignored students' right to free speech. These disagreements eventually led to protests that showed the difficulties in determining the limits of free speech.

As demonstrated by the Harry Potter book burning, the relationship between religion and free speech is often a challenging one. This became clearer after the editors of a Danish newspaper decided to test the limits of free speech in 2005. The editors encouraged artists to draw and submit pictures of the prophet Muhammad (c. 570–632), a sacred figure in the religion of Islam. Prophets are messengers of God who are believed to have been called by God to do his work. Muslims, who are followers of Islam, are discouraged from creating images of Muhammad. The decision to print the pictures led to angry protests and even violence in a number of Muslim countries.

The limits of free speech in relation to religion were tested again in 2015 after the offices of French magazine *Charlie Hebdo* were attacked by militant Islamists following the publication of cartoons showing the prophet Muhammad. The attack killed 12 people. In reaction, protesters in France and around the world marched in support of free speech. These marches emphasized the importance of standing up for freedom of speech even in the face of violence.

In 2017 the University of California, Berkeley (UCB), became a battleground in the fight over free speech in the United States. Protests first took place on the UCB campus when extreme right-wing speaker Milo Yiannopoulos (1984–) was scheduled to make an appearance there in early February. Protesters who objected to Yiannopoulos's appearance because of his controversial views rallied until school officials canceled the event. In March and April, similar protests occurred when pro–Donald Trump rallies were held on campus grounds.

The cancellation of another planned speech by conservative commentator Ann Coulter (1961–) in August led to demonstrations by right-wing protesters who argued that denying people like Coulter and Yiannopoulos the right to speak was a violation of free speech. Critics of the decision to block controversial conservatives from speaking on campus noted that UCB was the home of the free speech movement in the 1960s. They found the 2017 protests to be at odds with the school's past involvement in the struggle for free speech rights.

Free Speech

President Trump supporters are pepper sprayed during a clash with protesters at a "Patriots Day" free speech rally on April 15, 2017, in Berkeley, California. More than a dozen people were arrested after fistfights broke out at a park where supporters and opponents of Trump had gathered. © ELIJAH NOUVELAGE/GETTY IMAGES.

In an article for *Rolling Stone* magazine, political science professor Jack Citrin is quoted as saying: "This could have been a teaching moment for our students: that it is legitimate for people with views you find abhorrent to speak, and to debate them, and to do so with a superior argument. Instead, it ends up a moment where this provocateur gets exactly what he wanted." Citrin attended Berkeley during the free speech movement days.

Harry Potter Book Burning

LOCATION: Alamogordo, New Mexico

DATE: December 30, 2001

In late December 2001 members of the Christ Community Church in Alamogordo, New Mexico, made international headlines when they burned books from the Harry Potter series in a large bonfire. The Harry Potter series is a collection of young adult novels by British author J. K. Rowling. The books focus on a young boy named Harry who discovers that he is a wizard. Following this discovery, Harry attends a school for witches and wizards called Hogwarts. Throughout the books, Harry and his friends use magic to fight against a powerful dark wizard known as Voldemort.

U•X•L Protests, Riots, and Rebellions: Civil Unrest in the Modern World 177

The leader of the Christ Community Church, Pastor Jack Brock, took issue with the Harry Potter books. Although he had not read any of the four Harry Potter books that had been published at the time, Brock claimed that he had researched them. He said the books were satanic, or related to Satan (the devil). Brock then gave a sermon, or speech, to church members in which he discussed the Harry Potter books. He explained that he believed introducing children to ideas about witchcraft would destroy their lives. Brock and church members then participated in a book burning. Other residents of Alamogordo, however, came out and used their freedom of speech to protest the church's actions.

History of book burning

People have been burning books and other written materials for thousands of years. In the past, materials were burned as a way to control people. Long ago books were not easy to access. Many books were written by hand before the invention of printing presses in the 15th century. Because books were difficult to produce, only one or two copies of a book might have existed in a particular part of the world. Leaders who disagreed with the ideas found in such books could gather all the copies and burn them as way to censor, or limit, free speech. This prevented ideas that leaders disliked from spreading throughout their communities.

The first known book burning took place in China around 213 BCE. Chinese emperor Qin Shi Huang (pronounced Tin Sure Hwang; 259 BCE–210 BCE) ordered all of the history and philosophy books from outside his empire to be burned. The practice of book burning continued as the ancient Greeks and Romans burned Jewish and Christian religious texts. In the 16th century the Spanish burned the holy texts of the Maya after conquering them. The Maya are a native people who lived in Mexico and Central America hundreds of years ago.

Communists burned Western books in the Soviet Union in the early 20th century. Likewise, texts deemed pro-Communist were burned in the United States at the start of the Cold War (1945–1991). The Cold War was a period of great strain between the democratic United States and the Communist Soviet Union. Communism is a system of government in which one ruling party controls all businesses and means of production in a country. Such ideas were viewed as dangerous in the United States, where citizens freely elected leaders and private businesses were common.

Free Speech

Book Burnings in Nazi Germany, May 10, 1933

One of the most well-known book burnings occurred in Nazi Germany in May 1933. Politician Adolf Hitler (1889–1945) led the Nazi Party. The Nazi Party promoted the idea of German pride, and they wanted to rid the nation of anything they believed was "un-German." In their view, this included ridding the country of Jews, disabled individuals, Roma (Gypsies), and other people who were different from them. These beliefs eventually led to the deaths of millions of people in an event known as the Holocaust. Before the Holocaust began, Nazi officials started censoring ideas throughout Germany.

The Nazi Party officially came to power in 1933. Officials then began an effort to rid German culture of works that did not match the party's beliefs. The leader of this campaign was Nazi minister of propaganda Joseph Goebbels (1897–1945). Propaganda is the spread of ideas and information to promote a cause. Goebbels worked with the National Socialist German Students' Association. Together they identified materials by authors who wrote about ideas that went against Nazi politics. They then announced that these texts would be burned in an attempt to purify their society of un-German ideas.

Students in university towns across Germany gathered on May 10, 1933, and burned more than 25,000 books in huge bonfires. Many marched through the streets against the "anti-German spirit." The works of many German Jewish authors were included in the books that were burned. One of these authors was German Jewish poet Heinrich Heine (1797–1856). Heine famously warned that societies that burned books would also burn people in the end. Works of American authors such as Helen Keller (1880–1968) were burned because they promoted the rights of disabled people and women. More book burnings took place throughout Germany during the early summer of 1933. This was just the beginning of the Nazis' broad campaign of censorship before the start of World War II (1939–1945).

Modern book burnings are symbolic in nature. Books are widely available in the 21st century. The ideas they contain can easily spread across populations through the Internet and other media. People often burn books to show their opposition to the ideas authors express. Many people think that it is wrong to burn books and dangerous to limit freedom of expression in this way. Nevertheless, the right to burn a book is protected by the 1st Amendment of the US Constitution as a form of free speech.

Challenges to Harry Potter

The Harry Potter series is one of the most popular series of young adult novels in history. Since the first book was published in the United Kingdom in 1997, the books have been translated into dozens of languages. They have sold more than 400 million copies worldwide. The books were

Free Speech

Top Banned Books: 2000–2009

This primary source excerpt reveals the first 10 books on the American Library Association's list of the Top 100 Banned/Challenged Books: 2000–2009. The ALA monitors what books are being banned or challenged, and it presents a list each year. The Harry Potter series was on the list for more than 10 years.

Top 10 Banned/Challenged Books: 2000–2009: American Library Association

1. *Harry Potter* (series), by J. K. Rowling
2. *Alice* series, by Phyllis Reynolds Naylor
3. *The Chocolate War*, by Robert Cormier
4. *And Tango Makes Three*, by Justin Richardson/Peter Parnell
5. *Of Mice and Men*, by John Steinbeck
6. *I Know Why the Caged Bird Sings*, by Maya Angelou
7. *Scary Stories* (series), by Alvin Schwartz
8. *His Dark Materials* (series), by Philip Pullman
9. *ttyl; ttfn; l8r g8r* (series), by Lauren Myracle
10. *The Perks of Being a Wallflower*, by Stephen Chbosky

SOURCE: "Top 100 Banned/Challenged Books: 2000–2009." American Library Association, March 26, 2013. Available online at http://www.ala.org/advocacy/bbooks/top-100-bannedchallenged-books-2000-2009 (accessed October 12, 2017). Courtesy of American Library Association.

---

turned into a popular series of films that made billions of dollars at the box office. The series made Rowling into one of the wealthiest and most famous authors in the world. Seven Harry Potter books were published in all. Rowling has since written several companions to the series and a play that focuses on Harry's adult life.

Despite the success of the series, not everyone fell in love with the Harry Potter books. According to the American Library Association, Harry Potter was the most frequently banned or challenged series from 2000 to 2009. Reasons given for its being banned or challenged at schools and libraries included the fact that the series features violence and magic. Several characters die in the series. In addition, Harry and his friends must use magic to fight against the evil Voldemort.

Many people claimed that the material in the Harry Potter series went against their religious beliefs as Christians. Some individuals said that the books promoted satanic ideas to children. The witches and wizards in the series often try to do good works and fight against forces of darkness. Still, many opponents of the books believe that anything to do with the occult, or supernatural, is dangerous for young people.

Free Speech

The Harry Potter book burning in New Mexico

The events of December 30, 2001, in Alamogordo, New Mexico, were not originally supposed to involve a booking burning. About 500 members of the Christ Community Church were scheduled to gather to celebrate the coming new year. One of the events during the celebration was supposed to be a burning of materials that represented things members wanted to rid from their lives. Church members would also write their sins, or misdeeds, on pieces of paper and burn them in the bonfire.

The bonfire event went in a different direction after a discussion between a church member and Pastor Brock. The woman asked Brock whether she should buy her grandchildren the Harry Potter books for Christmas. At the time, four of the seven Harry Potter books had been published, and one of the movies had been released. Brock had not read any of the books. He told reporters who covered the book burning that he had researched them. From his research, Brock determined that the books were bad for children. According to the *Guardian* newspaper, he called the series "a masterpiece of satanic deception."

Before the book burning, Brock gave a sermon about the dangers of the Harry Potter series. He warned that the books encouraged children to practice witchcraft. Brock said that if members of the church had purchased the books for their children, then they should bring them to the

During a book burning in Alamogordo, New Mexico, sponsored by a church group in late 2001, people tossed Harry Potter books into a huge bonfire and also burned objects like Ouija boards, games, and other items they believed to be evil or offensive. © NEIL JACOBS/GETTY IMAGES.

bonfire event. Members brought about 30 copies of Harry Potter books and many other items. They burned books by authors such as Stephen King (1947–), J. R. R. Tolkien (1892–1973), and William Shakespeare (1564–1616). Compact discs (CDs) from artists such as AC/DC, Eminem (1972–), and the Backstreet Boys also were burned as church members sang hymns, including "Amazing Grace."

Before the bonfire took place, word about plans to burn Harry Potter books had spread throughout Alamogordo. Although the members of Christ Community Church were within their rights to burn the books, other residents of the town wanted to speak out against the event. About 800 protesters from within the community gathered across the street from the bonfire on the night of December 30. They used their freedom of speech to peacefully assemble and express their dislike of the church members' actions. The line of protesters stretched for nearly a quarter of a mile down the street.

Aftermath

The book burning and the protest against it gained international attention. Reporters from several media outlets covered the event and talked to people on both sides. Residents of Alamogordo said they knew it might be pointless to protest the book burning. Still, they wanted people around the world to know that they did not support what members of Christ Community Church were doing. The protesters did not discourage Brock and his fellow church members, though. The pastor said that the protesters were trying to make him and his church look bad. However, Brock claimed that the media coverage of the event allowed him to promote his church's beliefs to millions of people around the globe.

About 800 protesters from within the community gathered across the street from the bonfire on the night of December 30. They used their freedom of speech to peacefully assemble and express their dislike of the church members' actions.

After the protest, the Alamogordo Public Library extended a Harry Potter display that was meant to celebrate the release of the first film in November 2001. Library staff members told the press that they were against the book burning and that the Harry Potter books were available at their library. Following this, the library received many donations from supportive citizens.

The Harry Potter series continued to be banned and challenged in various communities throughout the early 21st century. On several occasions the series was the subject of book burnings in other areas of the United States. For her part, author Rowling was not concerned with criticisms against her work. According to the BBC, she rejected the idea that the books encouraged children to practice witchcraft. Rowling said that she had met with thousands of children who had read her books. She said that none of them ever told her they wanted to become a witch or wizard because of Harry Potter.

Muslim Protests of Danish Cartoons

LOCATION: Denmark and beyond

DATE: Mainly 2005–2008

Like the United States, the European nation of Denmark has laws in place to protect freedom of speech. In 2005 editors of the Danish newspaper *Jyllands-Posten* believed that this freedom was quietly being threatened. The editors thought that some people in Denmark were starting to censor, or edit, themselves in the name of political correctness. Political correctness is the act of avoiding certain language or activities that could offend a particular person or group. For this reason, the newspaper's editors decided to test the boundaries of Denmark's freedom of speech.

On September 30, 2005, the *Jyllands-Posten* printed a series of cartoons that showed the prophet Muhammad (c. 570–632). Muslims, or followers of the religion of Islam, believe that Muhammad is the messenger of God who founded Islam. Muslims generally avoid showing images of Muhammad in their artwork. They believe that such representations can interfere with people's relationship with God. Some of the *Jyllands-Posten* cartoons not only featured Muhammad but also displayed him in unflattering and disrespectful ways.

Many Muslims viewed the cartoons as an attack on Islam. Some accused the newspaper of blasphemy (pronounced BLASS-fuh-mee), or disrespect toward God and religion. A few months later, newspapers and magazines in other countries reprinted the cartoons, which gained more attention. Protests against the cartoons quickly began to spread. Some of the protests turned violent. Protesters rioted and tried to burn or damage government buildings. Other protests encouraged people to boycott, or stop buying and using, products from Denmark. Editors of the *Jyllands-Posten* apologized for the cartoons. However, they maintained that it was within their right to free speech to publish them. Protests continued for several years.

Background on Islamic beliefs

With about 1.8 billion followers, Islam is the world's second-largest religion after Christianity. Followers of Islam believe in one God, whom they call Allah. *Allah* is an Arabic word meaning "God." According to Islamic teachings, an angel named Gabriel gave the Koran, the holy book of Islam, to Muhammad in the 7th century CE. Muhammad then established Islam, which gained many followers before his death in 632. Since then, Islam has spread around the world. Muhammad's teachings continue to guide Muslims in many parts of their lives.

Muslims hold the prophet Muhammad in very high regard. However, they generally avoid creating physical representations of him, such as drawings or sculptures. Although the Koran does not outright forbid these works, Muslims are discouraged from creating them. Islamic teachings suggest that these pictures or statues could lead to idol worship, or the worship of a false god. They believe this form of worship weakens a person's relationship with God. Muslims consider images of Muhammad to be morally wrong for this reason.

A threat to free speech

Danish-born author Jytte Klausen (1954–) explains in her book *The Cartoons That Shook the World* that the decision to publish cartoons featuring Muhammad in the *Jyllands-Posten* began with a rumor. A Danish author had finished a children's book about Muhammad in the summer of 2005 but could not find an artist willing to illustrate the story. To the editors at the *Jyllands-Posten*, it seemed as though the illustrators feared that they might upset Muslims if they created images of Muhammad. The editors believed the artists were censoring themselves because of their fear. They saw this self-censorship as a threat to freedom of speech.

The editors decided to develop an assignment to see whether artists were truly afraid to express themselves freely. They sent a letter to more than 40 artists and, according to Klausen, asked them to "draw Muhammad, as you see him." Work was submitted by 12 artists. The newspaper published all 12 images on September 30, 2005, under the title "The Face of Muhammad."

Danish cartoonist Kurt Westergaard (1935–) drew the cartoon that received the most criticism. His cartoon became the most well known as a result of the protests. It shows the prophet Muhammad wearing a turban, a head covering made of a long piece of cloth, with a bomb in it. Muslims believed the cartoon suggested that Islam and the prophet Muhammad encourage violence and terror.

According to Klausen, "[Westergaard] intended his drawing to show that Muslim radicals use the Prophet's name to justify violence." A radical is someone who favors extreme measures to make a point or bring about change. Militant Islamist groups often support the overthrow of democratic governments. They want to replace democratic governments with a caliphate (pronounced kay-luh-FATE), a territory overseen by a Muslim religious and political leader. Westergaard wanted to show that these extremists sometimes carried out violent acts and then explained that God wanted them to commit these acts.

Critics said the cartoons promoted hatred of Islam and prejudice toward Muslims. They believed that the cartoons were meant to divide people of different faiths. Some defended the cartoons. They argued that the artists had the right to express themselves freely, even if some people found their images upsetting or disrespectful.

The protests begin

After the *Jyllands-Posten* printed the cartoons, many Muslims were upset. Some considered the images very insulting and said they amounted to blasphemy. Many people in Denmark did not necessarily agree with the content of the cartoons. However, they believed that the newspaper had the right to print them. The offices of the *Jyllands-Posten* received many letters to the editor criticizing the cartoons. Some of the cartoonists received death threats. On October 20, 2005, Muslim leaders filed a complaint with the head of the Danish government.

Within a few months, much of the protests over the cartoons had stopped. Then on January 10, 2006, a newspaper in Norway called *Magazinet* reprinted the cartoons. The editor of that paper, Vebjørn Selbekk (1969–), said that he reprinted the cartoons because he was "sick of the ongoing hidden erosion of the freedom of expression," according to John Ward Anderson in the *Washington Post*. Protests quickly began to spread in many nations with high Muslim populations. Protesters in India, Iran, Kuwait, Libya, and Saudi Arabia spoke out against the cartoons. Some burned Danish and Norwegian flags. Others called for boycotts of Danish goods.

Critics said the cartoons promoted hatred of Islam and prejudice toward Muslims. They believed that the cartoons were meant to divide people of different faiths. Some defended the cartoons.

Free Speech

In response to the publication of cartoon depictions of the prophet Muhammad, protests by Muslims erupted in many parts of the world. Here, Palestinian students burn a Danish flag in the West Bank city of Hebron in February 2006. © HAZEM BADER/AFP/GETTY IMAGES.

Soon the protests worsened. On January 30, 2006, 15 gunmen stormed into the offices of the European Union in Gaza, which borders Egypt and Israel. The gunmen demanded an apology for the cartoons. None of the gunmen fired his weapon, and no one was injured in the raid. A day later, the editor in chief of the *Jyllands-Posten*, Carsten Juste (1947–), apologized for the cartoons. He said the newspaper never meant to insult Muslims. In his apology, however, Juste maintained that the paper had not broken any laws and had the right to publish the cartoons.

The protests continue

The day after Juste's apology, newspapers in France, Germany, and Italy reprinted the cartoons. They wanted to show that they would not allow the right to free speech to be threatened. Three days later, Muslim protesters in Syria set fire to Danish and Norwegian embassies. An embassy is the office in one country where a representative of another country lives and works. Embassies in other nations were also attacked.

The cartoonists in Denmark, meanwhile, continued to receive death threats. Some, including Westergaard, needed constant police protection to keep them safe. Protests continued for several months. Each time a publication reprinted the cartoons, a new round of protests began.

By 2008 protests over the cartoons mostly had ended. Then on February 12, 2008, police in Denmark arrested several individuals who had formed a plan to kill Westergaard. In response to the news, several Danish newspapers reprinted one of the cartoons. Muslims immediately began to protest in Copenhagen, the capital city of Denmark. Other protests broke out in Gaza and Pakistan. Some of the protests were organized by militant Islamist groups.

The effects of the protests

Muslim protests of the Danish cartoons resulted in the deaths of at least 200 individuals. Many more were injured. Some were arrested for activities related to protesting. The editors of some newspapers in Muslim nations were jailed simply for reprinting the cartoons.

In 2010, five years after drawing one of the cartoons, Westergaard still feared for his safety. On January 1, an armed man broke into Westergaard's house intending to kill the cartoonist. Later that year, five men were arrested after police uncovered a planned attack on the offices of the *Jyllands-Posten*. In France a publication called *Charlie Hebdo* sparked similar protests. It has been attacked numerous times for publishing its own cartoons of Muhammad.

Numerous publications have reprinted the original Danish cartoons that sparked the Muslim protests. People around the world can view them online. Yet, some newspapers, such as the *New York Times* and the *Washington Post*, refused to reprint them. Yale University Press also refused to include the images in Klausen's book *The Cartoons That Shook the World*. They feared that doing so might lead to more protests.

These types of fears are among the main reasons why editors of the *Jyllands-Posten* published the cartoons in the first place. They believed that such fears lead to self-censorship, which limits free speech. They have maintained that publishing the cartoons was nothing more than an

Free Speech

Proposed Nazi March in Skokie, Illinois

Certain types of free speech can be offensive to some people. For many Muslims, the Muhammad cartoons were insulting and disrespectful. Nearly 30 years earlier, a protest of a different nature was being planned in Skokie, Illinois, which many people also found offensive. The planned protest involved the National Socialist Party of America. This group notified officials in Skokie that members intended to hold a rally. The National Socialists were a neo-Nazi group. *Nazi* refers to a political party that dates back to Germany during World War II (1939–1945). The Nazis believed in white supremacy. They carried out the Holocaust in which millions of people, particularly Jewish individuals, were killed during World War II. Nazis used a swastika, a cross with the ends bent at right angles in the same direction, as their symbol.

Many Holocaust survivors lived in Skokie, a village of about 60,000 people. At the time of the proposed march, Skokie had one of the largest populations of Holocaust survivors in the United States. The National Socialists intended to hold a demonstration in Skokie while wearing uniforms like those the Nazis wore during World War II. They planned to carry flags displaying swastikas, a symbol of hate. Authorities believed that Skokie residents who saw the swastikas would experience feelings of anger for the pain and suffering their families endured during the Holocaust. Officials believed this would lead to violence in the community. Skokie officials tried to stop the group from demonstrating. The National Socialists sued the village of Skokie for trying to deny their rights.

A court ruled that the group could not demonstrate in Nazi uniforms or display swastikas. The National Socialists appealed the decision, and the case went through more state and federal courts. The case finally went to the US Supreme Court in June 1977. In a 7–2 ruling, the Supreme Court said that the National Socialists had the right to demonstrate. The court upheld a lower court's decision. Groups that promote hate have the right to assemble and express their 1st Amendment rights. They also have the right to display symbols that stand for hate, such as the swastika. Denying a group's

exercise of their right to free speech. In the past they had published cartoons criticizing world leaders, such as US President George W. Bush (1946–), and the pope, the leader of the Catholic Church. They did not think that Islam or the prophet Muhammad should be above such criticism. They have stated that their goal in publishing the images was not to insult Islam or offend Muslims but to see how "free" free speech truly was.

After the protests, the *Jyllands-Posten* editors admitted that free speech can become irresponsible. People have to identify the line between responsible and irresponsible free speech and try to avoid crossing it.

Free Speech

right to display the symbol as a matter of free speech goes against the Constitution. The National Socialists were finally granted permission to demonstrate in Skokie, but the group decided against it. The members instead staged a demonstration in downtown Chicago.

Neo-Nazi leader Frank Collin appeared in a news conference about the proposed march on Skokie. He announced that he was canceling the rally in the heavily Jewish suburb. Collin said that there was no need for the march because the Nazis had achieved their free speech rights by being allowed to demonstrate in Chicago. © BETTMANN/GETTY IMAGES.

"Je Suis Charlie" Protests

LOCATION: France and other countries worldwide

DATE: January 2015

The "Je suis Charlie" (pronounced jeh swee shar-LEE) protests of January 2015 were a response to a terrorist attack on the offices of the French

Free Speech

magazine *Charlie Hebdo* earlier that month. Terrorism is the use of fear and violence to achieve political goals. Militant Islamists killed 12 people at the magazine for drawing cartoons of the prophet Muhammad. Muhammad founded the religion of Islam. Many Muslims, or followers of Islam, thought the cartoons showed a great disrespect for Muhammad and their religion.

The French phrase *Je suis Charlie* means "I am Charlie" in English. The phrase was meant to show support for the magazine and its right to free speech in printing the cartoons. The protests held around the world after the magazine attack called for people everywhere to respect free speech. Protesters believed *Charlie Hebdo* should be able to publish cartoons of any nature without fear of attack. Magazine supporters claimed that giving in to terrorist demands would mean the end of free speech.

In the weeks after the terrorist attack, Muslims worldwide started protesting *Charlie Hebdo*. Although these Muslims opposed terrorism, they wanted people to avoid mocking the prophet Muhammad. Magazine supporters argued that no one should ever limit free speech due to fear of violence. Muslims continued to ask that the world publicly respect their prophet and their religion.

Charlie Hebdo

Charlie Hebdo is a French satirical magazine. Satire is the use of humor to make fun of human nature. *Charlie Hebdo*'s publishers founded the

Muslim demonstrators protest in central London in February 2015 to denounce the use of images of the prophet Muhammad that appeared in the French magazine Charlie Hebdo. *Some sects of the Islamic religion prohibit visual depictions of Muhammad.*
© AFP/GETTY IMAGES.

magazine in 1970. They intended to use it to publish articles about politics and religion. *Charlie Hebdo* closed in the 1980s because it ran out of money. The magazine opened again in 1992. It continued publishing satirical stories on world events into the 21st century.

Charlie Hebdo generated controversy in 2006. That year, the magazine republished cartoons of the Islamic prophet Muhammad that the Danish newspaper *Jyllands-Posten* had published in 2005. Muslims consider Muhammad to be Allah's last prophet. *Allah* is the Arabic word for "God."

The cartoons angered some Muslims who saw them. Muslims respect the prophet Muhammad and thought the newspaper had attacked the religion of Islam by publishing the cartoons. Some Muslims tried to get *Charlie Hebdo* to stop making fun of Islam after the magazine reprinted the cartoons in 2006. *Charlie Hebdo*'s publishers said they could print the cartoons because they had a right to free speech.

Charlie Hebdo's publishers continued to print cartoons about Islam over the next few years even though they knew the cartoons angered many Muslims. In late 2011 the magazine published more cartoons about Muhammad and Islam. Early that November, *Charlie Hebdo*'s offices in Paris were destroyed when someone threw a bomb into a window. French politicians agreed that *Charlie Hebdo* had the legal right to publish cartoons concerning Islam. However, they questioned whether it was safe for the magazine to do so.

2015 *Charlie Hebdo* attack

Two men with guns attacked the *Charlie Hebdo* offices in Paris on January 7, 2015. The men were brothers who were born in France but were of Algerian (pronounced al-JEER-ee-en) ancestry. The brothers were Muslims. It was later revealed that the brothers had been trained to use weapons by al-Qaeda (pronounced al-KI-da). Al-Qaeda is a militant Islamist group based in the Middle East.

The brothers shot and killed 12 people at the *Charlie Hebdo* offices. Most were employees of the magazine. While attacking the offices, the brothers claimed they were seeking revenge on the magazine for offending the prophet Muhammad. The attackers then left the offices. French police later found the brothers, who were killed in a gunfight with law enforcement.

Free Speech

Many people around the world attended silent vigils to condemn the terror attack on the magazine staff of Charlie Hebdo; *12 people were killed in the January 2015 attack.*
© HADRIAN/ SHUTTERSTOCK.COM.

Protests begin

Later on January 7, French citizens started posting the phrase "Je suis Charlie" on social media websites. The phrase is French for "I am Charlie." The phrase was meant to show support for the employees of *Charlie Hebdo* and others who had been killed that day. "Je suis Charlie" became famous around the world in the days following the attack. People in numerous countries adopted the phrase to protest attacks on free speech.

The protests started in Paris the weekend after the attack. Nearly 4 million people marched through the city streets. Many held signs reading "Je suis Charlie." The protesters claimed they were marching to oppose terrorism and to defend free speech. They said the French people enjoyed the right to free speech and should not stop expressing themselves due to fear of terrorist violence.

The protests were not limited to France. Citizens of other nations around the world protested in support of free speech that same weekend. Americans in the US state of Georgia marched while carrying the French flag and signs reading "Je suis Charlie." Citizens of Lebanon protested with signs reading "Freedom of Speech" and "We are not afraid."

Other people similarly protested terrorism and supported free speech in countries such as Cyprus, South Africa, and Spain. In Egypt journalists gathered and silently held up pens to show how important it was for *Charlie Hebdo* and other publications to be allowed to express themselves freely. Protesters in London, England, described their reasons for marching by saying that journalists should have the right to say whatever they want, even if their opinions offended people.

Muslims protest in response

At the same time people around the world began showing their support for *Charlie Hebdo*, Muslims in France and elsewhere started protesting. They protested for a different reason, however. French Muslims claimed they loved the prophet Muhammad and wanted the world to respect their religion. They also said they opposed terrorism and loved France.

Muslims in the United Kingdom felt the same way. At protests in London, Muslims said that *Charlie Hebdo* had abused its freedom of speech by making fun of the prophet Muhammad. At the same time, British Muslims opposed the terrorist attack on *Charlie Hebdo*. Protesters said such attacks were against the laws of Islam.

On January 14, 2015, one week after the shooting, *Charlie Hebdo* published its next issue, the first since the attack. The magazine featured another cartoon of Muhammad. This time Muhammad held a sign reading "Je suis Charlie."

The new cartoon angered Muslims around the world. It inspired new waves of protests by Muslims who again believed the magazine was making fun of the prophet Muhammad. In the African country of Niger (pronounced NI-jur), Muslims publicly protested *Charlie Hebdo* by burning the French flag and setting other fires. Four people died and many others were injured in the protests.

Muslims in other countries also joined in protests. In the African country of Senegal (pronounced sen-a-GOL), Muslims marched with signs bearing the last name of the brothers who had attacked the *Charlie Hebdo* offices. The Muslims were showing that they agreed that the magazine's cartoons of Muhammad were offensive. The same was true in the Palestinian city of Gaza. There, Muslims protested *Charlie Hebdo* near the city's French Cultural Center. Muslims burned the French flag during the protests. Police were forced to stop protesters from becoming violent.

After the protests

The worldwide protests against *Charlie Hebdo* eventually ended. The magazine's editor later said the publication would no longer print cartoons of the prophet Muhammad. He said this was because *Charlie*

Hebdo had accomplished what it had intended, which was to draw cartoons in any way it wanted as a sign of free speech. The editor also said that no one would defend the magazine if it printed another Muhammad cartoon after the 2015 attack.

In January 2017 French journalist Zineb El Rhazoui (pronounced zin-eb el rah-ZOO-ee; c. 1982–), who worked for *Charlie Hebdo*, left the magazine because it refused to satirize Islam anymore. She said the magazine had given in to terrorists' demands by becoming afraid to depict Muhammad. Rhazoui claimed the old *Charlie Hebdo* disappeared in the 2015 attack. Since then, she said, the magazine had given up some of its freedom of speech.

Some non-Muslims also opposed *Charlie Hebdo*'s publishing of the cartoons about Islam. People from Western Europe, the Middle East, Latin America, and other parts of the world thought the magazine's cartoons of Muhammad were disrespectful and cruel. The magazine's editors said more people around the world criticized their cartoons after the 2015 terrorist attack than ever before. Still, employees of the magazine said their cartoons did not deserve to be met with violence.

Yale Student Protests on Free Speech

LOCATION: Yale University, New Haven, Connecticut

DATE: November 9 and 12, 2015

In late October and early November 2015, a series of events at Yale University led to protests from students on campus. The protesters questioned whether freedom of speech should be viewed as more important than issues of racial sensitivity. Racial sensitivity involves understanding the experiences of people of other races.

These events gained national attention. Students held a march on November 9, 2015, to protest racial insensitivity at Yale. The march itself was in response to two incidents that occurred at the end of October. One involved a fraternity party at which a black female student was turned away and told that the event was for "white girls only." A fraternity is a social organization for male students.

The second incident involved a resident hall staff member's reply to an e-mail sent out by the school's Intercultural Affairs Council (IAC). This council attempts to make the campus more welcoming to students from all racial and ethnic backgrounds. Just before Halloween, the IAC sent an e-mail asking students to consider how wearing costumes that represent other cultures might offend minority students. The council specifically addressed costumes that include feathered headdresses, to represent Native Americans, and ones that involve blackface. Dressing in blackface involves a white person using makeup to appear black.

Erika Christakis (pronounced kriss-ta-kiss; c. 1964–), a lecturer and staff member at the university's Silliman College, wrote a response to the IAC's e-mail. She said that policing students' choice of Halloween costumes blocked their right to free speech. Christakis said that college students should be allowed to make mistakes, even offensive ones, and attempt to learn from them. Her response was sent to every student in Silliman College. Her words set off a debate regarding free speech and racial sensitivity. However, racial issues had been increasing at Yale throughout 2015.

Yale history

Yale University is one of the oldest and most well-known colleges in the United States. It was founded in 1702 when slavery was still common. Over the years the college has retained some of its ties to slavery. One such tie involves the residential colleges at Yale. The university has 12 residential colleges. Students spend all four years living at their assigned college. Each college has a master, or head, and a dean. The master is responsible for making his or her college a welcoming and safe environment for all students. The dean helps students deal with educational matters.

Symbols of Yale's ties to slavery, particularly at the residential colleges, became an ongoing issue. The issue was most evident at Calhoun College. The college was named after John C. Calhoun (1782–1850), a Yale graduate and the seventh vice president of the United States. Calhoun was a slave owner and a white supremacist, a person who believes that white people are better than people of other races. The fact that one of the residential colleges was named for Calhoun deeply troubled many students, especially black students. Some students and professors asked

Christakis said that policing students' choice of Halloween costumes blocked their right to free speech. Christakis said that college students should be allowed to make mistakes, even offensive ones, and attempt to learn from them.

the school to change the residential college's name. Others were concerned about the use of the term *master* for residential heads. In the past, slave owners were often referred to as masters. Yale's use of the term was not intended to be connected to the history of slavery. Nevertheless, some people objected to residential heads being called masters.

Yale in 2015

Several issues on both the national and local level increased racial tensions at Yale in 2015. Racial tension is hostility between two or more groups of different races. One factor was the growing Black Lives Matter movement. The organization wanted to bring awareness to and address racism in the United States, especially police violence against black individuals. Racism is the unfair treatment of people of a different race, usually based on the idea that one's own race or culture is better. In late January 2015, a black Yale student was involved in an incident with one of the university's police officers. The student, Tahj Blow (c. 1994–), was the son of *New York Times* columnist Charles M. Blow (1970–).

In an account told to his father, which was published in the *New York Times*, Tahj Blow said he was walking back to his room when an officer stopped him. The young man claimed the officer pointed his gun at him. Reports said the officer was looking for a robbery suspect. Blow apparently matched the suspect's description. That suspect was soon arrested elsewhere, and Blow was let go. The officer was never charged with any wrongdoing, but the event caused a stir at Yale. It also drew national attention due to Charles Blow's publication of his son's experience.

Throughout the year, concerns about the university's remaining ties to slavery increased as well. That summer a mass shooting at a black church in Charleston, South Carolina, by a white man left nine people dead. Following the shooting, South Carolina's governor called for the removal of the Confederate flag from outside the state capitol building. The Confederate flag is the flag that represented the South, which supported slavery, during the American Civil War (1861–1865). The event led to more discussions about whether Yale should abandon symbols of slavery that remained on campus, such as a statue of Calhoun.

At the same time, both students and teachers were concerned about the university's ability to keep racially diverse professors on staff. Racial diversity means including people of different racial backgrounds. Over several months, Yale announced the departure of several black professors, including poet Elizabeth Alexander (1962–). Alexander, who read one of her poems at the 2009 inauguration of President Barack Obama (1961–), graduated from Yale in 1984. She had worked at the university for 15 years before announcing in September 2015 that she would leave for Columbia University.

E-mails and a fraternity party

The week before Halloween, Yale's IAC sent an e-mail to all students about the upcoming holiday. The council urged students to be thoughtful when choosing their Halloween costumes. The IAC wanted students to consider how costumes that represented certain cultures—including black, Asian, or Latino cultures—would affect fellow students. Erika Christakis, an assistant master of Silliman College, took issue with the IAC's e-mail. Christakis's husband, Nicholas Christakis (1962–), was the master of Silliman and a professor. The couple lived at the residential college alongside students.

Erika Christakis wrote an e-mail response to the IAC's statement that went out to all the students at Silliman. She argued that students should be able to wear any costume they wanted, including racially insensitive ones. Christakis said that the IAC's suggestion that students censor their costumes was a way for the university to limit free speech. She suggested that students simply look away from costumes they found offensive. She said students could also explain why the costumes were inappropriate to the students who were wearing them. Around the same time, reports surfaced that a black student was turned away from a party at the Sigma Alpha Epsilon fraternity because she was not white. The fraternity denied this charge.

Both incidents heightened the already tense atmosphere on campus. Hundreds of students signed an open letter to Christakis. The letter explained that students were offended and discouraged by her e-mail. In the letter they explained that minority students on campus already felt as if they were treated differently because of their race. To have a college leader such as Christakis tell them to accept or ignore racist costumes in favor of free speech made them believe that she was not

Yale students and faculty rally to demand that the university become more inclusive to all students in November 2015. As debates about race and other social issues have created tension on campuses, college officials took steps to call out the importance of the free expression of ideas. © AP IMAGES/ARNOLD GOLD.

Free Speech

University of California, Berkeley, Free Speech Movement, 1964

One of the biggest campus protests concerning free speech took place at the University of California, Berkeley, in the fall of 1964. In September of that year, school officials announced that students would no longer be allowed to organize in a particular part of campus without permission. Additionally, students would not be able to enlist others in off-campus political activities, such as registering people to vote.

Many students complained that this limited their right to free speech. Some even held demonstrations. Weeks later, students from two civil rights groups, the Student Nonviolent Coordinating Committee and the Congress of Racial Equality (CORE), set up tables near Sather Gate without permission. These eight students were suspended. On October 1, a student with CORE, Jack Weinberg (1940–), set up a table with political information. Police arrested him after he refused to leave or identify himself. Hundreds of students gathered at the university's Sproul Plaza to protest the arrest. They surrounded the police car. Student activist Mario Savio (1942–1996) led the demonstration. After almost two days, the students and school officials reached an agreement. The university would not file charges against Weinberg. Officials also agreed to meet with students to discuss political activities on campus.

The peace at the university was short-lived. Talks between students and school officials fell through. The school officials opposed students' right to participate in political activities on campus. They even demanded the right to punish students who supported actions that led to illegal activities on or off campus. Officials put Savio and another student on probation, which is a trial period, for their actions in early October. Students continued to rally and demanded that the university take Savio and the other student off probation.

The largest protest occurred on December 2, when students marched to Sproul Hall, Berkeley's main administration building. A crowd of 6,000 listened to speeches from Savio and others and music from musicians including folk singer Joan Baez (1941–). Following the rally, students occupied Sproul Hall. They conducted a sit-in, refusing to leave the building until their demands were met. The following day, California Governor Pat Brown (1905–1996) ordered police to remove the protesters. About 800 students were arrested.

concerned about her students' well-being. In response to criticism, Christakis sent a link to an article printed in the *Atlantic*. The writers of the article claimed that modern college students were too sensitive. They argued that trying to protect students from issues such as racism left them unprepared for the real world.

In the days that followed, many students and some staff called for Christakis and her husband to resign from their positions at Silliman.

Free Speech

On December 3 students announced a strike. Nearly 900 members of the university's staff wrote to the governor to object to the use of police on campus. The unrest continued for days. On December 7, some 16,000 students, teachers, and supporters gathered to urge Berkeley's president, Clark Kerr (1911–2003), to meet the protesters' demands. Kerr announced that students' actions up to that day would not be punished. However, the protests continued. The following day, the school's Academic Senate, a group of professors and other staff, met. They voted that the university should meet the students' demand that the school not limit free speech or political action on campus. Ten days later, university officials finally agreed.

Folk singer Joan Baez performs at a rally for the Free Speech Movement at the University of California, Berkeley.
© TED STRESHINSKY/CORBIS/CORBIS VIA GETTY IMAGES.

A group of students even confronted Nicholas Christakis in a courtyard. Part of the exchange between him and a female student was uploaded to the Internet. In the video, the student argues that the Christakises should try to understand the experiences of black students. The student believed that the Christakises should be trying to make students feel comfortable in their campus homes rather than supporting free speech. Nicholas Christakis disagreed, and the student began yelling at him.

The marches

Yale president Peter Salovey (1958–) and Jonathan Holloway (1967–), the first black dean of the college, were both criticized for their slow responses to students' concerns regarding Christakis's e-mail. In the week that followed, Salovey spent four hours in a meeting with students. A group of about 200 students confronted Holloway, who listened to how they felt about what was happening on campus. Still, many undergraduates believed that Yale officials were not doing enough to make the university a safe place for students of all races.

On Monday, November 9, 2015, nearly two weeks after the IAC e-mail was sent, hundreds of Yale students and supporters marched across campus. They were attempting to bring awareness to what they viewed as a culture of racial insensitivity at the university. Many students argued that their right to feel safe and respected on campus was more important than others' right to wear racist costumes in the name of free speech. However, the issues related to Yale's ties to slavery and the lack of a diverse teaching staff also concerned protesters.

Three days later, on November 12, a group of 200 students marched to Salovey's home in the middle of the night. They read aloud a list of demands concerning the treatment of students. These demands included calling for more support for cultural centers and addressing the mental health and well-being of minority students. The students again called for the Christakises to resign from their positions at Silliman College.

They were attempting to bring awareness to what they viewed as a culture of racial insensitivity at the university. Many students argued that their right to feel safe and respected on campus was more important than others' right to wear racist costumes in the name of free speech.

Aftermath

Unrest continued at Yale throughout the fall of 2015. By December of that year, Erika Christakis announced that she would no longer be teaching at the university. The following spring the press reported that Christakis and her husband would no longer be serving as assistant and master at Silliman College. Nicholas Christakis retained his teaching position at the university.

In the spring of 2016, Yale dropped the master title for the heads of residential colleges. Nearly a year later, in February 2017, Salovey sent a letter announcing that Yale would rename Calhoun College. The college would instead honor Yale graduate Grace Murray Hopper (1906–1992). Hopper was a computer scientist and a high-ranking official in the US Navy. Many students and professors cheered the decision. Others criticized Yale for changing the name. These critics saw the change as an attempt to ignore history in favor of pleasing students.

For More Information

BOOKS

Allport, Alan, and Jennifer Horner. *Freedom of Speech*. 2nd ed. New York: Chelsea House, 2011.

Klausen, Jytte. *The Cartoons That Shook the World*. New Haven, CT: Yale University Press, 2009.

Steffens, Bradley, ed. *The Free Speech Movement*. San Diego, CA: Greenhaven Press, 2004.

PERIODICALS

Anderson, John Ward. "Cartoons of Prophet Met with Outrage." *Washington Post* (January 31, 2006). Available online at http://www.washingtonpost.com/wp-dyn/content/article/2006/01/30/AR2006013001316.html (accessed July 25, 2017).

Drezner, Daniel W. "A Clash between Administrators and Students at Yale Went Viral. Why That Is Unfortunate for All Concerned." *Washington Post* (November 9, 2015). Available online at https://www.washingtonpost.com/posteverything/wp/2015/11/09/a-clash-between-administrators-and-students-at-yale-went-viral-why-that-is-unfortunate-for-all-concerned/?utm_term=.bdfae3d5f34b (accessed July 25, 2017).

Grossman, Ron. "Flashback: 'Swastika War': When the Neo-Nazis Fought in Court to March in Skokie." *Chicago Tribune* (January 1, 2002). Available online at http://www.chicagotribune.com/news/opinion/commentary/ct-neo-nazi-skokie-march-flashback-perspec-0312-20170310-story.html (accessed July 25, 2017).

Hall, Sarah. "Harry Potter and the Sermon of Fire." *Guardian* (January 1, 2002). Available online at https://www.theguardian.com/world/2002/jan/01/books.harrypotter (accessed July 25, 2017).

Jaschik, Scott. "Racial Tensions Escalate." *Inside Higher Ed* (November 9, 2015). Available online at https://www.insidehighered.com/news/2015/11/09/racial-tensions-escalate-u-missouri-and-yale (accessed July 25, 2017).

"N. M. Pastor Leads Flock in 'Potter' Book Burning." *Deseret News* (December 31, 2001). Available online at http://www.deseretnews.com/article/886981/NM-pastor-leads-flock-in-Potter-book-burning.html (accessed July 25, 2017).

"Prophet Mohammed Cartoon Controversy: Timeline." *Telegraph* (May 4, 2015). Available online at http://www.telegraph.co.uk/news/worldnews/europe/france/11341599/Prophet-Muhammad-cartoons-controversy-timeline.html (accessed July 25, 2017).

Remnick, Noah. "Yale Grapples with Ties to Slavery in Debate over a College's Name." *New York Times* (September 12, 2015). Available online at https://

www.nytimes.com/2015/09/12/nyregion/yale-in-debate-over-calhoun-college-grapples-with-ties-to-slavery.html (accessed July 25, 2017).

Saincome, Matt. "Berkeley Riots: How Free Speech Debate Launched Violent Campus Showdown." *Rolling Stone* (February 6, 2017). Available online at http://www.rollingstone.com/culture/features/berkeley-riots-inside-the-campus-showdown-over-free-speech-w465151 (accessed October 17, 2017).

Ross, Winston. "Protests Hit Netherlands in Wake of Paris Attack." *Newsweek* (January 7, 2015). Available online at http://www.newsweek.com/protests-hit-netherlands-wake-paris-attack-297459 (accessed July 25, 2017).

Santora, Marc. "Yale Report Clears Police Officer in Encounter with Student." *New York Times* (March 5, 2015). Available online at https://www.nytimes.com/2015/03/05/nyregion/yale-report-clears-police-officer-in-encounter-with-student.html (accessed July 25, 2017).

Swarns, Rachel L. "Yale College Dean Torn by Racial Protests." *New York Times* (November 16, 2015). Available online at https://www.nytimes.com/2015/11/16/nyregion/yale-college-dean-torn-by-racial-protests.html (accessed July 25, 2017).

"Why Islam Prohibits Images of Muhammad." *Economist* (January 19, 2015). Available online at https://www.economist.com/blogs/economist-explains/2015/01/economist-explains-12 (accessed July 25, 2017).

WEBSITES

"Embassies Burn in Cartoon Protest." BBC News, February 4, 2006. http://news.bbc.co.uk/2/hi/middle_east/4681294.stm (accessed July 25, 2017).

"'Satanic' Harry Potter Books Burnt." BBC News, December 31, 2001. http://news.bbc.co.uk/2/hi/entertainment/1735623.stm (accessed July 25, 2017).

Smith, David, and Luc Torres. "Timeline: A History of Free Speech." *Guardian*, February 5, 2006. https://www.theguardian.com/media/2006/feb/05/religion.news (accessed July 25, 2017).

"Top 100 Banned/Challenged Books: 2000–2009." American Library Association, March 26, 2013. http://www.ala.org/bbooks/top-100-bannedchallenged-books-2000-2009 (accessed July 25, 2017).

"2015 Charlie Hebdo Attacks Fast Facts." CNN, December 22, 2016. http://www.cnn.com/2015/01/21/europe/2015-paris-terror-attacks-fast-facts/index.html (accessed July 25, 2017).

"Visual History: Free Speech Movement, 1964." University of California Regents. http://fsm.berkeley.edu/free-speech-movement-timeline/ (accessed July 25, 2017).

"What Does Free Speech Mean?" United States Courts. http://www.uscourts.gov/about-federal-courts/educational-resources/about-educational-outreach/activity-resources/what-does (accessed July 25, 2017).

"Yale Students March over Concerns of Racism." CBS News, November 9, 2015. http://www.cbsnews.com/news/yale-students-march-over-concerns-of-racism/ (accessed July 25, 2017).

7

Globalization

Battle in Seattle: WTO Protests **209**

Occupy Wall Street **216**

March against Monsanto **223**

Globalization occurs when countries around the world participate in a global economy through free trade and the easy flow of capital, or money. Free trade is business conducted among nations without major taxes or other limits. Taxes are funds people pay to their governments for public services. Countries that participate in the global economy depend on one another for money, products, or services they might not be able to obtain otherwise.

Early examples of globalization occurred in the late 15th and early 16th centuries. During this time, Europeans discovered North and South America and found new ways to expand their economies across continents. Some historians point out examples of globalization that occurred in ancient times, including trade between Asia and Europe. Globalization increased over many centuries. It expanded greatly in the 20th and 21st centuries. This development was due to increased plane travel, more free trade, and the use of the Internet.

In the 21st century, opinions on globalization vary. Some people feel countries benefit from participating in the global market. Supporters argue that globalization creates jobs and lowers the prices of products. Other people strongly oppose globalization. Some people claim that globalization takes jobs away from those in wealthy countries, like the United States, and sends the jobs to poorer nations where people receive less pay. This practice saves companies money. Opponents of globalization also argue that some international businesses have poor working conditions for their employees. In addition, critics claim these businesses harm the environment with their practices. Large factories, for example, can release harmful chemicals into the air.

People around the world protested the rise of globalization in the 20th and 21st centuries. Many protesters believe globalization helps

Globalization

> ### WORDS TO KNOW
>
> **Anarchist:** A person who rebels against authority and believes governments should be overthrown.
>
> **Capitalism:** An economic system in which land and wealth are mostly owned by private individuals.
>
> **Consumerism:** An economic concept based on buying and using goods.
>
> **Corporatism:** Occurs when big businesses become powerful enough to take control of the state.
>
> **Depression:** A period during which economic activity is limited and joblessness is widespread.
>
> **Developing countries:** A country that has a low standard of living, including low average annual income per person, high infant mortality rates, widespread poverty, and an underdeveloped economy. Most of these countries are located in Africa, Asia, and Latin America.
>
> **Free trade:** The buying and selling of goods and services between nations without any special taxes or rules to limit trade.
>
> **Globalization:** Occurs when countries do business on an international level.
>
> **Monopoly:** When a single company or person is the sole provider of a product or service.
>
> **Multinational company:** A company that does business in many countries around the world.
>
> **Recession:** A period when trade and economic production slow.
>
> **Tariff:** A tax or fee added to foreign products to make them more expensive.

companies gain wealth at the expense of workers and the environment. Despite protests, countries continued to globalize through free trade in the early 21st century.

Origins of globalization

Some historians believe globalization began when ancient cultures started trading with one another. Around 3000 BCE the Middle Eastern culture of Sumer in what is now Iraq traded its goods with the Indus culture of present-day Pakistan. The two economies depended on each other in this early example of globalization. This type of trade developed even further during the next few thousand years. Ancient trade routes allowed Asians and Europeans to buy and sell products and exchange ideas.

Globalization continued on a larger scale in the 15th and 16th centuries. At the time, many European countries started establishing colonies in foreign lands. Colonies are countries or regions controlled by a more powerful nation. Europeans brought their cultures and economies to their colonies in North America, South America, and elsewhere. This globalized the world even more.

The 19th century saw globalization expand rapidly due to the rise of industry. For example, British factories bought materials from India to make finished products. Companies then sold the finished products to people in Britain and other countries.

The world started to become highly globalized during the 20th century. Industries and free trade greatly expanded. Air travel allowed people and products to reach areas they could not in the past. People also started using the Internet more regularly in the late 20th century. This online network allowed people from around the world to communicate with one another instantly. Businesses could also sell their products to consumers across the globe thanks to the Internet.

Globalization in the 21st century

Globalization had developed further by the 21st century. It primarily took the form of free trade agreements among nations. Free trade agreements are deals that make it easier for partner countries to buy and sell goods to one another. These deals are meant to help all parties.

For example, a free trade agreement might reduce taxes on shipping goods among the countries that take part in the deal. The agreement may also require each party to invest in the economies of the other nations. To invest means to fund projects that are expected to produce even more money over time. In these ways, trade agreements help all nations involved in the partnership.

By the end of the 20th century, the United States had signed the North American Free Trade Agreement (NAFTA) with its neighbors, Canada and Mexico. NAFTA greatly increased trade among the three countries. By the early 21st century, almost every country in the world had become a member of some sort of free trade agreement. For instance, the United States had also formed agreements with nations in different parts of the world. These countries included Australia, El Salvador, Morocco, and Singapore.

The World Trade Organization (WTO) plays a major role in modern globalization. The body formed in 1995 to manage international trade. By 2016 the WTO had more than 160 members. This organization includes nearly every country in the world. The WTO ensures all member countries are following the international trade rules to which they have agreed. The WTO's rules cover the trade of goods, services, and other properties. The organization oversees the buying and selling of these products among members. It also works with members to find ways to increase their trade with other countries.

Some nations create trade agreements with the countries in their own regions of the world. These agreements allow countries to work together to grow the region's overall economy. If the region's economy is strong, the economies of the individual nations will thrive as well.

Globalization benefits

Globalization continues to be a topic of much debate. Supporters say that the practice helps national economies. Opponents believe that free trade agreements ignore the needs of individual workers. Advocates feel that national economies benefit from globalization in many ways. The first benefit is free trade agreements. These agreements help grow economies, and larger economies create more jobs. They also allow companies to compete with one another. Competition drives companies to make better products. It also lowers the prices of certain goods.

Another of globalization's benefits is in the way that international trade helps poor or developing countries. Developing countries are nations that are trying to add more industry to their economies. Wealthy nations assist developing countries by forming free trade agreements with them. The developing countries can then sell their goods to the wealthy nations and start building up their economies.

Globalization also helps people through cultural exchange. This is the sharing of information and ideas among different societies. This exchange occurs through international trade. Ideally, cultural exchange allows people to learn about other groups by trading with them. In this way, globalization helps build international relations as well.

Globalization disadvantages

Opponents of globalization claim the process is bad for national economies. Free trade is meant to reduce taxes and other limitations on goods shipped overseas. However, this is not always the case. In addition, free trade does not lower prices all the time. Sometimes high prices occur when countries change the value of their money so other nations will only want to purchase products from them. This practice is generally considered unfair.

One of the major issues some people have with globalization is that it helps large companies, or corporations, that send jobs overseas become wealthier. Large companies in wealthy nations such as the United States

CRITICAL THINKING QUESTIONS

1. Why are many environmentalists opposed to globalization?

2. Why was Monsanto drawn in to the debate over globalization?

3. What are the possible advantages to Monsanto's style of doing business? What are the disadvantages?

4. How might the practices of monopolies affect consumers? How do such methods affect other businesses?

5. Why would drug companies be opposed to the sale of generic drugs?

6. Why do you think the World Trade Organization is in favor of free trade? Do you think the Seattle protesters were against free trade? Explain.

7. What were some of the steps Seattle's mayor took to stop the protests?

8. How could the Occupy Wall Street movement have been more successful?

---

can save money by employing foreign workers in other countries. This is because American workers make more money and are more expensive to hire. Instead of paying an American worker $10 an hour, the corporation might be able to pay a foreign worker in a developing country $1 an hour. Experts refer to this practice as outsourcing. Outsourcing can create anxiety in a work environment. For example, corporations that employ Americans can threaten to outsource jobs if the workers do not take a pay cut. This benefits the company but not its employees.

Finally, many people have accused international corporations of having poor working conditions. Opponents claim many workers around the world receive little pay and work in unsafe environments. Such conditions include workplaces where employees face the possibility of injury or illness just by doing their jobs. Some corporations have their products made in developing countries that do not have tough environmental laws. This allows them to engage in business practices that harm the environment. This involves polluting natural resources such as soil and water.

Globalization protests

In the 1980s and 1990s, citizens of the United States, Germany, and other countries started publicly protesting globalization. Many protesters disliked that large corporations in their own countries outsourced jobs to poor nations, where labor was cheaper. The protesters were also concerned that international corporations were harming the environment.

Globalization

One of the first well-known public protests against globalization came to be known as the Battle in Seattle. This was a series of protests against the WTO in Seattle, Washington, in November and December 1999. The WTO was meeting in Seattle for one of its regular conferences. The protesters believed the WTO cared more about international trade than it did about workers and the environment. Police eventually broke up the protests, which had turned violent.

The Occupy Wall Street movement that began in 2011 is another example of a protest against globalization. This movement was not directly about international trade or trade agreements. It concerned the great amounts of wealth held by American corporations and the top 1 percent of the US population. Wall Street in New York City is the location of many of the United States' largest banks and other businesses. The Occupy Wall Street protesters were angry that a small percentage of the US population had so much money while many other Americans had very little.

Globalization became international news again in 2017. That year members of the G20 held their annual meeting in Hamburg, Germany. The G20 is a group of 20 countries that meets once a year to discuss economic and political issues. Members of the G20 include the United States, China, and Russia.

A fire caused by demonstrators during the G20 summit in Hamburg, Germany, burns behind police dressed in riot gear. © MARTINDEJA/SHUTTERSTOCK.COM.

People in Hamburg violently protested the G20 meeting in July 2017. They believed the G20 nations were allowing globalization to grow. The protesters opposed many parts of globalization. They did not like that wealthy people were becoming richer while others remained poor. The protesters also thought globalization helped extend wars because wealthy countries sold weapons to nations involved in the fighting. Police fought with the protesters in Hamburg until the two-day meeting was over and the demonstrations eventually ended.

The division of globalization

Globalization continued to divide people in the late 2010s. Although the practice helped many economies grow, opponents questioned whether such benefits outweighed globalization's disadvantages. For example, globalization led to the creation of millions of factory jobs in China. The factories make products that other countries buy. However, the chemicals produced in the factories are released into the air as smog. Smog is a combination of smoke, fog, and chemicals and is harmful to breathe. Supporters of globalization say this is an example of how globalization is both helpful and harmful. Opponents also express concern that some products made in China and other parts of Asia contain lead. The use of lead was banned from use in some countries because it causes health problems.

Battle in Seattle: World Trade Organization Protests

LOCATION: Seattle, Washington

DATE: November 28–December 3, 1999

In 1999 the leaders of the World Trade Organization (WTO) scheduled a meeting in Seattle, Washington. The WTO consists of more than 160 member nations from around the world that set the rules for global trade. The WTO meets every few years in a city in one of its member nations. The WTO's rules are supposed to make trade fair for all nations, but some people believe those rules hurt poor countries. They believe the organization's policies favor wealthy nations, harm the environment, and allow unfair treatment of workers.

At the 1999 meeting in Seattle, WTO representatives planned to discuss trade rules for the start of the new millennium. A millennium is a period of 1,000 years. Opponents of the WTO saw the 1999 meeting as important. They believed it was a chance to bring their cause to the attention of world leaders and push for change in global economic rules. Several groups from around the United States and other nations participated in demonstrations during the event. Much organization took place over the Internet, which was just beginning to become popular at the time.

Over the course of the WTO meeting, tens of thousands of people protested in Seattle. The organizers' goal was to hold peaceful marches and demonstrations. However, some protests turned violent and destructive. In some cases, police responded by firing tear gas and rubber bullets at the protesters. Tear gas is a substance that causes difficulty breathing and a burning feeling in a person's eyes. Rubber bullets can cause great pain, but they are not usually fatal. The protesters managed to disrupt the conference and forced the cancellation of several meetings. Police arrested hundreds of people, and Seattle suffered millions of dollars in damage.

The goals of the WTO

In the late 20th century, world economies were changing. New technology made it easier for countries around the globe to do business worldwide. Improvements in air and sea travel meant products could be shipped over longer distances. The Internet allowed people from different countries to communicate with each other in seconds. WTO members believed these changes would lead to an even greater increase in global trade.

The WTO planned to use its scheduled 1999 meeting in Seattle to discuss globalization. Members wanted to change some rules and create new ones to make sure nations could openly do business. In the past, many countries competed with rival nations for international trade. Many nations added a fee to foreign goods to make them more expensive. This fee, or tax, is called a tariff. Tariffs ensure that domestic products, or products made within a home country, are less expensive to purchase than foreign-made products. Some countries also limited the amount of foreign products that could be sold and created other restrictions.

The WTO argued strongly for free trade. Members believed that this process of removing or reducing tariffs and special restrictions would increase economic growth around the world. Stronger economies would then lead to more jobs and lower poverty levels. Many business and government leaders in the United States and other wealthy nations supported the WTO and its push for more free trade.

Issues of concern to protesters

Opponents of globalization and free trade believed that fewer restrictions on business would allow wealthy nations to take advantage of poorer ones. They argued that businesses looking to make higher profits would build factories in places where they could pay workers lower wages. The leaders of less developed countries would then compete with one another to attract businesses by offering cheaper labor. In addition to lower wages, countries could reduce costs by cutting back on spending for environmental safety. They could also save by failing to provide quality workplaces and benefits for employees.

Many people who opposed free trade felt that large international corporations hurt small businesses, especially in poorer nations. For example, agricultural companies that can grow more fruits and vegetables and sell them for a lower price can outsell local farmers who rely on their crops to make a living. Opponents thought this would destroy small farms and damage local traditions in certain regions. They also believed large companies were too forceful in trying to make customers spend money and buy their products. They saw this effort as promoting out-of-control consumerism, the idea that buying goods always benefits the economy.

Protests begin in Seattle

WTO members make decisions on global trade in meetings called ministerial conferences. The first ministerial conference was held in 1996 in Singapore. The 1999 conference in Seattle was the first held in the United States. Opponents of free trade viewed the United States as a symbol of globalization and greed. Both the WTO and the city of Seattle expected protests at the conference, but organizers believed they would be nonviolent. In comments made before the meeting, US President Bill Clinton (1946–) said he welcomed peaceful demonstrations in hopes of promoting a debate on the issues.

Both the WTO and the city of Seattle expected protests at the conference, but organizers believed they would be nonviolent. In comments made before the meeting, US President Bill Clinton said he welcomed peaceful demonstrations in hopes of promoting a debate on the issues.

Globalization

Banksy Street Art Protests

For many years, protesters have used graffiti to bring attention to various causes. Graffiti includes unapproved drawings, paintings, or writings created on public or private structures. Many people believe that graffiti is destruction of property, and there are many laws against it. In the early 1990s, an artist by the name of Banksy (c. 1975–) began leaving graffiti on buildings and public places in Bristol, England. He used a style of art called stenciling. First, the artist makes an image out of paper. Then the artist uses the paper as a stencil and spray-paints the image on a structure.

Banksy moved to London around 2000 and became famous for his street art. He also traveled around the world and left his art in foreign cities. He has never revealed his real name, and he created his art in secret. His works would just show up in public overnight to the surprise of onlookers. Many of Banksy's works make a statement about society. They often criticize the way governments work and how people live their lives. His art is sometimes humorous and sometimes disturbing.

Banksy focuses on consumerism in many of his works. One painting features hooded people worshipping a sign that reads, "Sale Ends Today." Another features a white sign with the words "The Joy of Not Being Sold Anything!" spray-painted on it. Still another pictures a man selling T-shirts that say, "Destroy Capitalism." Capitalism is an economic system in which land and wealth are mostly owned by private citizens. Capitalists often try to make more money by selling products to people.

Bansky's graffiti **Very Little Helps** *appeared in London around 2008.* © CHRISDORNEY/SHUTTERSTOCK.COM.

In 2008 Banksy painted an image of children saluting a flag made from a plastic bag from the British grocery store chain Tesco. Banksy named the artwork *Very Little Helps*, a reference to Tesco's corporate slogan, "Every little helps." In 2011 rioters protested the opening of a Tesco store in Bristol. Banksy released artwork of a gasoline bomb in a Tesco bottle. A spokesperson for Banksy said the work makes a statement about the abuse of corporate power.

The conference was scheduled to begin on November 30. The first protesters began gathering on November 26. Two groups of about 30 to 50 people peacefully marched through downtown Seattle. The next day, police arrested three people after they climbed down a wall by a busy freeway and hung an anti-WTO banner. On November 28 the first large protest was held. A crowd of about 500 people blocked downtown streets and forced some businesses to close. Police also reported that a group of protesters had taken over an abandoned building and locked themselves inside.

Many groups traveled to Seattle to demonstrate against the WTO. Several groups communicated through the Internet to plan their protests months in advance. The Internet allowed protest organizers to get their message out to more people. This meant that a large number of demonstrators from across the United States and around the world knew about the event. Not all the groups agreed on the issues or even had the same goals. Some people just wanted their voices heard, and others wanted to prevent the WTO meetings from happening.

Some groups focused on nonviolent protests and marched without causing problems. Several thousand members of the Sierra Club, an organization dedicated to preserving the environment, held a peaceful rally on November 29. Religious groups and organizations that fight for workers' rights also called for nonviolent protests. Other groups planned violent action and came prepared for police response. Hundreds of protesters gathered in downtown Seattle on November 29 and began smashing windows at a McDonald's restaurant. The protesters then began heading for the freeway. Police had permission to use tear gas to stop them. However, many of the protesters wore gas masks to protect themselves.

Protests grow larger

On November 30 thousands of protesters surrounded the Washington State Convention Center, the site of the scheduled WTO event. Demonstrators blocked WTO representatives as they attempted to enter the building. The protesters were well organized. They had a plan to make sure no one could get in or out of the convention center. They marched through city streets, locked arms with one another, and chained themselves to objects near the center.

Some of the protesters were anarchists. Anarchists believe that any form of authority is unfair and that people should overthrow their governments. Some anarchist groups set out to be destructive during the protest. The group broke windows, spray-painted slogans on buildings, and threw garbage into the streets. They targeted the city's

Globalization

Police confront the anti-WTO demonstrators as they protest in Seattle, Washington, in 1999. © KARIE HAMILTON/SYGMA VIA GETTY IMAGES.

businesses. The anarchists especially focused on stores of large corporations such as the shoemaker Nike and the coffee company Starbucks. Some protesters joined in the destruction while others tried to stop it.

By the early afternoon of November 30, more than 40,000 people were protesting in downtown Seattle. Organizers canceled the opening ceremonies of the WTO conference because of the unrest. Seattle's mayor, Paul Schell (1937–2014), ordered a state of emergency in the city. Police responded to the protests by firing tear gas and rubber bullets at the demonstrators. Some of the protesters wore gas masks and stood their ground against the police. They set fires in garbage containers and threw rocks, bottles, and other objects at the officers. The police eventually ran out of tear gas.

Law enforcement efforts moved many of the protesters away from the convention center area, allowing some WTO representatives to enter. Fighting between the police and demonstrators continued in other sections of the city, though. Mayor Schell ordered a 25-block "no-protest"

Eyewitness to Violence

This primary source excerpt is from a report prepared by the WTO Accountability Review Committee of Seattle, Washington, in August 2000. It contains information that Jim Compton obtained from Isak Bressler, who was an eyewitness to the World Trade Organization (WTO) protests in Seattle in 1999. Compton interviewed Bressler on August 7, 2000.

Isak Bressler is a 26 year old law student at Seattle University who met me in my office. His narrative report is attached. He was a legal observer at several street events during the WTO and wrote a careful account of his observations. I found him careful and credible in his presentation.

Bressler emphasized that he was witness to the Dec 1 events on Capitol Hill, in particular the confrontation at Pike and Broadway. He said that prior to the police action, the crowd was "bored and ready to go home." He said the gathering was boisterous but peaceful, and could not fairly be portrayed as any threat to public safety. I pressed him several times about whether there was any provocation from the crowd, or from hangers-on, and he said convincingly that it was not a hostile environment for anyone.

Bressler claims that the white van driven by police drove into the crowd at about 20 miles per hour. He believes the driver wanted a confrontation and was baiting the crowd. He says the panic ensuing from the van incident was what precipitated police use of teargas.

Bressler believes that police were emboldened by the fact that they wore no badges or identification, and could act anonymously.

He recounted his experience later the same evening during the confrontation near the QFC [Quality Food Center, a supermarket] at Republican and Broadway. He described a chaotic scene in which he was unable to approach police lines and never succeeded in asking questions.

Bressler says at no time did he hear any warnings to disperse or other announcements from police.

He was shot at close range by an officer firing a tear gas cannister, and says it did not appear to be accidental, as the officer was looking directly at him while firing. The cannister cut his head, caused profuse bleeding, and required four stitches.

Bressler described an officer who detained a medic on Broadway, and said he saw the woman "spread eagled" by the policeman with a hand on her shoulder and holding a nightstick in a menacing fashion. He believed the woman had been struck and injured, although he did not witness it.

SOURCE: Compton, Jim. "Interview with Isak Bressler." Report from the WTO Accountability Review Committee, City of Seattle, August 3, 2000. Available online at http://www.seattle.gov/archive/wtocommittee/interviews.htm#banerian (accessed October 12, 2017). Courtesy of Seattle.gov.

---

area around the convention center. He also made it illegal for anyone other than police officers to wear gas masks. One of the reasons the mayor wanted to keep the area around the convention center safe was because President Clinton was scheduled to attend the event on December 1.

Globalization

Arrests and the aftermath

Protests and rioting continued outside the no-protest area. Police again used tear gas, rubber bullets, and other methods to force the crowds back. Law enforcement officers arrested people trying to protest within the restricted area. More than 500 people were arrested on December 1 alone. Protesters then began demonstrating against the creation of the no-protest area and against the police. On December 2 officers stopped using tear gas and rubber bullets. They arrested only two people that day. Soon, the protests became less violent.

The WTO conference ended on December 3. WTO representatives failed to come to an agreement on free trade. Thousands of protesters cheered the result and staged a peaceful march in the city. Other protesters gathered outside the police station to demand the release of arrested activists. Officials later dropped charges against most of those arrested.

Three days after the end of the protest, Seattle's police chief resigned. He said he was responsible for the unrest because the police had failed to prepare for so many protesters. The protests caused more than $2 million in damage to the city. The city of Seattle was also sued and forced to pay hundreds of thousands of dollars to people injured by the police and to some of the arrested protesters.

The WTO protests in Seattle inspired other demonstrations against international trade and business organizations. A combination of protests and disagreements among the nations caused the 2003 WTO meetings in Mexico to collapse.

Police in other US cities and around the world also learned from the mistakes of the Seattle police. They made sure to prepare for future protests. Officers were also less likely to use methods such as tear gas and rubber bullets against protesters unless absolutely necessary.

Occupy Wall Street

LOCATION: New York City and cities around the world

DATE: Starting September 17, 2011

The Occupy Wall Street movement was a global protest against economic inequality. The movement started in New York City on September 17, 2011. Its aim was to draw attention to the imbalanced and unfair nature of capitalism, corporatism, and globalization. Capitalism is an economic system in which land and wealth are mostly owned by private citizens. Corporatism occurs when big businesses become powerful enough to take control of the state. Globalization occurs when countries conduct business on an international level.

The people behind Occupy Wall Street believed that an unjust economic system existed in the United States. This system enabled a tiny part of the American population to hold nearly all of the country's wealth and power. The Occupy Wall Street protesters famously referred to this tiny group of people as the "1 percent." The group called themselves and others like them the "99 percent."

The initial Occupy protest began when people gathered in Manhattan's Zuccotti Park to demonstrate against Wall Street. The protesters rallied against corrupt economic practices and the widespread inequality they caused. The demonstration continued for weeks. Some protesters even slept in the park overnight at times. As the Occupy movement gained attention, it eventually spread into more than 1,500 other cities across the United States and around the world. The initial New York protest ended after city officials forced demonstrators out of Zuccotti Park on November 15, 2011. Some activities of the movement continued into 2012 and beyond.

History of Wall Street

The Occupy movement was focused on Wall Street. This famous section of New York City serves as the financial center of the United States. It is home to the New York Stock Exchange (NYSE). A stock exchange is where stocks and bonds are traded to make money. Wall Street's growth as the nation's leading financial center began in the mid-19th century. Before that time, New York was competing with Philadelphia, Pennsylvania; Boston, Massachusetts; and Hartford, Connecticut, to become America's financial capital. New York first pulled ahead of the other cities in that race during the American Civil War (1861–1865). New York played a key role in overseeing the financial aspects of the war. Because of this, its reputation as an economic center grew. It would still be several decades before Wall Street as it is known today truly began to emerge.

In the late 19th century, banker J. P. Morgan (1837–1913) and other major figures in the New York financial community worked to build the modern banking system. Their efforts raised Wall Street's standing in the

The people behind Occupy Wall Street believed that an unjust economic system existed in the United States. This system enabled a tiny part of the American population to hold nearly all of the country's wealth and power.

financial world even further. The United States became a creditor nation, or a country whose investments in foreign nations exceed the investments made in it by other countries. After World War I (1914–1918), Wall Street officially took its place as the primary center of US finance.

Anti–Wall Street movements Wall Street also became a target for people who took issue with capitalism and the workings of the US economy. Early on in Wall Street's rise to power, many people began to question the important roles that banks and other organizations played in the US economy. This led to the first notable anti–Wall Street movement, which was called the Populist movement.

The Populist movement began in the South and Midwest. It was a reaction to the increasing amount of control Wall Street had over the nation's financial power. Populists feared that Wall Street's growing political influence would threaten US democracy. Around the same time, the rising US labor movement began calling attention to problems like low wages and poor working conditions. The role Wall Street played in labor issues began to be questioned.

In the 20th century, many political groups viewed Wall Street as a symbol of everything that was wrong with capitalism. Some held protests to voice their concerns. Early in the century, reformers called on the government to watch over Wall Street more closely. They thought the government should take a more direct role in policing Wall Street's activities. In the 1930s many people blamed Wall Street for causing the Great Depression. This economic disaster left millions of Americans with little or no money. Many people also lost their jobs. In the 1960s and 1970s, other social movements took aim at Wall Street banks for treating people unfairly based on their income level or race.

In the 1930s many people blamed Wall Street for causing the Great Depression. This economic disaster left millions of Americans with little or no money.

Wall Street and inequality One of the longest-running and most serious criticisms of Wall Street is that it directly contributes to economic inequality. Since its beginnings, Wall Street has approached business in a way that has caused wide gaps in wealth and income among people at different levels of US society. While people at the upper levels got wealthier, others were mostly left behind. Although the level of economic inequality improved somewhat in the mid-20th century, it began to worsen again in the 1970s. This trend continued into the early 21st century.

Occupy Wall Street

The Occupy Wall Street movement was formed in response to several issues. The main problem was growing economic inequality. The Great Recession worsened this problem. This was a global economic downturn that occurred between December 2007 to June 2009. The Great Recession damaged the US economy. It also made life more difficult for those who were already struggling financially. As a result, some people lost their jobs, their homes, and large amounts of the money they were saving for retirement.

While all of this was going on in the United States, other important events that helped to inspire the Occupy movement began to unfold elsewhere in the world. In 2011 a series of pro-democracy protests took place in northern Africa and the Middle East. These movements, known as the Arab Spring, led to the fall of several governments in the region. Other countries had problems with debt and began to reduce government services.

The US economic problems and the effectiveness of the Arab Spring moved activists Kalle Lasn (1942–) and Micah White (1982–) to take action. They began what would become the Occupy Wall Street movement in June 2011. The pair worked for a Canadian magazine called *Adbusters*. They set up the details for a movement designed to shed light on the role Wall Street and the banking industry were playing in America's economic struggles. They called for a protest in the heart of New York's financial district. This would create a great deal of attention and send a powerful message about the need for change.

The Occupy Wall Street movement officially began when about 1,000 protesters gathered in Zuccotti Park on September 17, 2011. Zuccotti Park is located in the heart of New York's financial district. The park offered protesters an ideal public space for taking a stand against Wall Street's questionable practices. Once in the park, protesters built a camp, where many slept overnight.

The first Occupy protesters and those who followed later included people from all backgrounds. Teenagers, college students and graduates, unemployed people, discouraged workers, retirees, the homeless, and others were part of the movement. They argued that Wall Street banks and other big businesses were getting rich while ordinary people were struggling to live. They believed this was unfair, and they wanted the US government to do something about it.

Globalization

Occupy Wall Street: Declaration of Principles

This primary source excerpt contains a sampling of some of the principles that the Occupy Wall Street protesters rallied around. These principles were created by the New York City General Assembly of Occupy Wall Street.

DECLARATION OF THE OCCUPATION OF NEW YORK CITY

As we gather together in solidarity to express a feeling of mass injustice, we must not lose sight of what brought us together. We write so that all people who feel wronged by the corporate forces of the world can know that we are your allies. . . .

- They have taken our houses through an illegal foreclosure process, despite not having the original mortgage.
- They have taken bailouts from taxpayers with impunity, and continue to give Executives exorbitant bonuses.
- They have perpetuated inequality and discrimination in the workplace based on age, the color of one's skin, sex, gender identity and sexual orientation.
- They have poisoned the food supply through negligence, and undermined the farming system through monopolization.
- They have profited off of the torture, confinement, and cruel treatment of countless animals, and actively hide these practices.
- They have continuously sought to strip employees of the right to negotiate for better pay and safer working conditions.
- They have held students hostage with tens of thousands of dollars of debt on education, which is itself a human right.
- They have consistently outsourced labor and used that outsourcing as leverage to cut workers' healthcare and pay.
- They have influenced the courts to achieve the same rights as people, with none of the culpability or responsibility.
- They have spent millions of dollars on legal teams that look for ways to get them out of contracts in regards to health insurance.
- They have sold our privacy as a commodity.

The protest grows The protest continued in the days that followed the initial gathering. More people came to Zuccotti Park every day, and the movement slowly began to gain more media attention. As time passed, a growing number of activist organizations, labor unions, and celebrities expressed their support of Occupy Wall Street. A number of marches throughout the financial district were also held. These attracted even more attention to the Occupy cause.

As the Occupy movement grew, so too did the strain between protesters and the police. Activists sometimes clashed with police officers who tried to break up the protest or enforce certain rules. Officers arrested many protesters. During a march across the Brooklyn Bridge on October 1, police arrested about 700 protesters.

- They have used the military and police force to prevent freedom of the press.
- They have deliberately declined to recall faulty products endangering lives in pursuit of profit.
- They determine economic policy, despite the catastrophic failures their policies have produced and continue to produce.
- They have donated large sums of money to politicians, who are responsible for regulating them.
- They continue to block alternate forms of energy to keep us dependent on oil.
- They continue to block generic forms of medicine that could save people's lives or provide relief in order to protect investments that have already turned a substantial profit.
- They have purposely covered up oil spills, accidents, faulty bookkeeping, and inactive ingredients in pursuit of profit.
- They purposefully keep people misinformed and fearful through their control of the media.
- They have accepted private contracts to murder prisoners even when presented with serious doubts about their guilt.
- They have perpetuated colonialism at home and abroad.
- They have participated in the torture and murder of innocent civilians overseas.
- They continue to create weapons of mass destruction in order to receive government contracts.

To the people of the world,

We, the New York City General Assembly occupying Wall Street in Liberty Square, urge you to assert your power....

Join us and make your voices heard!

SOURCE: NYC General Assembly. "Declaration of the Occupation of New York City." Available online at https://archive.org/details/DeclarationOfTheOccupationOfNewYorkCity (accessed October 14, 2017). Courtesy of NYC General Assembly.

Within the first few weeks, the Occupy movement became so popular that it began to spread beyond New York City. By October additional Occupy protests sprang up in San Francisco, California; Houston, Texas; Tampa, Florida; and other cities across the United States. Later in the month, the Occupy movement went global with protests in some European and Asian cities.

The New York protest continued for another month. Finally, on November 15, city officials closed the Zuccotti Park camp. Although this shut down energized the protest for a short time, it eventually marked the beginning of the Occupy movement's end. In the months that followed, the Occupy movement slowly faded away. The last camps across the country and around the world were broken up during the winter of 2012.

Globalization

The Occupy Wall Street movement spread to various cities in the United States and other parts of the world. Here, demonstrators march in the Occupy protest in downtown Los Angeles in October 2011.
© GERRY BOUGHAN/SHUTTERSTOCK.COM.

Results

Occupy Wall Street was both a success and a failure. It succeeded in bringing attention to the problem of economic inequality. It also encouraged people to stand up for what they believed. However, it failed to achieve any real change. Critics say this was because the Occupy movement lacked both organized leadership and real goals.

While the immediate success of Occupy Wall Street was limited, its long-term accomplishments were much greater. The Occupy movement proved that it was possible for ordinary people to make their opinions heard. Over time, this led to an increase in activism related to many social concerns. Inspired by the Occupy movement, activists held a large Washington, DC, protest against the Keystone XL pipeline in late 2011. Occupy Wall Street also succeeded in drawing attention to the damaging influence of wealth on politics and sparked a movement in favor of reducing that influence.

In 2016 about 100 members of the original Occupy Wall Street demonstration gathered to celebrate the fifth anniversary of the movement. The group met in a park in New York City, where they listened to speeches. Later they marched to police headquarters. Many of them said that for them the movement never ended. They continued to try to effect change whenever possible.

Globalization

March against Monsanto

LOCATION: 436 cities in 52 countries

DATE: May 25, 2013

On May 25, 2013, people around the world marched in opposition to Monsanto, a multinational company headquartered in the United States. Organizers said close to 2 million people participated in related protests held in 436 cities in 52 countries worldwide. Protesters said they were concerned about Monsanto's control over world agriculture. They also worried about the company's production of genetically modified food. Scientists sometimes change the genes, or traits, of certain organisms. They do this to make the organisms more useful. For instance, scientists may try to create plants that are resistant to insects or produce more crops.

Not everyone believes that genetic modification is a good idea, though. Those protesting Monsanto wanted government officials to create laws that would force the company to label any food developed from a genetically modified organism (GMO). They also hoped to publicize what they believed to be the possible dangers of GMOs to both the environment and human health.

Monsanto is one of the largest companies specializing in agricultural production. It is also one of the biggest sellers of genetically modified seeds. Monsanto has created genetically modified versions of canola, corn, cotton, soybeans, and other crops. The company is also a large producer of insecticides, which are chemicals that poison insects and other pests. Insecticides are sometimes called pesticides, a broader category that also includes herbicides. The company also makes herbicides, which are chemicals that kill weeds. Years ago, an earlier version of the Monsanto corporation was one of the companies that produced the herbicide Agent Orange for the US government. Dow Chemical was another. During the Vietnam War (1954–1975), soldiers used the chemical to clear away plants in the Vietnam jungles. Scientists later discovered that Agent Orange increased soldiers' risk of cancer.

Concerns about Monsanto products

One of Monsanto's first successes was the creation of seeds that are resistant to Roundup, one of the company's herbicides. In 1980 the US Supreme Court gave Monsanto the right to patent its seeds. This meant that only Monsanto could sell seeds that its scientists had developed. Farmers who wanted these resistant seeds had to buy them from Monsanto. The farmers also had to agree not to use seeds gathered from previous harvests when planting the next year's crops. Instead, they had to buy new seeds every year. Critics argued that this gave Monsanto too much power. For example, if the resistant seeds blew onto another farmer's fields, Monsanto could sue that farmer to prevent him or her from using the seeds.

Some people also worry about Monsanto's environmental record. Such people feel that Monsanto's actions have negatively affected global agriculture and human health. For instance, some scientists believe that Roundup can increase the risk of cancer. In 2017 the state of California added the main ingredient in Roundup, an herbicide called glyphosate (pronounced GLI-fuh-sayt), to its list of cancer-causing chemicals. In addition, studies in Africa showed that glyphosate might reduce men's ability to produce children. The company, however, contends the product is safe. Many anti-GMO activists worry that glyphosates and other pesticides may make their way into the food supply. If this happens, these chemicals could make many people sick.

Some people believe that genetically modified seeds may even be dangerous. Insects that help fertilize both genetically modified and natural plants can create hybrid plants. Hybrid plants have characteristics from both parents. These plants may breed with plants elsewhere. This can result in genetically modified plants mixing in with natural crops. Some studies have suggested that genetically modified plants could possibly make animals and insects such as butterflies and bees sick. Many health advocates are concerned about the effects of GMOs on humans as well. As of 2017, only a few studies reviewing the risks of GMOs to animals and humans had been conducted. At the time, there were still many questions about whether GMOs could harm human and animal health.

Another concern is that Monsanto has bought many competing agricultural companies. This has made the company the largest producer of many varieties of seeds. Critics have expressed concern about the worldwide dependence on Monsanto agricultural products. Some people believe this could be particularly problematic if scientists someday discover that genetically modified seeds are dangerous. Anti-globalization activists have opposed Monsanto because they worry that the company has too much power. These activists believe that Monsanto has strong control over the food supply because the company sells such a high percentage of seeds.

Benefits of Monsanto products Monsanto contends that its seeds and chemicals serve valuable purposes. The company argues that its genetically modified seeds produce more crops than non-GMO seeds. This allows farmers who use Monsanto products to have greater harvests. They can sell more food, which enables them to make more money. Increased harvests also provide more food in developing nations that might have food supply shortages.

Monsanto also argues that studies linking GMOs to health problems are exaggerated. They point out that some of the scientific research linking GMOs to various health issues has been disproven. Defenders of Monsanto's work with GMOs note that modifying plants is not a new practice. In fact, farm crops often look very little like their wild relatives. This occurs because humans have used various methods over time to create larger fruits and vegetables that taste better. They feel that the science behind GMOs is merely another way of programming seeds to have desirable traits. Many studies of GMO crops indicate that they are nutritionally the same as non-GMO crops. The resistance of GMO crops to damaging insects has meant that fewer insecticides are necessary. GMO plants are also less likely to carry toxins created by fungi. In addition, the US government has stated that Monsanto's products are safe for people to eat.

Since Monsanto uses herbicide-resistant seeds, the methods necessary to raise them are different. Farmers use a practice called no-till farming to plant the seeds. No-till farming is a planting method in which the farmer does not need to disturb the soil by plowing it. This practice has several advantages that are friendly to the environment. It reduces soil erosion, a problem in which the most valuable soil is lost over time. No-till farms also require less machinery, so less pollution is created. The practice also reduces the amount of greenhouse gases

Anti-globalization activists have opposed Monsanto because they worry that the company has too much power. These activists believe that Monsanto has strong control over the food supply because the company sells such a high percentage of seeds.

Globalization

Protests against Big Pharma over HIV/AIDS Drugs

Anti-globalization marches also target other major corporations. For example, in 2001 activists gathered to protest the fact that many HIV/AIDS patients did not have access to affordable lifesaving drugs. HIV (human immunodeficiency virus) is the virus that causes AIDS (acquired immunodeficiency syndrome). AIDS is a disease that weakens the immune system. Many protesters focused their efforts on big multinational pharmaceutical companies. Pharmaceutical companies make drugs. Opponents have nicknamed these companies "Big Pharma." Critics feel that Big Pharma companies intentionally raise prices of drugs to make huge profits. Such practices make drugs unaffordable to many people, particularly those in poorer countries. People with HIV/AIDS face much higher risks of illness and death if they do not have access to necessary medicines.

Protesters were particularly worried about a court case in South Africa. Thirty-nine drugmakers sued the South African government to prevent the country from buying the cheapest available drugs to treat HIV/AIDS patients. Many of these drugs were generic. Generic drugs often have the same or a similar formula as brand-name drugs but are far less expensive. Such drugs are less profitable for drug companies. In addition to their lawsuit, many drug companies placed pressure on South Africa by closing factories and reducing investments there. They pushed their own governments to threaten South Africa with trade limits.

In response, activists gathered on March 5, 2001, to protest against Big Pharma companies. More than 200 participants gathered in New York City and marched to the GlaxoSmithKline and Bristol-Myers Squibb headquarters, two of the drug companies involved in the South African lawsuit. Other related protests were held around the world, including one in South Africa. The protests and the resulting publicity created enormous public pressure on the drug companies involved in the lawsuit. The US government decided to drop its public support of these companies on this issue. On April 20,

---

released into the atmosphere. Greenhouse gases can build in Earth's upper atmosphere and trap heat. The increase in greenhouse gases caused by human activity has been linked to global warming and climate change.

March against Monsanto

American homemaker Tami Canal came up with the idea for the March against Monsanto. Canal was motivated by the narrow failure of a proposed bill on the 2012 California ballot called Proposition 37. This bill would have required food companies to label products containing

Globalization

2001, the companies agreed to end their legal case and allow South Africa to purchase generic drugs. The decision enabled other African countries to pursue similar methods of buying less expensive AIDS drugs without challenge.

HIV/AIDS activists are among several thousand people marching through the streets of Pretoria, South Africa, in 2001. They are protesting the high cost of lifesaving drugs, saying that profits are more important to drug manufacturers than people. © ANNA ZIEMINSKI/AFP/GETTY IMAGES.

GMOs. On February 28, 2013, she started an Internet campaign and called on her friends to join her in staging a rally against Monsanto. Her online posts received even more publicity and support than she expected. Within a few months, Canal's cause was taken up by several activist organizations. Among the organizations that offered support to Canal's idea were the Anti-Media and A Revolt. Both groups support anti-globalization causes. Anti-globalists hope to reduce the amount of power that multinational corporations have over the international economy. These organizations helped to publicize the march.

Organizers had a number of goals they wanted to achieve through the march. First, they hoped to protect the global food supply from possibly

Globalization

Protesters rallied in the streets against the Monsanto corporation, accusing the company of producing genetically modified foods that the protesters believe are unsafe. © IRA BOSTIC/SHUTTERSTOCK.COM.

dangerous chemicals sold by Monsanto. Second, they wanted to protect small farmers who could not afford Monsanto products from being persuaded by the large company to use them. Third, organizers wanted to protect the environment from chemical pollution and promote organic alternatives. Organic products are grown without the use of pesticides and chemical fertilizers.

Protesters also wanted to emphasize the influence that massive multinational corporations like Monsanto had on national governments. They further intended to demonstrate that Monsanto was increasingly becoming a monopoly. A monopoly occurs when one company or person is the sole provider of a product or service. When there is no competition, there is no one to challenge a company's actions. This means the monopoly can control prices and use unfair practices.

Activists in cities on all six populated continents participated in marches. This broad support was a reflection of Monsanto's international standing among many global activists. In Argentina, where Monsanto sold nearly 100 percent of the country's soy and grain seeds, protesters gathered in the city of Buenos Aires. In the United States, marchers carrying posters protested in many cities across the country. Organizers noted that their events occurred without the violence that sometimes happens at other anti-globalization and environmental protests. In fact, no arrests were reported at any of the 436 related events. At many protests, activists handed out pamphlets and listened to speeches.

Organizers noted that these marches were not intended to make Monsanto look bad. Instead, protesters wanted to bring attention to the possible dangers of both GMO products and the chemicals produced by the company. In response to these marches, Monsanto acknowledged the rights of protesters to hold rallies. However, the company suggested that protesters' concerns were misplaced. Monsanto also released a statement that noted how GMOs helped boost the global food supply and expressed the company's support of small farmers.

Effects of the protests

Organizers of the march were encouraged by the turnout. They hoped to build on this widespread support to pressure politicians to change laws regarding GMOs. A second march was held on October 12, 2013, and included hundreds of marchers in several cities around the world. A third march took place on May 21, 2014, in 382 cities across six continents. Additional marches were held in 2015, 2016, and 2017.

The protesters' cause was taken up by several politicians and celebrities. The labeling of GMOs was among the campaign issues of Vermont Senator Bernie Sanders (1941–) during his 2016 presidential campaign. Other supporters of the March against Monsanto included American actor Gwyneth Paltrow (1972–) and Canadian singer Neil Young (1945–). Paltrow founded a company named GOOP that promotes the use of GMO-free products. Young recorded an album called *The Monsanto Years* (2015), which features several songs about GMOs and activism.

Thanks to the efforts of activists, lawmakers made changes to how GMOs are distributed in the United States. In 2016 Congress passed a law requiring companies to label products containing GMOs. However, those labels can be in the form of "QR codes," which are little boxes printed on the packaging. Customers would have to scan those codes with their smartphones to find out more about the GMO content. The measure received support from members of both the Republican and Democratic Parties. This law passed despite a campaign against it by Monsanto and other companies. Experts believe these companies spent millions in their efforts to oppose laws that supported the labeling of GMOs on food products. Anti-Monsanto activists and small farmers welcomed this bill. As of 2016, 64 countries had similar laws. However, politicians including Sanders and Oregon Senator Jeff Merkley (1956–) expressed concern that the language of the US bill was not clear and would easily allow companies to find loopholes.

Nevertheless, many people were interested in purchasing non-GMO products. Whole Foods, one of the largest supermarket chains in the United States, reported that sales of non-GMO foods rose by 15 to 30 percent since the store began labeling GMO products in 2013. On the other hand, Monsanto has seen its global sales drop since 2013. This is likely a result of the protests against the company and the resulting negative publicity.

For More Information

BOOKS

Fass, Paula S. *Children of a New World: Society, Culture, and Globalization.* New York: New York University Press, 2007.

Gitlin, Todd. *Occupy Nation: The Roots, the Spirit, and the Promise of Occupy Wall Street.* New York: HarperCollins, 2012.

PERIODICALS

Burton, Lynsi. "WTO Riots in Seattle: 15 Years Ago." *Seattle Post Intelligencer* (November 29, 2014). Available online at http://www.seattlepi.com/local/article/WTO-riots-in-Seattle-15-years-ago-5915088.php (accessed July 25, 2017).

Collins, Mike. "The Pros and Cons of Globalization." *Forbes* (May 6, 2015). Available online at https://www.forbes.com/sites/mikecollins/2015/05/06/the-pros-and-cons-of-globalization/#60ffb291ccce (accessed July 27, 2017).

Ellsworth-Jones, Will. "The Story behind Banksy." *Smithsonian* (February 2013). Available online at http://www.smithsonianmag.com/arts-culture/the-story-behind-banksy-4310304/ (accessed July 26, 2017).

Federoff, Nina. "Can We Trust Monsanto with Our Food?" *Scientific American* (July 25, 2013). Available online at https://www.scientificamerican.com/article/can-we-trust-monsanto-with-our-food/ (accessed July 25, 2017).

Leonhardt, Megan. "The Lasting Effects of Occupy Wall Street, Five Years Later." *Money* (September 16, 2016). Available online at http://time.com/money/4495707/occupy-wall-street-anniversary-effects/ (accessed July 27, 2017).

Levitin, Michael. "The Triumph of Occupy Wall Street." *Atlantic* (June 10, 2015). Available online at https://www.theatlantic.com/politics/archive/2015/06/the-triumph-of-occupy-wall-street/395408/ (accessed July 27, 2017).

"Marchers in over 400 Cities Protest Monsanto." *Washington Post* (May 25, 2013). Available online at https://www.washingtonpost.com/politics/marchers-in-over-400-cities-protest-monsanto/2013/05/25/938dd988-c59b-11e2-914f-a7aba60512a7_story.html?utm_term=.cd0efcd95a22 (accessed July 25, 2017).

"Millions March against GM Crops." *Guardian* (May 25, 2013). Available online at https://www.theguardian.com/environment/2013/may/26/millions-march-against-monsanto (accessed July 25, 2017).

Smith, Noah. "The Dark Side of Globalization: Why Seattle's 1999 Protesters Were Right." *Atlantic* (January 6, 2014). Available online at https://www.theatlantic.com/business/archive/2014/01/the-dark-side-of-globalization-why-seattles-1999-protesters-were-right/282831/ (accessed July 27, 2017).

Xia, Rosanna. "Hundreds in L.A. March in Global Protest against Monsanto, GMOs." *Los Angeles Times* (May 25, 2013). Available online at http://articles.latimes.com/2013/may/25/local/la-me-ln-monsanto-protest-20130525 (accessed July 25, 2017).

WEBSITES

"Agent Orange: Background on Monsanto's Involvement." Monsanto, April 7, 2017. https://monsanto.com/company/media/statements/agent-orange-background/ (accessed October 4, 2017).

"AIDS Drugs for Africa March & Rally." ACT Up, March 5, 2001. http://www.actupny.org/reports/march5.html (accessed July 25, 2017).

"Globalization." *National Geographic*, March 28, 2011. https://www.nationalgeographic.org/encyclopedia/globalization/ (accessed July 27, 2017).

Prentice, Chris. "U.S. GMO Food Labeling Bill Passes Senate." Reuters, July 7, 2016. http://www.reuters.com/article/us-usa-food-gmo-vote-idUSKCN0ZO08N (accessed July 25, 2017).

Smith, Natalie. "What Is Occupy Wall Street?" Scholastic. http://www.scholastic.com/browse/article.jsp?id=3756681 (accessed July 27, 2017).

"World Trade Organization Protests in Seattle." Seattle.gov. https://www.seattle.gov/cityarchives/exhibits-and-education/digital-document-libraries/world-trade-organization-protests-in-seattle (accessed July 25, 2017).

Research and Activity Ideas

Animal Rights

Some of the animals discussed in this chapter include whales, elephants, and monkeys. Choose one animal mentioned in the chapter, or select an animal you would like to learn more about. Research that animal on the Internet or in the school library. Create a poster that includes a picture of the animal and facts about it. Be sure to include information about where the animal lives, what makes it unique, and how it interacts with humans. Present your poster to the rest of the class, and explain why you chose the animal you did.

Civil Rights, African American

The Freedom Riders protested segregation in the southern United States. The Freedom Riders' protests helped bring about the desegregation of public transportation. Many Freedom Riders were threatened and some were beaten for their protests. Write an editorial to a newspaper about why you think the Freedom Riders' protests were important and should be remembered today. Include specific details about the Freedom Riders and explain specific outcomes of their protests.

Civil Rights, Hispanic and Latino

Dolores Huerta was the cofounder of the National Farm Workers Association, which later became United Farm Workers (UFW). Huerta advocated for workers' rights throughout her life. Use the Internet or school library resources to research Huerta's life. Write a paragraph describing one event in which Huerta participated or one part of her life story that most interests you. Share your writing with the group.

Economic Discontent

The citizens of the United Kingdom launched campaigns for and against Britain's break from the European Union, which became known as "Brexit." Demonstrate the opposing sides by organizing into two groups: one to research economic arguments in support of leaving the European Union and the other to research economic arguments in support of staying in the European Union. With your group, prepare a speech explaining why the UK should leave or stay in the European Union. Then choose one representative from each group to present the speech to the whole class.

Environment

The Pacific Climate Warriors tried to prevent coal ships from leaving an Australian port in 2014. Use the Internet or school library resources to search for images of the Pacific Climate Warriors' protest. Have the class vote on one image to print. Post the image at the front of the class. Then, break into small groups to discuss what the image shows and how the people in the picture most likely felt. With your group, write a journal entry from the point of view of one of the protesters in the picture. Explain how that person felt during the protest and why that person wanted to protest. Also describe what the person hoped to change by protesting.

Free Speech

In 2001 a church group burned Harry Potter books. People have burned and banned books for many reasons throughout history. Use the Internet or your school library to learn about one of these banned books: *The Absolutely True Diary of a Part-Time Indian, The Adventures of Huckleberry Finn, The Call of the Wild, The Catcher in the Rye, Go Ask Alice, The Handmaid's Tale, I Know Why the Caged Bird Sings, The Outsiders,* or *Twilight*. Read about the history of the book and why it is considered controversial. Pretend leaders in your community are planning to ban the book you chose from the community library. Write and present a speech about why they should or should not ban the book from the library's shelves.

Globalization

Banksy is an artist whose works have shared messages about many topics, including globalization. Do you agree or disagree with Banksy's opinions about consumerism and globalization? Use the Internet or the school library to find images of anti-globalization artwork. Imagine that you are an artist. Create a piece of art in response to Bansky's art shown in this chapter. You may create a drawing, a painting, or a collage with pictures from magazines or the Internet. Present your artwork to the class.

Gun Control/Gun Rights

The Black Panther protest of 1967 and the "I Will Not Comply" rally in 2014 both supported gun rights. However, these protests had different goals and different methods pertaining to gun rights. Create a compare-contrast chart on a poster. Fill in details about each protest to show how they were similar and how they were different. Present your poster to the class.

Human Rights

In 1971 prisoners at the Attica prison rioted in response to overcrowding, lack of food, and a lack of medical care. The riot ended in a great deal of violence. In 2016 prisoners from at least a dozen prisons in the United States commemorated the Attica Prison Riot by refusing to work. Use the Internet or your school library to research this protest from 2016. Which conditions were the prisoners protesting in 2016? How did those conditions compare to the conditions at Attica in 1971? How did the 2016 protest differ from the 1971 protest? How was it similar? Write a two-paragraph essay comparing and contrasting the conditions both groups were protesting.

Immigrant Rights

The 1844 riots in Philadelphia focused on Irish immigrants, most of whom were Catholic. The 2017 travel ban protests focused mostly on Middle Eastern and African immigrants, most of whom were Muslim. Use the Internet or the school library to research immigration in the United States from the early 1800s to the present. How have immigration rates from various parts of the world changed over time? How did this change most likely affect protests for immigrants' rights? What role has religion or race played in who was allowed into the country? Write a short essay

RESEARCH AND ACTIVITY IDEAS

(a couple of paragraphs) about how changes in immigration over time have affected protests for immigrants' rights in the United States.

Independence Movements

Imagine that you are a citizen of India in 1930. You want India to have independence from the United Kingdom. One day you see Mohandas Gandhi and a few hundred followers marching toward the sea. Some of them tell you about their plans to collect salt. You decide to join the march. Write a letter to a friend about your experience on the Salt March with Gandhi. Tell your friend why you joined the march and how you felt after collecting salt. Describe to your friend your hope for the future of India.

Indigenous Peoples' Rights

Imagine that you have a friend from another part of the world who learned about the Dakota Access Pipeline and the protests by the Standing Rock Sioux in the news. Your friend wants to learn more about the protests. He or she wants to know about the protesters' goals. Gather information about the protest from the chapter. Use the Internet or your school library to do research if you need more information. Then, write a two-paragraph email to your friend explaining the reasons for the protests, the protesters' goals, and the outcome of the protests.

Labor Rights

In 1936 and 1937 workers at a General Motors plant went on strike. Imagine that you are a newspaper journalist living in Flint, Michigan, in the 1930s. You just learned that the workers at General Motors have gone on strike. Write a newspaper article about the strike. Include at least one made-up quotation from a striking worker in your article. If you need more information about the strike, use the Internet or school library resources to research the topic.

LGBTQ Rights

The Stonewall Riots are one of the earliest protests for LGBTQ rights. Since then, many important events have helped shape the LGBTQ rights movement. Use the Internet or school library resources to research important events that happened around the world and shaped this movement. Then create a timeline poster starting in the 1960s and ending in the present. Mark at least 10 important events that happened in the LGBTQ rights movement during that time.

Political/Government Uprisings

The Arab Spring started in December 2010 in Tunisia. Many protests followed the one in Tunisia. The effects of the Arab Spring are still being felt in the Middle East today. Use the Internet or the school library to research the events of the Arab Spring. Make a poster with a timeline listing the most important events from the Arab Spring. Start the timeline in 2010 and end it in the present. Present your timeline to the class and compare it to the timelines your classmates made. Discuss with classmates how the timelines are similar or different.

Racial Conflict

In 1976 thousands of black students in Soweto, South Africa, protested unfair government laws. Imagine that you are a news reporter covering the Soweto uprising. You have an opportunity to interview a number of protesters after the uprising ends. Write a list of questions you would ask them about their protest. Then make up answers that you think the protesters might give based on what you have read. Share your questions and answers with a small group.

Reproductive Rights

Reproductive rights differ from one country to another. Track the reproductive rights of different countries around the world. Organize into five groups and have each group choose a different continent (Africa, Asia, Europe, North America, and South America). Try to determine which country on your chosen continent offers the most reproductive rights and which country offers the fewest reproductive rights. Use the Internet or your school library to research the reproductive rights in different countries. With your group, prepare a two-minute presentation about the reproductive rights in the countries you studied. Share your presentation with the class.

Resistance to Nazis

The White Rose movement published informational pamphlets as a way to resist Nazis. Consider the information the White Rose movement most likely included in its pamphlets. Organize into small groups. Imagine you are members of the White Rose movement, and you are designing another pamphlet to hand out in Germany. Use the Internet or school library resources to research the White Rose movement's pamphlets. Make a similar pamphlet with your group. Include information in the pamphlet that you want other Germans to know about the Nazis. Present your finished pamphlets to the class.

Slavery

Enslaved Africans were unable to protest to gain their freedom. People who escaped enslavement, however, often wanted to share their stories. They wanted people to understand the horrors of slavery and the terrible conditions enslaved people faced. Many enslaved people who were freed or who escaped wrote stories about their lives. Using the Internet or the school library, find one of these stories written by Frederick Douglass, Olaudah Equiano, Harriet Ann Jacobs, Solomon Northup, William Wells Brown, Briton Hammon, or Mary Prince. Read part of the story. Write a paragraph explaining how anti-slavery protesters could have benefited from reading the story.

War

In 1965 a group of students in Des Moines, Iowa, decided to wear black arm bands to protest the Vietnam War. Their school tried to stop them. In response, the students' families sued the school. The court case, *Tinker v. Des Moines*, eventually reached the US Supreme Court. Imagine that you are a lawyer defending one of the students in *Tinker v. Des Moines*. Write a one- or two-paragraph statement that you want to present in the courtroom to support your client's protest. Be sure to include information about why the students protested and why you think they should be allowed to take part in such a protest.

Women's Rights

Both the women from Saudi Arabia who were involved in the Baladi campaign in 2015 and the American women who were involved in the women's suffrage protest in 1918 were protesting to gain the right to vote. Talk about the two protests with a partner. Discuss what one of the Saudi protesters and one of the American protesters might say to each other about their protests if they could meet each other. Write down notes about this imaginary conversation. Then, perform a short skit in front of the class to show what the two protesters might say when talking about their protests.

Where to Learn More

Books

Amison Lüsted. *Tiananmen Square Protests*. Edina, MN: ABDO, 2011.

Arsenault, Raymond. *Freedom Riders: 1961 and the Struggle for Racial Justice*. New York: Oxford University Press, 2006.

Bledsoe, Karen E. *Consumption and Waste*. New York: Bloomsbury, 2014.

Çinar, Özgür Heval. *Conscientious Objection to Military Service in International Human Rights Law*. New York: Palgrave Macmillan, 2013.

Cunningham, Anne. *Critical Perspectives on Gun Control*. Berkeley Heights, NJ: Enslow, 2017.

David, Laurie, and Cambria Gordon. *The Down-to-Earth Guide to Global Warming*. New York: Scholastic, 2007.

Fredrickson, George M. *Racism: A Short History*. Princeton, NJ: Princeton University Press, 2002.

Gitlin, Todd. *Occupy Nation: The Roots, the Spirit, and the Promise of Occupy Wall Street*. New York: HarperCollins Publishers, 2012.

Henderson, Timothy J. *The Mexican Wars for Independence*. New York: Hill and Wang, 2009.

Jenkins, Henry. *Convergence Culture: Where Old and New Media Collide*. New York: New York University Press, 2006.

Kelly, Nigel. *The Fall of the Berlin Wall: The Cold War Ends*. Rev. ed. Chicago: Heinemann, 2006.

Kinsbruner, Jay. *Independence in Spanish America: Civil Wars, Revolutions, and Underdevelopment*. Albuquerque: University of New Mexico Press, 2000.

Laine, Carolee. *Book Banning and Other Forms of Censorship*. Minneapolis, MN: ABDO, 2017.

Lennox, Corinne, and Damien Short, eds. *Handbook of Indigenous Peoples' Rights*. New York: Routledge, 2016.

Mize, Ronald L., and Grace Peña Delgado. *Latino Immigrants in the United States*. Cambridge, UK: Polity Press, 2012.

Oberg, Michael Leroy. *Native America: A History*. 2nd ed. Hoboken, New Jersey: Wiley-Blackwell, 2017.

Parks, Rosa. *Rosa Parks: My Story*. New York: Penguin, 1992.

Poehlmann, Tristan. *The Stonewall Riots: The Fight for LGBT Rights*. Minneapolis, MN: ABDO, 2017.

Reagan, Leslie J. *When Abortion Was a Crime: Women, Medicine, and Law in the United States, 1867–1973*. Berkeley: University of California Press, 1998.

Regan, Tom. *The Case for Animal Rights*. 2nd ed. Berkeley: University of California Press, 2004.

Robinson, J. Dennis. *Striking Back: The Fight to End Child Labor Exploitation*. Mankato, MN: Compass Point Books, 2010.

Rosinsky, Natalie M. *The Kent State Shootings*. Minneapolis: Compass Point Books, 2009.

Singer, Peter. *Animal Liberation: The Definitive Classic of the Animal Movement*. 40th anniversary ed. New York: Open Road Media, 2015.

Shuter, Jane. *Resistance to the Nazis*. Chicago: Heinemann, 2003.

Skocpol, Theda, and Vanessa Williamson. *The Tea Party and the Remaking of Republican Conservatism*. Oxford, UK: Oxford University Press, 2012.

Skurzynski, Gloria. *Sweat and Blood: A History of U.S. Labor Unions*. Minneapolis, MN: Twenty-First Century Books, 2009.

Stienstra, Deborah. *Women's Movements and International Organizations*. New York: St. Martin's Press, 1994.

Townsend, Riley M. *The European Migrant Crisis*. Morrisville, NC: Lulu, 2015.

Periodicals

Abend, Lisa. "In Spain, Human Rights for Apes." *Time* (July 18, 2008). Available online at http://content.time.com/time/world/article/0,8599,1824206,00.html (accessed July 10, 2017).

Abouzeid, Rania. "Bouazizi: The Man Who Set Himself and Tunisia on Fire." *Time* (January 21, 2011). Available online at http://content.time.com/time/magazine/article/0,9171,2044723,00.html (accessed August 18, 2017).

Aisch, Gregor, and K. K. Rebecca Lai. "The Conflicts along 1,172 Miles of the Dakota Access Pipeline." *New York Times* (March 23, 2017). Available online at https://www.nytimes.com/interactive/2016/11/23/us/dakota-access-pipeline-protest-map.html (accessed August 21, 2017).

Alexander, Harriet. "Who Is Chelsea Manning and Why Is She Being Released from Prison?" *Telegraph* (May 17, 2017). Available online at http://www.telegraph.co.uk/news/2017/05/17/chelsea-manning-released-prison/ (accessed September 20, 2017).

Anderson, John Ward. "Cartoons of Prophet Met with Outrage." *Washington Post* (January 31, 2006). Available online at http://www.washingtonpost.com/wp-dyn/content/article/2006/01/30/AR2006013001316.html (accessed July 25, 2017).

Archibold, Randal C. "Immigrants Take to U.S. Streets in Show of Strength." *New York Times* (May 2, 2006). Available online at http://www.nytimes.com/2006/05/02/us/02immig.html (accessed July 17, 2017).

"A Background Guide to 'Brexit' from the European Union." *Economist* (February 24, 2016). Available online at https://www.economist.com/blogs/graphicdetail/2016/02/graphics-britain-s-referendum-eu-membership (accessed July 24, 2017).

Bacon, John, and Alan Gomez. "Protests against Trump's Immigration Plan Rolling in More than 30 Cities." *USA Today* (January 29, 2017). Available online at https://www.usatoday.com/story/news/nation/2017/01/29/homeland-security-judges-stay-has-little-impact-travel-ban/97211720/ (accessed August 3, 2017).

Blair, David. "The World Has Over 45 Million Slaves—Including 1.2 Million in Europe—Finds New Study." *Telegraph* (May 31, 2016). Available online at http://www.telegraph.co.uk/news/2016/05/31/the-world-has-over-45-million-slaves---including-12-million-in-e/ (accessed August 28, 2017).

Blythe, Anne. "NC Law Replacing HB2 Is Still a Bathroom Bill That Discriminates, Challengers Claim." *News & Observer* (July 21, 2017). Available online at http://www.newsobserver.com/news/politics-government/state-politics/article162850673.html (accessed August 22, 2017).

Burton, Lynsi. "WTO Riots in Seattle: 15 Years Ago." *Seattle Post Intelligencer* (November 29, 2014). Available online at http://www.seattlepi.com/local/article/WTO-riots-in-Seattle-15-years-ago-5915088.php (accessed July 25, 2017).

"Casting Ballots, Saudi Women Proudly 'Make History.'" *Times of Israel* (December 13, 2015). Available online at http://www.timesofisrael.com/casting-ballots-saudi-women-proudly-make-history (accessed August 21, 2017).

Chertoff, Emily. "Occupy Wounded Knee: A 71-Day Siege and a Forgotten Civil Rights Movement." *Atlantic* (October 23, 2012). Available online at https://www.theatlantic.com/national/archive/2012/10/occupy-wounded-knee-a-71-day-siege-and-a-forgotten-civil-rights-movement/263998/ (accessed August 21, 2017).

Cobb, James C. "The Voting Rights Act at 50: How It Changed the World." *Time* (August 6, 2015). Available online at http://time.com/3985479/voting-rights-act-1965-results/ (accessed July 18, 2017).

Cohen, Sascha. "The Day Women Went on Strike." *Time* (August 26, 2015). Available online at http://time.com/4008060/women-strike-equality-1970 (accessed August 21, 2017).

Collins, Mike. "The Pros and Cons of Globalization." *Forbes* (May 6, 2015). Available online at https://www.forbes.com/sites/mikecollins/2015/05/06/the-pros-and-cons-of-globalization/#60ffb291ccce (accessed July 27, 2017).

"Dalit Anger Singes West India." *Times of India* (December 1, 2006). Available online at https://www.pressreader.com/india/the-times-of-india-new-delhi-edition/20061201/281552286366605 (accessed September 21, 2017).

Davis, Julie Hirschfeld, and Helene Cooper. "Trump Says Transgender People Will Not Be Allowed in the Military." *New York Times* (July 26, 2017). Available online at https://www.nytimes.com/2017/07/26/us/politics/trump-transgender-military.html (accessed August 23, 2017).

Davis, Kenneth C. "America's True History of Religious Tolerance." *Smithsonian* (October 2010). Available online at http://www.smithsonianmag.com/history/americas-true-history-of-religious-tolerance-61312684/ (accessed August 1, 2017).

Day, Elizabeth. "#BlackLivesMatter: The Birth of a New Civil Rights Movement." *Guardian* (July 19, 2015). Available online at https://www.theguardian.com/world/2015/jul/19/blacklivesmatter-birth-civil-rights-movement (accessed September 15, 2017).

Drezner, Daniel W. "A Clash between Administrators and Students at Yale Went Viral. Why That Is Unfortunate for All Concerned." *Washington Post* (November 9, 2015). Available online at https://www.washingtonpost.com/posteverything/wp/2015/11/09/a-clash-between-administrators-and-students-at-yale-went-viral-why-that-is-unfortunate-for-all-concerned/?utm_term=.bdfae3d5f34b (accessed July 25, 2017).

Eddy, Melissa. "Big Anti-Immigration Rally in Germany Prompts Counterdemonstrations." *New York Times* (January 12, 2015). Available online at https://www.nytimes.com/2015/01/13/world/europe/big-anti-immigration-rally-in-germany-prompts-counterdemonstrations.html (accessed July 27, 2017).

"800 Arrested at Berkeley; Students Paralyze Campus." *Harvard Crimson* (December 4, 1964). Available online at http://www.thecrimson.com/article/1964/12/4/800-arrested-at-berkeley-students-paralyze/ (accessed July 25, 2017).

Eilperin, Juliet. "The Keystone XL Pipeline and Its Politics, Explained." *Washington Post* (February 4, 2014). Available online at https://www.washingtonpost.com/news/the-fix/wp/2013/04/03/the-keystone-xl-pipeline-and-its-politics-explained/?utm_term=.2b02fc9a65c7 (accessed July 22, 2017).

Ellingwood, Ken. "In Mexico City, Crowds Protest Drug Violence." *Los Angeles Times* (May 8, 2011). Available online at http://articles.latimes.com/2011/may/08/world/la-fg-mexican-violence-protest-20110509 (accessed July 18, 2017).

Engler, Mark, and Paul Engler. "How Did Gandhi Win? Lessons from the Salt March." *Dissent* (October 10, 2014). Available online at https://www.dissentmagazine.org/blog/gandhi-win-lessons-salt-march-social-movements (accessed August 2, 2017).

Erb, Kelly Phillips. "Considering the Death Penalty: Your Tax Dollars at Work." *Forbes* (May 1, 2014). Available online at https://www.forbes.com/

sites/kellyphillipserb/2014/05/01/considering-the-death-penalty-your- tax-dollars-at-work/#3dbe69c7664b (accessed September 7, 2017).

Federoff, Nina. "Can We Trust Monsanto with Our Food?" *Scientific American* (July 25, 2013). Available online at https://www.scientificamerican.com/article/can-we-trust-monsanto-with-our-food/ (accessed July 25, 2017).

Fitz, Nicholas. "Economic Inequality: It's Far Worse than You Think." *Scientific American* (March 31, 2015). Available online at https://www.scientificamerican.com/article/economic-inequality-it-s-far-worse-than-you-think/ (accessed July 28, 2017).

Ford, Matt. "Can Europe End the Death Penalty in America?" *Atlantic* (February 18, 2014). Available online at https://www.theatlantic.com/international/archive/2014/02/can-europe-end-the-death-penalty-in-america/283790/ (accessed September 7, 2017).

Gaffey, Conor. "South Africa: What You Need to Know about the Soweto Uprising 40 Years Later." *Newsweek* (June 16, 2016). Available online at http://www.newsweek.com/soweto-uprising-hector-pieterson-memorial-471090 (accessed September 15, 2017).

Gopalakrishnan, Amulya, and Vaibhav Ganjapure. "10 Years Later, Khairlanji Shows How Caste Crimes Fester." *Times of India* (September 28, 2016). Available online at http://timesofindia.indiatimes.com/city/nagpur/10-years-later-Khairlanji-shows-how-caste-crimes-fester/articleshow/54568908.cms (accessed September 19, 2017).

Gordon, Noah. "The Little Rock Nine: How Far Has the Country Come?" *Atlantic* (September 25, 2014). Available online at https://www.theatlantic.com/politics/archive/2014/09/the-little-rock-nine/380676/ (accessed July 18, 2017).

Greenhouse, Steven. "With Day of Protests, Fast-Food Workers Seek More Pay." *New York Times* (November 30, 2012). Available online at http://www.nytimes.com/2012/11/30/nyregion/fast-food-workers-in-new-york-city-rally-for-higher-wages.html?mcubz=3 (accessed August 25, 2017).

Gregory, Alice. "A Brief History of the Zoot Suit: Unraveling the Jazzy Life of a Snazzy Style." *Smithsonian* (April 2016). Available online at http://www.smithsonianmag.com/arts-culture/brief-history-zoot-suit-180958507 (accessed September 15, 2017).

Grossman, David. "The Dakota Pipeline Controversy Explained." *Popular Mechanics* (January 24, 2017). Available online at http://www.popularmechanics.com/technology/infrastructure/a23658/dakota-pipeline-protests (accessed August 21, 2017).

Grossman, Ron. "Flashback: 'Swastika War': When the Neo-Nazis Fought in Court to March in Skokie." *Chicago Tribune* (January 1, 2002). Available online at http://www.chicagotribune.com/news/opinion/commentary/ct-neo-nazi-skokie-march-flashback-perspec-0312-20170310-story.html (accessed July 25, 2017).

WHERE TO LEARN MORE

Hall, Sarah. "Harry Potter and the Sermon of Fire." *Guardian* (January 1, 2002). Available online at https://www.theguardian.com/world/2002/jan/01/books.harrypotter (accessed July 25, 2017).

Havard, Kate, and Lori Aratani. "Nearly 1,000 March in D.C. for Gun Control." *Washington Post* (January 26, 2013). Available online at https://www.washingtonpost.com/local/trafficandcommuting/newtown-residents-among-those-at-dc-march-for-gun-control/2013/01/26/1813a3f6-67cb-11e2-85f5-a8a9228e55e7_story.html?utm_term=.c1c727450d42 (accessed August 8, 2017).

Hendel, John. "The Freedom Riders for Civil Rights, Half a Century Later." *Atlantic* (May 4, 2011). Available online at https://www.theatlantic.com/national/archive/2011/05/the-freedom-riders-for-civil-rights-half-a-century-later-life-photos/238342/ (accessed July 18, 2017).

Herszenhorn, David M. "Armenia, on Day of Rain and Sorrow, Observes 100th Anniversary of Genocide." *New York Times* (April 24, 2015). Available online at https://www.nytimes.com/2015/04/25/world/europe/armenian-genocide-100th-anniversary.html?mcubz=1&module=ArrowsNav&contentCollection=Europe&action=keypress&region=FixedLeft&pgtype=article (accessed September 8, 2017).

Herszenhorn, David M., and Emmarie Huetteman. "House Democrats' Gun-Control Sit-In Turns into Chaotic Showdown with Republicans." *New York Times* (June 23, 2016). Available online at https://www.nytimes.com/2016/06/23/us/politics/house-democrats-stage-sit-in-to-push-for-action-on-gun-control.html (accessed August 8, 2017).

Hingston, Sandy. "Bullets and Bigots: Remembering Philadelphia's 1844 Anti-Catholic Riots." *Philadelphia Magazine* (December 17, 2015). Available online at http://www.phillymag.com/news/2015/12/17/philadelphia-anti-catholic-riots-1844/ (accessed August 1, 2017).

Holmes, Steven A. "Disabled Protest and Are Arrested." *New York Times* (March 14, 1990). Available online at http://www.nytimes.com/1990/03/14/us/disabled-protest-and-are-arrested.html (accessed September 21, 2017).

Iracheta, Michelle. "Houston Group Protests Texas' Death Penalty." *Houston Chronicle* (October 26, 2014). Available online at http://www.chron.com/news/houston-texas/houston/article/Houston-group-protests-Texas-death-penalty-5848226.php (accessed September 7, 2017).

Iyengar, Rishi. "6 Questions You Might Have about Hong Kong's Umbrella Revolution." *Time* (October 5, 2014). Available online at http://time.com/3471366/hong-kong-umbrella-revolution-occupy-central-democracy-explainer-6-questions/ (accessed August 21, 2017).

Jacobs, Andrew. "Gay Festival in China Pushes Official Boundaries." *New York Times* (June 15, 2009). Available online at http://www.nytimes.com/2009/06/15/world/asia/15shanghai.html (accessed August 16, 2017).

Jaschik, Scott. "Racial Tensions Escalate." *Inside Higher Ed* (November 9, 2015). Available online at https://www.insidehighered.com/news/2015/

11/09/racial-tensions-escalate-u-missouri-and-yale (accessed July 25, 2017).

Kafanov, Lucy. "Turkey, Armenians Battle over Genocide 100 Years Later." *USA Today* (April 23, 2015). Available online at https://www.usatoday.com/story/news/world/2015/04/23/turkey-armenia-genocide-massacre-anniversary/26261059/ (accessed September 8, 2017).

Kaleem, Jaweed. "The Death Penalty Has Long Divided Americans. Here's Why Those Who Oppose It Are Winning." *Los Angeles Times* (April 27, 2017). Available online at http://www.latimes.com/nation/la-na-death-penalty-arkansas-20170427-htmlstory.html (accessed September 7, 2017).

Kifner, John. "Armenian Genocide of 1915: An Overview." *New York Times*, n.d. Available online at http://www.nytimes.com/ref/timestopics/topics_armeniangenocide.html?mcubz=0 (accessed September 8, 2017).

Koch, Wendy. "Tens of Thousands Demand Action on Climate Change." *USA Today* (February 17, 2013). Available online at https://www.usatoday.com/story/news/nation/2013/02/17/climate-change-rally-human-pipeline/1925719/ (accessed July 22, 2017).

Kopel, David. "The Warsaw Ghetto Uprising: Armed Jews vs. Nazis." *Washington Post* (October 10, 2015). Available online at https://www.washingtonpost.com/news/volokh-conspiracy/wp/2015/10/10/the-warsaw-ghetto-uprising-armed-jews-vs-nazis/?utm_term=.914e605236fd (accessed August 8, 2017).

Levitin, Michael. "The Triumph of Occupy Wall Street." *Atlantic* (June 10, 2015). Available online at https://www.theatlantic.com/politics/archive/2015/06/the-triumph-of-occupy-wall-street/395408/ (accessed July 27, 2017).

Liu, Melinda. "China Gay-Pride Event Meets Obstacles." *Newsweek* (June 12, 2009). Available online at http://www.newsweek.com/china-gay-pride-event-meets-obstacles-80291 (accessed August 16, 2017).

Lueck, Thomas J. "Threats and Responses: Protests; Candlelight Vigils Are Held around the World to Oppose Military Action against Iraq." *New York Times* (March 17, 2003). Available online at http://www.nytimes.com/2003/03/17/world/threats-responses-protests-candlelight-vigils-are-held-around-world-oppose.html?mcubz=1 (accessed September 22, 2017).

"Marchers in over 400 Cities Protest Monsanto." *Washington Post* (May 25, 2013). Available online at https://www.washingtonpost.com/politics/marchers-in-over-400-cities-protest-monsanto/2013/05/25/938dd988-c59b-11e2-914f-a7aba60512a7_story.html?utm_term=.cd0efcd95a22 (accessed July 25, 2017).

McCarthy, Tom. "Under the Umbrellas: What Do Hong Kong's Protesters Want from China?" *Guardian* (September 29, 2014). Available online at https://www.theguardian.com/world/2014/sep/29/hong-kong-democracy-protests-china-umbrellas-police (accessed August 21, 2017).

McFadden, Robert D. "The Republicans: The Convention in New York—The March; Vast Anti-Bush Rally Greets Republicans in New York." *New York Times* (August 30, 2004). Available online at http://www.nytimes.com/

2004/08/30/us/republicans-convention-new-york-march-vast-anti-bush-rally-greets-republicans.html?mcubz=1 (accessed September 22, 2017).

Mejia, Brittny, et al. "Armenian Genocide: Massive March Ends at Turkish Consulate in L.A." *Los Angeles Times* (April 24, 2015). Available online at http://www.latimes.com/local/lanow/la-me-ln-armenian-genocide-march-los-angeles-20150424-story.html (accessed September 8, 2017).

Meyer, Robinson. "The Standing Rock Sioux Claim 'Victory and Vindication' in Court." *Atlantic* (June 14, 2017). Available online at https://www.theatlantic.com/science/archive/2017/06/dakota-access-standing-rock-sioux-victory-court/530427/ (accessed August 21, 2017).

"Millions March against GM Crops." *Guardian* (May 25, 2013). Available online at https://www.theguardian.com/environment/2013/may/26/millions-march-against-monsanto (accessed July 25, 2017).

Minder, Raphael. "Animal Welfare Activists to Protest Bullfighting in Spain." *New York Times* (August 20, 2010). Available online at http://www.nytimes.com/2010/08/21/world/europe/21iht-spain.html (accessed July 12, 2017).

Patterson, Romaine. "Let Westboro Baptist Have Their Hate Speech. We'll Smother It with Peace." *Washington Post* (March 6, 2011). Available online at http://www.washingtonpost.com/wp-dyn/content/article/2011/03/04/AR2011030406330.html (accessed August 14, 2017).

Peters, Jeremy W., et al. "Pence Tells Anti-Abortion Marchers That 'Life Is Winning.'" *New York Times* (January 27, 2017). Available online at https://www.nytimes.com/2017/01/27/us/politics/march-for-life.html (accessed August 30, 2017).

"Prophet Mohammed Cartoon Controversy: Timeline." *Telegraph* (May 4, 2015). Available online at http://www.telegraph.co.uk/news/worldnews/europe/france/11341599/Prophet-Muhammad-cartoons-controversy-timeline.html (accessed July 25, 2017).

Rayman, Noah. "6 Things You Should Know about the Tiananmen Square Massacre." *Time* (June 4, 2014). Available online at http://time.com/2822290/tiananmen-square-massacre-facts-time/ (accessed August 23, 2017).

Remnick, Noah. "Yale Grapples with Ties to Slavery in Debate over a College's Name." *New York Times* (September 12, 2015). Available online at https://www.nytimes.com/2015/09/12/nyregion/yale-in-debate-over-calhoun-college-grapples-with-ties-to-slavery.html (accessed July 25, 2017).

Richmond, Emily. "Civics Lessons from the House Democrats' Sit-in." *Atlantic* (June 28, 2016). Available online at https://www.theatlantic.com/education/archive/2016/06/civics-lessons-from-the-house-democrats-sit-in/489167/ (accessed August 8, 2017).

Ross, Winston. "Protests Hit Netherlands in Wake of Paris Attack." *Newsweek* (January 7, 2015). Available online at http://www.newsweek.com/protests-hit-netherlands-wake-paris-attack-297459 (accessed July 25, 2017).

Rothman, Lily. "What We Still Get Wrong about What Happened in Detroit in 1967." *Time* (August 3, 2017). Available online at http://time.com/4879062/detroit-1967-real-history/ (accessed September 15, 2017).

Sanchez, Raf. "WikiLeaks Q & A: Who Is Bradley Manning and What Did He Do?" *Telegraph* (July 30, 2013). Available online at http://www.telegraph.co.uk/news/worldnews/wikileaks/10210160/WikiLeaks-Q-and-A-who-is-Bradley-Manning-and-what-did-he-do.html (accessed September 20, 2017).

Santora, Marc. "Yale Report Clears Police Officer in Encounter with Student." *New York Times* (March 5, 2015). Available online at https://www.nytimes.com/2015/03/05/nyregion/yale-report-clears-police-officer-in-encounter-with-student.html (accessed July 25, 2017).

Smith, Mitch. "Standing Rock Protest Camp, Once Home to Thousands, Is Razed." *New York Times* (February 23, 2017). Available online at https://www.nytimes.com/2017/02/23/us/standing-rock-protest-dakota-access-pipeline.html (accessed July 22, 2017).

Smith, Noah. "The Dark Side of Globalization: Why Seattle's 1999 Protesters Were Right." *Atlantic* (January 6, 2014). Available online at https://www.theatlantic.com/business/archive/2014/01/the-dark-side-of-globalization-why-seattles-1999-protesters-were-right/282831/ (accessed July 27, 2017).

Stack, Liam. "A Brief History of Deadly Attacks on Abortion Providers." *New York Times* (November 29, 2015). Available online at https://www.nytimes.com/interactive/2015/11/29/us/30abortion-clinic-violence.html (accessed August 31, 2017).

Steinfels, Peter. "Paris, May 1968: The Revolution That Never Was." *New York Times* (May 11, 2008). Available online at http://www.nytimes.com/2008/05/11/world/europe/11iht-paris.4.12777919.html (accessed July 24, 2017).

Steyn, Paul. "African Elephant Numbers Plummet 30 Percent, Landmark Survey Finds." *National Geographic* (August 31, 2016). Available online at http://news.nationalgeographic.com/2016/08/wildlife-african-elephants-population-decrease-great-elephant-census/ (accessed July 11, 2017).

Swarns, Rachel L. "Yale College Dean Torn by Racial Protests." *New York Times* (November 15, 2015). Available online at https://www.nytimes.com/2015/11/16/nyregion/yale-college-dean-torn-by-racial-protests.html (accessed July 25, 2017).

"Tiananmen Square 25 Years On: 'Every Person in the Crowd Was a Victim of the Massacre.'" *Guardian* (June 1, 2014). Available online at https://www.theguardian.com/world/2014/jun/01/tiananmen-square-25-years-every-person-victim-massacre (accessed August 23, 2017).

"A Timeline of the Dakota Access Oil Pipeline." *U.S. News & World Report* (February 22, 2017). Available online at https://www.usnews.com/news/north-dakota/articles/2017-02-22/a-timeline-of-the-dakota-access-oil-pipeline (accessed August 21, 2017).

Tremlett, Giles. "Spain Protesters Vote to Dismantle Puerta del Sol Tent City." *Guardian* (June 8, 2011). Available online at https://www.theguardian.com/

world/2011/jun/08/spain-protesters-dismantle-puerta-sol (accessed August 1, 2017).

"Why Islam Prohibits Images of Muhammad." *Economist* (January 19, 2015). Available online at https://www.economist.com/blogs/economist-explains/2015/01/economist-explains-12 (accessed July 25, 2017).

Wilkinson, Tracy. "New Report Raises Chilling Possibility That Mystery of 43 Mexican Students' Disappearance Will Never Be Solved." *Los Angeles Times* (April 25, 2016). Available online at http://www.latimes.com/world/mexico-americas/la-fg-mexico-students-20160425-story.html (accessed July 18, 2017).

Winkler, Adam. "The Secret History of Guns." *Atlantic* (September 2011). Available online at https://www.theatlantic.com/magazine/archive/2011/09/the-secret-history-of-guns/308608/ (accessed August 8, 2017).

Woo, Elaine. "'60s 'Blowouts': Leaders of Latino School Protest See Little Change." *Los Angeles Times* (March 7, 1988). Available online at http://articles.latimes.com/1988-03-07/local/me-488_1_lincoln-high-school-graduate (accessed July 13, 2017).

Worthington, Danika. "Meet the Disabled Activists from Denver Who Changed a Nation." *Denver Post* (July 5, 2017). Available online at http://www.denverpost.com/2017/07/05/adapt-disabled-activists-denver/ (accessed September 21, 2017).

Yee, Vivian, Kenan Davis, and Jugal K. Patel. "Here's the Reality about Illegal Immigrants in the United States." *New York Times* (March 2, 2017). Available online at https://www.nytimes.com/interactive/2017/03/06/us/politics/undocumented-illegal-immigrants.html (accessed July 19, 2017).

Yong, Ed. "How the March for Science Finally Found Its Voice." *Atlantic* (April 23, 2017). Available online at https://www.theatlantic.com/science/archive/2017/04/how-the-march-for-science-finally-found-its-voice/524022/ (accessed July 22, 2017).

Websites

"About." 18th Annual March to Abolish the Death Penalty – Oct 28, 2017. http://marchforabolition.org/about-2/ (accessed September 7, 2017).

Badcock, James. "Will Spain Ever Ban Bullfighting?" BBC News, December 3, 2016. http://www.bbc.com/news/world-europe-38063778 (accessed July 12, 2017).

Batha, Emma. "Europe's Refugee and Migrant Crisis in 2016. In Numbers." World Economic Forum, December 5, 2016. https://www.weforum.org/agenda/2016/12/europes-refugee-and-migrant-crisis-in-2016-in-numbers (accessed July 27, 2017).

Black, Richard. "Copenhagen Climate Accord: Key Issues" BBC News, December 19, 2009. http://news.bbc.co.uk/2/hi/science/nature/8422186.stm (accessed July 22, 2017).

Botelho, Greg. "Arab Spring Aftermath: Revolutions Give Way to Violence, More Unrest." CNN, March 2015. http://www.cnn.com/2015/03/27/middleeast/arab-spring-aftermath/index.html (accessed August 18, 2017).

"Chicano Movement." Brown University. http://www.brown.edu/Research/Coachella/chicano.html (accessed July 13, 2017).

"Civil Rights at Stonewall National Monument." National Park Service, October 17, 2016. https://www.nps.gov/places/stonewall.htm (accessed August 17, 2017).

Connolly, Katie. "What Exactly Is the Tea Party?" BBC News, September 16, 2010. http://www.bbc.com/news/world-us-canada-11317202 (accessed July 14, 2017).

Convention on International Trade in Endangered Species of Wild Fauna and Flora (CITES). https://www.cites.org/ (accessed July 10, 2017).

"Czech Republic Slovakia: Velvet Revolution at 25." BBC News, November 17, 2014. http://www.bbc.com/news/world-europe-30059011 (accessed August 4, 2017).

"The Death Penalty in United States of America." Cornell Center on the Death Penalty Worldwide, March 10, 2014. http://www.deathpenaltyworldwide.org/country-search-post.cfm?country=united+states+of+america (accessed September 7, 2017).

Dwyer, Colin. "Protests against Planned Parenthood Rouse Dueling Rallies Nationwide." National Public Radio, February 11, 2017. http://www.npr.org/sections/thetwo-way/2017/02/11/514717975/protests-against-planned-parenthood-rouse-dueling-rallies-nationwide (accessed August 31, 2017).

"Episode 337: The Secret Document That Transformed China." *Planet Money*, National Public Radio, May 14, 2014. http://www.npr.org/sections/money/2014/05/14/312488659/episode-337-the-secret-document-that-transformed-china (accessed July 19, 2017).

Fessenden, Marissa. "How a Nearly Successful Slave Revolt Was Intentionally Lost to History." *Smithsonian*. http://www.smithsonianmag.com/smart-news/its-anniversary-1811-louisiana-slave-revolt-180957760 (accessed August 25, 2017).

"45.8 Million People Are Enslaved across the World." Global Slavery Index, May 30, 2016. https://www.globalslaveryindex.org/media/45-8-million-people-enslaved-across-world/ (accessed August 28, 2017).

"The Freedom Rides: CORE Volunteers Put Their Lives on the Road." Congress of Racial Equality (CORE). http://www.core-online.org/History/freedom%20rides.htm (accessed July 18, 2017).

Friedman, Gail. "March of the Mill Children." Encyclopedia of Greater Philadelphia. http://philadelphiaencyclopedia.org/archive/march-of-the-mill-children/ (accessed August 25, 2017).

Gamboa, Suzanne. "For Latinos, 1965 Voting Rights Act Impact Came a Decade Later." NBC News, August 6, 2015. http://www.nbcnews.com/

news/latino/latinos-1965-voting-rights-act-impact-came-decade-later-n404936 (accessed July 20, 2017).

"The Global Divide on Homosexuality." Pew Research Center, June 4, 2013. http://www.pewglobal.org/2013/06/04/the-global-divide-on-homosexuality/ (accessed August 16, 2017).

"Globalization." *National Geographic*, March 28, 2011. https://www.nationalgeographic.org/encyclopedia/globalization/ (accessed July 27, 2017).

Goodman, Al. "Thousands of Spaniards Call for Economic Reform in New Protest." CNN, June 19, 2011. http://www.cnn.com/2011/WORLD/europe/06/19/spain.protests/ (accessed August 1, 2017).

"The Grito de Lares: The Rebellion of 1868." Library of Congress. https://www.loc.gov/collections/puerto-rico-books-and-pamphlets/articles-and-essays/nineteenth-century-puerto-rico/rebellion-of-1868 (accessed July 31, 2017).

"Gun Violence." Brady Campaign to Prevent Gun Violence. http://www.bradycampaign.org/gun-violence (accessed August 8, 2017).

"Hate Crimes Law." Human Rights Campaign. http://www.hrc.org/resources/hate-crimes-law (accessed August 15, 2017).

Hersher, Rebecca. "Key Moments in the Dakota Access Pipeline Fight." National Public Radio, February 22, 2017. http://www.npr.org/sections/thetwo-way/2017/02/22/514988040/key-moments-in-the-dakota-access-pipeline-fight (accessed August 21, 2017).

"Hispanics in the US Fast Facts." CNN, March 31, 2017. http://www.cnn.com/2013/09/20/us/hispanics-in-the-u-s-/index.html (accessed July 27, 2017).

"History—Incident at Wounded Knee." US Marshals Service. https://www.usmarshals.gov/history/wounded-knee/ (accessed August 21, 2017).

"Hong Kong Protests: Timeline of the Occupation." BBC News, December 11, 2014. http://www.bbc.com/news/world-asia-china-30390820 (accessed August 21, 2017).

"How the United States Immigration System Works." American Immigration Council, August 12, 2016. https://www.americanimmigrationcouncil.org/research/how-united-states-immigration-system-works (accessed July 19, 2017).

"India's Dalits: Between Atrocity and Protest." Human Rights Watch, January 12, 2007. https://www.hrw.org/news/2007/01/12/indias-dalits-between-atrocity-and-protest (accessed September 21, 2017).

"Indigenous Peoples." The World Bank. http://www.worldbank.org/en/topic/indigenouspeoples (accessed August 21, 2017).

International Congress of Women. "Final Programme." Gothenburg University Library. http://www.ub.gu.se/kvinndata/portaler/fred/samarbete/pdf/program_1915.pdf (accessed September 8, 2017).

Johnson, Troy. "We Hold the Rock." National Park Service, February 27, 2015. https://www.nps.gov/alca/learn/historyculture/we-hold-the-rock.htm (accessed August 21, 2017).

Jones, Owen. "The People Are Revolting—the History of Protest." BBC. http://www.bbc.co.uk/timelines/ztvxtfr (accessed August 15, 2017).

Kauffman, Stephen. "They Abandoned Their Wheelchairs and Crawled Up the Capitol Steps." ShareAmerica, March 12, 2015. https://share.america.gov/crawling-up-steps-demand-their-rights/ (accessed September 21, 2017).

Kennedy, Merrit. "A Look at Egypt's Uprising, 5 Years Later." National Public Radio, January 25, 2016. http://www.npr.org/sections/thetwo-way/2016/01/25/464290769/a-look-at-egypts-uprising-5-years-later (accessed August 15, 2017).

Kim, Inga. "The 1965–1970 Delano Grape Strike and Boycott." United Farm Workers, March 7, 2017. http://ufw.org/1965-1970-delano-grape-strike-boycott (accessed August 25, 2017).

Kurtzleben, Danielle. "100 Days In, Women's March Still Inspires. But Can the Enthusiasm Hold?" National Public Radio, April 28, 2017. http://www.npr.org/2017/04/28/525764938/100-days-in-womens-march-still-inspires-but-can-the-enthusiasm-hold (accessed August 21, 2017).

Lee, Brianna, and Danielle Renwick. "Mexico's Drug War." Council on Foreign Relations, May 25, 2017. https://www.cfr.org/backgrounder/mexicos-drug-war (accessed July 18, 2017).

Lee, Trymaine. "Justice for All: Thousands March against Police Violence." MSNBC, July 21, 2015. http://www.msnbc.com/msnbc/justice-all-thousands-expected-march-washington-against-police-violence (accessed September 15, 2017).

Lewis, Jerry M., and Thomas R. Hensley. "The May 4 Shootings at Kent State University: The Search for Historical Accuracy." Kent State University. http://www.kent.edu/may-4-historical-accuracy (accessed September 7, 2017).

"LGBT Rights Milestones Fast Facts." CNN, July 4, 2017. http://www.cnn.com/2015/06/19/us/lgbt-rights-milestones-fast-facts/index.html (accessed August 23, 2017).

"Little Rock Central High School: Crisis Timeline." National Park Service. https://www.nps.gov/chsc/learn/historyculture/timeline.htm (accessed July 18, 2017).

López, Gustavo, and Kristen Bialik. "Key Findings about U.S. Immigrants." Pew Research Center, May 3, 2017. http://www.pewresearch.org/fact-tank/2017/05/03/key-findings-about-u-s-immigrants/ (accessed July 17, 2017).

"Malala's Story." Malala Fund. https://www.malala.org/malalas-story (accessed August 21, 2017).

Malik, Asad. "Charles Deslondes and the American Uprising of 1811." Pan-African Alliance. https://www.panafricanalliance.com/charles-deslondes (accessed August 25, 2017).

WHERE TO LEARN MORE

"Māori Land Rights." Museum of New Zealand. http://sites.tepapa.govt.nz/sliceofheaven/web/html/landrights.html (accessed August 21, 2017).

"March for Science." EarthDay.org, April 22, 2017. http://www.earthday.org/marchforscience/ (accessed July 22, 2017).

"March on Washington for Jobs and Freedom." National Park Service. https://www.nps.gov/articles/march-on-washington.htm (accessed July 18, 2017).

"The Matthew Shepard and James Byrd, Jr., Hate Crimes Prevention Act of 2009." US Department of Justice. https://www.justice.gov/crt/matthew-shepard-and-james-byrd-jr-hate-crimes-prevention-act-2009-0 (accessed August 15, 2017).

Meincke, Paul. "Protests Mark 100th Anniversary of Armenian Massacres." ABC News 7, April 24, 2015. http://abc7chicago.com/news/protests-mark-100th-anniversary-of-armenian-massacres-/679914/ (accessed September 8, 2017).

Michals, Debra. "Ruby Bridges (1954–)." National Women's History Museum, 2015. https://www.nwhm.org/education-resources/biography/biographies/ruby-bridges (accessed July 18, 2017).

"The Modern Environmental Movement." Public Broadcasting Service. http://www.pbs.org/wgbh/americanexperience/features/earth-days-modern-environmental-movement/ (accessed July 22, 2017).

"Murder in Mississippi." Public Broadcasting Service. http://www.pbs.org/wgbh/americanexperience/features/freedomsummer-murder/ (accessed July 18, 2017).

"Muslims Protest Danish Muhammad Cartoons." NBC News, February 15, 2008. http://www.nbcnews.com/id/23186467/ns/world_news-europe/t/muslims-protest-danish-muhammad-cartoons/#.WW9wZITyuUl (accessed July 25, 2017).

National Rifle Association (NRA). https://home.nra.org/ (accessed August 8, 2017).

"1943: Zoot Suit Riots." *National Geographic.* https://www.nationalgeographic.org/thisday/jun3/zoot-suit-riots (accessed September 15, 2017).

"Obergefell v. Hodges." Oyez. https://www.oyez.org/cases/2014/14-556 (accessed August 18, 2017).

"The Official Harvey Milk Biography." Milk Foundation. http://milkfoundation.org/about/harvey-milk-biography (accessed August 22, 2017).

"Our History." Royal Society for the Prevention of Cruelty to Animals (RSPCA). https://www.rspca.org.uk/whatwedo/whoweare/history (accessed July 11, 2017).

Pao, Maureen. "Cesar Chavez: The Life behind a Legacy of Farm Labor Rights." National Public Radio, August 12, 2016. http://www.npr.org/2016/08/02/488428577/cesar-chavez-the-life-behind-a-legacy-of-farm-labor-rights (accessed July 14, 2017).

Pilgrim, David. "What Was Jim Crow." Ferris State University, September 2000. https://ferris.edu/HTMLS/news/jimcrow/what/ (accessed August 23, 2017).

"Polish Resistance and Conclusions." United States Holocaust Memorial Museum. https://www.ushmm.org/learn/students/learning-materials-and-resources/poles-victims-of-the-nazi-era/polish-resistance-and-conclusions (accessed August 2, 2017).

"The Raid on Harpers Ferry." Public Broadcasting Service. http://www.pbs.org/wgbh/aia/part4/4p2940.html (accessed August 21, 2017).

Ravitz, Jessica. "The Surprising History of Abortion in the United States." CNN, June 27, 2016. http://www.cnn.com/2016/06/23/health/abortion-history-in-united-states/index.html (accessed August 31, 2017).

"Rescue in Denmark." United States Holocaust Memorial Museum. https://www.ushmm.org/outreach/en/article.php?ModuleId=10007740 (accessed August 2, 2017).

"Rock Hill, South Carolina, Students Sit-In for US Civil Rights, 1960." Global Nonviolent Action Database at Swarthmore College. http://nvdatabase.swarthmore.edu/content/rock-hill-south-carolina-students-sit-us-civil-rights-1960 (accessed July 18, 2017).

"'Satanic' Harry Potter Books Burnt." BBC News, December 31, 2001. http://news.bbc.co.uk/2/hi/entertainment/1735623.stm (accessed July 25, 2017).

Schwartz, Daniel. "What Happened after the Arab Spring?" CBC News, August 4, 2014. http://www.cbc.ca/news/world/what-happened-after-the-arab-spring-1.2723934 (accessed August 18, 2017).

"September 11th Terror Attacks Fast Facts." CNN, August 24, 2017. http://www.cnn.com/2013/07/27/us/september-11-anniversary-fast-facts/index.html (accessed September 22, 2017).

"Shanghai to Show Pride with Gay Festival." BBC News, June 6, 2009. http://news.bbc.co.uk/1/hi/world/asia-pacific/8083672.stm (accessed August 16, 2017).

Smith, Natalie. "What Is Occupy Wall Street?" Scholastic. http://www.scholastic.com/browse/article.jsp?id=3756681 (accessed July 27, 2017).

"Spain's Indignados Protest Here to Stay." BBC News, May 15, 2012. http://www.bbc.com/news/world-europe-18070246 (accessed July 18, 2017).

"Syrian War Monitor Says 465,000 Killed in Six Years of Fighting." Reuters, March 13, 2017. http://www.reuters.com/article/us-mideast-crisis-syria-casualties-idUSKBN16K1Q1 (accessed August 18, 2017).

"Timeline: Iraq War." BBC News, July 5, 2016. http://www.bbc.com/news/magazine-36702957 (accessed September 22, 2017).

"Timeline: Tiananmen Protests." BBC News, June 2, 2014. http://www.bbc.com/news/world-asia-china-27404764 (accessed August 23, 2017).

WHERE TO LEARN MORE

"Tinker v. Des Moines Independent Community School Dist." Cornell Law School. https://www.law.cornell.edu/supremecourt/text/393/503 (accessed August 31, 2017).

"Topics in Chronicling America—The Haymarket Affair." Library of Congress. https://www.loc.gov/rr/news/topics/haymarket.html (accessed August 25, 2017).

"Trafficking in Persons Report." US Department of State, June 2017. https://www.state.gov/documents/organization/271339.pdf (accessed August 23, 2017).

"Treblinka Death Camp Revolt." United States Holocaust Memorial Museum. https://www.ushmm.org/research/the-center-for-advanced-holocaust-studies/miles-lerman-center-for-the-study-of-jewish-resistance/medals-of-resistance-award/treblinka-death-camp-revolt (accessed July 31, 2017).

"The Triangular Slave Trade: Overview." BBC. http://www.bbc.co.uk/bitesize/ks3/history/industrial_era/the_slave_trade/revision/2/ (accessed August 28, 2017).

Tuysuz, Gul. "What Is Sharia Law?" CNN, August 16, 2016. http://www.cnn.com/2016/08/16/world/sharia-law-definition/index.html (accessed August 21, 2017).

"2015 Charlie Hebdo Attacks Fast Facts." CNN, December 22, 2016. http://www.cnn.com/2015/01/21/europe/2015-paris-terror-attacks-fast-facts/index.html (accessed July 25, 2017).

"The 2016 ITUC Global Rights Index: The World's Worst Countries for Workers." International Trade Union Confederation (ITUC). https://www.ituc-csi.org/IMG/pdf/ituc-violationmap-2016-en_final.pdf (accessed August 25, 2017).

"The Velvet Revolution, November 1989." Association for Diplomatic Studies and Training. http://adst.org/2015/10/the-velvet-revolution-november-1989 (accessed August 4, 2017).

"Warsaw." United States Holocaust Memorial Museum. https://www.ushmm.org/wlc/en/article.php?ModuleId=10005069 (accessed August 8, 2017).

Weeks, Linton. "Whatever Happened to the Anti-War Movement?" National Public Radio, April 15 2011. www.npr.org/2011/04/15/135391188/whatever-happened-to-the-anti-war-movement (accessed September 22, 2017).

"What Are Human Rights?" United Nations Human Rights Office of the High Commissioner. http://www.ohchr.org/EN/Issues/Pages/WhatareHumanRights.aspx (accessed September 19, 2017).

"What Does Free Speech Mean?" US Courts. http://www.uscourts.gov/about-federal-courts/educational-resources/about-educational-outreach/activity-resources/what-does (accessed July 25, 2017).

"What Is Fracking and Why Is It Controversial?" BBC News, December 16, 2015. http://www.bbc.com/news/uk-14432401 (accessed July 22, 2017).

"What Is the Americans with Disabilities Act (ADA)?" ADA National Network. https://adata.org/learn-about-ada (accessed September 21, 2017).

"White Rose." United States Holocaust Memorial Museum. https://www.ushmm.org/wlc/en/article.php?ModuleId=10007188 (accessed August 4, 2017).

"WikiLeaks Fast Facts." CNN. http://www.cnn.com/2013/06/03/world/wikileaks-fast-facts/index.html (accessed September 20, 2017).

"Woman Suffrage Timeline (1840–1920)." National Women's History Museum. https://www.nwhm.org/education-resources/history/woman-suffrage-timeline (accessed August 21, 2017).

"World Trade Organization Protests in Seattle." Seattle.gov. https://www.seattle.gov/cityarchives/exhibits-and-education/digital-document-libraries/world-trade-organization-protests-in-seattle (accessed July 25, 2017).

"Yale Students March over Concerns of Racism." CBS News, November 9, 2015. http://www.cbsnews.com/news/yale-students-march-over-concerns-of-racism/ (accessed July 25, 2017).

Zhou, David. "Operation Rescue Activists Resist Abortion Clinic in Wichita, Kansas (Summer of Mercy), 1991." Global Nonviolent Action Database, April 30, 2012. http://nvdatabase.swarthmore.edu/content/operation-rescue-activists-resist-abortion-clinic-wichita-kansas-summer-mercy-1991 (accessed August 28, 2017).

Other

Blackfish. Documentary. Directed by Gabriela Cowperthwaite. New York: Magnolia Pictures, 2013.

Britches. Documentary. Directed by Lori Gruen, Norfolk, VA: PETA, 1986.

A Day without a Mexican. DVD. Directed by Sergio Arau. Los Angeles: Altavista Films, 2004.

Gasland. Documentary. Directed by Josh Fox. Brooklyn, NY: International WOW Company, 2010.

An Inconvenient Truth. Documentary. Directed by Davis Guggenheim. Los Angeles: Paramount Pictures, 2006.

The Ivory Game. Documentary. Directed by Richard Ladkani and Kief Davidson. Vienna, Austria: Terra Mater Factual Studios, 2016.

General Index

Italic type indicates volume numbers; **boldface** indicates main entries. Illustrations are marked by (ill.).

A

A21 Campaign, *3:* 647
Abdullah bin Abdulaziz al Saud, King of Saudi Arabia, *3:* 715–716
Abernathy, Ralph, *1:* 36 (ill.)
Ableism, *2:* 276
Abolition of slavery, *2:* 267–268; *3:* 511–512. *See also* **Slavery**
    Harpers Ferry Raid (1859), *3:* 638–643, 642 (ill.)
    Mauritania, *3:* 643
    United Kingdom, *3:* 637
    United States, *3:* 633
    Washington, D.C., *3:* 633
Abolitionist movement, *3:* 622, 638, 639
Aboriginal Land Rights Protest (1988), *2:* 375–379, 378 (ill.). *See also* **Indigenous peoples' rights**
Aboriginals, *2:* 365–366, 375–379
Abortion, *3:* 549. *See also* **Reproductive rights**
    anti-abortion laws, *3:* 552–553
    blocking access to clinics, *3:* 557–558, 562–568, 566–567
    history, *3:* 551–553
    late-term, *3:* 566
    legalization of, *3:* 575–576
Abzug, Bella, *3:* 560
ACCD (American Coalition of Citizens with Disabilities), *2:* 279
ACLU (American Civil Liberties Union), *2:* 460, 461–462, 464

ACT UP, HIV/AIDS demonstration, *2:* 433 (ill.)
Activists
    animal rights, *1:* 4, 7–11, 10 (ill.), 12–13, 25–26
    labor, *1:* 75–76
    scientists, *1:* 168
ADA (United States. Americans with Disabilities Act), *2:* 277, 280–283
ADAPT (American Disabled for Accessible Public Transit), *2:* 279–280, 283
Addams, Jane, *3:* 660, 660 (ill.)
ADL (Anti-Defamation League), *2:* 446
Afghanistan War, *3:* 681–682
    civilian casualties, *3:* 684
    refugees, *2:* 319
AFL (American Federation of Labor), *2:* 409
Africa
    child labor, *2:* 399
    slavery, *3:* 620–621
African American civil rights, *1:* **35–70**, 36 (ill.), 39 (ill.), 45 (ill.), 52 (ill.), 53 (ill.), 56 (ill.), 58 (ill.), 61 (ill.), 65 (ill.). *See also* Civil rights; **Racial conflict**
    Bridges, Ruby, *1:* 53, 53 (ill.)
    desegregation in Birmingham, Alabama, *1:* 62
    Freedom Rides (1961), *1:* 54–59, 56 (ill.)
    Little Rock Nine Crisis (1957), *1:* 47–52, 52 (ill.)
    Lunch Counter Protest, McCrory's (1961), *1:* 59–63, 61 (ill.)
    March on Washington for Jobs and Freedom (1963), *1:* 39 (ill.), 63–69, 65 (ill.)

lxix

GENERAL INDEX

Mississippi Summer Project/Freedom Summer Voter Registration, *1:* 58, 58 (ill.)
Montgomery Bus Boycott (1955–1956), *1:* 36 (ill.), 42–47
African Americans
  racial discrimination, *1:* 36–37; *3:* 512, 513–515
  violence against, *1:* 38, 40, 56–57, 56 (ill.), 58, 62; *3:* 526–527
  voting rights, *1:* 40
African slave trade, *3:* 620–621, 621 (ill.)
  end of, *3:* 622
  triangular trade, *3:* 621
Afrikaans, *3:* 534–535
Afrikaners, *3:* 533
Agent Orange, *1:* 223
Agha-Soltan, Neda, *3:* 490–491, 491 (ill.)
Agricultural Workers Organizing Committee (AWOC), *2:* 418
Ahmadinejad, Mahmoud, *3:* 490
AIM (American Indian Movement), *2:* 364–365, 371–372
AIM (American Indian Movement) Occupation of Wounded Knee (1973), *2:* 364–365, 367–375, 374 (ill.). *See also* **Indigenous peoples' rights**
Airports, anti-Trump travel ban protests, *2:* 330–331, 330 (ill.)
Alabama
  desegregation, *1:* 62
  Freedom Rides, *1:* 56, 56 (ill.), 57
  Montgomery Bus Boycott (1955–1956), *1:* 36 (ill.), 42–47
Alamagordo, NM, book burning, *1:* 181 (ill.)
Alamagordo Public Library, *1:* 182
Alcatraz, occupation by Native Americans, *2:* 370–371, 371 (ill.)
Alexander the Great, *2:* 430
Alexis, Aaron, *2:* 253
ALF (Animal Liberation Front), *1:* 7–11
  activists, *1:* 10 (ill.)
  debate over methods, *1:* 11
  founding, *1:* 8
  use of arson, *1:* 10–11
Allende, Salvador, *1:* 106–107, 107 (ill.)
Alliance of Small Island States (AOSIS), *1:* 146, 147
Allred, Gloria, *3:* 577 (ill.)

Alt Right, *3:* 542, 543
Amazon rain forest, *2:* 366, 379–384
Amazonian indigenous peoples, *2:* 366, 379–384. *See also* Indigenous peoples
Ambedkar, Bhimrao Ramji, *2:* 291–293, 295
American Airlines Flight 11, *3:* 677, 678
American Airlines Flight 77, *3:* 677
American Civil Liberties Union (ACLU), *2:* 460, 461–462, 464
American Coalition of Citizens with Disabilities (ACCD), *2:* 279
American Federation of Labor (AFL), *2:* 409
American Horse, *2:* 373
American Indian Movement (AIM), *2:* 364–365, 371–372
American Indian Movement (AIM) Occupation of Wounded Knee (1973), *2:* 364–365, 367–375, 374 (ill.)
American Library Association, *1:* 180
American Protestant Association, *2:* 315, 316
American Psychiatric Association (APA), *2:* 432
American Recovery and Reinvestment Act (ARRA), *1:* 113
American Republican Association, *2:* 315
American Revolutionary War (1775–1783), *2:* 233, 335–337; *3:* 471. *See also* United States
American Society for the Prevention of Cruelty to Animals (ASPCA), *1:* 3
  circus animals, *1:* 29
  position on ALF methods, *1:* 11
American War of Independence (1775–1783), *2:* 233, 335–337; *3:* 471. *See also* United States
American westward expansion, *3:* 638, 639–640. *See also* United States
Americans for Responsible Solutions, *2:* 248
Americans with Disabilities Act (ADA), *2:* 277, 280–283
Amherst, NY, Operation Rescue protests, *3:* 562–568
Amnesty International, *3:* 474
Anarchists, *1:* 213–214
Ancient Greece
  free speech, *1:* 172
  slavery, *3:* 617–619
Anderson, John Ward, *1:* 185

Andry, Manuel, *3:* 625–627
Angel Action, *2:* 449–451, 449 (ill.), 451
Anielewicz, Mordechai, *3:* 605
Animal cruelty, *1:* 4
Animal experimentation, *1:* 7–11. *See also* **Animal rights**
Animal Liberation: A New Ethics for Our Treatment of Animals (1975), *1:* 3–4
Animal Liberation Front (ALF), *1:* 7–11
    activists, *1:* 10 (ill.)
    debate over methods, *1:* 11
    founding, *1:* 8
    use of arson, *1:* 10–11
Animal rights, *1:* **1–33**, 6 (ill.), 10 (ill.), 13 (ill.), 17 (ill.), 23 (ill.), 24 (ill.)
    Bilbao Anti-bullfighting Protest (2010), *1:* 12–18, 17 (ill.)
    Blackfish Documentary and SeaWorld Protests (2013-2014), *1:* 25–31
    Circus animals, *1:* 5, 29, 29 (ill.)
    Global March for Elephants and Rhinos, *1:* 18–25, 24 (ill.)
    Greenpeace and whaling, *1:* 22–23, 23 (ill.)
    ongoing fight for, *1:* 4–5
    PETA antifur campaign, *1:* 12–13, 13 (ill.)
    protests, *1:* 5–7
    UCR Lab Raid (1985), *1:* 7–11
Animal rights activists, *1:* 4
    ALF, *1:* 10 (ill.)
    anti-fur campaign, *1:* 12–13
    SeaWorld protests, *1:* 25–26
    UCR lab raid, *1:* 7–11
Animal rights movement
    history, *1:* 1–7
    modern, *1:* 3–4
Animal rights organizations, *1:* 2–3
Animal Welfare Act of 1966, *1:* 3
Anima-Naturalis, *1:* 17, 17 (ill.)
Anniston, Alabama, *1:* 56
Anthony, Susan B., *3:* 697 (ill.), 713
Anti-abortion laws, *3:* 552–553, 561, 580
Anti-abortion protesters, *3:* 558, 564 (ill.), 567 (ill.)
Anti-Catholicism, *2:* 313
Anti-Defamation League (ADL), *2:* 446
Antifa, *3:* 542

Anti-fur campaign, *1:* 12–13, 13 (ill.)
Anti-gay laws. *See also* **LGBTQ rights**
    protests against in Russia, *2:* 455 (ill.)
    Russia, *2:* 454–455
    United States, *2:* 432
Anti-gay protests
    counterprotests, *2:* 448, 449–451
    Westboro Baptist Church, *2:* 448, 449–451, 451
Anti-immigrant riots, *2:* 328–329, 329 (ill.)
Anti-Islam movement, *2:* 322–323
Anti-migrant protests
    Dresden, Germany, *2:* 321, 323 (ill.)
    Warsaw, Poland, *2:* 323
Anti-slavery Day, *3:* 647
Anti-slavery petitions, *3:* 628–634
Anti-war protests, *3:* **651–692**, 656 (ill.), 660 (ill.), 667 (ill.), 668 (ill.), 679 (ill.), 674 (ill.), 679 (ill.), 682 (ill.), 686 (ill.). *See also* Pacifists
    burning draft cards, *3:* 666–667, 667 (ill.)
    Candlelight Vigils against Invasion of Iraq (2003), *3:* 676–683, 682 (ill.)
    Democratic National Convention (DNC) (1968), *3:* 656 (ill.)
    International Congress of Women, *3:* 657–663, 660 (ill.)
    Iraq War (2003–2011), *3:* 657, 682 (ill.)
    Manning, Chelsea, and WikiLeaks, *3:* 684–690, 686 (ill.)
    One Thousand Coffins Protest (2004), *3:* 678–679, 679 (ill.)
    Student Armband Protest of Vietnam War (1965–1969), *3:* 663–668, 668 (ill.)
    United States, *3:* 653–657
    Vietnam War (1954–1975), *3:* 655–656, 663–668, 669–676
AOSIS (Alliance of Small Island States), *1:* 146, 147
APA (American Psychiatric Association), *2:* 432
Apartheid, *3:* 531, 534, 539. *See also* Desegregation/Segregation; Racial discrimination
Apprentices, *2:* 395
Arab Spring, *1:* 90, 120, 219; *3:* 486–493. *See also* **Political/Government uprisings**
    Bahrain, *3:* 489
    Egypt, *3:* 495
    Libya, *3:* 489–490

GENERAL INDEX

origins, *3:* 487–488
spread of, *3:* 489–490
Syria, *3:* 491–493, 492 (ill.)
Tunisia, *2:* 318–319
Yemen, *3:* 488–489
Argentina, March against Monsanto, *1:* 228
Aristophanes, *3:* 651–652
Arizona, mass shooting, *2:* 248
Arkansas, school integration, *1:* 47–52
Armenia
genocide survivors, *2:* 298–300, 299
history, *2:* 297–298
Armenian Genocide Protests (2015), *2:* 297–302, 301 (ill.). *See also* Genocide; **Human rights**
Army of God, *3:* 558
ARRA (United States. American Recovery and Reinvestment Act), *1:* 113
Arson, *1:* 10–11
Aryan race, *3:* 598–599
Asia. *See also* Specific Asian countries
independence movements, *2:* 339–340
use of rhino horn, *1:* 19
Asia for Educators, *3:* 569
Asner, Ed, *3:* 560
ASPCA (American Society for the Prevention of Cruelty to Animals), *1:* 3
circus animals, *1:* 29
position on ALF methods, *1:* 11
Assad, Bashar al-, *2:* 319; *3:* 487, 491–492
Assange, Julian, *3:* 685, 687
Assassination attempts, Hitler, Adolf, *3:* 590–591
Assault weapons, *2:* 234–235
Athens (city state), *1:* 172
Athletes, protests by, *3:* 516–517
Atkins v. Virginia, *2:* 285
Atlantic, *1:* 198
ATSIC (Aboriginal and Torres Strait Islander Commission), *2:* 379
Attica Prison Riot (1971), *2:* 270–276, 274 (ill.). *See also* **Human rights**
investigation and outcome, *2:* 275–276
manifesto of demands, *2:* 273
prisoner conditions, *2:* 271–272
Austerity measures, Spain, *1:* 116–122, 117–118, 121

Austin, TX, March to Abolish the Death Penalty, *2:* 287
Australia
aboriginals, *2:* 365–366, 375–379
land rights protests, *2:* 375–379
pro-migrant rallies, *2:* 318–325
Australia Day, *2:* 365–366, 375, 376–377
Australian aboriginals, *2:* 365–366, 375–379
Automobile industry, working conditions, *2:* 408–409
AWOC (Agricultural Workers Organizing Committee), *2:* 418
Axis Powers, *3:* 585

B

Background checks, *2:* 236, 252. *See also* **Gun control/Gun rights**
federal law, *2:* 253
gun shows, *2:* 257
private sales, *2:* 256
Washington (state), *2:* 253–254
Baez, Joan, *1:* 68, 198, 199 (ill.); *3:* 670
Bahrain, Arab Spring, *3:* 489
Baladi campaign, *3:* 699, 714–718, 716 (ill.). *See also* **Women's rights**
goals of, *3:* 716–717
leaders, *3:* 716 (ill.)
Balch, Emily G., *3:* 660
Bald and Golden Eagle Protection Act, *1:* 135
Baldwin, James, *1:* 68
Baldwin-Felts, *2:* 410
Banks, Dennis, *2:* 372, 374, 390–391
Banksy, *1:* 212, 212 (ill.)
Banned books, *1:* 180. *See also* Censorship
Baptist War (1831–1832), *3:* 634–638. *See also* **Slavery**
Barbagelata, John, *2:* 443
Bassey, Nnimmo, *1:* 148
Bates, Berke, M.M., *3:* 543
Bates, Daisy, *1:* 50–51
Battle in Seattle, World Trade Organization Protests (1999), *1:* 209–216, 214 (ill.). *See also* **Globalization**

Battle of Blair Mountain (1921), *2:* 410–411
Battle of Matewan, *2:* 410
Battle of Stalingrad (1943), *3:* 594–595, 609. *See also* World War II (1939–1945)
Bavaud, Maurice, *3:* 590–591
Bear Runner, Oscar, *2:* 374 (ill.)
Bearbaiting, *1:* 2
Beijing, China, Tiananmen Square protests, *3:* 473–478, 476 (ill.)
Belarus, human rights protests, *2:* 270
Belo Monte Dam, *2:* 381, 384
Belvis, Segundo Ruiz, *2:* 344–345
Ben Ali, Zine El-Abidine, *3:* 488, 495
Bergh, Henry, *1:* 3
Berlin, Germany
    division of, *3:* 480
    fall of the Berlin Wall (1989), *3:* 478–486
Berlin Wall, *3:* 483 (ill.)
    building of, *3:* 482–483
    fall of, *3:* 485–486
    history, *3:* 478–479
    Reagan, Ronald speech, *3:* 484–485
Bernard, Sheila C., *3:* 530–531
Betances, Ramón Emeterio, *2:* 344–345, 345 (ill.)
Bhopal, India
    torch rally, *1:* 136 (ill.)
    toxic chemical spills, *1:* 136
Bhotmange family, *2:* 293–294, 296
Bialystok Ghetto, Poland, *3:* 607
Bias, danger of, *1:* 167
Bible, *2:* 314–316
Biden, Joe, *2:* 250
Big Pharma, *1:* 226–227, 227 (ill.)
Biko, Steve, *3:* 532–533
Bilbao (Spain) Anti-bullfighting Protest (2010), *1:* 12–18, 17 (ill.). *See also* **Animal rights**
bin Laden, Osama, *3:* 681
Binghamton, NY, Operation Rescue protests, *3:* 563
Birmingham, AL
    desegregation, *1:* 62
    Freedom Rides, *1:* 56, 57
Birth control, *3:* 550. *See also* One child policy; **Reproductive rights**
    access to information, *3:* 553, 575
    China, *3:* 568–574

health insurance plans and, *3:* 556
laws limiting, *3:* 555
oral contraceptives, *3:* 558–559
Birth rate, China, *3:* 569, 573
Bisexuals. *See* LGBTQ people
Black armbands, *3:* 664, 665
Black consciousness movement, *3:* 532–533
Black Lives Matter, *2:* 244; *3:* 515, 539
    demonstrators, *3:* 540 (ill.)
    origins, *3:* 540–544
Black Panthers, *2:* 239–245, 240–241, 243 (ill.)
Blackfish (2013), *1:* 4–5, 25–31, 28, 30
Blair Mountain, Battle of (1921), *2:* 410–411
Blake, James F., *1:* 44–45
Blankenship, Geraldine Green, *2:* 413
Blasphemy, *1:* 183
Blow, Charles M., *1:* 196
Blow, Tahj, *1:* 196
Blowouts, Mexican American students, *1:* 77–82
Blue Star Boy, Suzanne, *2:* 247–249
Bly, Nellie, *2:* 278, 278 (ill.)
Boehner, John, *1:* 115
Boko Haram, *3:* 700, 722–723
Bolívar, Simón, *2:* 338, 338 (ill.)
Book burning. *See also* Censorship; **Free speech**
    Alamagordo, New Mexico, *1:* 181 (ill.)
    Harry Potter (book series), *1:* 175, 177–183, 181 (ill.)
    history, *1:* 178–179
    Mayan texts, *1:* 178
    Nazi Germany, *1:* 179
    protests against in Alamagordo, *1:* 182
Boston Harbor, *2:* 337 (ill.)
Boston Tea Party (1773), *1:* 99, 111–112; *2:* 336–337, 337 (ill.); *3:* 471
Bouazizi, Mohamed, *3:* 487–488
Boutilier v. Immigration and Naturalization Service, *2:* 432
Boycotts. *See also* Protests
    defined, *1:* 35
    Delano Grape Strike and Boycott, *2:* 414–422, 421 (ill.)
    farm produce, *1:* 78–79
    Great American, *1:* 88
    Japan, *1:* 126–127

Montgomery Bus Boycott (1955–1956), *1:* 35, 36 (ill.)
NCAA, of North Carolina, *2:* 460–461
North Carolina, *2:* 461–462
South African products, *3:* 538
Boynton v. Virginia, 1: 55
Brady, James, *2:* 236
Brady Campaign to Prevent Gun Violence, *2:* 236–237, 250
Brady Handgun Violence Prevention Act, *2:* 236–237, 253
Brancheau, Dawn, *1:* 26, 27 (ill.)
Brando, Marlon, *1:* 68; *2:* 375
Brazil
Malê Revolt of 1835, *3:* 626–627
Preservation of Amazon Rain Forest Awareness Campaign, *2:* 379–384
Bressler, Isak, *1:* 215
Brexit, *1:* 103–104, 103 (ill.), 122–129, 124 (ill.). *See also* **Economic discontent**
demonstrations, *1:* 103 (ill.), 124 (ill.), 125–128
EU anniversary demonstration, *1:* 127–128
May, Theresa, speech, *1:* 128–129
referendum, *1:* 124–125
Bridges, Ruby, *1:* 53, 53 (ill.)
Bring Back Our Girls, *3:* 722–723
demonstrators, *3:* 723 (ill.)
Obama, Michelle, speech, *3:* 700–701
Britches, *1:* 8, 9
Britches (1986), *1:* 9
British colonies, *2:* 336–337. *See also* Colonization; United Kingdom
Australia, *2:* 376
Hong Kong, *3:* 499
India, *2:* 347–349
women's rights, *3:* 693–695
British East India Company (EIC), *2:* 347–348
British Raj, *2:* 348–349
Brock, Jack, *1:* 178, 181–182
Brotherhood of Sleeping Car Porters, *1:* 64
Brown, John, *3:* 640–643, 640 (ill.), 642 (ill.)
anti-slavery activity in Kansas, *3:* 640
Douglass, Frederick speech, *3:* 641
Harpers Ferry Raid, *3:* 641–643, 642 (ill.)
Brown, Minnijean, *1:* 50, 51

Brown v. Board of Education, 1: 38–39, 49
BUC (Buffalo United for Choice), *3:* 565
Buchanan, James, *3:* 642
Buenos Aires, Argentina, March against Monsanto, *1:* 228
Buffalo, NY, Operation Rescue protests, *3:* 562–568
Buffalo United for Choice (BUC), *3:* 565
Bull Moose Party, *3:* 710
Bullbaiting, *1:* 1–2
Bullfighting, *1:* 6, 12–13, 14–15 (ill.)
arguments against, *1:* 15
Bilbao, Spain, protest, *1:* 16–18, 17 (ill.)
interview with former bullfighter, *1:* 16
Burgdorf, Robert L., Jr., *2:* 282
Burma. *See* Myanmar
Burns, Lucy, *3:* 710
Burwell v. Hobby Lobby, 3: 555
Bush, George H.W., *2:* 281; *3:* 478
Bush, George W., *1:* 112
position on reproductive rights, *3:* 561
protests at RNC, *3:* 678–679
speech on Iraq invasion, *3:* 680–681

C

Cacerolaza protests, *1:* 106–107. *See also* **Economic discontent**
Caesar, Julius, *3:* 469, 469 (ill.)
Cairo, Egypt, Tahrir Square Protests (2011), *3:* 495–498, 496 (ill.)
Calderón, Felipe, *1:* 91, 94–95
Calhoun, John C., *1:* 195
California. *See also* East Los Angeles, CA; Los Angeles, CA
Black Panthers protest Mulford Act, *2:* 239–245, 243 (ill.)
Delano Grape Strike and Boycott (1965–1970), *2:* 414–422, 421 (ill.)
occupation of Alcatraz (1969–1970), *2:* 370–371, 371 (ill.)
protest against Trump travel bans, *2:* 327, 330 (ill.)
San Bernardino terrorist attack, *2:* 328
San Diego SeaWorld protest, *1:* 30

California. Mulford Act, *2:* 242–243, 244
California. Senate. Resolution No. 16 (2017), *2:* 327
California redwoods, *1:* 152
California State Capitol, Sacramento, CA, *2:* 239–245, 243 (ill.)
Cameron, David, *1:* 124–125; *2:* 321
Camus, Albert, *1:* 93
Canada
    indigenous peoples, *2:* 365 (ill.), 382
    land rights protests, *2:* 365 (ill.), 382
Candlelight Vigils against Invasion of Iraq (2003), *3:* 676–683, 682 (ill.). *See also* **War protests**
Capital punishment, *2:* 284–285. *See also* **Human rights**
    declining use, 289
    history, *2:* 285
    legal challenges to, *2:* 285–286
    support and opposition, *2:* 286–287
Capitalism, *1:* 212
Capitol Crawl (1990), *2:* 276–284, 282 (ill.). *See also* **Human rights**
Carlos, John, *3:* 516, 517 (ill.)
Carpenter, Mary Chapin, *3:* 729
Carson, Rachel, *1:* 135
Carter, Jimmy, *1:* 143; *2:* 280–281
Cartoons, of Muhammad, *1:* 184–187
The Cartoons That Shook the World (2009), *1:* 184, 187
CAS International, *1:* 17, 17 (ill.)
The Case for Animal Rights (1983), *1:* 4
Casper, WY, anti-gay protests by WBC, *2:* 448
Caste systems, *2:* 290–291
    discrimination, *2:* 296
    India, *2:* 290–297
Castro, Fidel, *1:* 106
Castro, Sal, *1:* 80, 82
Castro Village Association, *2:* 442
Catalonia, Spain, *1:* 17–18
Catholic Church, *1:* 173
Cats, animal testing, *1:* 10 (ill.)
Catt, Carrie Chapman, *3:* 710, 711
La Causa, *1:* 78
Cavanagh, Jerome, *3:* 528
CCP (Chinese Communist Party), *1:* 105, 107

Censorship, *1:* 171. *See also* Banned books; Book burning
    Catholic Church, *1:* 173
    Nazi Germany, *1:* 179
CERCLA (United States. Comprehensive Environmental Response, Compensation, and Liability Act), *1:* 143
Chaillot Prize, *3:* 716 (ill.)
Chaney, James Earl, *1:* 58, 58 (ill.)
Charlie Hebdo, *1:* 176, 187, 190–191
    publication of Muhammad cartoons, *1:* 191
    terrorist attack on offices, *1:* 191
Charlotte Magazine, *2:* 462, 463
Charlottesville Protests (2017), *3:* 542–543, 543 (ill.). *See also* **Racial conflict**
Chávez, César
    Delano Grape Strike and Boycott (1965–1970), *2:* 414–415, 419–421, 421 (ill.)
    Hispanic and Latino civil rights, *1:* 75–76, 78–79, 79 (ill.), 86
    state holiday, *1:* 79
Chechnya, *2:* 454–455
Chemical weapons, use in Syria, *3:* 492
Chen Guangcheng, *3:* 571
Chernobyl nuclear accident, *1:* 136–137
Cherokees, *2:* 386–387
Chicago, IL
    DNC anti-war protests, *3:* 656 (ill.)
    Haymarket Square Riot, *2:* 418–419
Chicano movement, *1:* 76, 79
Child, Lydia Maria, *3:* 697 (ill.)
Child labor, *2:* 393–394, 400–401, 400 (ill.), 402–403, 403 (ill.). *See also* **Labor rights**
    Africa, *2:* 399
    labor laws, *2:* 407
    Mother Jones's "Children's Crusade," *2:* 399–407, 406 (ill.)
    NYC protest of 1909, *2:* 402–403, 403 (ill.)
    textile mills, *2:* 400 (ill.)
Children
    cruelty to animals, *1:* 4
    disabled, *2:* 277–278
    Love Canal protests, *1:* 143 (ill.)
    runaway, *3:* 645

GENERAL INDEX

Children's Crusade of 1903, *2:* 399–407, 406 (ill.). See also **Labor rights**
Chile, *Cacerolaza* protests, *1:* 106–107
China, *1:* 103
  birth rate, *3:* 569, 573
  book burning, *1:* 178
  collective farms and communes, *1:* 108–110
  Cultural Revolution (1966), *1:* 108
  economic reforms, *1:* 110–111
  farmers' secret agreement, *1:* 105–111, 109 (ill.)
  fur production, *1:* 12, 13
  history, *1:* 105–108
  ivory trade, *1:* 25
  labor rights, *2:* 398
  LGBTQ rights, *2:* 452–453, 458
  one child policy, *3:* 568–574
  relationship with Hong Kong, *3:* 499–500
  rhino horn, *1:* 19
  sanctions by United States, *3:* 478
  Shanghai Pride Festival (2009), *2:* 452–458, 456 (ill.)
  Tiananmen Square protests, *3:* 473–478, 476 (ill.)
  transgender rights, *2:* 452–453
China Daily, 2: 455, 457
Chinese Classification of Mental Disorders, 2: 452
Chinese Communist Party (CCP), *1:* 105, 107
Chinese farmers
  one child policy, *3:* 570
  secret agreement, *1:* 105–111, 109 (ill.)
Chinese immigrants. See also Immigrants and immigration
  riots against, Denver, Colorado, *2:* 328–329, 329 (ill.)
  United States, *2:* 307, 415–416
Chinese traditional medicine, *1:* 19
Chinese workers, working conditions, *2:* 398
Christ Community Church, Alamagordo, New Mexico, *1:* 175, 177–183
Christakis, Erika, *1:* 195, 197–198, 200
Christakis, Nicholas, *1:* 197–198, 200
Christian X, King of Denmark, *3:* 600
Christmas Rebellion (1831–1832), *3:* 634–638. See also **Slavery**

Cigar workers, *1:* 85 (ill.)
  strikes, *1:* 84
  violence against, *1:* 84
Circus animals, *1:* 5, 29, 29 (ill.)
CITES (Convention on International Trade in Endangered Species of Wild Fauna and Flora), *1:* 21
Citizen journalism, *3:* 490–491
Citizens for a Sound Economy, *1:* 111
Citrin, Jack, *1:* 177
City of Hope National Medical Center, *1:* 9
Civic Forum, *2:* 355
Civil disobedience, *1:* 139. See also Nonviolent resistance
  "I Will Not Comply" Rally, *2:* 254
  Indian independence movement, *2:* 346–347, 349, 350
Civil rights. See also **African American civil rights**; **Free speech**; **Hispanic and Latino civil rights**; **Human rights**; **Indigenous peoples' rights**; **LGBTQ rights**
  defined, *1:* 71
  DOJ lawsuit against North Carolina, *2:* 463
  farm workers, *1:* 78–79
  summary of laws, *1:* 41
Civil rights, African American. See **African American civil rights**
Civil rights, Hispanic and Latino. See **Hispanic and Latino civil rights**
Civil Rights Act of 1957, *1:* 41
Civil Rights Act of 1960, *1:* 41
Civil Rights Act of 1964, *1:* 40, 41, 69
Civil Rights Act of 1968, *1:* 40, 41
Civil rights movement, *1:* 35–36, 38–42, 42
  Freedom Rides, *1:* 54–59, 56 (ill.)
  Hispanic and Latino, *1:* 75–76
  legislation, *1:* 40–41
  origins, *1:* 38–39
  resulting legislation, *1:* 40–41
  United States, *3:* 472
Civilian casualties, *3:* 684, 686
Cleary, John, *3:* 674 (ill.)
Cleveland, Ohio, *1:* 135–136
Climate change. See also **Environment**; Global warming
  COP 15, *1:* 144–145
  greenhouse gases, *1:* 137, 145, 157
  island nations, *1:* 157–158
  US attitudes about, *1:* 164, 164 (ill.)

Climate deniers, *1:* 165–166
Climate Justice Action (CJA), *1:* 145, 146
Climate Justice Now (CJN), *1:* 146
Climate refugees, *1:* 159
Clinton, Bill, *1:* 52
    Gay and Lesbian Pride Month, *2:* 441
    gays in military policy, *2:* 434
    gun control laws, *2:* 253
    position on reproductive rights, *3:* 561
    support of gun control sit-in, *2:* 259
    WTO meeting, *1:* 211
Clinton, Hillary Rodham, *2:* 426; *3:* 578, 699, 725–726
Clovis, Sam, *1:* 168
Coal miners and coal mining
    environmental impact, *1:* 159
    global warming, *1:* 159
    strikes, *2:* 410–411
    working conditions, *2:* 312
Cockfighting, *1:* 2
Code Noir, *3:* 624
Coffee, Linda, *3:* 576
Cold War (1945–1991), *1:* 178; *3:* 479, 483, 484, 486, 655
Collective farms, *1:* 108–110
Collin, Frank, *1:* 189 (ill.)
Collins, Susan, *2:* 260
Colonization, *1:* 204; *2:* 335. *See also* British colonies; French colonies; Portuguese colonies; Spanish colonies
    impact on indigenous peoples, *2:* 361, 375–376
    impact on Native Americans, *2:* 362–363, 386–387
    North America, *1:* 72
    prison colonies, *2:* 376
    South America, *1:* 72; *3:* 533
Colorado, A Day without Immigrants protests, *1:* 88
Columbus, Christopher, *2:* 343
Comfort Women (Korean), protests, *2:* 269 (ill.)
Communes, *1:* 108–110
Communism and communists, *2:* 352; *3:* 587, 663–664, 669
    Chile, *1:* 106
    China, *1:* 107–108
    resistance to Nazis, *3:* 587–588

Compensated Emancipation Act, *3:* 633, 633 (ill.)
Comprehensive Environmental Response, Compensation, and Liability Act (CERCLA), *1:* 143
Compton, Jim, *1:* 215
Comstock Act, *3:* 553, 575
Conception, *3:* 562
Confederate symbols, *3:* 515–517
Congress of Racial Equality (CORE), *1:* 54–57
    Berkeley free speech movement, *1:* 198
    sit-ins, *1:* 60–61, 62
Congressional Union for Woman Suffrage, *3:* 710
Connecticut, Sandy Hook mass shooting, *2:* 246–247
Conscientious objectors, *3:* 652–653
Constitution of India, *2:* 292
Consumerism, *1:* 212
Contraceptives, *3:* 549
Convention on International Trade in Endangered Species of Wild Fauna and Flora (CITES), *1:* 21
Cooper, Roy, *2:* 462, 463
COP 15 (Conference of the Parties 15), *1:* 144–145, 145–146, 146–148. *See also* **Environment**
Copenhagen, Denmark, protests (2009), *1:* 144–151, 150 (ill.). *See also* **Environment**
    clashes with police, *1:* 148–150
    protest groups plan, *1:* 146–148
    response of Danish government, *1:* 147–150
Copernicus, Nicolaus, *1:* 173
CORE (Congress of Racial Equality), *1:* 54–57
    Berkeley free speech movement, *1:* 198
    sit-ins, *1:* 60–61, 62
Cornell Center on the Death Penalty Worldwide, *2:* 284
Coulter, Ann, *1:* 176
Cowperthwaite, Gabriela, *1:* 26–27
Cree First Nations, *2:* 382. *See also* Indigenous peoples
Creedence Clearwater Revival, *3:* 670
Criminal justice system, human rights abuses, *2:* 270–271
Cruz, Sophie, *3:* 729
C-SPAN, *2:* 259
Cuba, independence movements, *2:* 338–339
Cuernavaca, Mexico, *1:* 91 (ill.), 93–94
Cullen, H. Jay, *3:* 542–543

GENERAL INDEX

Cullors, Patrice, *3:* 541
Cultural exchange, *1:* 206
Cultural Revolution (1966), *1:* 108; *3:* 473. See also China
Cultural studies, Los Angeles Unified School District, *1:* 82
Cuomo, Mario, *2:* 382
Cuyahoga River, *1:* 135–136
Cyrus the Great, King of Persia, *2:* 265
Czech Republic, *2:* 357–358
Czech resistance (World War II), *3:* 589
Czechoslovakia
    independence movements, *2:* 341–342, 352–358
    invasion of 1968, *2:* 354 (ill.)
    under Soviet Union, *2:* 353–354

D

Dakota Access Pipeline (DAPL), *1:* 140; *2:* 384, 385
    Native American opposition, *1:* 144; 366–367, 367 (ill.), 384–391, 388 (ill.)
    Trump, Donald, *2:* 367
Dakota Access Pipeline (DAPL) Protest (2016–2017), *2:* 366–367, 367 (ill.), 384–391, 388 (ill.). See also **Indigenous peoples' rights**
    Dennis Banks, *2:* 390–391
    Native Americans, *2:* 367 (ill.), 388 (ill.)
Dalit Protests in India (2006), *2:* 290–297, 295 (ill.). See also **Human rights**
Dalits, *2:* 290, 291–293, 295 (ill.)
    continuing discrimination, *2:* 296–297
    murder of family in Khairlanji, India, *2:* 293–294
    violence against, *2:* 293–294, 297
Dallas, TX, Huey P. Newton Gun Club demonstrations, *2:* 244
Dams
    land rights protests by Cree First Nations, *2:* 382
    land rights protests by Kayapo, *2:* 379–384
Dandi March, *2:* 346–352, 351 (ill.)
Danish Jews, *3:* 597, 601–602
Danish resistance (World War II), *3:* 589, 597–602
DAPL (Dakota Access Pipeline), *1:* 140; *2:* 384, 385
    Native American opposition, *1:* 144
    Trump, Donald, *2:* 367

DAPL (Dakota Access Pipeline) Protest (2016–2017), *2:* 366–367, 367 (ill.), 384–391, 388 (ill.). See also **Indigenous peoples' rights**
    Dennis Banks, *2:* 390–391
    Native Americans, *2:* 367 (ill.)
Dart, Justin, Jr., *2:* 282
Davis, Sammy, Jr., *1:* 68
Davison, Emily Wilding, *3:* 705, 705 (ill.)
A Day without a Mexican (2004), *1:* 86
A Day without a Woman (2017), *3:* 731
A Day without Immigrants, *1:* 83–89, 88 (ill.)
DDT, *1:* 135
De Klerk, F.W., *3:* 539
Death camps, *3:* 585–586, 587, 604–605, 608–609
Death penalty, *2:* 284–285. See also **Human rights**
    declining use, *2:* 289
    history, *2:* 285
    legal challenges to, *2:* 285–286
    support and opposition, *2:* 286–287
Declaration of Independence, *2:* 337
Declaration of Sentiments, *3:* 708, 709 (ill.)
Declaration of the Rights of Animals, *1:* 3
Declaration of the Rights of Man and of the Citizen, *2:* 267
Defense of Marriage Act, *2:* 438
Deforestation, *1:* 138
DeGeneres, Ellen, *2:* 434
Delano (CA) Grape Strike and Boycott (1965–1970), *2:* 414–422, 421 (ill.). See also **Labor rights**
Democracia Real Ya (DRY), *1:* 116, 120
Democracy, *3:* 467, 493, 669
Democratic Congressional Representatives Sit-in for Gun control (2016), *2:* 256–260, 259 (ill.). See also **Gun control/Gun rights**
Democratic National Convention (DNC), *3:* 564, 656 (ill.)
Deng, Xiaoping, *1:* 108, 110
Denmark
    Holocaust Resistance in Denmark (1943), *3:* 597–602, 601 (ill.)
    Nazi occupation, *3:* 598–600
    Nazi occupation ends, *3:* 602
    protests against *Jyllands-Posten* cartoons, *1:* 183–188
    response to Copenhagen protests, *1:* 147–148

Denver, CO, A Day without Immigrants protests, *1:* 88
Deportations
    to death camps, *3:* 604–605
    to Mexico by the United States, *1:* 74
Derby Day Protest (1913), *3:* 705
Des Moines, IA, Vietnam War protest (1965–1969), *3:* 663–668
Desegregation/Segregation, *1:* 38–39, 42. *See also* Apartheid
    Birmingham, Alabama, *1:* 62
    Little Rock, Arkansas, *1:* 47–52
    national defense jobs, *1:* 64
Desertification, *1:* 138
Deslondes, Charles, *3:* 625–627
Detroit Riots (MI) (1967), *3:* 524–530, 528 (ill.). *See also* **Racial conflict**
    aftermath, *3:* 529–530
    origins in "blind pig," *3:* 525
    Romney, George, interview, *3:* 530–531
Developing countries, advantages of globalization, *1:* 206
Development, Relief, and Education for Alien Minors Act (United States. DREAM Act), *1:* 89
Diagnostic and Statistical Manual of Mental Disorders, *2:* 432
Dickinson, Anna E., *3:* 697 (ill.)
Dictators, *3:* 467–468
Disability rights, *2:* 276–284. *See also* **Human rights**
    ADA passage, *2:* 280–283
    legislation, *2:* 278–279
    ongoing efforts, *2:* 283–284
    organizations, *2:* 279–280
Disabled children, education, *2:* 277–278
Discrimination. *See also* Racial discrimination
    against LGBTQ people, *2:* 431, 432, 436, 454–455
    Mexican American students, *1:* 79–80
District of Columbia. *See* Washington, D.C.
DNC (Democratic National Convention), *3:* 564, 656 (ill.)
"Don't Ask, Don't Tell," *2:* 434, 435
Douglass, Frederick, *3:* 638, 641
Dowell, Denzil, *2:* 241
Draft cards, burning, *3:* 666–667, 667 (ill.)

Draft (military)
    United States Civil War, *3:* 526, 654
    Vietnam War, *3:* 666
Drag shows, *2:* 457
DREAM Act, *1:* 89
Dresden, Germany, anti-migrant protests, *2:* 321, 323 (ill.)
Drug trade
    Mexico, *1:* 75, 90, 91
    violence, *1:* 91–92
DRY (Democracia Real Ya), *1:* 116, 120
Dubček, Alexander, *2:* 353
Dublin, Ireland, Easter Rebellion (1916), *3:* 480–481, 481 (ill.)
Duckwitz, Georg Ferdinand, *3:* 600–601
Duncan, Arne, *2:* 249
Dunlop, Marion Wallace, *3:* 704, 706
Durant, William C., *2:* 408
Dutilleux, Jean-Pierre, *2:* 381–382
Dylan, Bob, *1:* 68; *3:* 670

E

Earth Day, *1:* 136, 164; *3:* 730–731
Earth Liberation Front (ELF), *1:* 11
Earthquakes, *1:* 154
East Los Angeles, CA. *See also* California; Los Angeles, CA
    blowouts, *1:* 77–82
    commemoration of East LA blowouts, *1:* 81 (ill.)
    Mexican American students, *1:* 77
Easter Rebellion (1916), *3:* 480–481, 481 (ill.). *See also* **Political/Government uprisings**
Eckford, Elizabeth, *1:* 50–51, 52 (ill.)
Eckhardt, Christopher, *3:* 664, 665
Economic discontent, *1:* **99–131**, 103 (ill.), 109 (ill.), 114 (ill.), 119 (ill.), 121 (ill.), 124 (ill.). *See also* **Globalization**
    Brexit, *1:* 103, 103 (ill.), 122–129, 124 (ill.)
    Cacerolazo Protests in Chile (1971), *1:* 106–107
    15-M Movement (2011), *1:* 116–122, 121 (ill.)
    Porkulus Protests, Tea Party (2009–2010), *1:* 111–116, 114 (ill.)
    Rice Riots of 1918 (Japan), *1:* 126–127

GENERAL INDEX

Secret Document of the Farmers of Xiaogang (1978), *1:* 105–111, 109 (ill.)
student protests in France (May 1968), *1:* 118–119, 119 (ill.)
Economic inequality, *1:* 208
   protest against, *1:* 216–217
   Wall Street, *1:* 218
Ecoterrorism, *1:* 11. See also Terrorism
Education
   for disabled children, *2:* 277–278
   discrimination against Mexican American students, *1:* 79–80
   for girls and women, *3:* 718–724
Education for All Handicapped Children Act, *2:* 278
Educational Issues Coordinating Committee (EICC), *1:* 82
EEC (European Economic Community), *1:* 123
Egypt
   labor rights, *2:* 398
   post-revolution, *3:* 497–498
   Tahrir Square Protests (2011), *3:* 493–498, 495–498, 496 (ill.)
Egyptian Revolution (2011), *3:* 488, 493–498, 496 (ill.). See also **Political/Government uprisings**
EIA (United States. Energy Information Administration), *1:* 155
EIC (British East India Company), *2:* 347–348
EICC (Educational Issues Coordinating Committee), *1:* 82
8888 Uprising, Myanmar (1988), *3:* 502–503, 503 (ill.)
Eilperin, Juliet, *1:* 141
Eisenhower, Dwight D., *1:* 48, 52
El Rhazoui, Zineb, *1:* 194
Elections
   disputed, Iran, *3:* 490
   source of unrest in Hong Kong, *3:* 499–500
   US presidential (2016), *3:* 725–726
Elephants
   poaching, *1:* 18–19, 25
   population decline, *1:* 20–22
   postage stamp, *1:* 29 (ill.)
   in Ringling Bros. circus, *1:* 29, 29 (ill.)
ELF (Earth Liberation Front), *1:* 11

Elizabeth I, Queen of England, *1:* 173; *2:* 347
Elser, Georg Johann, *3:* 591
Emancipation Proclamation, *3:* 633
Emergency Economic Stabilization Act of 2008, *1:* 112
Emerson, Ralph Waldo, *2:* 387, 387 (ill.)
Encyclopedia of Environmental Issues, *3:* 573
Endangered Species Act, *1:* 136
Energy Transfer Partners, *2:* 384, 385, 386–387
England. Bill of Rights, *1:* 173; *2:* 266–267
ENGOs (Environmental nongovernmental organizations), *1:* 146
Enlightenment, *2:* 265–267
Environment, *1:* **133–170**, 135 (ill.), 136 (ill.), 142 (ill.), 143 (ill.), 150 (ill.), 153 (ill.), 155 (ill.), 161 (ill.), 162 (ill.), 165 (ill.). See also Climate change; Global warming
   Copenhagen Protests (2009), *1:* 144–151, 150 (ill.)
   Forward on Climate Rally (2013), *1:* 139–144, 142 (ill.)
   Fukushima nuclear power protests, *1:* 160–161, 161 (ill.)
   Global Frackdown (2014), *1:* 151–156, 155 (ill.)
   Gore, Al, *1:* 148–149
   Hill, Julia "Butterfly," *1:* 152, 153 (ill.)
   human impact, *1:* 137–138
   Love Canal, NY, *1:* 136, 143, 143 (ill.)
   March for Science (2017), *1:* 163–168, 165 (ill.)
   Pacific Climate Warriors Blockade (2014), *1:* 157–163, 162 (ill.)
   21st century challenges, *1:* 137–138
Environmental movement
   history, *1:* 133–137
   methods, *1:* 138–139
Environmental nongovernmental organizations (ENGOs), *1:* 146
Environmentalists, *1:* 133, 138–139
EPA (United States. Environmental Protection Agency), *1:* 136
Equal pay, *3:* 728–729
Equal Rights Amendment (ERA), *3:* 558–559
Equanimal, *1:* 17, 17 (ill.)
Espionage, *2:* 285
Estonia, independence movements, *2:* 348
Ethnicity, *3:* 509

EU (European Union)
    exit of United Kingdom, *1:* 103–104, 122–129
    immigrants and immigration, *2:* 309–310
    refugee crisis, *2:* 324–325
    refugees, *2:* 319–321
Europe, pro-migrant rallies, *2:* 318–325, 324 (ill.)
European Court of Human Rights, *2:* 454
European Economic Community (EEC), *1:* 123
European Union (EU)
    exit of United Kingdom, *1:* 103–104, 122–129
    immigrants and immigration, *2:* 309–310
    refugee crisis, *2:* 324–325
    refugees, *2:* 319–321
Euroscepticism, *1:* 125
Eviction protests, *1:* 120
Evidence-based policies, *1:* 163–164
Executions
    declining use, 2890
    lethal injection, 2890
    Texas, *2:* 284

F

FACE Act (United States. Freedom of Access to Clinic Entrances Act), *3:* 568
Fair Housing Act of 1968, *1:* 40, 41
Fair Labor Standards Act of 1938, *2:* 397–398, 407
Fairchild, Morgan, *3:* 560
Fall of the Berlin Wall (1989), *3:* 478–486, 483 (ill.). *See also* **Political/Government uprisings**
Fallata, Iman, *3:* 716 (ill.)
Famines, *3:* 569
Farage, Nigel, *1:* 125
Farm workers. *See also* Workers
    civil rights, *1:* 78–79
    labor unions, *1:* 75–76
    Mexican, *1:* 75 (ill.)
    working conditions, *2:* 416
Fast Food Forward, *2:* 424, 425
Fast-food Workers' Strike (2012), *2:* 422–426, 424 (ill.). *See also* **Labor rights**
    global recognition, *2:* 425
    sit-ins, *2:* 425
Faubus, Orbal, *1:* 48, 50–52

Fawcett, Millicent, *3:* 703
FBI (United States. Federal Bureau of Investigation), *3:* 686–687, 725
Federal Assault Weapons Ban, *2:* 234–235
Federal Society of Journeymen Cordwainers, *2:* 396
Federalists, *1:* 175
Feld Entertainment, *1:* 29
Feminists, *3:* 558. *See also* **Women's rights**
Ferdinand II, King of Spain, *2:* 343
Ferrera, America, *3:* 729
Feudal societies, *3:* 469–470, 619–620
Fields, James Alex, *3:* 542
15-M Movement, *1:* 90, 116–122, 121 (ill.). *See also* **Economic discontent**
Fight for $15, *2:* 422
Fight to Stop Human Trafficking, *3:* 643–647. *See also* **Slavery**
Filipino workers, *2:* 416, 418–419. *See also* Workers
Final Solution, *3:* 608
Finding Dory, *1:* 28
Firearms Owners' Protection Act, *2:* 234
First Landing Day (Australia), *2:* 365–366, 375, 376–377
Fisher Body Plant No. 1, Flint, MI, *2:* 410
Fisher Body Plant No. 2, Flint, MI, *2:* 410
Fitz, Nicholas, *1:* 100
Flag burning, Palestinian students, *1:* 186 (ill.)
Flint (MI) Sit-Down Strike against General Motors (1936–1937), *2:* 407–414, 412 (ill.). *See also* **Labor rights**
Florida
    mass shootings at Pulse nightclub, *2:* 257
    Tea Party movement, *1:* 114 (ill.)
    Ybor City Cigar Strike (1931), *1:* 84
Floyd, John, *3:* 632
Fonda, Jane, *3:* 560
Food & Water Watch, *1:* 155
Food labeling, *1:* 229–230
Forced abortions, *3:* 571
Forced labor, *3:* 644–646
Forced sterilization, *3:* 571
Force-feeding, *3:* 702, 706, 713
Ford v. Wainwright, *2:* 285
Fort Myers, FL, Tea Party movement, *1:* 114 (ill.)

Forward on Climate Rally (2013), *1:* 139–144, 142 (ill.). *See also* **Environment**
Fossey, Dian, *1:* 20
Foundation Day (Australia), *2:* 365–366, 375, 376–377
Fox, Helen, *3:* 703–704
Fox, Maggie, *3:* 556
Fracking, *1:* 151–154; *2:* 385. *See also* **Environment**
   bans on, *1:* 156
   environmental impact, *1:* 154–155
   origins, *1:* 153–154
   toxic wastes, *1:* 153–154
France
   attack on *Charlie Hebdo* offices, *1:* 191
   student protests of 1968, *1:* 118–119, 119 (ill.)
Frantz (William) Elementary School, *1:* 53
Free blacks, *3:* 630–632. *See also* African Americans
Free speech, *1:* **171–202**, 177 (ill.), 181 (ill.), 186 (ill.), 189 (ill.), 190 (ill.), 192 (ill.), 197 (ill.), 199 (ill.). *See also* Civil rights
   Banned book list, *1:* 180
   Harry Potter Book Burning (2001), *1:* 177–183, 181 (ill.)
   history of, *1:* 171–174
   "Je Suis Charlie" protests (2015), *1:* 189–194, 192 (ill.)
   limits of, *1:* 171, 175–177
   Muslim protests against *Charlie Hebdo*, *1:* 190 (ill.), 193
   Muslim protests of Danish cartoons (2005–2008), *1:* 183–188, 186 (ill.)
   Nazi Book Burning, *1:* 179
   proposed Skokie neo-Nazi march, *1:* 188–189, 189 (ill.)
   religion and, *1:* 176, 183
   Supreme Court decisions, *3:* 667–668
   United States, *1:* 173–174
   University of California, Berkeley, *1:* 176–177, 177 (ill.), 198–199, 199 (ill.)
   Yale Student Protests (2015), *1:* 194–201, 197 (ill.)
Free Syrian Army, *3:* 492
Free trade. *See also* **Globalization**
   defined, *1:* 203
   opponents of, *1:* 211

Free trade agreements, *1:* 205–206
Freedom of Access to Clinic Entrances Act (FACE Act), *3:* 568
Freedom of religion, *2:* 265
Freedom of speech. *See* **Free speech**
Freedom Riders, *1:* 39, 56 (ill.)
Freedom Rides (1961), *1:* 39, 54–59, 56 (ill.). *See also* **African American civil rights**
   first ride, *1:* 56–57
   origins, *1:* 54–55
Freedom Sunday, *3:* 647
French colonies. *See also* Colonization
   Haitian Revolution (1791–1804), *3:* 625
   independence movements, *2:* 338
   slavery in, *3:* 624–625
French resistance (World War II), *3:* 589
French Revolution (1789–1799), *2:* 267; *3:* 471
French Student Protests of 1968, *1:* 118–119, 119 (ill.)
Friedan, Betty, *3:* 558, 728, 729 (ill.)
Friendship Junior College, *1:* 59, 61
Friendship Nine, *1:* 59, 61, 63
Frost, Robert, *1:* 149
Fryberg, Jaylen, *2:* 253
Fugitive Slave Law, *3:* 631
Fukushima nuclear power protests, *1:* 160–161, 161 (ill.)
Fulton, Sybrina, *3:* 545–546
Fur farms, *1:* 11
Furman v. Georgia, *2:* 285
Furs, PETA protests against, *1:* 12–13, 13 (ill.)

G

G20 Summit, Hamburg, Germany (2017), *1:* 208–209, 208 (ill.)
Gandhi, Mahatma, *1:* 78; *2:* 340–341, 341, 351 (ill.)
   Indian independence movement, *2:* 348–352
   Salt March, *2:* 341–342, 346–352, 351 (ill.)
   speech before the Salt March, *2:* 349
Gandhi, Mohandas. *See* Gandhi, Mahatma
Gandhi's Salt March (1930), *2:* 340–341, 346–352, 351 (ill.). *See also* **Independence movements**
Garfield High School, East LA, *1:* 81

Garner, Eric, *3:* 541–542, 544–545
Garner, Esaw, *3:* 546
Garza, Alicia, *3:* 541
Gasland (2010), *1:* 154
Gaulle, Charles de, *1:* 118–119
Gay and Lesbian Alliance against Defamation (GLAAD), *2:* 458
Gay and Lesbian Pride Month, *2:* 441
Gay pride
  parades, *2:* 441
  Shanghai Pride Festival, *2:* 452–458, 456 (ill.)
Gaye, Marvin, *3:* 670
Gays. *See* LGBTQ people
Gdansk Shipyard Strike, Poland (1980), *2:* 356–357, 357 (ill.)
Gender identity, *2:* 429, 435
Genderqueer, *2:* 429–430
General Motors Co. (GM)
  Flint Sit-Down Strike, *2:* 407–414, 412 (ill.)
  working conditions, *2:* 408–409
Genetically modified organisms (GMOs), *1:* 224
  food, *1:* 223
  labeling, *1:* 229–230
  seeds, *1:* 223
Genocide, *2:* 297, 300. *See also* Holocaust
George III, King of Great Britain, *2:* 376
Gerber, Henry, *2:* 432
German immigrants, *2:* 307. *See also* Immigrants and immigration
Germany. *See also* Nazi Germany
  anti-migrant protests, *2:* 321, 323 (ill.)
  Fukushima nuclear energy protests, *1:* 161 (ill.)
  Nazi resistance, *3:* 592–597
  nuclear energy policy, *1:* 161
  post-World War II division, *3:* 479–481
  reunification, *3:* 486
Gestapo, *3:* 592, 593, 594. *See also* Nazi Germany
Ghettos, *3:* 602
  Bialystok, Poland, *3:* 607
  Warsaw, Poland, *3:* 602–605
Ghost dance, *2:* 369, 369 (ill.)
Giffords, Gabrielle, *2:* 248, 248 (ill.)
Giumarra, John, Sr., *2:* 421 (ill.)
GLAAD (Gay and Lesbian Alliance against Defamation), *2:* 458

Glacier Point, Yosemite Valley, *1:* 135 (ill.)
Global Frackdown (2014), *1:* 151–156, 155 (ill.). *See also* **Environment**
Global March for Elephants and Rhinos (GMFER), *1:* 18–25, 24 (ill.). *See also* **Animal rights**
Global Recession of 2008, *1:* 219
  Spain, *1:* 104–105, 116–117
  United States, *1:* 112–113
Global Slavery Index, *3:* 623
Global warming, *1:* 145, 159. *See also* Climate change; **Environment**
Globalization, *1:* **203–231**, 208 (ill.), 212 (ill.), 214 (ill.), 222 (ill.), 227 (ill.), 228 (ill.). *See also* **Economic discontent**
  Banksy street art protests, *1:* 212, 212 (ill.)
  Battle in Seattle, World Trade Organization protests (1999), *1:* 209–216, 214 (ill.)
  benefits and disadvantages, *1:* 206–207
  Big Pharma, *1:* 226–227, 227 (ill.)
  history, *1:* 204–205
  March against Monsanto (2013), *1:* 223–230, 228 (ill.)
  Occupy Wall Street (2011), *1:* 216–222, 222 (ill.)
  21st century, *1:* 205–206
Glover, Danny, *3:* 678
Glyphosate, *1:* 224
GM (General Motors Co.)
  Flint Sit-Down Strike, *2:* 407–414, 412 (ill.)
  working conditions, *2:* 408–409
GMFER (Global March for Elephants and Rhinos), *1:* 18–25, 24 (ill.). *See also* **Animal rights**
GMOs (Genetically modified organisms), *1:* 224
  foods, *1:* 223
  labeling, *1:* 229–230
  seeds, *1:* 223
Goddard, Colin, *2:* 249–250
Goebbels, Joseph, *1:* 179
Goldsmith, Judy, *3:* 559–560
Goodman, Andrew, *1:* 58, 58 (ill.)
Gorbachev, Mikhail, *3:* 476, 478, 484, 485
Gore, Al, *1:* 148–149
Gorillas, *1:* 20
Gorsuch, Neil, *3:* 579
Govea, Jessica, *2:* 417
Graffiti, *1:* 212

GENERAL INDEX

Graves, Goddard C., *3:* 667 (ill.)
Gray, Freddie, *3:* 544
Gray, Nellie, *3:* 559
Gray, Vincent, *2:* 250
Great American Boycott, *1:* 88. *See also* Boycotts
Great Britain. Tea Act, *2:* 336–337
Great Depression, *1:* 74, 218; *2:* 409, 419
Great Recession. *See* Global Recession of 2008
Green, Ernest, *1:* 50, 52
Green, Jay J., *2:* 413
Greenhouse gases. *See also* **Environment**
    from agriculture, *1:* 225–226
    climate change, *1:* 137, 145, 157
    Newcastle Harbor, New South Wales, *1:* 160–161
Greenpeace, *1:* 22–23, 23 (ill.)
Greensboro, NC, sit-ins, *1:* 59, 60
Greenwich Village, NY, *2:* 436–437, 441
Greenwood, Grace, *3:* 697 (ill.)
Grito de Lares (1868), *2:* 340, 342–346. *See also* **Independence movements**
Guangdong, China, *3:* 570–573
Guangxi, China, *3:* 570–573
Guardian, 1: 158, 181
Guggenheim Museum, Bilbao, Spain, *1:* 12, 16–18
Guiliani, Rudolph, *3:* 680
Gun Control Act, *2:* 234
Gun control laws
    background checks, *2:* 253
    California, *2:* 242–243
    history in the United States, *2:* 233–235
Gun control/Gun rights, *2:* **233–262**, 237 (ill.), 238 (ill.), 243 (ill.), 248 (ill.), 249 (ill.), 254 (ill.), 259 (ill.)
    Black Panthers Protest Mulford Act (1967), *2:* 239–245, 243 (ill.)
    Democratic Congressional Representatives Sit-in for Gun Control (2016), *2:* 256–260, 259 (ill.)
    demonstrators, *2:* 237 (ill.), 238 (ill.)
    gun control arguments, *2:* 235–237
    gun rights arguments, *2:* 237–238
    Huey P. Newton Gun Club demonstrations, *2:* 244
    "I Will Not Comply" Rally (2014), *2:* 252–256, 254 (ill.)
    March on Washington for Gun Control (2013), *2:* 246–252, 249 (ill.)
    Seale, Bobby, on Mulford Act, *2:* 240, 242
    Vocal Majority Tour (2016), *2:* 248, 248 (ill.)
Gun ownership
    history in United States, *2:* 233–235
    United States, *2:* 235, 235 (ill.)
Gun shows, *2:* 257
Gunn, David, *3:* 554
Gutenberg, Johannes, *1:* 172
Guttmacher Institute, *3:* 556

H

The Hague, Netherlands, International Congress of Women (1915), *3:* 657–663, 660 (ill.)
Haitian Revolution (1791–1804), *2:* 338; *3:* 625
Hamid bin Isa Al Khalifa, King of Bahrain, *3:* 489
Hamilton, Alice, *3:* 660
Handguns, *2:* 235
Harbor blockades, *1:* 157–163
Harding, Warren G., *2:* 411
Harpers Ferry Raid (1859), *3:* 638–643, 642 (ill.). *See also* **Slavery**
Harry Potter Book Burning (2001), *1:* 177–183, 181 (ill.). *See also* **Free speech**
Harry Potter (book series), *1:* 175
    book burning, *1:* 177–183, 181 (ill.)
    opposition to, *1:* 179–180
Hate crimes
    expanding definition, *2:* 447–448, 451
    laws, *2:* 434, 446, 450
    United States, *3:* 518 (ill.)
Hate groups, *3:* 518 (ill.), 542
Hatfield, Sid, *2:* 410
Hatshepsut, *2:* 430–431
Havel, Václav, *2:* 355, 356
Hawke, Bob, *2:* 378–379
Haymarket Square Riot (1886), *2:* 418–419, 419 (ill.)
HDI (Human Development Index), *1:* 102
Health insurance plans, birth control and, *3:* 555, 556
Heart (music group), *1:* 30
Heine, Heinrich, *1:* 179
Heller, Aron, *3:* 610

Henderson, Russell, *2:* 447, 451
Henry VII, King of England, *2:* 265
Henry VIII, King of England, *1:* 173; *2:* 285
Heston, Charlton, *1:* 68
Heydrich, Reinhard, *3:* 589
Heyer, Heather, *3:* 542
Heymann, Lida Gustava, *3:* 660
Hidalgo, Miguel, *2:* 338
Hill, Julia "Butterfly," *1:* 152, 153 (ill.)
Himmler, Heinrich, *3:* 604, 605
Hinckley, John, Jr., *2:* 236–237
Hinduism, *2:* 290–291
Hispanic and Latino civil rights, *1:* **71–98**, 76 (ill.), 81 (ill.), 88 (ill.), 91 (ill.), 95 (ill.). *See also* Civil rights
   Day without Immigrants protests (2006), *1:* 83–89, 88 (ill.)
   Day without Latinos (2006), *1:* 87
   early history, *1:* 73
   East LA blowouts (1968), *1:* 77–82, 81 (ill.)
   Mexican Indignados movement, *1:* 90–96, 91 (ill.), 95 (ill.)
   Sicilia, Javier, *1:* 90, 91 (ill.), 92–93, 94
   Tlatelolco Massacre (1968), *1:* 94, 95
   Ybor City Cigar Strike (1931), *1:* 84–85
Hispanics and Latinos. *See also* Mexican Americans
   definitions, *1:* 71
   United States population, *1:* 75–76
Hitler, Adolf, *1:* 179; *3:* 479–480, 585–586, 590–591, 592, 607
HIV/AIDS
   demonstrations, *2:* 433 (ill.)
   drugs protests, *1:* 226–227, 227 (ill.)
   epidemic, *2:* 433–434
Hobby Lobby, *3:* 555
Holloway, Jonathan, *1:* 200
Holocaust, *1:* 179; *2:* 297; *3:* 586, 613. *See also* Genocide
Holocaust Resistance in Denmark (1943), *3:* 597–602, 601 (ill.). *See also* **Resistance to Nazis**
Homosexuality. *See also* LGBTQ people
   as mental disorder, *2:* 432, 452
   opposition to by WBC, *2:* 448, 452
   as personality disorder, *2:* 432
Hong Kong
   relationship with China, *3:* 499–500

   Umbrella Revolution (2014), *3:* 498–505, 500 (ill.), 504 (ill.)
Hopper, Grace Murray, *1:* 200
Horn, Jerry, *3:* 560
Houston, TX
   anti-abortion demonstrators, *3:* 564 (ill.)
   March to Abolish the Death Penalty, *2:* 287
HPI (Human Poverty Index), *1:* 102
Hu Yaobang, *3:* 473–474
Huerta, Dolores, *1:* 75, 76 (ill.), 78, 86; *2:* 414–415, 419–420
Human development, *1:* 101–102
Human Development Index (HDI), *1:* 102
Human migrations, *2:* 305–306
Human Poverty Index (HPI), *1:* 102
Human rights, *2:* **263–304**, 269 (ill.), 274 (ill.), 278 (ill.), 282 (ill.), 287 (ill.), 295 (ill.), 301 (ill.). *See also* Civil rights; Disability rights; **Immigrant rights**
   Americans with Disabilities Act (ADA), *2:* 277, 280–283
   Armenian Genocide Protests, *2:* 297–302, 301 (ill.)
   Attica Prison Riot (1971), *2:* 270–276, 274 (ill.)
   Bly, Nellie, investigation of mental hospital, *2:* 278, 278 (ill.)
   Capitol Crawl (1990), *2:* 276–284, 282 (ill.)
   Dalit Protests in India (2006), *2:* 290–297, 295 (ill.)
   definition and nature of, *2:* 263
   history, *2:* 264–268
   March to Abolish the Death Penalty, *2:* 284–289, 287 (ill.)
   Strangeways Prison Riot (1990), *2:* 271
Human Rights Campaign, *2:* 458
Human trafficking, *3:* 623, 643–647. *See also* **Slavery**
Humane Society of the United States, *1:* 11
Hunger strikes, *3:* 476, 701–702
   Manning, Bradley/Chelsea, *3:* 689
   Pankhurst, Sylvia, *3:* 704 (ill.)
   by Suffragettes in Prison, *3:* 701–707
   Women's Suffrage Protest at the White House, *3:* 713
Hunt, Jane, *3:* 708
Hussein, Saddam, *3:* 682

GENERAL INDEX

Hutton, Bobby, *2:* 245
Hyde Amendment, *3:* 578
Hydro-Quebec, *2:* 382

I

"I Have a Dream" speech, *1:* 39, 63, 68
"I Will Not Comply" Rally (2014), *2:* 252–256
    See also **Gun control/Gun rights**
IAT (Indians of All Tribes), *2:* 370–371
Idle No More, *2:* 365 (ill.)
Iglesias, Pablo, *1:* 121–122
Iguala, Mexico, *1:* 95–96
IJM (International Justice Mission), *3:* 647
Illinois
    DNC anti-war protests, *3:* 656 (ill.)
    Haymarket Square Riot, *2:* 418–419
    proposed Skokie neo-Nazi march, *1:* 188–189
ILO (International Labour Organization), *3:* 644
Immigrant rights, *2:* **305–334**, 313 (ill.), 317 (ill).
    323 (ill.), 324 (ill.), 329 (ill.), 330 (ill.). *See also*
    Human rights
    anti-Chinese riots, Denver, CO (1980),
      2: 328–329, 329 (ill.)
    California. Senate. Resolution No. 16 (2017),
      2: 327
    Molly Maguires, *2:* 312–313, 313 (ill.)
    Nativist Riots (1844), *2:* 311–318, 317 (ill.)
    Patriotic Europeans against the Islamization of
      the West (PEGIDA), *2:* 322–323, 323 (ill.)
    Pro-migrant Rallies in Europe and Australia
      (2015-2016), *2:* 318–325, 324 (ill.)
    Protests against President Trump's Travel Ban
      (2017), *2:* 325–332, 330 (ill.)
Immigrants and immigration. *See also* Refugees
    Chinese, *2:* 307, 328–329, 329 (ill.), 415–416
    Day without Immigrants protests, *1:* 83–89
    EU (European Union), *2:* 309–310
    German, *2:* 307
    Irish, *2:* 307, 312, 314
    Latin American, *2:* 308–309
    Mexican, *2:* 308–309
    undocumented immigrants, *1:* 74, 83–84; *2:* 325
    United Kingdom, *1:* 123, 124
    United States, *1:* 74, 83–85; *2:* 306–309

INC (Indian National Congress), *2:* 348–349
Income inequality, *1:* 99–100
Indentured servants, *3:* 510–511, 694
Independence movements, *2:* **335–359**, 345 (ill.),
    337 (ill.), 345 (ill.), 351 (ill.), 354 (ill.), 357 (ill.)
    Asia, *2:* 339–340
    Cuba, *2:* 338–339
    Czechoslovakia, *2:* 341–342, 352–358, 354 (ill.)
    Estonia, Singing Revolution, *2:* 348
    French colonies, *2:* 338; *3:* 625
    Gandhi leads Salt March (1930), *2:* 340–341,
      346–352, 351 (ill.)
    Gdansk Shipyard Strike, Poland (1980),
      2: 356–357, 357 (ill.)
    Grito de Lares (1868), *2:* 342–346, 345 (ill.)
    history, *2:* 335–340
    India, *2:* 340–341, 346–352
    Jamaica, *2:* 339
    Mexico, *2:* 338
    Puerto Rico, *2:* 342–346
    Spanish colonies, *2:* 338–339
    Velvet Revolution (1989), *2:* 352–358
India
    caste systems, *2:* 290–297
    colonial history, *2:* 347–349
    Dalit protests, *2:* 290–297, 295 (ill.)
    8888 anniversary protest, *3:* 503 (ill.)
    independence movements, *2:* 340–341, 346–352
    reservation system, *2:* 292–293, 294–295
India. Constitution, *2:* 292
India. National Crime Record Bureau, *2:* 296–297
Indian Mutiny (1857–1858), *2:* 348
Indian National Congress (INC), *2:* 348–349
Indian reservations. *See also* Native Americans
    land rights, *2:* 362–363
    Pine Ridge Reservation, *2:* 370, 372, 374
    Standing Rock Reservation, *2:* 369, 370, 384
Indians of All Tribes (IAT), *2:* 370–371
Indigenous Australians. *See* Aboriginals
Indigenous peoples. *See also* Native Americans
    Amazonian, *2:* 366, 379–384
    Canada, *2:* 365 (ill.)
    Copenhagen protests, *1:* 146, 149
    Cree First Nations, *2:* 382
    impact of colonization, *2:* 361, 375–376

GENERAL INDEX

Kayapo, *2:* 366, 380–384
land rights, *2:* 361
New Zealand, *2:* 364
Pacific Climate Warriors Blockade, *1:* 162, 162 (ill.)
South Africa, *3:* 532–533, 534
Taino, *2:* 343
Indigenous peoples' rights, *2:* **361–392**, 365 (ill.), 367 (ill.), 369 (ill.), 371 (ill.), 374 (ill.), 378 (ill.), 383 (ill.), 388 (ill.). *See also* Civil rights
    Aboriginal Land Rights Protest (1988), *2:* 365–366, 375–379, 378 (ill.)
    AIM Occupation of Wounded Knee (1973), *2:* 364–365, 367–375, 374 (ill.)
    Cree First Nations dam protest, *2:* 382
    Dakota Access Pipeline Protest (2016–2017), *2:* 366–367; 367 (ill.), 384–391, 388 (ill.)
    history, *2:* 362–364
    occupation of Alcatraz, *2:* 370–371, 371 (ill.)
    Preservation of Amazon Rain Forest Awareness Campaign (1989), *2:* 366, 379–384, 383 (ill.)
    Trail of Tears protest, *2:* 386–387, 387 (ill.)
Indignados movement, *1:* 90–96
Indigo Girls, *3:* 729
Individuals with Disabilities Education Act (IDEA), *2:* 278
Industrial Revolution, *1:* 133–134; *2:* 393, 395, 395 (ill.)
Industrialization, *2:* 400
International Congress of Women (1915), *3:* 657–663, 660 (ill.). *See also* Anti-war protests
    goals of, *3:* 661
    impact of, *3:* 661–663
    resolutions, *3:* 662
International Justice Mission (IJM), *3:* 647
International Labour Organization (ILO), *2:* 407; *3:* 644
International March for Elephants, *1:* 22–23. *See also* **Animal rights**
International Union, United Automobile, Aerospace and Agricultural Implement Workers of America, *2:* 414. *See also* UAW (United Auto Workers)
International Whaling Commission (IWC), *1:* 22
International Woman Suffrage Alliance, *3:* 658
International Workers Day, *1:* 86

Internet
    citizen journalism, *3:* 490–491
    role in organizing protests, *1:* 213
Interstate Commerce Commission, *1:* 54–55, 57, 59
Iowa, Student Armband Protest of Vietnam War (1965–1969), *3:* 663–668, 668 (ill.)
IPCC (United Nations. Intergovernmental Panel on Climate Change), *1:* 137, 148
Iranian demonstrators, violence against, *3:* 490–491, 491 (ill.)
Iranian Green Movement (2009), *3:* 490–491, 491 (ill.)
Iraq War (2003–2011), *3:* 682–683
    anti-war protests, *3:* 657, 682 (ill.)
    Bush, George W., speech, *3:* 680–681
    Candlelight Vigils against Invasion of Iraq (2003), *3:* 676–683
    civilian casualties, *3:* 684
Ireland
    Brexit demonstrations, *1:* 126
    Easter Rebellion (1916), *3:* 480–481, 481 (ill.)
Irish immigrants, *2:* 307, 312, 314. *See also* Immigrants and immigration
Irish Republican Brotherhood, *3:* 480
Irish War of Independence (1919–1921), *3:* 481
Irwin, Lord, *2:* 351
Islam, *1:* 184
Islamic extremists, *2:* 326–328
Islamic law, *3:* 715, 718, 719
Islamization, *2:* 322
Island nations, *1:* 146
    climate change, *1:* 157–158
    Pacific Climate Warriors Blockade, *1:* 162
Ivory trade, *1:* 18–19
IWC (International Whaling Commission), *1:* 22

J

Jackson, Jesse, *3:* 678
Jackson, Mahalia, *1:* 67, 68
Jackson, MS, Freedom Rides, *1:* 57
Jacobs, Aletta, *3:* 657, 658–659
"Jail, no bail," *1:* 61

GENERAL INDEX

Jamaica
    Christmas Rebellion/Baptist War (1831–1832), *3:* 634–638
    history, *3:* 634–635
    independence movements, *2:* 339
James II, King of England, *1:* 173; *2:* 266
Japan
    nuclear energy policy, *1:* 160
    rice riots of 1918, *1:* 126–127
    Tokyo Big March, *1:* 160
Jati, *2:* 291
"Je Suis Charlie" Protests (2015), *1:* 189–194, 192 (ill.). *See also* **Free speech**
    Muslim protests against *Charlie Hebdo*, *1:* 190 (ill.), 193
    pro free speech, *1:* 192–193
Jefferson County Courthouse, West Virginia, *2:* 411 (ill.)
Jewish Combat Organization (ZOB), *3:* 604–606, 605
Jewish Holocaust, *1:* 179; *2:* 297; *3:* 586, 613. *See also* Genocide
Jews
    assistance to, *3:* 588–589
    Danish, *3:* 597, 601–602
    under Nazis, *3:* 585–586, 607
Jim Crow laws, *1:* 37, 43–44. *See also* Racial discrimination
    changes to, *1:* 48
    school segregation, *1:* 48–49
    segregation, *1:* 55
John, King of England, *3:* 470
Johnson, Lyndon B., *1:* 69
    civil rights, *1:* 40
    Detroit Riots, *3:* 529
Jones, Mary Harris
    crusade against child labor, *2:* 399–407, 406 (ill.)
    excerpt from autobiography, *2:* 404–405
    Kensington textile mill strike, *2:* 401–403
Journey of Reconciliation (1947), *1:* 55
Judd, Ashley, *3:* 729
July 20 Plot (1944), *3:* 591
Juste, Carsten, *1:* 186
Justice for All March (2014), *3:* 515, 539–546, 545 (ill.). *See also* **Racial conflict**
Jyllands-Posten, *1:* 183–188, 191

K

Kadhem, Laila al-, *3:* 716 (ill.)
Kaepernick, Colin, *3:* 515, 516–517, 517 (ill.)
Kansas
    Brown, John, anti-slavery activity, *3:* 640
    debate over slavery, *3:* 640
    Summer of Mercy Protest, *3:* 566–567
Kayany Foundation, *3:* 724
Kayapo, *2:* 366, 380–384. *See also* Indigenous peoples
Keelan, Jennifer, *2:* 282 (ill.)
Keller, Helen, *1:* 179
Kelly, Mark, *2:* 248, 248 (ill.)
Kennedy, Anthony, *2:* 439
Kennedy, John F., *1:* 54
    assassination, *2:* 234
    Freedom Rides, *1:* 57, 59
    March on Washington, *1:* 66–67
Kennedy, Robert, *1:* 57, 69
Kennedy (John F.) International Airport, *2:* 330
Kenrick, Francis Patrick, *2:* 314–315, 316
Kensington Textile Mill Strike (1903), *2:* 401–403
Kent State University student protests, *3:* 669–676, 674 (ill.). *See also* Anti-war protests
Kenya, Global March for Elephants and Rhinos, *1:* 22–23, 24 (ill.)
Kerner Commission, *3:* 529–530
Kerr, Clark, *1:* 199
Kerr, Stanley, *2:* 299
Keys, Alicia, *3:* 729
Keystone XL project, *1:* 139, 140–141, 144
Khairlanji, India, Dalit family murder, *2:* 293–294
Kifner, John, *3:* 672–673
Killer whales, *1:* 4–5
    SeaWorld protests, *1:* 25–31
    treatment by SeaWorld, *1:* 26–27, 30–31
King, Martin Luther, Jr., *1:* 36, 78
    assassination, *1:* 41, 69
    Birmingham, AL, desegregation, *1:* 62
    civil rights movement, *1:* 75; *3:* 472
    "I Have a Dream" speech, *1:* 39
    March on Washington, *1:* 63, 67, 68
    Montgomery bus boycott, *1:* 36 (ill.), 45–46, 47

King, Rodney, *3:* 522
KKK (Ku Klux Klan), *1:* 47, 58; *3:* 542
Klausen, Jytte, *1:* 184, 185
KMT (Kuomintang), *1:* 107
Knights of Labor, *2:* 397
Koch, Charles, *1:* 111
Koch, David, *1:* 111
Kopp, James C., *3:* 563–564
Koran, *3:* 498, 715, 718
Kozachenko, Kathy, *2:* 433
Krause, Allison, *3:* 675
Ku Klux Klan (KKK), *1:* 47, 58; *3:* 542
Kulach, Adam, *3:* 716 (ill.)
Kuomintang (KMT), *1:* 107
Kyoto Protocol, *1:* 146

L

Labeling, genetically modified organisms, *1:* 229–230
Labor activists, *1:* 75–76
Labor Day, *2:* 402
Labor laws, *2:* 393
  child labor, *2:* 407
  United States, *2:* 397–398
Labor movement, *2:* 395–398, 401
Labor rights, *2:* **393–428**, 395 (ill.), 400 (ill.), 403 (ill.), 406 (ill.), 411 (ill.), 412 (ill.), 419 (ill.), 421 (ill.), 424 (ill.). *See also* Child labor; Workers
  Battle of Blair Mountain strike (1921), *2:* 410–411, 411 (ill.)
  Delano Grape Strike and Boycott (1965–1970), *2:* 414–422, 421 (ill.)
  Fast-Food Workers' Strike (2012), *2:* 422–426, 424 (ill.)
  Flint Sit-down Strike against General Motors (1936–1937), *2:* 407–414, 412 (ill.)
  Haymarket Square Riot (1886), *2:* 418–419, 419 (ill.)
  Mother Jones's "Children's Crusade" (1903), *2:* 399–407, 406 (ill.)
  Solidarity movement, *2:* 356–357, 357 (ill.)
  United States, *2:* 394
  worldwide, *2:* 398–399
Labor unions, *2:* 396–397
  employer resistance to, *2:* 397–398
  farmworkers, *1:* 75–76

Lafayette, LA, mass shooting, *2:* 251
Lake Oahe, *2:* 386
Lakota Sioux, *2:* 369, 369 (ill.), 370, 372. *See also* Native Americans
Lam, Carrie, *3:* 504–505
Lambda Legal, *2:* 433, 464
Land rights
  Indian reservations, *2:* 362–363
  indigenous peoples, *2:* 361
  Māori, *2:* 363–364
Land rights protests, *2:* 364–367. *See also* **Indigenous peoples' rights**
  Aboriginals, *2:* 365–366
  Amazonian indigenous peoples, *2:* 366, 379–384
  Australia, *2:* 375–379
  Canada, *2:* 365 (ill.)
  Cree First Nations, *2:* 382
  Native Americans, *2:* 364–365, 366–367, 384–391, 388 (ill.)
Lanza, Adam, *2:* 246–247, 253
Laramie, WY
  anti-gay protests by Westboro Baptist Church, *2:* 449–451
  murder of Matthew Shepard, *2:* 445–446
The Laramie Project, 2: 456–457
Las Vegas, NV, mass shootings, *2:* 260
Lasn, Kalle, *1:* 219
Latin America, *1:* 71, 72
Latin American immigrants, *2:* 308–309. *See also* Immigrants and immigration; Mexican Americans
Latino civil rights. *See* **Hispanic and Latino civil rights**
Latinos. *See* Hispanics and Latinos
Law Center to Prevent Gun Violence, *2:* 256
Law Enforcement Officers Protection Act, *2:* 234
Lebanon, Yousafzai, Malala, All-Girls School, *3:* 718–724
Lectors, *1:* 84, 85 (ill.)
Lee, Robert E., *3:* 642
Lee, Ronnie, *1:* 8
Lemay, Tiffany, *2:* 454
Lennon, John, *3:* 670, 671 (ill.)
Lesbians, *2:* 430. *See also* LGBTQ people
Lethal injection, *2:* 289. *See also* Death penalty
Leung, Trini, *3:* 474–475
Leung Chun-ying, *3:* 500–501, 504–505

GENERAL INDEX

Levi-Strauss, Claude, *1:* 166
Lewis, John, *1:* 56, 66–67, 68; *2:* 258, 259 (ill.)
LGBTQ people. *See also* Homosexuality
    definition, *2:* 429–430
    discrimination against, *2:* 431, 432, 436, 454–455
    lesbians, *2:* 430
    transgender people, *2:* 429, 435
LGBTQ rights, *2:* **429–466**, 433 (ill.), 439 (ill.), 440 (ill.), 444 (ill.), 449 (ill.), 455 (ill.), 456 (ill.), 461 (ill.), 463 (ill.). *See also* Civil rights
    China, *2:* 452–453, 458
    history, *2:* 430–431
    Marriage equality, *2:* 438–439, 439 (ill.)
    modern movement, *2:* 431–435
    NCAA boycott of North Carolina, *2:* 460–461, 461 (ill.)
    organizations, *2:* 432, 436
    protests against, *2:* 445–452
    Protests of North Carolina House Bill 2 (2016), *2:* 458–464, 461 (ill.), 463 (ill.)
    Russia, *2:* 454–455, 455 (ill.)
    Shanghai Pride Festival (2009), *2:* 452–458, 456 (ill.)
    Stonewall Riots (1969), *2:* 435–441, 440 (ill.)
    Westboro Baptist Church Protests of Matthew Shepard (1998–1999), *2:* 445–452, 449 (ill.)
    White Night Riots (1979), *2:* 441–445, 444 (ill.)
Li Peng, *3:* 475
Li Yinhe, *2:* 452
Liberal Democratic Party (Japan), *1:* 160
Libya
    Arab Spring, *3:* 489–490
    civil war, *3:* 490
Lincoln, Abraham, *3:* 654, 654 (ill.)
Little Rock, AR, school integration, *1:* 47–52
Little Rock Central High School, *1:* 47–52
Little Rock Nine Crisis (1957), *1:* 47–52, 52 (ill.). *See also* **African American civil rights**
Livermore, Mary, *3:* 697 (ill.)
Lloyd George, David, *3:* 705
Lobbyists, *1:* 139
Locke, John, *2:* 266
Loeak, Milañ, *1:* 158
London, UK, anti-fracking protesters, *1:* 155 (ill.)

Longley, Kristin, *2:* 413
Los Angeles, CA. *See also* California; East Los Angeles, CA
    Armenian genocide protests, *2:* 301 (ill.), 302
    A Day without Immigrants protests, *1:* 88
    King, Rodney, riots, *3:* 522–523, 523 (ill.)
    March for Women's Lives (1986), *3:* 556–561
    Occupy Wall Street demonstration, *1:* 222 (ill.)
    race riots (1992), *3:* 522–523, 523 (ill.)
    Watts Riots, *3:* 514 (ill.)
    Zoot Suit Riots, *3:* 518–524, 521 (ill.)
Los Angeles Race Riots (1992), *3:* 522–523, 523 (ill.)
Los Angeles Unified School District
    cultural studies introduced, *1:* 82
    discrimination in education, *1:* 79–80
Loughner, Jared Lee, *2:* 248
Louisiana
    mass shooting, *2:* 251
    school desegregation, *1:* 53
    slavery, *3:* 624–625
Louisiana Rebellion (German Coast) (1811), *3:* 623–628. *See also* **Slavery**
Love, William T., *1:* 143
Love Canal, NY, *1:* 136, 143, 143 (ill.)
Lowell, Arthur, *2:* 413
Luddites, *2:* 395 (ill.)
Lunch Counter Protest, McCrory's (1961), *1:* 59–63, 61 (ill.). *See also* **African American civil rights**
Luther, Martin, *2:* 312
Lyden, Jack, *2:* 450
Lysistrata, *3:* 651–652

M

Macy's Thanksgiving Parade, *1:* 28, 30
Madonna, *3:* 729
Mafia, *2:* 436–437
Magazinet, *1:* 185
Magna Carta (1215), *2:* 265; *3:* 470
Maharashtra, India, *2:* 296
Malala Fund, *3:* 724
Malala Yousafzai All-Girls School, *3:* 718–724
El Malcriado: The Voice of the Farm Worker, *2:* 417

Malê Revolt of 1835, *3:* 626–627, 627 (ill.). *See also* **Slavery**
Mallory, Tamika, *3:* 728
Malloy, Annie E., *3:* 660 (ill.)
Manama, Bahrain, *3:* 489
Manchester, England, Strangeways Prison riot, *2:* 271
Mandela, Nelson, *3:* 539
Manning, Bradley/Chelsea, *3:* 684–690, 686 (ill.). *See also* Transgender people
    arrest and trial, *3:* 686–688
    communication with WikiLeaks, *3:* 685–686
Mao Zedong, *1:* 107, 108; *3:* 473, 569
Māori, land rights, *2:* 363–364
March against Monsanto (2013), *1:* 223–230, 228 (ill.). *See also* **Globalization**
March for Life (1986), *3:* 558, 559
March for Life Education and Defense Fund, *3:* 559
March for Marriage, *2:* 439 (ill.)
March for Science (2017), *1:* 163–168, 165 (ill.); *3:* 730–731. *See also* **Environment**
March for Women's Lives (1986), *3:* 556–561, 557 (ill.), 559. *See also* **Reproductive rights**
March of the Mill Children, *2:* 399–407, 406 (ill.). *See also* **Labor rights**
March on Washington for Gun Control (2013), *2:* 246–252, 249 (ill.). *See also* **Gun control/Gun rights**
March on Washington for Jobs and Freedom (1963), *1:* 39, 39 (ill.), 63–69, 65 (ill.); *3:* 472. *See also* **African American civil rights**
    King Jr., Martin Luther, *1:* 63, 67, 68
    leaders, *1:* 65–66, 65 (ill.)
    Lewis, John, *1:* 66–67
    origins, *1:* 64
March to Abolish the Death Penalty, *2:* 284–289, 287 (ill.). *See also* **Human rights**
Marine Mammal Protection Act, *1:* 136
Maroons, *3:* 636
Marriage equality, *2:* 434
    defined, *2:* 430
    legal battle, *2:* 438–439
    Washington, D.C., protest against, *2:* 439 (ill.)
Married women, rights of, *3:* 693–695
Marshall, Thurgood, *1:* 39

Marshall Islands, *1:* 158
Martin, Richard, *1:* 2
Martin, Trayvon, *3:* 540–541
Martin's Act, *1:* 2
Mary II, Queen of England, *1:* 173
Marysville Pilchuck High School shootings, *2:* 253
Mass shootings, *2:* 239, 253–254, 257
    Lafayette, Louisiana, *2:* 251
    Las Vegas, Nevada, *2:* 260
    Obama, Barack speech, *2:* 251
    Sandy Hook Elementary School, *2:* 246–247
    Tucson, Arizona, *2:* 248
    Umpqua Community College, *2:* 251
    Virginia Tech, *2:* 249
Mateen, Oscar, *2:* 257
Matewan Massacre (1921), *2:* 410
Mattachine Society, *2:* 432
Matters, Muriel, *3:* 703–704
Matthew Shepard and James Byrd, Jr., Hate Crimes Prevention Act, *2:* 450, 451
Mauritania, abolition of slavery, *3:* 643
Maximilian, Saint, *3:* 652
Maximilianus, *3:* 652
May, Theresa, *1:* 125, 128–129
May Day, *1:* 86
Mayan texts, book burning, *1:* 178
McAuliffe, Terry, *3:* 542
McCartney, Stella, *1:* 12–13
McCormick Reaper Works, *2:* 418
McCorvey, Norma, *3:* 576–577, 577 (ill.)
McCoy, Rose, *1:* 28, 30
McCrory, Pat, *2:* 459
McCrory's Lunch Counter Protest (1961), *1:* 59–63, 61 (ill.). *See also* **African American civil rights**
McDonald's, *2:* 422, 424, 425
McGuire, Barry, *3:* 670
McKinney, Aaron, *2:* 447, 451
M'Clintock, Mary Ann, *3:* 708
McSpadden, Lesley, *3:* 545–546
Means, Russell, *2:* 372, 374
Mechanics' Union of Trade Associations, *2:* 396–397
Medicaid, *2:* 283–284; *3:* 578
Medina, Francisco Ramírez, *2:* 345

Melchior, Bent, *3:* 598–599, 599 (ill.)
Meltdowns. *See* Nuclear accidents
Mental institutions, *2:* 278
Mercado, Mark, *2:* 255–256
Merkel, Angela, *1:* 161; *2:* 321, 322
Merkley, Jeff, *1:* 230
Methane gas, *1:* 159
Metropolitan Coalition against Nukes, *1:* 160
Mexican American students
    discrimination in education, *1:* 79–80
    East LA blowouts, *1:* 77–82
Mexican-American War (1846–1848), *1:* 73
Mexican Americans. *See also* Hispanics and Latinos
    racial conflict, *3:* 518–524
    racial discrimination, *3:* 519
    Zoot Suit Riots, *3:* 512 (ill.), 521 (ill.)
Mexican farm workers, *1:* 75 (ill.). *See also* Workers
Mexican immigrants, *2:* 308–309. *See also* Immigrants and immigration
Mexican Indignados movement, *1:* 90–96
Mexican students
    demonstrations, *1:* 95 (ill.)
    murder of in Iguala, *1:* 95–96
    Tlatelolco massacre, *1:* 94
    violence against, *1:* 90, 94
Mexican workers, *2:* 416, 418–419. *See also* Workers
Mexico
    drug trade, *1:* 75, 90, 91
    independence movements, *2:* 338
    Indignados movement, *1:* 90–96
    Tlatelolco Massacre (1968), *1:* 94, 95
    war on drugs, *1:* 91–95
Mexico City, Mexico, *1:* 93–94
MIA (Montgomery Improvement Association), *1:* 45–46
Michigan
    Detroit Riots (1967), *3:* 524–530
    strike against GM, *2:* 407–414, 412 (ill.)
Middle Ages
    political/government uprisings, *3:* 469–470
    slavery, *3:* 619–620
Middle East, Arab Spring, *1:* 90; *3:* 486–493
Middle Eastern refugees, *2:* 318–319
Migrant workers, *2:* 415, 416. *See also* Workers

Military draft
    United States Civil War, *3:* 526, 654
    Vietnam War, *3:* 666
Military servicemen, Zoot Suit Riots, *3:* 520–522
Milk (2008), *2:* 445
Milk, Harvey, *2:* 433, 441, 442, 445
Mill, John Stuart, *3:* 703
Miller, David, *3:* 666
Miller, Hannah, *2:* 454
Miller, Jeffrey, *3:* 675
Minimum wage, *2:* 422–423, 426. *See also* **Labor rights**
Minks, *1:* 11
Mississippi, Freedom Rides, *1:* 57
Mississippi Summer Project/Freedom Summer Voter Registration, *1:* 58, 58 (ill.). *See also* **African American civil rights**
Mitchell, George P., *1:* 154
Molly Maguires, *2:* 312–313, 313 (ill.)
Moms Demand Action, *2:* 238 (ill.)
Monáe, Janelle, *3:* 729
Monkeys, animal testing, *1:* 7–8, 10
Monopolies, *1:* 224–225, 228
Monsanto Co., *1:* 223–230
    concerns about products, *1:* 224–225
    product benefits, *1:* 225–226
Montgomery, AL
    bus boycott, *1:* 42–47
    Freedom Rides, *1:* 57
Montgomery Bus Boycott (1955–1956), *1:* 36 (ill.), 42–47. *See also* **African American civil rights**
Montgomery Improvement Association (MIA), *1:* 45–46
Moore, Gwen, *2:* 425
Moore, Michael, *3:* 678, 729
Moore, Tim, *2:* 462
Morgan, Ephraim, *2:* 410
Morgan, J.P., *1:* 217–218
Morgan v. Virginia, *1:* 55
Morsi, Mohamed, *3:* 498
Moscone, George Richard, *2:* 441, 442, 443, 445
Mother Jones
    crusade against child labor, *2:* 399–407, 406 (ill.)
    excerpt from autobiography, *2:* 404–405
    Kensington textile mill strike, *2:* 401–403

Mother Jones's "Children's Crusade" (1903), *2:* 399–407, 406 (ill.). *See also* **Labor rights**
Mothershed, Thelma, *1:* 50
Mott, Charles Stewart, *2:* 408
Mott, Lucretia, *3:* 697 (ill.), 708
Movement for Peace with Justice and Dignity, *1:* 93
Mubarak, Hosni, *3:* 488, 494, 496–497
Muhammad, images of, *1:* 176, 183, 184, 190
Muir, John, *1:* 135, 135 (ill.)
Mulford, Donald, *2:* 242–243
Mulford Act (California), *2:* 242–243, 244
Múnera, Álvaro, *1:* 16
Murder. *See also* Violence
    of Dalit family in Khairlanji, India, *2:* 293–294
    by pro-life advocates, *3:* 554–555, 563–564, 567
Murphy, Christopher, *2:* 258
Murphy, Frank, *2:* 412
Muslim Brotherhood, *3:* 498
Muslim protesters
    against *Charlie Hebdo* use of images of Muhammad, *1:* 190 (ill.), 193
    Muhammad cartoons, *1:* 186–187, 186 (ill.)
Muslim Protests of Danish Cartoons, *1:* 183–188, 186 (ill.). *See also* **Free speech**
Muslims, Trump travel bans, *2:* 325–326, 328–329, 330 (ill.)
Mutawa, 3: 715
Myanmar
    8888 Uprising (1988), *3:* 502–503
    violence against the Rohingya, *3:* 503

N

NAACP (National Association for the Advancement of Colored People)
    founding, *1:* 35
    legal actions, *1:* 38–39
    March on Washington, *1:* 65
    Montgomery bus boycott, *1:* 44
NAFTA (North American Free Trade Agreement), *1:* 205
Naidu, Sarojina, *2:* 351 (ill.)
NAN (National Action Network), *3:* 539, 544

Nat Turner's Rebellion (1831–1832), *3:* 628–634, 629 (ill.). *See also* **Slavery**
National Action Network (NAN), *3:* 539, 544
National Advisory Commission on Civil Disorders, *3:* 529–530
National American Woman Suffrage Association (NAWSA), *3:* 710
National Association for the Advancement of Colored People (NAACP)
    founding, *1:* 35
    legal actions, *1:* 38–39
    March on Washington, *1:* 65
    Montgomery bus boycott, *1:* 44
National Center for Missing and Exploited Children, *3:* 645
National Child Labor Committee, *2:* 407
National Collegiate Athletic Association (NCAA), *2:* 460–461, 461 (ill.)
National Conference of Dalit Organizations, *2:* 295 (ill.), 296
National Council on the Handicapped (NCH), *2:* 282
National defense jobs, desegregation, *1:* 64
National Democratic Party (Egypt), *3:* 495
National Family Planning Program, *3:* 577–578
National Farm Workers Association (NFWA), *1:* 75, 78; *2:* 419
National Firearms Act, *2:* 234
National Football League (NFL), *3:* 515
National Geographic, 1: 21–22
National Guard, *2:* 275, 389
    Arkansas, *1:* 48, 50–52, 52 (ill.)
    Michigan, *3:* 528, 528 (ill.), 531
    Ohio, *3:* 674–675
National Instant Criminal Background Check System, *2:* 253
National Labor Relations Act of 1935, *2:* 397
National Socialist German Workers' Party (Nazi Party), *3:* 585, 592, 607
National Socialist Party of America, *1:* 188
National Socialists German Students' Association, *1:* 179
National Urban League (NUL), *1:* 35
National Women's Party (United States), *3:* 698 (ill.), 710, 712 (ill.)

GENERAL INDEX

National Youth Peace Prize (Pakistan), *3:* 719
Nationwide Tea Party Coalition, *1:* 114
Native Americans. *See also* Indian reservations; Indigenous peoples
  Dakota Access Pipeline Protest, *2:* 366–367, 367 (ill.), 384–391, 388 (ill.)
  impact of colonization, *2:* 362–363, 386–387
  Lakota Sioux, *2:* 369, 369 (ill.), 370, 372
  land rights protests, *2:* 364–365, 366–367, 384–391, 388 (ill.)
  occupation of Alcatraz, *2:* 370–371, 371 (ill.)
  opposition to oil pipelines, *1:* 144
  slavery, *3:* 624
  Standing Rock Sioux, *2:* 384–385, 387–388, 388 (ill.)
  treaties with federal government, *2:* 368, 386
  treatment in the United States, *2:* 368–369
Nativism, *2:* 314
Nativist Riots (1844), *2:* 311–318, 317 (ill.). *See also* **Immigrant rights**
  eyewitness account, *2:* 314–315
  Protestant-Catholic conflict, *2:* 312–313
NATO (North Atlantic Treaty Organization), *3:* 490
NAWSA (National American Woman Suffrage Association), *3:* 710
Nazi Germany, *3:* 585–586, 592. *See also* Germany; Gestapo; **Resistance to Nazis**
  book burnings, *1:* 179
  deportations to death camps, *3:* 604–605
Nazi Party (National Socialist German Workers' Party), *3:* 585, 592, 607
Nazis, *1:* 188. *See also* Neo-Nazis
NCAA (National Collegiate Athletic Association), *2:* 460–461, 461 (ill.)
NCH (National Council on the Handicapped), *2:* 282
Ne Win, *3:* 502–503
Nelson, Willie, *1:* 30
Neo-Nazis, *1:* 188–189; *3:* 542, 543 (ill.). *See also* Nazis
Neumann-Ortiz, Christine, *1:* 87
Nevada, mass shootings, *2:* 260
New Delhi, India, 8888 anniversary protest, *3:* 503 (ill.)

New Mexico, Alamagordo book burning, *1:* 181 (ill.)
New Orleans, LA, school desegregation, *1:* 53
New York, NY
  child labor protest of 1909, *2:* 402–403, 403 (ill.)
  draft riots of 1863, *3:* 526–527, 527 (ill.)
  Occupy Wall Street, *1:* 216–222
  One Thousand Coffins Protest (2004), *3:* 678–679, 679 (ill.)
  racial conflict, *3:* 526–527
New York. State Police, *2:* 275
New York Act (1866), *1:* 3
New York City Draft Riots (1863), *3:* 526–527, 527 (ill.), 654. *See also* **Racial conflict**
New York Communities for Change (NYCC), *2:* 422, 423, 424
New York (state)
  Love Canal, *1:* 136, 143, 143 (ill.)
  Operation Rescue protests, *3:* 562–568, 563
New York State Liquor Authority, *2:* 436
New York Times, *3:* 555–556
New Zealand, indigenous peoples, *2:* 364
Newcastle Harbor, New South Wales, *1:* 160–161
Newman, Paul, *1:* 68
Newsweek, *2:* 452
Newton, Huey P., *2:* 240, 242
Newton (Huey P.) Gun Club, *2:* 244
Newtown, Connecticut, mass shooting, *2:* 246–247
NFL (National Football League), *3:* 515
NFWA (National Farm Workers Association), *1:* 75, 78; *2:* 419
Nigeria, Boko Haram kidnappings, *3:* 700, 722–723
Nixon, Richard M., *2:* 371
  decision to invade Cambodia, *3:* 671
  expansion of Vietnam War, *3:* 656
  moves to end Vietnam War, *3:* 676
  Women's Equality Day, *3:* 729
No Taxpayer Funding for Abortion and Abortion Insurance Full Disclosure Act, *3:* 580
NOAA (United States. National Oceanic and Atmospheric Administration), *1:* 136
Nobel Peace Prize
  Gore, Al, speech, *1:* 148–149
  Suu Kyi, Aung San, *3:* 503
  Yousafzai, Malala, *3:* 718, 720–721

xciv U•X•L Protests, Riots, and Rebellions: Civil Unrest in the Modern World

Nonviolent resistance, *2:* 341, 420–421. *See also* Civil disobedience
Norman, Peter, *3:* 516, 517 (ill.)
North America
  British colonies, *2:* 336–337
  colonization, *1:* 72
North American Free Trade Agreement (NAFTA), *1:* 205
North Atlantic Treaty Organization (NATO), *3:* 490
North Carolina
  boycott, *2:* 461–462
  NCAA boycott, *2:* 460–461
  sit-ins, *1:* 59, 60
  transgender rights, *2:* 458–464
North Carolina. General Assembly. HB2, *2:* 458–459
  protests, *2:* 458–464, 461 (ill.), 463 (ill.)
  repeal, *2:* 463–464
North Carolina. General Assembly. HB142, *2:* 460, 464
North Dakota
  Dakota Access Pipeline protest, *2:* 366–367, 367 (ill.), 388 (ill.)
  land rights protests, *2:* 384–391, 388 (ill.)
North Vietnam, *2:* 340 (ill.). *See also* Vietnam
Northern Ireland, Brexit demonstrations, *1:* 126
Norway
  publication of cartoons of Muhammad, *1:* 185
  whaling, *1:* 22–23
No-till farming, *1:* 225–226
NOW (National Organization for Women), *3:* 554, 558–561, 560–561, 728
NPS (United States. National Park Service), *1:* 135
NRA (National Rifle Association), *2:* 238–239, 245, 250, 252, 257
Nuclear accidents
  Chernobyl, Ukraine, *1:* 136–137
  Fukushima, Japan, *1:* 160–161
Nuclear power plants, post-Fukushima protests, *1:* 160–161, 161 (ill.)
NUL (National Urban League), *1:* 35
Nunez, David, *2:* 255–256
NUWSS (National Union of Women's Suffrage Societies), *3:* 703

NYCC (New York Communities for Change), *2:* 422, 423, 424
Nye, Bill, *1:* 165 (ill.)

O

Oakes, Richard, *2:* 370
Oakland, CA, Global Frackdown, *1:* 156
Obama, Barack, *1:* 76 (ill.), 113
  Dakota Access Pipeline, *2:* 385
  declares Stonewall Inn a national landmark, *2:* 441
  hate crimes laws, *2:* 451
  Keystone XL project, *1:* 139, 141, 144
  Manning, Chelsea, sentence reduction, *3:* 685, 690
  on mass shootings, *2:* 251
  minimum wage, *2:* 422–423, 426
  repeal of "Don't Ask, Don't Tell," *2:* 435
  support of gun control sit-in, *2:* 259
Obama, Michelle, *3:* 700–701, 727
Obergefell, Jim, *2:* 438–439
Obergefell v. Hodges, *2:* 434, 438–439
Occupation of Alcatraz (1969–1970), *2:* 370–371, 371 (ill.)
Occupy Central with Love and Peace, *3:* 500–501
Occupy Wall Street (2011), *1:* 216–222, 222 (ill.). *See also* **Globalization**
  declaration of principles, *1:* 220–221
  expansion beyond NYC, *1:* 220–221, 222 (ill.)
  origins, *1:* 219
Ochs, Phil, *3:* 670
Ogallala Aquifer, *1:* 141
Ohio, Kent State University student protests, *3:* 669–676, 674 (ill.)
Oil leaks, *1:* 140
Oil pipelines, *1:* 140–141, 142. *See also* Dakota Access Pipeline (DAPL); Keystone XL project
Olympic Games, Mexico City (1968), *3:* 516, 517 (ill.)
One child policy, *3:* 568. *See also* Birth control; **Reproductive rights**
  enforcement of, *3:* 570–572
  introduction of, *3:* 569–570
  results of, *3:* 573
  revision of, *3:* 573–574

One Child Policy Riots (2007), *3:* 568–574, 572 (ill.)
One Million Moms for Gun Control, *2:* 248
One Thousand Coffins Protest (2004), *3:* 678–679, 679 (ill.). *See also* Anti-war protests
Open carry, *2:* 235. *See also* **Gun control/Gun rights**
  Black Panthers protest, *2:* 239–245, 243 (ill.)
  Huey P. Newton Gun Club demonstrations, *2:* 244
Operation Rescue (1992), *3:* 562–568. *See also* **Reproductive rights**
  demonstrators, *3:* 564 (ill.), 567 (ill.)
  history, *3:* 562–563
  methods, *3:* 563–564
Operation Save America, *3:* 563
Opletal, Jan, *2:* 355
Orcas, *1:* 4–5
  SeaWorld protests, *1:* 25–31
  treatment by SeaWorld, *1:* 26–27, 30–31
Orestiada, Greece, pro-migrant rally, *2:* 324 (ill.)
Origliasso, Jessica, *1:* 13 (ill.)
Origliasso, Lisa, *1:* 13 (ill.)
Orlando, FL, mass shootings at Pulse nightclub, *2:* 257
O'Sullivan, Michael, *1:* 28
Oswald, Lee Harvey, *2:* 234
Oswald, Russell, *2:* 273
Ottoman Empire, *2:* 297–300
Outsourcing, *1:* 207
Oxfam, *1:* 100
Oxford, Mississippi, *1:* 58

P

Pacific Climate Warriors Blockade (2014), *1:* 157–163, 162 (ill.). *See also* **Environment**
Pacific Lumber Company, *1:* 152
Pacifists, *3:* 652, 661. *See also* Anti-war protests
Paddock, Stephen, *2:* 260
PAH (Platform for People Affected by Mortgages), *1:* 120
Palestinian students, flag burning, *1:* 186 (ill.)
Paltrow, Gweneth, *1:* 229
Pankhurst, Emmeline, *3:* 703
Pankhurst, Sylvia, *3:* 704 (ill.)

Pantaleo, Daniel, *3:* 541–542, 544–545
Pantsuit Nation, *3:* 726
Parent, Elena, *2:* 238 (ill.)
Paris, France
  attack on *Charlie Hebdo* offices, *1:* 191
  student protests of 1968, *1:* 118–119, 119 (ill.)
Paris Agreement, *1:* 168
Paris Peace Accords, *3:* 676
Parks, Rosa, *1:* 36 (ill.), 42–43, 45 (ill.), 47
Partial-Birth Abortion Act, *3:* 561
Partisans, *3:* 589
Patents, genetically modified seeds, *1:* 224
Patriot Guard Riders, *2:* 452
Patriotic Europeans against the Islamization of the West (PEGIDA), *2:* 322–323, 323 (ill.)
Patterson, Romaine, *2:* 449
Pattillo, Melba, *1:* 50
Paul, Alice, *3:* 698 (ill.), 710, 713
Paul, Rand, *1:* 115–116
PayPal, *2:* 462
Pearse, Patrick, *3:* 480
Peasants' Revolt of 1381, *3:* 470
PEGIDA (Patriotic Europeans against the Islamization of the West), *2:* 322–323, 323 (ill.)
Pence, Mike, *3:* 559, 578–579
Penn, Sean, *2:* 445
Pennsylvania
  Kensington textile mill strike, *2:* 401–403
  Nativist Riots (1844), *2:* 311–318, 317 (ill.)
Peño Nieto, Enrique, *1:* 95, 96
Pentagon terror attack (2001), *2:* 326; *3:* 677–680. *See also* Terrorism
People for the Ethical Treatment of Animals (PETA)
  antifur campaign, *1:* 12–13, 13 (ill.)
  circus animals, *1:* 29
  founding, *1:* 4
  SeaWorld protests, *1:* 30
  support for ALF, *1:* 11
People's Climate March, *1:* 156
Perez, Carmen, *3:* 728
Periscope, *2:* 259
Perry, John B., *2:* 314–315
Perry, Rick, *2:* 288
Pesticides, *1:* 135, 224

PETA (People for the Ethical Treatment of Animals)
   antifur campaign, *1:* 12–13, 13 (ill.)
   circus animals, *1:* 29
   founding, *1:* 4
   SeaWorld protests, *1:* 30
   support for ALF, *1:* 11
Peter, Paul, and Mary, *3:* 670
Pethick-Lawrence, Emmeline, *3:* 660 (ill.), 661
Pew Research Center, *2:* 308, 453; *3:* 541 (ill.)
Pharmaceutical industry, *1:* 226–227, 227 (ill.)
Phelps, Fred, *2:* 446, 448
Philadelphia, PA, Nativist Riots (1844), *2:* 311–318, 317 (ill.)
Phipps, Benjamin, *3:* 629 (ill.)
Picketing, *3:* 563
Pieterson, Hector, *3:* 537
Pine Ridge Reservation, *2:* 370, 372, 374
Pixar Animation Studios, *1:* 28
Planned Parenthood, *3:* 558, 574, 575–576, 728.
   See also **Reproductive rights**
   anti-abortion demonstrators, *3:* 564 (ill.)
   debate over government funding for, *3:* 577–579
   pro-choice supporters, *3:* 579 (ill.)
   protests (2017), *3:* 574–580, 579 (ill.)
Planned Parenthood of Southeastern Pennsylvania v. Casey, *3:* 561
Platform for People Affected by Mortgages (PAH), *1:* 120
Plessy v. Ferguson, *1:* 48–49
Poaching
   elephants, *1:* 18–19, 25
   gorillas, *1:* 20
   rhinos, *1:* 18–19, 25
Podemos, *1:* 121–122
Poitier, Sidney, *1:* 68
Poland, Bialystok Ghetto, *3:* 607
Poland. Home Army, *3:* 589–590, 604
Polaris Project, *3:* 644, 646
Police
   impact of police shootings, *3:* 541 (ill.)
   racial discrimination, *3:* 513–514
   Watts Riots, *3:* 514 (ill.)
Police brutality, *3:* 525
Polish Home Army, *3:* 589–590, 604

Polish resistance (World War II), *3:* 589–590, 590 (ill.)
Political prisoners, *3:* 706
Political/Government uprisings, *3:* 467–507, 476 (ill.), 481 (ill.), 483 (ill.), 491 (ill.), 492 (ill.), 496 (ill.), 500 (ill.), 503 (ill.), 504 (ill.)
   Arab Spring and the Syrian Civil Uprising (2011), *3:* 486–493, 492 (ill.)
   causes of, *3:* 467–468
   Easter Rebellion (1916), *3:* 480–481, 481 (ill.)
   8888 Uprising, Myanmar (1988), *3:* 502–503, 503 (ill.)
   Fall of the Berlin Wall (1989), *3:* 478–486, 483 (ill.)
   history, *3:* 469–472
   Iranian Green Movement (2009), *3:* 490–491, 491 (ill.)
   Middle Ages, *3:* 469–470
   Tahrir Square Protests (Egyptian Revolution, 2011), *3:* 493–498, 496 (ill.)
   Tiananmen Square Protests (1989), *3:* 473–478, 476 (ill.)
   Umbrella Revolution (2014), *3:* 498–505, 500 (ill.), 504 (ill.)
PoliticsNation, *3:* 544
Pollution, *1:* 134–135
Pompeo, Mike, *3:* 690
Popular Party (Spain), *1:* 121, 122
Populist movement, *1:* 218
Porkulus protests, Tea Party, *1:* 111–116, 114 (ill).
   See also **Economic discontent**
Portuguese colonies. *See also* Colonization
   slave rebellions, *3:* 626–627
   slave trade, *3:* 621
   slavery, *3:* 511
Potter (Harry) Book Burning (2001), *1:* 177–183
Potter (Harry) (book series), *1:* 175
   book burning, *1:* 177–183
   opposition to, *1:* 179–180
Poverty, *1:* 101
Prague Spring, *2:* 353, 354 (ill.)
Preservation of Amazon Rain Forest Awareness Campaign (1989), *2:* 379–384
Presidential elections, *3:* 725–726
Presidential Medal of Freedom, *1:* 76 (ill.), 79

GENERAL INDEX

El Primer Congreso Mexicanista, *1:* 73
Prison colonies, *2:* 376. *See also* Colonization
Prisoners' rights, *2:* 270–276. *See also* **Human rights**
Prisons, human rights abuses, *2:* 270–271
Probst, Christoph, *3:* 593, 596
Pro-choice groups, *3:* 550–551, 554, 556, 574, 579 (ill.). *See also* **Reproductive rights**
Pro-democracy protests. *See* **Political/Government uprisings**
Progressive Party (United States), *3:* 710
Prohibition (1920–1933), *2:* 233–234
Project Confrontation, *1:* 62
Pro-life groups, *3:* 550, 554, 557, 574. *See also* **Reproductive rights**
  March for Life, *3:* 559
  murder by, *3:* 554–555
Pro-migrant rallies. *See also* **Immigrant rights**
  Europe and Australia, *2:* 318–325, 324 (ill.)
  Orestiada, Greece, *2:* 324 (ill.)
Protest literature, *3:* 631
Protest songs, *3:* 670–671
Protestant Reformation, *2:* 312–313
Protestants, *2:* 312
#ProtestPP, *3:* 574, 579–580
Protests. *See also* Boycotts; Riots; Sit-ins; Student protests
  African American civil rights, *1:* 35–70
  animal rights, *1:* 1–33
  athletes, *3:* 516–517
  economic discontent, *1:* 99–131
  environment, *1:* 133–170
  free speech, *1:* 171–202
  globalization, *1:* 203–231
  gun control/gun rights, *2:* 233–262, 237 (ill.), 238–239, 238 (ill.)
  Hispanic and Latino civil rights, *1:* 71–98
  HIV/AIDS drugs, *1:* 226–227
  human rights, *2:* 263–304
  immigrant rights, *2:* 305–334
  independence movements, *2:* 335–359
  indigenous peoples' rights, *2:* 361–392
  labor rights, *2:* 393–428
  LGBTQ rights, *2:* 429–466
  Mexican American students, *1:* 77–82
  political/government uprisings, *3:* 467–507
  racial conflict, *3:* 509–548
  reproductive rights, *3:* 549–583
  resistance to Nazis, *3:* 585–615
  slavery, *3:* 617–649
  in sports, *3:* 516–517
  tax, *1:* 111–116
  war, *3:* 651–692
  whaling, *1:* 22–23
  women's rights, *3:* 693–732
Protests against President Trump's travel ban (2017), *2:* 325–332, 330 (ill.). *See also* **Immigrant rights**
Protests of North Carolina House Bill 2 (2016), *2:* 458–464, 463 (ill.). *See also* **LGBTQ rights**
PSOE (Spanish Socialist Workers' Party), *1:* 120–121
Puerta del Sol, Madrid, Spain, *1:* 119, 121 (ill.)
Puerto Rico
  independence movements, *2:* 342–346
  as Spanish colony, *2:* 343–344
Pulse nightclub shootings, *2:* 257
Purple Teardrop Campaign, *3:* 646–647
Putin, Vladimir, *2:* 454

Q

Qaddafi, Mu'ammar al-, *3:* 488–489
al-Qaeda, *1:* 191
Qatar, labor rights, *2:* 398–399
Qin Shi Huang, *1:* 178
Qing Dynasty, *1:* 105–106
QR codes, *1:* 229
Quakers, *3:* 630, 652
Queer, *2:* 429. *See also* LGBTQ people
Quinn, William, *2:* 274

R

Race and racism, *3:* 509–510. *See also* White supremacists
  motivation for Zoot Suit riots, *3:* 523
  myth of racial superiority, *3:* 512–513

Racial conflict, *3:* **509–548**, 512 (ill.), 514 (ill.), 517 (ill.), 521 (ill.), 523 (ill.), 527 (ill.), 528 (ill.), 535 (ill.), 540 (ill.), 543 (ill.), 545 (ill.). *See also* **African American civil rights**; Black Lives Matter
  Black Consciousness Movement, *3:* 532–533
  Charlottesville Protests (2017), *3:* 542–543, 543 (ill.)
  Detroit Riots (1967), *3:* 524–530, 528 (ill.)
  Justice for All March (2014), *3:* 539–546, 545 (ill.)
  Los Angeles Race Riots (1992), *3:* 522–524, 523 (ill.)
  Mexican Americans, *3:* 518–524
  New York City Draft Riots (1863), *3:* 526–527, 527 (ill.)
  Soweto Uprising (1976), *3:* 530–539, 535 (ill.)
  Sports, protests in, *3:* 516–517, 517 (ill.)
  United States, *3:* 515–518
  Zoot Suit Riots (1943), *3:* 512, 512 (ill.), 518–524, 521 (ill.)
Racial discrimination, *1:* 35. *See also* Apartheid; Discrimination; Jim Crow laws
  African Americans, *1:* 36–37; *3:* 512, 513–515
  bus service, *1:* 54–59
  Mexican Americans, *3:* 519
  police, *3:* 513–514
  segregation and, *1:* 42
  South Africa, *3:* 513
Racial profiling, *3:* 539
Racial sensitivity, *1:* 194, 200
Racial superiority, *3:* 509–510, 512–513
Rain forests, *2:* 366, 379–380
Randolph, A. Philip, *1:* 64, 65–66, 68
Rankin, Jeannette, *3:* 711
Raoni (1977), *2:* 382
Raoni Metuktire, *2:* 366, 380–381, 383 (ill.)
Ray, Gloria, *1:* 50, 51
Reagan, Leslie J., *3:* 552
Reagan, Ronald, *2:* 245, 281
  Berlin Wall speech, *3:* 484–485
  position on reproductive rights, *3:* 559
  reproductive rights, *3:* 558
Redwoods, *1:* 152
Reed (Walter) Medical Center, *3:* 688–689, 689 (ill.)
Refugees. *See also* Immigrants and immigration
  Afghanistan, *2:* 319

  camps, *2:* 319–320, 320
  climate, *1:* 159
  crisis in Europe, *2:* 309–310, 324–325
  dangerous journeys, *2:* 323–324
  defined, *2:* 320
  EU (European Union), *2:* 319–321
  Middle Eastern, *2:* 318–319
  Syrian, *2:* 319, 321; *3:* 493, 720–724
Regan, Tom, *1:* 4
Reich, Robert, *2:* 425
Reid, Eric, *3:* 517 (ill.)
Religion, free speech and, *1:* 176, 183
Religious freedom, *2:* 311
Reproductive health services, *3:* 575
Reproductive rights, *3:* **549–583**, 557 (ill.), 564 (ill.), 567 (ill.), 572 (ill.), 577 (ill.), 579 (ill.). *See also* Abortion; Pro-choice groups; Pro-life groups; **Women's rights**
  debate over, *3:* 549–550
  history, *3:* 551–555
  laws limiting, *3:* 555
  March for Life (1986), *3:* 558, 559
  March for Women's Lives (1986), *3:* 556–561, 557 (ill.)
  McCorvey, Norma, *3:* 576–577, 577 (ill.)
  One Child Policy Riots (2007), *3:* 568–574, 572 (ill.)
  ongoing fight over, *3:* 555–556
  Operation Rescue (1992), *3:* 562–568, 564 (ill.)
  Planned Parenthood Protests (2017), *3:* 574–580, 579 (ill.)
  Summer of Mercy Protest (1991), *3:* 566–567
Republican National Convention (RNC), *3:* 564, 678
Reservation system
  India, *2:* 292–293
  private businesses, *2:* 294–295
Resistance to Nazis, *3:* **585–615**, 590 (ill.), 593 (ill.), 596 (ill.), 601 (ill.), 606 (ill.), 611 (ill.). *See also* Nazi Germany
  beginnings, *3:* 587–588
  Holocaust Resistance in Denmark (1943), *3:* 597–602, 601 (ill.)
  peaceful resistance, *3:* 588–589
  Treblinka Death Camp Revolt (1943), *3:* 607–614, 611 (ill.)

GENERAL INDEX

violent resistance, *3:* 590–591
  Warsaw Ghetto Uprising (1943), *3:* 602–607, 606 (ill.)
  White Rose Movement (1942–1943), *3:* 592–597, 593 (ill.), 596 (ill.)
Revolutionary Committee of Puerto Rico, *2:* 344–345
Rhino horn, *1:* 19
Rhinos
  poaching, *1:* 18–19, 25
  population decline, *1:* 21–22
Rhodes, James A., *3:* 674–675
Rice Riots of 1918 (Japan), *1:* 126–127
Richards, Cecile, *3:* 579, 728
Rig Veda, *2:* 290–291
Ringling Bros. and Barnum & Bailey Circus, *1:* 5, 29, 29 (ill.)
Riots. *See also* Protests; Violence
  anti-immigrant, *2:* 328–329
  Detroit Riots (MI) (1967), *3:* 524–530, 528 (ill.)
  Los Angeles Race Riots (1992), *3:* 522–523, 523 (ill.)
  Nativist riots, Philadelphia, Pennsylvania, *2:* 311–318, 317 (ill.)
  New York City Draft Riots (1863), *3:* 526–527, 527 (ill.), 654
  One Child Policy Riots (2007), *3:* 568–574, 572 (ill.)
  Rice Riots of 1918, *1:* 126–127
  Stonewall Riots (1969), *2:* 432–433, 435–441, 440 (ill.)
  White Night Riots (1979), *2:* 441–445, 444 (ill.)
  Zoot Suit Riots (1943), *3:* 512, 512 (ill.), 518–524, 521 (ill.)
RNC (Republican National Convention), *3:* 564, 678
Roberts, John, *1:* 87
Roberts, Terrence, *1:* 50
Robinson, Jackie, *1:* 68
Rock Hill, SC, Freedom Rides, *1:* 56
Rockefeller, Nelson, *2:* 273, 275
Roe v. Wade, 3: 554, 556, 575–576. *See also* McCorvey, Norma.
Roeder, Scott, *3:* 567
Rohingya, violence against, *3:* 503
Rolling Stone, 1: 177
Roman Empire (27 BCE–476 CE), *2:* 305–306; *3:* 617–619
Romney, George, *3:* 528, 529, 530–531
Roosevelt, Franklin D., *1:* 64; *2:* 277, 407, 414
Roosevelt, Theodore, *1:* 135 (ill.); *2:* 399, 405; *3:* 710
Roper v. Simmons, 2: 285
Rose Parade, SeaWorld protests, *1:* 30,
Rowling, J.K., *1:* 175, 177, 182–183
Royal Society for the Prevention of Cruelty to Animals (RSPCA), *1:* 2–3
RSPCA (Royal Society for the Prevention of Cruelty to Animals), *1:* 2–3
Rubio, Marco, *1:* 115
Rudd, Kevin, *2:* 379
Runaway children, *3:* 645
Russia, *2:* 454–455, 455 (ill.). *See also* Soviet Union
Rustin, Bayard, *1:* 65–66
Ryan, Paul, *1:* 115; *2:* 260

S

Sacramento, CA, Black Panthers protest Mulford Act, *2:* 239–245, 243 (ill.)
Sacred Stone Camp, *2:* 367, 387–388
Sadler, Barry, *3:* 671
Salazar, Sonia, *1:* 81 (ill.)
Saleh, Ali Abdullah, *3:* 488–489
Salman bin Abdulaziz al Saud, King of Saudi Arabia, *3:* 717
Salovey, Peter, *1:* 200
Salt Acts, *2:* 341
Same-sex marriage, *2:* 430, 434, 438–439, 439 (ill.)
San Bernardino, CA, terrorist attack, *2:* 328
San Diego, CA, SeaWorld protest, *1:* 30
San Francisco Chronicle, 2: 245
Sanctions, *3:* 538
Sanders, Bernie, *1:* 229, 230; *2:* 426
Sandy Hook Elementary School mass shooting, *2:* 246–247
Sanger, Margaret, *3:* 558, 575
Santelli, Rick, *1:* 113
Sappho, *2:* 430
Sarsour, Linda, *3:* 728

Satrom, LeRoy, *3:* 674
Saudi Arabia
    Baladi campaign, *3:* 699, 714–718, 716 (ill.)
    women's rights, *3:* 714–715
Saudi Arabia. Shura Council, *3:* 716
Savage, Adam, *1:* 166–167
Save the Rhino, *1:* 21
Savio, Mario, *1:* 198
Schell, Paul, *1:* 214–215
Scheuer, Sandra, *3:* 675
Schmidt, Douglas, *2:* 444
Schmorell, Alexander, *3:* 593, 596
Scholl, Hans, *3:* 588, 592, 593, 596
Scholl, Sophie, *3:* 588, 592, 593, 593 (ill.), 595–596, 596
School segregation. *See also* Desegregation/Segregation
    Little Rock, AR, *1:* 47–52
    New Orleans, LA, *1:* 53
Schroeder, William, *3:* 675
Schwerner, Michael Henry, *1:* 58, 58 (ill.)
Schwimmer, Rosika, *3:* 660
Science Champions, *1:* 168
Scientific American, *1:* 100
Scientists, as activists, *1:* 168
Scott, Elizabeth, *2:* 254–255
Sea level rise, *1:* 137, 146, 157–158. *See also* **Environment**
Seale, Bobby, *2:* 240, 242
Seaman, Elizabeth Cochrane, *2:* 278
Seattle, Washington, WTO protests, *1:* 209–216, 214 (ill.)
SeaWorld
    protests against, *1:* 25–31, 28, 30
    treatment of orcas, *1:* 26–27, 30–31
Secret Document of the Farmers of Xiaogang (1978), *1:* 105–111, 109 (ill.). *See also* **Economic discontent**
Seeds, genetically modified, *1:* 223
Seeger, Pete, *3:* 670
Segregation. *See* Desegregation/Segregation
Seim, Gavin, *2:* 254
Selbekk, Vebjørn, *1:* 185
Self-censorship, *1:* 184, 187
Semiautomatic weapons, *2:* 247
Seneca Falls Convention (1848), *3:* 696, 708, 708 (ill.)

Seneca Falls Convention (1848). Declaration of Sentiments, *3:* 708, 709 (ill.)
Sensenbrenner, James, Jr., *1:* 84–86, 87
Serfdom, *3:* 619–620
Service Employees International Union, *2:* 424
Sex reassignment surgery, *2:* 452–453
Sexual orientation, *2:* 429
Sexual predators, *2:* 459
Shanghai Pride Festival (2009), *2:* 452–458, 456 (ill.). *See also* **LGBTQ rights**
Shapi Township, Guangdong, China, *3:* 572
Sharia, *3:* 715, 718, 719
Sharpe, Samuel, *3:* 634, 635–637, 635 (ill.)
Sharpeville Massacre (1960), *3:* 534
Sharpton, Al, *3:* 539, 544, 546
Shekau, Abubaka, *3:* 722
Sheldrick (David) Wildlife Trust, *1:* 22
Shepard, Judy, *2:* 446, 450
Shepard, Matthew, *2:* 434, 446–447
    The Laramie Project, *2:* 456–457
    murder of, *2:* 445–446, 447
Shepard (Matthew) and James Byrd, Jr., Hate Crimes Prevention Act, *2:* 450, 451
Shepard (Matthew) Foundation, *2:* 447
Shook, Teresa, *3:* 726–727
Sicilia, Javier, *1:* 90, 91 (ill.), 92–93, 94
Sicilia, Juan Francisco, *1:* 92
Sidewalk counseling, *3:* 563
Sierra Club, *1:* 135, 213
Silent Spring (1962), *1:* 135
Singer, Peter, *1:* 3–4
Singh, Manmohar, *2:* 296
Singing Revolution (1988), *2:* 348
Single women, rights of, *3:* 693–695
Sisi, Abdel Fattah el-, *3:* 498
Sit-ins, *1:* 59–63; *2:* 256–257. *See also* Protests
    Democratic Congressional Representatives for Gun Control, *2:* 256–260, 259 (ill.)
    fast-food workers strikes, *2:* 425
    redwood trees, *1:* 152, 153 (ill.)
    University of California Berkeley, *1:* 198
Sitting Bull, *2:* 369
Skokie, Illinois, proposed neo-Nazi march, *1:* 188–189, 189 (ill.)
Slater, Amber, *2:* 242

GENERAL INDEX

Slave codes, *3:* 624
Slave rebellions, *3:* 623–624
    Christmas Rebellion/Baptist War (1831–1832), *3:* 634–638
    Louisiana Rebellion (German Coast), *3:* 623–628
    Malê Revolt of 1835, *3:* 626–627
    Turner's (Nat) rebellion (1831), *3:* 628–634, 629 (ill.)
Slave trade, *3:* 620–621, 621 (ill.)
    end of, *3:* 622
    triangular trade, *3:* 621
Slavery, *1:* 35, 36–37; *3:* 510–511, **617–649,** 619 (ill.), 621 (ill.), 629 (ill.), 633 (ill.), 635 (ill.), 639 (ill.), 640 (ill.), 642 (ill.), 644 (ill.), 647 (ill.).
    See also Abolition of slavery; Human trafficking
    Africa, *3:* 620–621
    American westward expansion, *3:* 638, 639–640
    ancient world, *3:* 617–619, 619 (ill.)
    Christmas Rebellion/Baptist War (1831–1832), *3:* 634–638, 635 (ill.)
    Fight to Stop Human Trafficking, *3:* 643–647, 644 (ill.)
    Harpers Ferry Raid (1859), *3:* 638–643, 642 (ill.)
    Louisiana Rebellion (German Coast) (1811), *3:* 623–628
    Malê Revolt of 1835, *3:* 626–627, 627 (ill.)
    Middle Ages, *3:* 619–620
    modern, *3:* 623
    Nat Turner's Rebellion/Anti-slavery petitions, *3:* 628–634, 629 (ill.). 633 (ill.)
    Native Americans, *3:* 624
    slave ships, *3:* 621, 621 (ill.)
    symbols of at Yale, *1:* 195, 196
Sleepy Lagoon murder, *3:* 520
Slovakia, *2:* 357–358
Smeal, Eleanor, *3:* 559–560
Smith, Molly, *2:* 247–249
Smith, Tommie, *3:* 516, 517 (ill.)
SNCC (Student Nonviolent Coordinating Committee), *1:* 57, 58
    Berkeley free speech movement, *1:* 198
    March on Washington, *1:* 65
    sit-ins, *1:* 60
Socialism, *3:* 587
Socialists, resistance to Nazis, *3:* 587–588

Society for Human Rights, *2:* 432
Solidarity movement, *2:* 356. *See also* **Labor rights**
Soroptimist International, *3:* 644 (ill.), 646–647
South Africa
    black consciousness movement, *3:* 532–533
    boycotts, *3:* 538
    brief history, *3:* 532–533
    HIV/AIDS drugs protests, *1:* 226–227, 227 (ill.)
    indigenous peoples, *3:* 532–533, 534
    racial discrimination, *3:* 513
    Soweto Uprising (1976), *3:* 530–539, 535 (ill.)
    student protests, *3:* 530–539, 535 (ill.)
    violence against blacks, *3:* 513
South America, *1:* 71, 72
South Carolina, Freedom Rides, *1:* 56
South Dakota
    AIM Occupation of Wounded Knee (1973), *2:* 367–375, 374 (ill.)
    Wounded Knee Massacre (1890), *2:* 369–370, 369 (ill.), 373
South Vietnam, *2:* 340 (ill.). *See also* Vietnam
Southern Christian Leadership Council, *1:* 65
Southern Poverty Law Center (SPLC), *2:* 446
Soviet Union. *See also* Russia
    book burning, *1:* 178
    break-up, *3:* 486
    control of Czechoslovakia, *2:* 353–354
    Estonian revolution, *2:* 348
    invasion of Czechoslovakia, *2:* 354 (ill.)
Soviet Union. Red Army, *2:* 354 (ill.)
Soweto Uprising (1976), *3:* 530–539, 535 (ill.). *See also* **Racial conflict**
    effects of, *3:* 538–539
    eyewitness account, *3:* 536–537
    spreading unrest, *3:* 537–538
Spain
    austerity measures, *1:* 117–118, 121
    Bilbao Anti-bullfighting Protest (2010), *1:* 12–18, 17 (ill.)
    15-M movement, *1:* 90, 116–122, 121 (ill.)
    Global Recession of 2008, *1:* 104–105, 116–117
Spanish colonies. *See also* Colonization
    independence movements, *2:* 338–339
    Puerto Rico, *2:* 343–344
    slave trade, *3:* 621
    slavery, *3:* 511

Spanish Socialist Workers' Party (PSOE), *1:* 120–121
Spanish-American War (1898), *2:* 338–339, 346
SPLC (Southern Poverty Law Center), *2:* 446
Sports, protests in, *3:* 516–517, 517 (ill.)
Spring of Life, *3:* 562, 564–565
    counterprotests, *3:* 565
    results of protest, *3:* 566–568
Springsteen, Bruce, *2:* 462
Stalingrad, Battle of (1943), *3:* 594–595, 609
Stand for Freedom, *3:* 647
Standing Rock Pipeline Protest (2016). *See* Dakota Access Pipeline (DAPL) Protest; **Indigenous peoples' rights**
    Dennis Banks, *2:* 390–391
    Native Americans, *2:* 367 (ill.)
Standing Rock Reservation, *2:* 369, 370, 384
Standing Rock Sioux, *2:* 384–385, 387–388, 388 (ill.). *See also* Native Americans
Stanton, Elizabeth Cady, *3:* 696, 697 (ill.), 708, 708 (ill.), 710
Starr, Edwin, *3:* 670
Stauffenberg, Claus von, *3:* 591
Steinem, Gloria, *3:* 560, 728
Sterilization, *3:* 549
Sting, *2:* 366, 383, 383 (ill.)
Stonewall Inn, *2:* 432, 436–437, 439, 441
Stonewall Riots (1969), *2:* 432–433, 435–441, 440 (ill.). *See also* **LGBTQ rights**
Stookey, N. Paul, *1:* 68
Stowe, Harriet Beecher, *3:* 631, 631 (ill.), 638
Strangeways Prison Riot (1990), *2:* 271
Street art, *1:* 212, 212 (ill.)
Strikes, *2:* 397. *See also* **Labor rights**; Protests
    cigar workers, *1:* 84
    coal miners, *2:* 410–411
    Delano Grape Strike and Boycott, *2:* 414–422
    equal pay for women, *3:* 728–729
    fast-food workers, *2:* 422–426, 424 (ill.)
    Flint strike against General Motors, *2:* 407–414, 412 (ill.)
    Gdansk Shipyard, Poland, *2:* 356–357, 357 (ill.)
    Kensington textile mill, *2:* 401–403
    legalization, *2:* 409
    McCormick Reaper Works, *2:* 418
    slaves, *3:* 634, 635–636
    University of California Berkeley, *1:* 199
Stroop, Jürgen, *3:* 605, 606
Student Armband Protest of Vietnam War (1965–1969), *3:* 663–668, 668 (ill.). *See also* Anti-war protests
Student Nonviolent Coordinating Committee (SNCC), *1:* 57, 58
    Berkeley free speech movement, *1:* 198
    March on Washington, *1:* 65
    sit-ins, *1:* 60
Student Protest at Kent State (1970), *3:* 669–676, 674 (ill.). *See also* Anti-war protests
    eyewitness account, *3:* 672–673
    wounded student, *3:* 674 (ill.)
Student protests. *See also* Protests
    counterprotests in Charlottesville, VA, *3:* 542
    Hong Kong, *3:* 500–501
    Kent State (1970), *3:* 669–676, 674 (ill.)
    Paris, France, *1:* 118–119, 119 (ill.)
    Soweto uprising, *3:* 530–539, 535 (ill.)
    Student Armband Protest of Vietnam War (1965–1969), *3:* 663–668, 668 (ill.)
    Vietnam War, *3:* 669–676
    White Rose movement, *3:* 588
The Suffragette, *3:* 705 (ill.)
Suffragettes. *See* Women's suffrage movement
Suffragists. *See* Women's suffrage movement
Summer of Mercy Protest (1991), *3:* 566–567
Sumner, Gordon, *2:* 366, 383, 383 (ill.)
Sun Yat-sen, *1:* 107
Supreme Court (United States). *See* United States. Supreme Court
Survivors, Armenian genocide, *2:* 299
Suu Kyi, Aung San, *3:* 502–503, 503 (ill.)
Sweden
    escape of Danish Jews to, *3:* 597, 601 (ill.)
    Melchior, Bent, escape to, *3:* 598–599
Sydney, Australia, aboriginal land rights protest, *2:* 375–379
Syria
    Arab Spring, *3:* 491–493, 492 (ill.)
    civil war, *2:* 319; *3:* 492–493, 720–721
Syrian refugees, *2:* 319, 321; *3:* 493, 720–724. *See also* Refugees

GENERAL INDEX

T

Tahrir Square protests (2011), *3:* 493–498, 494–495, 496 (ill.). *See also* **Political/Government uprisings**
Taigman, Kalman, *3:* 610
Taino (indigenous people), *2:* 343. *See also* Indigenous peoples
Taliban, *3:* 681, 719
Tariffs, *1:* 210
TARP (United States. Troubled Asset Relief Program), *1:* 112
Tax protests, *1:* 111–116
Tea Party movement, *1:* 103–104, 111–116, 114 (ill.)
    demonstration in Fort Myers, Florida, *1:* 114 (ill.)
    first events, *1:* 113–114
    membership statistics, *1:* 114–115
    mid-term elections of 2010, *1:* 115
Tema, Sophie Topsie, *3:* 536–537
Terauchi Masatake, *1:* 127, 127 (ill.)
Terra nullius, *2:* 376
Terrorism, *1:* 190; *2:* 285
    animal rights, *1:* 4
    ecoterrorism, *1:* 11
    fears of, *2:* 310
    San Bernardino, California, *2:* 328
    Syria, *3:* 489
    United States, *2:* 326
    World Trade Center/Pentagon terror attack (2001), *3:* 677–680
Terrorist watch list, *2:* 257, 260
Testerman, Cabell, *2:* 410
Texas
    executions, *2:* 284
    Huey P. Newton Gun Club demonstrations, *2:* 244
    March to Abolish the Death Penalty, *2:* 287, 287 (ill.)
Textile mills, child labor, *2:* 400 (ill.)
Thebes, *3:* 469
Thomas, Jefferson, *1:* 50
Thoreau, Henry David, *1:* 133
350.org, *1:* 157, 161

Tiananmen Square protests, *3:* 473–478, 476 (ill.). *See also* **Political/Government uprisings**
    eyewitness account, *3:* 474–475
    origins, *3:* 473–474
    use of military force, *3:* 477–478
Tilikum, *1:* 5, 26, 27 (ill.), 31
Tillard, Violet, *3:* 703–704
Tiller, George, *3:* 566–567
Timberlake, Justin, *2:* 423
Times of India, *2:* 296
Tinker, John, *3:* 664, 665, 668, 668 (ill.)
Tinker, Mary Beth, *3:* 664, 665, 668, 668 (ill.)
Tinker v. Des Moines Independent Community School District, *3:* 657, 667–668
Title X, *3:* 577–578
Tlatelolco Massacre (1968), *1:* 94, 95. *See also* **Hispanic and Latino civil rights**
Tokyo Big March, *1:* 160
Tometi, Opal, *3:* 541
Torture, *3:* 686
Toxic chemical spills, Bhopal, India, *1:* 136
Toxic wastes
    fracking, *1:* 153–154
    Love Canal, *1:* 136, 143
Trafficking Victims Protection Act (TVPA), *3:* 646
Trail of Tears protest, *2:* 386–387
TransCanada, *1:* 140
Transgender people, *2:* 429, 435. *See also* LGBTQ people; Manning, Bradley/Chelsea
Transgender rights, *2:* 435. *See also* **LGBTQ rights**
    China, *2:* 452–453
    North Carolina, *2:* 458–464
Travers, Mary, *1:* 68
Treason, *2:* 285
Treaty of New Echota, *2:* 386
Treblinka
    closing of, *3:* 613–614
    deportations to, *3:* 604, 606
Treblinka Death Camp Revolt (1943), *3:* 607–614. *See also* **Resistance to Nazis**
Tree sitting, *1:* 152
Tresckow, Henning von, *3:* 591
Trial by jury, *2:* 265
Triangular trade, *3:* 621
Trick (music group), *1:* 30

Troubled Asset Relief Program (TARP), *1:* 112
Trump, Donald, *1:* 89, 115
    ban on transgender people in military, *2:* 435
    birth control and health insurance plans, *3:* 556
    Charlottesville protests, *3:* 543
    climate change policies, *1:* 165–166
    criticism of NFL protesters, *3:* 515
    Dakota Access Pipeline, *2:* 367, 385, 391
    election of 2016, *3:* 725–726
    immigration policy, *2:* 310
    Keystone XL project, *1:* 139, 144
    reproductive rights, *3:* 578
    supporters, *1:* 177 (ill.)
    women's protest marches, *3:* 724–731
Trump travel bans (2017). *See also* **Immigrant rights**
    airport protests, *2:* 330–331, 330 (ill.)
    countries excluded in first travel ban, *2:* 326 (ill.)
    demonstrations against, *2:* 330 (ill.)
    lawsuit against, *2:* 331–332
    Muslims, *2:* 325–326
    protests against, *2:* 325–332, 330 (ill.)
    worldwide protests, *2:* 331
Tubman, Harriet, *3:* 639 (ill.)
Tucson, AZ, mass shooting, *2:* 248
Tunisia
    Arab Spring, *2:* 318–319; *3:* 487–488
    democracy in, *3:* 493
Tunisian Revolution, *3:* 488, 495
Turkey
    American protests against, *2:* 302
    Armenian genocide denial, *2:* 300–301
Turner, Nat, *3:* 628–629, 629 (ill.)
Turner's (Nat) Rebellion (1831–1832), *3:* 628–634, 629 (ill.). *See also* **Slavery**
Turning Hawk, *2:* 373
Tuvalu, *1:* 147
TVPA (United States. Trafficking Victims Protection Act), *3:* 646
12th Street Riots, Detroit, MI, *3:* 524–530, 528 (ill.)
    aftermath, *3:* 529–530
    origins in "blind pig," *3:* 525
    Romney, George, interview, *3:* 530–531
"Twinkie defense," *2:* 444

U

UAW (United Auto Workers), *2:* 408, 409, 414
UCR (University of California, Riverside)
    animal experimentation, *1:* 7–8
    lab raid to protest animal testing, *1:* 7–11
UFW (United Farm Workers), *2:* 414–415, 420
Umbrella Revolution (2014), *3:* 498–505, 500 (ill.), 504 (ill.). *See also* **Political/Government uprisings**
Umpqua Community College, mass shootings, *2:* 251
Unauthorized immigration. *See* Undocumented immigrants
Uncle Tom's Cabin, *3:* 631, 638
Underground Railroad, *3:* 639
Undocumented immigrants, *1:* 74, 83–84; *2:* 325. *See also* Immigrants and immigration
UNFCCC (United Nations. Framework Convention on Climate Change), *1:* 137, 145
Union of Concerned Scientists, *1:* 168
Unitarians, *3:* 652
United Airlines Flight 93, *3:* 677
United Airlines Flight 175, *3:* 677, 678
United Auto Workers (UAW), *2:* 408, 409, 414
United Farm Workers of America, *1:* 78
United Farm Workers (UFW), *2:* 414–415, 420
United for Peace and Justice, *3:* 678–679
United Kingdom. *See also* British colonies
    abolition of slavery, *2:* 268; *3:* 637
    anti-fracking protesters, *1:* 155 (ill.)
    Easter Rebellion, *3:* 480–481
    exit from EU, *1:* 103–104, 122–129
    immigrants and immigration, *1:* 123, 124
    Industrial Revolution, *2:* 395, 395 (ill.)
    women's suffrage movement, *3:* 471–472, 697–698, 701–707
United Kingdom. Act to Prevent the Cruel and Improper Treatment of Cattle in the United Kingdom (1822), *1:* 2
United Kingdom. Cat and Mouse Act, *3:* 706
United Kingdom. Equal Suffrage Act, *3:* 707
United Kingdom. Health and Morals of Apprentices Act of 1802, *2:* 395

United Kingdom. Pease's Act, *1:* 2
United Kingdom. Prisoners (Temporary Discharge for Ill-Health) Act, *3:* 706
United Kingdom. Representation of the People Act, *3:* 706–707
United Kingdom. Slavery Abolition Act of 1833, *2:* 268; *3:* 637
United Nations
    abolition of slavery, *3:* 643
    environmental protection, *1:* 137
    human rights, *2:* 264, 268–269
    measurement of human development, *1:* 101–102
United Nations. Climate Change Conference, *1:* 144–145
United Nations. Framework Convention on Climate Change (UNFCCC), *1:* 137, 145
United Nations. Intergovernmental Panel on Climate Change (IPCC), *1:* 137, 148
United States. *See also* American Revolutionary War (1775–1783); United States Civil War (1861–1865); Specific states and cities
    abolition of slavery, *2:* 268; *3:* 633
    anti-gay laws, *2:* 432
    anti-war protests, *3:* 653–657
    attitudes about climate change, *1:* 164, 164 (ill.)
    book burning, *1:* 178
    child labor, *2:* 401
    civil rights movement, *3:* 472
    Day without Immigrants protests, *1:* 83–89
    free speech, *1:* 173–174
    gun control, *2:* 233–235
    gun ownership, *2:* 233–235, 235 (ill.)
    gun protests, *2:* 238–239
    hate crimes, *3:* 518 (ill.)
    hate groups, *3:* 518 (ill.)
    Hispanic and Latino population, *1:* 75–76
    immigrants and immigration, *1:* 74, 83–85; *2:* 306–309
    immigration policy, *1:* 83–85, 89; *2:* 416
    income inequality, *1:* 99–100
    labor laws, *2:* 397–398
    labor rights, *2:* 394
    migrant workers, *2:* 415
    presidential election of 2016, *3:* 725–726
    racial conflict, *3:* 515–518
    recession of 2008, *1:* 112–113
    sanctions against China, *3:* 478
    slavery, *3:* 622
    Tea Party movement, *1:* 103–104
    terrorism, *2:* 326
    treatment of Native Americans, *2:* 368–369
    undocumented immigrants, *1:* 74; *2:* 325
    westward expansion, *1:* 72–73
    women in early United States, *3:* 696
    women's rights movement, *3:* 696–698
    women's suffrage movement, *3:* 707–713
United States. American Recovery and Reinvestment Act (ARRA), *1:* 113
United States. Americans with Disabilities Act (ADA), *2:* 277, 280–283
United States. Animal Welfare Act of 1966, *1:* 3
United States. Army Corp of Engineers, *2:* 385, 389–390
United States. Bald and Golden Eagle Protection Act, *1:* 135
United States. Bill of Rights, *1:* 174; *2:* 267
United States. Brady Handgun Violence Prevention Act, *2:* 236–237, 253
United States. Centers for Disease Control and Prevention, *3:* 556
United States. Chinese Exclusion Act, *2:* 329, 416
United States. Civil Rights Act of 1957, *1:* 41
United States. Civil Rights Act of 1960, *1:* 41
United States. Civil Rights Act of 1964, *1:* 40, 41, 69
United States. Civil Rights Act of 1968, *1:* 40, 41
United States. Comprehensive Environmental Response, Compensation, and Liability Act (CERCLA), *1:* 143
United States. Comstock Act, *3:* 553, 575
United States. Congress. House of Representatives, *2:* 256–260, 259 (ill.)
United States. Congress. HR 4437, *1:* 83–85, 89
United States. Constitution. 1st Amendment, *1:* 174–175
United States. Constitution. 2nd Amendment, *2:* 237, 252, 254–255
United States. Constitution. 13th Amendment, *2:* 268; *3:* 622, 633
United States. Constitution. 14th Amendment, *1:* 46, 49; *3:* 709

United States. Constitution. 15th Amendment, *3:* 709–710

United States. Constitution. 19th Amendment, *3:* 698 (ill.), 708, 713

United States. Defense of Marriage Act, *2:* 438

United States. Department of Justice (DOJ), *2:* 463

United States. DREAM Act (Development, Relief, and Education for Alien Minors Act), *1:* 89

United States. Education for All Handicapped Children Act, *2:* 278

United States. Emergency Economic Stabilization Act of 2008, *1:* 112

United States. Endangered Species Act, *1:* 136

United States. Energy Information Administration (EIA), *1:* 155

United States. Environmental Protection Agency (EPA), *1:* 136

United States. Fair Housing Act of 1968, *1:* 40, 41

United States. Fair Labor Standards Act of 1938, *2:* 397–398, 407

United States. Federal Assault Weapons Ban, *2:* 234–235

United States. Federal Bureau of Investigation (FBI), *3:* 686–687, 725

United States. Firearms Owners' Protection Act, *2:* 234

United States. Freedom of Access to Clinic Entrances Act (FACE Act), *3:* 568

United States. Gun Control Act, *2:* 234

United States. Individuals with Disabilities Education Act (IDEA), *2:* 278

United States. Interstate Commerce Commission, *1:* 54–55, 57, 59

United States. Law Enforcement Officers Protection Act, *2:* 234

United States. Marine Mammal Protection Act, *1:* 136

United States. Matthew Shepard and James Byrd, Jr., Hate Crimes Prevention Act, *2:* 450, 451

United States. National Firearms Act, *2:* 234

United States. National Guard, *2:* 275, 389

United States. National Guard (Arkansas), *1:* 48, 50–52, 52 (ill.)

United States. National Guard (Michigan), *3:* 528, 528 (ill.), 531

United States. National Guard (Ohio), *3:* 674–675

United States. National Instant Criminal Background Check System, *2:* 253

United States. National Institutes of Health, *1:* 9–10

United States. National Labor Relations Act (Wagner Act), *2:* 397, 409

United States. National Oceanic and Atmospheric Administration (NOAA), *1:* 136

United States. National Park Service (NPS), *1:* 135

United States. No Taxpayer Funding for Abortion and Abortion Insurance Full Disclosure Act, *3:* 580

United States. Partial-Birth Abortion Act, *3:* 561

United States. Supreme Court
    abortion rights, *3:* 554
    death penalty, *2:* 285
    defining free speech, *1:* 175
    LGBTQ rights, *2:* 432
    marriage equality, *2:* 434, 438–439
    neo-Nazi march, *1:* 188–189
    right to free speech, *3:* 667–668

United States. Trafficking Victims Protection Act (TVPA), *3:* 646

United States. Troubled Asset Relief Program (TARP), *1:* 112

United States. Voting Rights Act of 1965, *1:* 40, 41, 58, 69

United States Civil War (1861–1865), *2:* 268. *See also* United States
    anti-war protests, *3:* 653–654
    impact on women's rights movement, *3:* 709–710
    military draft, *3:* 526

Universal Declaration of Human Rights (UDHR), *2:* 268–269, 290; *3:* 646

University of California, Berkeley, *1:* 176–177, 177 (ill.), 198–199, 199 (ill.)
    free speech movement (1964), *1:* 198–199, 199 (ill.)
    free speech rally, *1:* 176–177, 177 (ill.)

University of California, Riverside
    animal experimentation, *1:* 7–8
    lab raid to protest animal testing, *1:* 7–11

University of Maine. Basketball team, *2:* 460, 461 (ill.)

University of Munich, *3:* 588, 593, 595, 597

University of Pennsylvania. Head Injury Lab, *1:* 9

Untouchability, *2:* 292. *See also* Dalits

Uprising of 1967 (Detroit, MI), *3:* 524–530, 528 (ill.)
    aftermath, *3:* 529–530
    origins in "blind pig," *3:* 525
    Romney, George, interview, *3:* 530–531

Urbanization, *2:* 400

V

Van Buren, Martin, *2:* 387 (ill.)
Varna, *2:* 291
Velvet Divorce, *2:* 357–358
Velvet Revolution (1989), *2:* 341–342, 352–358. *See also* **Independence movements**
Venezuela, human rights protests, *2:* 269
Vera, Raul, *1:* 91 (ill.)
Vietnam
  independence movements, *2:* 339–340
  partition, *2:* 340 (ill.)
Vietnam War (1954–1975), *2:* 339–340; *3:* 664–665, 669–671
  anti-war protests, *3:* 655–656, 663–668, 669–676
  Nixon ends war, *3:* 676
  protest songs, *3:* 670–671
  student protests, *3:* 669–676
Villas Boas, Leonardo, *2:* 380–381
Villas Boas, Orlando, *2:* 380–381
Violence. *See also* Murder; Riots
  against African Americans, *1:* 38, 40, 56–57, 56 (ill.), 58, 62; *3:* 526–527
  against black South Africans, *3:* 513
  against cigar workers, *1:* 84
  against Dalits, *2:* 293–294, 297
  drug trade, *1:* 91–92
  against Iranian demonstrators, *3:* 490–491
  against Mexican students, *1:* 90, 94
  against Myanmar protesters, *3:* 502
  racial conflict, *3:* 512
  against Rohingya, *3:* 503
  against Tiananmen Square protesters, *3:* 477–478
  against women's health clinics, *3:* 558
  against WTO protesters, *1:* 215
Virginia
  anti-slavery petitions, *3:* 628–634
  Charlottesville Protests (2017), *3:* 542–543, 543 (ill.)
  debate over slavery, *3:* 628, 632
  Harpers Ferry Raid (1859), *3:* 638–643, 642 (ill.)
  Turner's (Nat) Rebellion (1831), *3:* 628–634, 629 (ill.)
Virginia Tech, mass shooting, *2:* 249
Virginia Yearly Meeting of the Society of Friends, *3:* 630
Vocal Majority Tour (2016), *2:* 248, 248 (ill.)
Votes for Women, 3: 703
Voting rights, *1:* 40, 58. *See also* Civil rights; Women's suffrage movement
Voting Rights Act of 1965, *1:* 40, 41, 58, 69

W

Wade, Henry, *3:* 576
Wagner Act, *2:* 397, 409
Walentynowicz, Anna, *2:* 356
Walesa, Lech, *2:* 356, 357 (ill.)
Walk for Freedom, *3:* 647
Walk Free Foundation, *3:* 623
Walkouts, Mexican American students, *1:* 77–82
Wall Street
  economic inequality, *1:* 218
  history, *1:* 217–218
  Occupy Wall Street movement (2011), *1:* 216–222
  opposition movements, *1:* 218
Walls, Carlotta, *1:* 50
Walter Reed Medical Center, *3:* 688–689, 689 (ill.)
War on drugs, Mexico, *1:* 91–95
War on Terror, *3:* 681–682
War protests, *3:* **651–692**, 656 (ill.), 660 (ill.), 667 (ill.), 668 (ill.), 671 (ill.), 674 (ill.), 679 (ill.), 682 (ill.), 686 (ill.)
  burning draft cards, *3:* 666–667, 667 (ill.)
  Candlelight Vigils against Invasion of Iraq (2003), *3:* 676–683, 682 (ill.)
  International Congress of Women (1915), *3:* 657–663, 660 (ill.)
  Manning, Chelsea, and WikiLeaks, *3:* 684–690, 686 (ill.)
  One Thousand Coffins Protest (2004), *3:* 678–679, 679 (ill.)
  protest songs, *3:* 670–671
  Student Armband Protest of Vietnam War (1965–1969), *3:* 663–668, 668 (ill.)
  Student Protest at Kent State (1970), *3:* 669–676, 674 (ill.)
Warren, Earl, *3:* 522–523
Warren, Elizabeth, *3:* 728

Warsaw, Poland
   anti-migrant protests, *2:* 323
   Polish resistance, *3:* 590 (ill.)
Warsaw Ghetto, *3:* 602–605
   creation of, *3:* 604
   deportations to death camps, *3:* 604–605
Warsaw Ghetto Uprising (1943), *3:* 590, 602–607, 606 (ill.). *See also* **Resistance to Nazis**
   end of the uprising, *3:* 606
   Willenberg, Samuel, *3:* 612
Washington, D.C.
   abolition of slavery, *3:* 633
   Capitol Crawl (1990), *2:* 276–284
   Forward on Climate rally (2013), *1:* 139–144, 142 (ill.)
   Justice for All March (2014), *3:* 515, 539–546, 545 (ill.)
   LGBTQ rights demonstrations, *2:* 433 (ill.)
   March for Gun Control (2013), *2:* 246–252
   March for Science (2017), *1:* 163–168, 165 (ill.)
   March for Women's Lives (1986), *3:* 556–561, 557 (ill.)
   Women's March on Washington (2017), *3:* 724–731, 730 (ill.)
   Women's Suffrage Protest at the White House (2017), *3:* 707–713, 712 (ill.)
Washington, D.C. Compensated Emancipation Act, *3:* 633, 633 (ill.)
Washington Post, 1: 141, 185; *3:* 688
Washington (state)
   background checks, *2:* 253–254
   WTO protests, *1:* 209–216, 214 (ill.)
Water pollution, *1:* 154
Watts Riots, *3:* 514 (ill.)
Weddington, Sarah, *3:* 576
Weiland, Hannah, *1:* 13
Weinberg, Jack, *1:* 198
West Virginia, Battle of Blair Mountain strike, *2:* 410–411
Westboro Baptist Church
   anti-gay protests, *2:* 449 (ill.), 451
   as hate group, *2:* 446
   protests of Matthew Shepard, *2:* 445–452
Westergaard, Kurt, *1:* 184–185, 187
Westwood, Vivienne, *1:* 13

WFL (Women's Freedom League), *3:* 703–704
Wheels of Justice March (1990), *2:* 282
When Abortion Was a Crime (1997), *3:* 552
Whistle-blowers, *3:* 684, 688
White, Dan, *2:* 441–442, 443–444
White, Micah, *1:* 219
White Night Riots (1979), *2:* 441–445, 444 (ill.). *See also* **LGBTQ rights**
White Rose Movement (1942–1943), *3:* 588, 592–597, 593 (ill.), 596 (ill.). *See also* **Resistance to Nazis**
   capture of leaders, *3:* 594–595
   methods, *3:* 594
   monument at University of Munich, *3:* 596 (ill.)
   origins, *3:* 593
White supremacists, *3:* 516–517, 542–543, 543. *See also* Race and racism
WHO (World Health Organization), *1:* 101; *3:* 550
Whole Women's Health v. Hellerstedt, 3: 555
Wichita, KS, Summer of Mercy Protest, *3:* 566–567
WikiLeaks and, Manning, Bradley/Chelsea, *3:* 684–690, 686 (ill.)
Wilde, Oscar, *2:* 430
Wildfire (ship), *3:* 621 (ill.)
Wilkins, N.B., *2:* 329
Wilkins, Roy, *1:* 51
Will and Grace, 2: 434
Willenberg, Samuel, *3:* 610, 611 (ill.), 612–613, 613 (ill.)
William Frantz Elementary School, *1:* 53
William III, King of England, *1:* 173
Willingham, Cameron Todd, *2:* 288
Wilson, Woodrow, *3:* 663, 710, 712
Wilson (Woodrow) High School, East LA, *1:* 81
Woman's Rights Convention (1848), *3:* 696, 708, 708 (ill.)
Woman's Rights Convention (1848). Declaration of Sentiments, *3:* 708, 709
Women's Equality Day, *3:* 713, 729
Women's Freedom League (WFL), *3:* 703–704
Women's health clinics, blocking access to, *3:* 557–558, 562–568, 566–567
Women's International League for Peace and Freedom, *3:* 661

Women's March on Washington (2017), *3:* 559, 724–731
   demonstrators, *3:* 730 (ill.)
   sister marches, *3:* 729–730
Women's Peace Congress (1915), *3:* 657–663, 660 (ill.)
   goals of, *3:* 661
   impact of, *3:* 661–663
   resolutions, *3:* 662
Women's rights, *3:* **693–732**, 697 (ill.), 698 (ill.), 704 (ill.), 705 (ill.), 708 (ill.), 709 (ill.), 712 (ill.), 716 (ill.), 719 (ill.), 723 (ill.), 729 (ill.), 730 (ill.).
   See also **Reproductive rights**
   Baladi campaign, *3:* 714–718, 716 (ill.)
   Bring Back Our Girls, *3:* 700–701, 722–723, 723 (ill.)
   British colonies, *3:* 693–695
   delayed by World War I, *3:* 658
   to education, *3:* 718–724
   Equal Rights Amendment, *3:* 558–559
   Hunger Strikes by Suffragettes in Prison, *3:* 701–707, 704 (ill.)
   Saudi Arabia, *3:* 714–715
   Seneca Falls Convention (1848), *3:* 696, 708, 708 (ill.)
   single v. married, *3:* 693–695
   21st century, *3:* 699–700
   Women's March on Washington (2017), *3:* 724–731, 730 (ill.)
   Women's Strike for Equality (1970), *3:* 728–729, 729 (ill.)
   Women's Suffrage Protest at the White House (1917), *3:* 707–713, 712 (ill.)
   Yousafzai, Malala, All-Girls School, *3:* 718–724
Women's Social and Political Union (WSPU), *3:* 703, 705
Women's Strike for Equality (1970), *3:* 728–729, 729 (ill.)
Women's suffrage movement, *3:* 696–698. *See also* Voting rights
   Derby Day Protest (1913), *3:* 705
   division over tactics, *3:* 703
   Hunger Strikes by Suffragettes in Prison, *3:* 701–707, 704 (ill.)
   impact of United States Civil War, *3:* 709–710
   impact of World War I (1914–1918), *3:* 710–711
   leaders, *3:* 697 (ill.)
   Saudi Arabia, *3:* 714–718
   United Kingdom, *3:* 471–472, 697–698, 701–707
   United States, *3:* 696–698, 707–713
Women's Suffrage Protest at the White House (1917), *3:* 707–713, 712 (ill.)
Woodrow Wilson High School, East LA, *1:* 81
Woolworth's, Greensboro, NC, *1:* 60
Work hours, *2:* 393
Workers. *See also* **Labor rights**
   farm, *1:* 75–76, 75 (ill.), 78–79; *2:* 416
   Fast-food Workers' Strike, *2:* 422–426, 424 (ill.)
   Filipino, *2:* 416, 418–419
   Mexican, *2:* 416, 418–419
   migrant, *2:* 415, 416
Workers' rights. *See* **Labor rights**
Working conditions
   Chinese workers, *2:* 398
   coal mining, *2:* 312
   farm workers, *2:* 416
   General Motors Co., *2:* 408–409
   labor laws, *2:* 397–398
   migrant workers, *2:* 416
World Bank, *2:* 381, 384
World Conservation Congress, *1:* 21
World Day against Trafficking in Persons, *3:* 647
World Economic Forum, *2:* 323
World Health Organization (WHO), *1:* 101; *3:* 550
World Trade Center terror attack (2001), *2:* 326; *3:* 677–680. *See also* Terrorism
World Trade Organization (WTO). Accountability Review Committee of Seattle, Washington, *1:* 215
World War I (1914–1918), *2:* 298
   anti-war efforts, *3:* 655
   impact on women's suffrage movement, *3:* 658, 710–711
World War II (1939–1945), *1:* 74; *3:* 585, 607, 655
   Battle of Stalingrad, *3:* 594–595
   Germany, *3:* 479–481
Wounded Knee, SD
   AIM occupation (1973), *2:* 364–365, 367–375, 374 (ill.)
   massacre (1890), *2:* 369–370, 373
Wright, Martha, *3:* 708
WSPU (Women's Social and Political Union), *3:* 703, 705

WTO (World Trade Organization), *1:* 205–206
   goals, *1:* 210–211
   protests in Seattle, Washington, *1:* 209–216
WTO (World Trade Organization). Accountability Review Committee of Seattle, Washington, *1:* 215
Wuchang Revolt (1911), *1:* 106
Wyoming
   anti-gay protests by WBC, *2:* 448, 449–451
   murder of Matthew Shepard, *2:* 445–446

X

Xiaogang, China, *1:* 103
   collective farms and communes, *1:* 108–110
   farmers' secret agreement, *1:* 105–111, 109 (ill.)
Xingu River, *2:* 379–381

Y

Yale University
   history, *1:* 195–196
   racial tensions, *1:* 196–199
   student protests on free speech, *1:* 194–201, 197 (ill.)
Yale University. Calhoun College, *1:* 195, 200
Yale University. Intercultural Affairs Council, *1:* 195, 197
Yarrow, Peter, *1:* 68
Ybor City Cigar Strike (1931), *1:* 84–85
Yemen, Arab Spring, *3:* 488–489
Yiannopoulos, Milo, *1:* 176
York County Prison Farm, *1:* 62
Young, Neil, *3:* 670
Young Turks, *2:* 298
Yousafzai, Malala, *3:* 700–701, 718–720, 719 (ill.), 720–721
Yousafzai, Malala, All-Girls School, *3:* 718–724

Z

Zhou Enlai, *1:* 108
Zimmerman, George, *3:* 540–544
ZOB (Jewish Combat Organization), *3:* 604–606, 605
Zoot Suit Riots (1943), *3:* 512, 512 (ill.), 518–524, 521 (ill.). *See also* **Racial conflict**
Zoot suits, *3:* 519–520
Zuccotti Park, *1:* 219